D1453228

Turf Weeds and Their Control

Related Society Publications

Turfgrass, Agronomy Monograph 32

Contributions from Breeding Forage and Turf Grasses, CSSA Special Publication Number 15

CSSA Slide Sets
  The Botanical Characteristics of Turfgrasses
  Diseases of Turfgrasses
  Maintenance of Athletic Turf
  Microbiology of Turf Soils
  Roadside Turfgrass
  Safety in Pesticide Application
  Soil Fumigation and Sterilization
  Thatch in Turfgrass
  Turfgrass Insects

For more information on these titles, please contact the ASA, CSSA, SSSA Headquarters Office; Attn: Marketing; 677 South Segoe Road; Madison, WI 53711-1086. Phone: (608) 273-8080 ext. 322. Fax: (608) 273-2021.

Turf Weeds and Their Control

Editor
Alfred J. Turgeon

Managing Editor
David M. Kral

Associate Editor
Marian K. Viney

American Society of Agronomy, Inc.
Crop Science Society of America, Inc.
Madison, Wisconsin, USA

1994

Library of Congress Cataloging-in-Publication Data

Turf weeds and their control / editor, Alfred J. Turgeon ; associate
  editor, Marian K. Viney.
      p.   cm.
  Includes bibliographical references and index.
  ISBN 0-89118-120-2
    1. Turfgrasses—Weed control. 2. Turf management. I. Turgeon,
A. J. (Alfred J.), 1943–   . II. Viney, Marian K.
  SB608.T87T86   1994
  635.9′642958—dc20   94-4166
                                                                    CIP

Printed in the United States of America

CONTENTS

1 Weed Taxonomy   1

DAVID W. HALL, LAMBERT B. McCARTY, AND TIM R. MURPHY

2 Ecology of Turfgrass Weeds   29

T. L. WATSCHKE AND R. E. ENGEL

3 Herbicide Action and Metabolism   37

DONALD PENNER

4 Turfgrass Phytotoxicity from Preemergence Herbicides   71

L. M. CALLAHAN

FOREWORD

The turf industry, a $25 billion industry in the U.S. in 1992, ranking as one of the larget agricultural industries, has a co-commitment to support the environmental quality and value of turf to home owners, businesses, recreational, and public areas. The expanded use of turf, combined with expansion in the scientific and technical knowledge about turf taxonomy and ecology, the development of new chemistries and techniques for herbicide application, and the growing concern of society over the fate of pesticides and their environmental impact reflect the need for a treatise on turf weeds and their control. The subjects covered in this book embody in a microcosm the multidimensional nature of agriculture in all of its complexity—scientific, technical, environmental, and social.

The Crop Science Society of America and the American Society of Agronomy believe that turf and other crops should be managed in an environmentally, socially, and economically acceptable manner based on sound scientific principles. Further, these societies recognize and emphasize the value of turf-based environments in promoting the wise use of natural resources, and in water and soil conservation. The authors of the chapters of this book are industry and university leaders in their respective subject matter areas. They have given us their best perspectives in a very dynamic field. The American Society of Agronomy and the Crop Science Society of America extend a special acknowledgment and gratitude to the many authors of this book for providing the users a comprehensive approach to weed management in turf.

VERNON B. CARDWELL, *President*
Crop Science Society of America

CALVIN O. QUALSET, *President*
American Society of Agronomy

PREFACE

The classical definition of a weed is: *a plant growing out of place or growing where it is not desired.* According to the Weed Science Society of America, the currently accepted definition is: *any plant that is objectionable or interferes with the activities or welfare of man.* Within the context of a turfgrass community, the definition can be expanded to: *an undesirable plant because of its negative impact on the esthetic appearance, soil stabilizing capacity, or overall utility of a turf.*

The control of weeds in turfgrass communities may include virtually any practice designed to prevent weed emergence or to effect shifts toward desirable turfgrasses and away from undesirable vegetation. Historically, turfgrass weed control has been heavily dependent upon properly establishing well adapted turfgrasses and creating an environment conducive to their healthy, vigorous growth. As the components of a strategy for resisting weed invasion generally correspond to measures for achieving and maintaining acceptable turf quality, *cultural* control of turf weeds has generally been synonymous with proper turfgrass culture.

Herbicides may be used to control existing weed populations or to enhance the turf's resistance to weed invasion. Because of the role that herbicides often play in tuf weed control strategies, several chapters were developed covering their action and metabolism, formulations, application methods, and practical uses. As some herbicides (especially preemergence types) may cause injury, reduced growth or loss of competitive capacity of selected turfgrasses, a chapter devoted exclusively to this subject was included. Finally, implicit in all current recommendations on the use of herbicides for turf weed control is the avoidance of unacceptable environmental consequences; thus, a chapter on the environmental fate of herbicides was developed to address this concern.

Because managing weeds usually involves a combination of chemical and cultural methods, it should be based on a knowledge of the specific weeds to be controlled, the habitats in which they are likely to occur and the means by which they enter and persist in a turfgrass community. This information is covered in the three chapters on weed taxonomy, ecology, and control; and constitutes the foundation on which a turf weed control program should be constructed.

A. J. TURGEON
Editor

CONTRIBUTORS

George B. Beestman — Senior Research Associate, DuPont Agricultural Products, Wilmington, DE 19880-0402

B. E. Branham — Associate Professor, Department of Crop and Soil Sciences, Michigan State University, East Lansing, MI 48824

Lloyd M. Callahan — Professor, Department of Ornamental Horticulture, University of Tennessee, Knoxville, TN 37996-4500

Ralph E. Engel — Emeritus Professor, Box 339, Milltown, NJ 08850

David W. Hall — Senior Botanist, KBN Engineering and Applied Sciences, Inc., Gainesville, FL 32605

William J. Kowite — Senior Research Scientist, Rhone-Poulenc Ag Products, Research Triangle Park, NC 27709

Lambert B. McCarty — Associate Professor of Environmental Horticulture, Department of Environmental Horticulture, University of Florida, Gainesville, FL 32611-0670

Tim R. Murphy — Associate Professor, Crop and Soil Sciences Department, The University of Georgia, The Georgia Experiment Station, Griffin, GA 30223-1797

Donald Penner — Professor, Department of Crop and Soil Sciences, Michigan State University, East Lansing, MI 48824

Thomas F. Reed — Spraying Systems Company, P. O. Box 7900, Wheaton, IL 60189

Steve Titko — Manager, Development and Technical Services, Scotts/Hyponex, Marysville, OH 43041

Thomas L. Watschke — Professor of Tufgrass Science, Agronomy Department, Pennsylvania State University, University Park, Pennsylvania 16802

Chapter 1

Weed Taxonomy

DAVID W. HALL, *KBN Engineering and Applied Sciences, Gainesville, Florida*

LAMBERT B. McCARTY, *University of Florida, Gainesville, Florida*

TIM R. MURPHY, *University of Georgia, Griffin, Georgia*

A common goal shared by most turfgrass managers is to establish and maintain a vigorous, high quality, attractive turf. Limiting the deleterious effects of insects, disease-inciting pathogens and weeds and promoting desirable growth through proper watering, fertilization, mowing, and cultural practices, are necessary components of a balanced turfgrass management program.

Weeds are the major pests on many turfgrass sites. Weeds compete with turfgrasses for growing space, sunlight, soil moisture, and plant nutrients. Additionally, weeds detract from the natural beauty of turfgrasses due to differences in color, size, shape, and growth habit. Weed species such as lawn burweed [*Soliva pterosperma* (Juss.) Less] and khakiweed (*Alternanthera pungens* HBK) produce fruit with sharp-tipped spines and can cause injuries to humans. On golf courses, goosegrass [*Eleusine indica* (L.) Gaertn.] and other weeds disrupt the uniform surface of putting greens and interfere with ball roll.

Effective turfgrass weed control strategies are dependent upon correctly identifying the problem weed, its life cycle and preferred habitat. Weed species differ in their susceptibility to herbicides and other weed control strategies. For example, oryzalin has been shown to be more effective for controlling large crabgrass [*Digitaria sanguinalis* (L.) Scop.] than goosegrass (8).

I. HISTORY

Historically, plant identification has been conducted by professional taxonomists or systematic botanists. Taxonomy can be defined as the theory and practice of classifying organisms in established categories (7). Systemat-

ic botanists study the kinds and diversity of plants and examine or catego-
rize any and all relationships between them. Takhtajan (12) has estimated
that 250 000 flowering plants occur in the world; however, numerous plant
species exist that have not been classified. The science of plant taxonomy
includes the identification, nomenclature and classification of plants and is
often synonymous with systematic botany (6). Traditionally, plant taxonomy has been based on the recognition and classification of floral and other
reproductive structures of plant species. The reproductive structures of plants
are morphologically less variable than vegetative structures such as leaves.
Weed identification in turf is complicated by the fact that mowing continually removes the floral parts of most weeds with erect or semierect growth
habits. In these situations, identification is primarily based on the appearance and form of vegetative structures such as leaves and stems. Thorough
discussions and reviews of principles, practices, techniques, theory, and other
topics relevant to plant taxonomy can be found in such texts as: *Taxonomy
of Vascular Plants* by G. Lawrence (6), *Principles of Angiosperm Taxonomy* by P. Davis and V. Heywood (4), *Plant Taxonomy and Biosystematics*
by C. Stace (11), and *The Evolution and Classification of Flowering Plants*
by A. Cronquist (3).

II. IDENTIFICATION METHODS

Turfgrass weeds can be identified by the use of classical plant taxonomy books such as *Manual of the Vascular Flora of the Carolinas* (10), *Gray's
Manual of Botany* (5), *Manual of the Vascular Plants of Texas* (2), and *A
California Flora* (9), weed identification guides or manuals that contain photographs or line drawings of various species, or by sending the plant to a
turfgrass weed scientist or plant taxonomist. Classical plant taxonomy books
primarily use dichotomous keys that are based on reproductive structures
for plant identification. These keys use a series of paired statements about
flowers, fruits, leaves, or other anatomical structures that are answered yes
or no. The series of statements ultimately ends with the name of a plant species
that has the characteristics indicated by the yes answers (1). Usually it is necessary to have a specimen in flower or fruit to effectively use the keys of a
classical plant taxonomy book. Additionally, the botanical terminology employed in these texts and the lack of photographs and line drawings, usually
limit the use to persons trained in plant taxonomy.

Weed identification manuals that have been published by universities,
chemical companies, professional organizations, and private authors are extremely useful to identify commonly found turfgrass weeds. These manuals
usually contain high quality photographs or line drawings of the various turfgrass weed species showing pertinent vegetative identification characteristics.
Some of these guides contain keys for identification that are based entirely
on vegetative material and enable the user to find the name of the plant
without using flowers or fruits. Recently several user friendly computer ori-
ented identification systems have been developed.

The first step in utilizing these manuals is to classify the unknown plant as either a grass-like or broadleaf plant. In nearly all classification schemes, virtually all turf weeds in the USA are angiosperms (subdivision Angiospermae). This subdivision is divided into two broad groups: monocotyledoneae (monocots) and dicotyledoneae (dicots). The monocots are primarily grass-like plants and the dicots are primarily broadleaf plants. Grass-like and broadleaved plants are usually easy to recognize vegetatively. This natural separation is a convenient starting point for weed identification. Grass-like plants include grasses (Poaceae), sedges (Cyperaceae), and rushes (Juncaceae). Grasses have relatively narrow (longer than wide), two-ranked (arise from the stem in two different angles), alternate leaves with parallel veins, usually differentiated into a blade, sheath and ligule, and round or flattened stems with hollow internodes. The leaf sheath of grasses is usually split or open, and wraps around the stem with the edges meeting or slightly overlapping. Sedges differ from grasses by the presence of three-ranked leaves that often lack ligules, and have solid triangular stems (three-sided). The leaf sheath of sedges is closed and surrounds the stem like a cylinder. Rushes differ from grasses and sedges in that the leaves are mostly basal, linear and round or flat in cross-section. The leaf sheath of rushes usually is split or open and stems may be solid or hollow.

Broadleaf plants may have an alternate, opposite or whorled leaf attachment. Leaves have netted venation and may be classified as simple (not divided into individual leaflets) or compound (divided into two or more leaflets).

Two common turfgrass weeds that do not fit into grass-like or broadleaf plant groups are wild garlic (*Allium vineale* L.) and wild onion (*Allium canadense* L.). Refer to the descriptions of key identifying features for these weeds provided in this chapter.

After the unknown plant has been placed into the grass-like or broadleaf category, photographs or line drawings of the species contained in the manual can be compared with the unknown plant. When an apparent match is made, the key identifying features described for the species shown in the manual should be reviewed and compared with the unknown specimen. If the photograph and description of the species in the manual match that of the unknown species there is a high probability that the unknown species or weed has been correctly identified.

Weed identification manuals are useful but do have limitations. Unlike classical taxonomic floral manuals, that contain thousands of species, weed identification books may only contain 25 to 300 or so species. Often these manuals are adapted to a specific region of the USA. Users of these manuals often become frustrated when it becomes apparent that a manual does not contain weed species common to the region of interest. Nonetheless, weed identification manuals are extremely beneficial in identifying common turfgrass weeds.

Weeds that cannot be identified should be packaged and shipped to a county extension agent, turfgrass weed scientist, or plant taxonomist. A representative plant sample that includes leaves, stems, flowers or fruits, and roots should be submitted. Try to wash or knock off any soil contained in the root mat. Weeds can be placed between newspapers or cardboard and mailed through normal delivery services. Fresh, nonpressed specimens should never be sealed in plastic bags or shipped with wet foliage. During the warm months of the year specimens quickly decay and become unidentifiable. Information on the habitat, location, and the extent of distribution of the weed infestation should also be included with the specimen. There are perhaps >300 turfgrass weeds in the USA. Those included in this chapter are among the most common. Descriptions of plant families can be found in the various regional floras and particularly in Lawrence (6). Lawrence (6) and many of the regional floras contain illustrations that will aid identification.

III. GRASS AND GRASS-LIKE PLANTS

A. Cyperaceae

Green Kyllinga (Perennial Kyllinga) (Color Plate 1-1)
Cyperus brevifolius (Rottb.) Hassk. [*Kyllinga brevifolius* Rottb.]
    Mat forming perennial to 15 cm (6 in.) tall from reddish purple rhizomes. Leaves and stems, dark green. Seedhead simple, nearly round or oblong, with usually three short leaves just below. Reproduces by seeds and rhizomes. Found in low areas or where moisture is in excess. Of sporadic occurrence from Delaware and Rhode Island south through the Carolinas. Common from Georgia into south Florida, west to Texas and California. Also occurs in Hawaii, Mexico, Central and South America, the West Indies, Africa, Asia, Indonesia, Australia, and Europe.

Annual Sedge (Color Plate 1-2)
Cyperus compressus L.
    Annual. Seedhead with a few long leaves at the top of a bare stem. Clusters of flat spikes on short to long stalks. Spikes greenish, sometimes shining, up to 2.5 cm (1 in.) long. Reproduces by seeds. Found in sandy, moist, disturbed areas. Occurs from Minnesota, Ohio, and New York south through Florida and west to Texas. Also found in Bolivia, Ecuador, and Brazil.

Yellow Nutsedge (Yellow Nutgrass) (Color Plate 1-3)
Cyperus esculentus L.
    Rapidly spreading, perennial with three-ranked basal leaves. Leaves flat or slightly corrugated, usually as long or longer than flowering stem, with long attenuated tip. Seedhead yellowish-brown or straw colored, formed at end of triangular stem. Tubers round, lacking hairs and formed at ends of whitish rhizomes. Does not form chains of tubers. Tubers sweet to taste. Reproduces primarily by tubers. Found throughout the USA. Also found in Canada, the West Indies, Mexico, Central and South America, Europe, Africa, Asia, and Hawaii.

Globe Sedge (Color Plate 1–4)
Cyperus globulosus Aubl.
   Perennial with densely tufted stems. Leaf blades flat, smooth, dense, bright green. Seedhead branches at top of stem. Seeds in loose globe-like clusters. Reproduces by seeds. Occurs commonly in turf and most other moist to dry sandy habitats. Found from Virginia south into Florida and west to Texas, Oklahoma, and Missouri. Also occurs in the West Indies, Central and South America, Indonesia, Thailand, Japan, and China. Very similar to Cylindric Sedge (*Cyperus retrorsus* Chapm.), which differs by having seeds in cylindric clusters.

Purple Nutsedge (Color Plate 1–5)
Cyperus rotundus L.
   Rapidly-spreading, perennial with three-ranked basal leaves. Leaves flat or slightly corrugated, usually shorter than flowering stem, abruptly tapering at tip. Seedhead purple to reddish brown, formed at end of triangular stem. Tubers oblong, covered with hairs, and found in chains connected by brown, wiry rhizomes. Tubers bitter to taste. Reproduces primarily by tubers. Found north to Kentucky and West Virginia, west to Central Texas and in southern California. Also occurs in the West Indies, Mexico, Central and South America, Europe, Africa, Asia, and Hawaii.

B. Gramineae

Quackgrass (Color Plate 1–6)
Agropyron repens (L.) Beauv. [*Elymus repens* (L.) Gould]
   Green or silvery perennial from underground, yellowish runners. Leaf blades flat and usually sparsely hairy on the upper surface. Seedheads stiffly erect. Flowers in clusters, 4 to 6 per cluster. Flowers up to 1 cm long, often with a stiff hair at the tip. Reproduces by seeds and runners. Fields, pastures and disturbed areas. North Carolina, Oklahoma, Colorado, and California, northward in the USA. Native to Europe and Asia. Canada, Alaska, Hawaii, the Middle East, India, Japan, Australia, and South America.

Creeping Bentgrass (Photo not available)
Agrostis stolonifera L. var. *palustris* (Huds.) Farw. (*A. palustris* Huds.)
   Perennial with long aboveground runners. Leaf sheaths smooth. Leaf blades sandpapery. Seedheads with branches pressed upward against the stalk. Flowers on separate stalks, about 2 mm long. Reproduces by seeds and runners. Found in moist to wet areas. Scattered throughout the USA north of Florida. Canada, Alaska, Hawaii. Native to Europe. Widely introduced into cooler regions of the world.

Bushy Bluestem (Bushy Broomgrass, Bushy Beardgrass) (Color Plate 1–8)
Andropogon glomeratus (Walt.) BSP.
   Perennial with several tall stems from a basal crown. Leaf sheaths flattened and keeled. Flowers green to reddish-purple, becoming straw colored

upon maturity. Seeds with white silky hairs, paired. Reproduces by seeds. Differs from broomsedge in that the seedheads are very dense and bushy in a cluster at the top of the stem. Found only in wet areas of old fields, pastures and roadside ditches. Occurs from Massachusetts to Michigan, throughout the Atlantic coastal and southeastern states and Florida. Also occurs in Ontario, the West Indies, Mexico, Central America and Colombia. Naturalized in California, Hawaii, Japan, and Australia.

Broomsedge (Broomgrass, Sagegrass) (Color Plate 1–9)
Andropogon virginicus L.
   Perennial with several tall stems from a basal crown. Leaf sheaths flattened and keeled. Flowers green to reddish-purple, becoming straw colored upon maturity. Seeds with white silky hairs, paired. Reproduces by seeds. Differs from bushy bluestem in that the seedheads are longer with scattered flowers. Found in old fields, roadsides and pastures. Occurs in the Northeastern, Southeastern and Middle Atlantic States, throughout Florida to Texas, Utah, and Nevada. Also found in the West Indies and Central America.

Carpetgrass (Color Plate 1–10)
Axonopus affinis Chase
   Mat-forming perennial from somewhat flattened, smooth stolons. Leaf blade, smooth on both surfaces, tip rounded; few long hairs present on leaf sheath margin and at base of blade margin. Seedhead resembles crabgrass spp., with two to five ascending spikes. Uppermost two branches usually paired. Reproduces by seeds and stolons. Most common on low, moist sites. Often seeded as a companion grass to centipedegrass. Common in the coastal plain of the Gulf states, north to North Carolina, and west to Arkansas, and Oklahoma. Also occurs in Central and South America, India, Australia, and Southern Africa.

Alexandergrass (Creeping Signalgrass) (Color Plate 1–11)
Brachiaria plantaginea (Link) A.S. Hitchc.
   Summer annual with prostrate, creeping smooth stems, rooting at nodes. Leaf blades usually smooth, flat and wide. Leaf sheath often with hairs on margin. Seedhead branches spreading like signal flags with seeds on underside. Occurring in turf and disturbed habitats. Reproduces by seeds. Found in peninsula of Florida, Georgia and isolated places in New Jersey, Pennsylvania, and Hawaii. Also found in Mexico, Central America, and South America. Native to Tropical America.

Broadleaf Signalgrass (Color Plate 1–12)
Brachiaria platyphylla (Griseb.) Nash
   Spreading, highly-branched summer annual rooting at lower nodes. Leaf blade short and wide, smooth on both surfaces, often partly folded or creased near the tip. Spikelets on underside of two to six ascending branches. Angle of branches resembles a signal flag. Reproduces by seeds. May be common

during turfgrass establishment. Found throughout the Southeast from North Carolina into Florida and west to Oklahoma and Texas.

Smallflowered Alexandergrass (Color Plate 1-13)
Brachiaria subquadripara (Trin.) A.S. Hitchc.
   Perennial from stolons. Leaf blade and sheath hairy. Flowering branches ascending, to 45 cm (18 in.) tall. Seedheads with two to seven branches or fingers. Seeds located under and appressed to the branch. Angle of branches resembling a signal flag. Reproduces by seeds and stolons. Found in lawns, cultivated fields, disturbed areas, and hammocks. Occurs throughout peninsula of Florida. Introduced into Africa, Mexico, Costa Rica, and the West Indies. Native to India, Burma, Malaysia, Java, some Pacific Islands, and Australia.

Field Sandbur (Coast Sandspur, Field Sandspur) (Color Plate 1-14)
Cenchrus incertus M.A. Curtis [*C. pauciflorus* Benth.]
   Annual or short-lived perennial with erect or ascending stems. Leaf blades flat to slightly folded, sandpapery to the touch. Seedheads in spikes of burs with flat spines. Burs finely hairy with one to three seeds. Reproduces by seeds. Found in any open sandy site. Occurs from Virginia along the coast to California, inland to Oklahoma and Arkansas. Also occurs in the West Indies, Mexico to coastal Central and South America, South Africa, and the Philippines.

Bermudagrass (Color Plate 1-15)
Cynodon dactyon (L.) Pers.
   Perennial with underground and aboveground runners. Leaf sheaths and blades smooth to hairy. Leaf blades flat to folded and rolled. Seedheads with 3 to 9 branches, all joined at the same point. Flowers underneath the branches, flattened, 2 to 3 mm long. Reproduces by underground and aboveground runners and seeds. Fields, pastures, roadsides, wet areas, disturbed areas. Occurs throughout the USA. Native to Eurasia. Introduced into Canada and all warmer areas of the world.

Orchardgrass (Color Plate 1-16)
Dactylis glomerata L.
   Tufted perennial. Stems bent at base. Leaf blade, V-shaped in cross section near base, prominent midrib on underside, margins rough to the touch. Visible sharp-pointed membranous ligule at base of blade. Seedheads green, densely clustered. Reproduces by seeds. An introduced cool-season forage grass found throughout most of North America, except peninsula of Florida. Also found in Europe, Asia, Australia, South America, and Hawaii. Native to the Old World.

Crowfootgrass (Color Plate 1-17)
Dactyloctenium aegyptium (L.) Willd.
   Tufted summer annual with upwardly bent stems. Leaves with row of hairs extending outward from the margin at the base of blade. Spikelets ar-

ranged on two to five fingers at tip of the stem. Outer tips of fingers extended giving seedhead a crowfoot appearance. Reproduces by seeds. Fairly common in low maintenance areas in the coastal plain and piedmont regions of the southern states, north to New York, and west to California. Also found in the West Indies, Central and South America, Australia, Europe, Asia, Tropical Africa, and Hawaii.

Tropical Crabgrass (Color Plate 1-18)
Digitaria bicornis (Lam.) Roem. & Schult. ex Loud.
Annual bending and rooting at lower nodes. Leaf sheaths and blades hairy. Blades usually 6 cm (>2 in.) long. Visible membranous ligule at base of leaf blade. Differs from large and southern crabgrass in that seedhead branches all join stem at same point. Reproduces by seeds. Found throughout the Gulf Coastal Plain to Texas. Thought to be introduced from the Old World.

Smooth Crabgrass (Color Plate 1-19)
Digitaria ischaemum (Schreb. ex Schweig.) Schreb. ex Muhl.
Tufted or prostrate, spreading summer annual. Leaves smooth on both surfaces. Leaf sheath smooth, few long hairs at collar. Visible membranous ligule at base of leaf blade. Seedhead with two to six finger-like branches. Reproduces by seeds. Found throughout the USA and the world.

Large Crabgrass and Southern Crabgrass (Color Plate 1-20)
Digitaria sanguinalis (L.) Scop. and *Digitaria ciliaris* (Retz.) Koel.
Tufted, or prostrate to spreading summer annual with branched stems that root at the nodes. Leaf blade, longer than 5 cm (2 in.), usually hairy on both surfaces, visible toothed membranous ligule at base of leaf. Leaf sheath with dense hairs. Spikelets in two to nine finger-like branches. Southern crabgrass is distinguished from large crabgrass on the basis of the length of the second glume (a bract at the base of a spikelet). These species differ from tropical crabgrass in that the seedhead branches arise from different points of attachment along the stalk. Both species reproduce by seeds. Southern crabgrass occurs northward on the coastal plain occasionally to Connecticut, more common southward east of the Appalachian region, throughout Florida, extending west into Texas and north into Kansas and Nebraska. Also occurs in the West Indies, Mexico, Central America, and South America. Large crabgrass is found throughout North America, except Florida, and the warm temperate regions of the world. Both species thought to be introduced from the Old World.

Goosegrass (Crowfoot, Silver Crabgrass) (Color Plate 1-21)
Eleusine indica (L.) Gaertn.
Tough, clumped summer annual, generally with a whitish to silverish coloration at the center of the plant. Leaf blade smooth on both surfaces, occasionally a few hairs near the base. Visible, short-toothed, membranous ligule at base of leaf blade. Spikelets in two rows on two to thirteen fingers.

Frequently a single finger below the terminal cluster of fingers. Reproduces by seeds. Found throughout the temperate and warm parts of the USA and throughout the warm temperate, subtropical and tropical areas of the world.

Tall Fescue (Color Plate 1–22)
Festuca arundinacea Schreb. [*F. elatior* L, sensu stricto]
Tufted perennial, rarely with thin, weak underground runners. Leaf sheaths smooth. Leaf blades flat, smooth. Seedheads 20 to 30 cm long. Flowers in clusters of 4 to 7. Flowers 4 to 7 mm long, with a stiff hair at the tip. Reproduces by runners and seeds. Pastures, roadsides, and disturbed moist areas. Throughout the USA. Native to Europe and Asia, Canada, and Hawaii. Widely introduced into most temperate areas of the world.

Nimblewill (Color Plate 1–23)
Muhlenbergia schreberi J.F. Gmel.
Delicate perennial with a reclining growth habit. Leaves very narrow, short, and hairless. Leaf collers hairy. Ligule a short, jagged membrane. Sheaths smooth. Panicle narrow, with ascending branches. Reproduces by seeds. Thrives in moist, shady sites. Often confused with bermudagrass. Occurs New Hampshire, south to central peninsula Florida, west to Texas, Arizona, Oklahoma, Kansas, Iowa, and Wisconsin, Eastern Canada.

Fall Panicum (Color Plate 1–24)
Panicum dichotomiflorum Michx.
Sprawling to erect summer annual. Stems bent and branched outward. Leaf blade smooth, occasionally hairy on the upper surface, with a distinct broad, light green midrib. Ligule a fringe of hairs. Seedhead purplish colored at maturity, open, and freely branched. Reproduces by seeds. Common during turfgrass establishment. Found from Maine, Michigan, and Minnesota, south into Florida and west to Texas, Arizona, California, and Hawaii. Also found in Europe.

Torpedograss (Color Plate 1–25)
Panicum repens L.
Perennial with creeping, sharply pointed rhizomes. Stems stiff and erect. Leaves folded or flat and sparsely hairy on upper surface. Seedheads with stiff, ascending or appressed branches. Reproduces primarily by rhizomes. Found in the Gulf Coast region of the southeast USA from Florida west into Texas. Also occurs in Tropical Africa, Tropical Asia, Europe, and Hawii.

Dallisgrass (Color Plate 1–26)
Paspalum dilatatum Poir.
Clumped perennial from short thick rhizomes. Leaf sheaths at base of plant sometimes rough hairy. Leaf blade, smooth on both surfaces, with a few long hairs at leaf base and behind ligule at base of leaf blade. Ligule tall, membranous, either sharply or bluntly tipped. Spikelets arranged in four rows on three to seven alternate branches. Reproduces by seeds and very short

rhizomes. Common throughout the southeastern states, north to Virginia, west to Arizona, California, the Pacific Northwest, and Hawaii. Also occurs in the West Indies, Central and South America, and Europe.

Bahiagrass (Color Plate 1-27)
Paspalum notatum Fluegge

Aggressive, mat-forming, warm-season perennial with shallow, often-exposed rhizomes. Leaves, primarily basal, somewhat folded, smooth on both surfaces or often hairy only at the collar. Ligule short, membranous. Seedheads with usually two or occasionally three branches. Seedhead branches usually paired. Spikelets in two rows on lower sides. Reproduces by seeds and rhizomes. Common primarily in the Gulf States, north to North Carolina and west to Texas. Also found in the West Indies, Central America, and Hawaii. Native to South America.

Vaseygrass (Color Plate 1-28)
Paspalum urvillei Steud.

Perennial with densely tufted stems. Leaf sheaths usually rough hairy. Leaf blades flat, smooth except for hairs at base of blade on upper surface. Ligule membranous, tall. Seedheads with four to thirty spreading branches. Branches with paired, hairy flowers in lines on the lower side. Reproduces by seeds. Occurring in ditches, fields, pastures, disturbed areas, and pinelands usually where the soil is moist to wet. Found from Virginia into Florida, west into Texas and southern California. Also found throughout the warm and tropical areas of the world and Europe. Native to South America.

Annual Bluegrass (Color Plate 1-29)
Poa annua L.

Small tufted to clumped winter annual with some perennial biotypes. Leaf blade smooth on both surfaces, with two distinct, clear lines, one on each side of the midrib. Leaf tip keeled or boat-shaped. Ligule membranous. Light green to whitish spikelets that lack cottony hairs, are arranged on branches, one to two per node, in dense to open flower clusters. Reproduces by seeds. Found throughout the world.

Yellow Foxtail (Color Plate 1-30)
Setaria pumila (Poir.) Roem. & Schult.; [*S. glauca* auct. non (L.) P. Beauv.; *S. lutescens* (Weig.) F.T. Hubbard]

Annual; stems ascending, but bending and rooting at base. Leaf sheaths with hairs on margins, otherwise smooth. Leaf blades sandpapery, small to long hairs on upper surface at base. Seedhead like a fox's tail, cylindric, bristly, 2 to 15 cm long, yellow at maturity. Seeds rough on the back. Reproduces by seeds. Fields, roadsides, disturbed areas, and open woods. Throughout the USA. Canada, the West Indies. Native to tropical and warm regions of the Old World.

Johnsongrass (Color Plate 1–31)
Sorghum halepense (L.) Pers.

Coarse perennial from long, thick, scaly, sharp pointed rhizomes. Stems erect, forming dense stands to 2 m (6 ft) tall. Leaf blade with prominent white midvein and hairs at base of upper surface. Prominent membranous ligule at base of leaf blade. Large, open seedhead often purple in color. Seeds hairy. Does not persist under close frequent mowing. Reproduces by seeds and rhizomes. Found from Massachusetts to Iowa, south into Florida, and west into Texas, Arizona, and California. Also found in the West Indies, Mexico, Central and South America, Hawaii, Europe, Africa, India, and Australia. Native from southern Eurasia east to India. Introduced into the warmer regions of the world as a forage species.

Smutgrass (Color Plate 1–32)
Sporobolus indicus (L.) R.Br. [*Sporobolus poiretii* (Roem. & Schult.) Hitchc.]

Tufted perennial with erect stems. Leaf blades flat to usually folded at base of plant becoming rounded toward tip. Seedhead very narrow or with spreading branches. Seeds infected with a black fungus (smut) or unaffected and brown. Reproduces by seeds. Occurs in turf, pastures, and roadsides. Found throughout the southeast USA, from Virginia into Florida and Texas, inland to Oklahoma and Missouri. Also found in the West Indies, Central and South America, Japan, and the Philippines. Native to Tropical America.

C. Liliaceae

Wild Onion (Color Plate 1–33)
Allium canadense L.

Perennial from a fibrous bulb. Plant with an onion odor. Leaves narrowly linear, soft, flattish, slightly keeled, shorter than scape, 1 to 3 mm wide, channeled. Flowers white to pink, replaced by bulblets. Reproduces by terminal bulblets. Found in meadows, woods, fields, and along roadsides. Florida to Texas, north to North Dakota, southeastern Canada, and eastern USA.

Wild Garlic (Color Plate 1–34)
Allium vineale L.

Cool-season perennial with slender, hollow cylindrical leaves. Leaves on the flowering stem up to half the height of the plant. Underground bulb bears offset bulblets that are flattened on one side and enclosed by a membrane. Flowers, greenish-white, small on short stems above aerial bulbils. Plant with distinctive garlic odor when crushed. Reproduces by seed, aerial bulbils, and underground bulblets. Found throughout most of the eastern and southern USA, north into Canada, west to Missouri and Arkansas; North Africa; Europe. Wild onion (*Allium canadense* L.) is often found on same sites as wild garlic. Wild onion can be distinguished from wild garlic by presence of a fibrous coat on the central bulb, no offset bulblets and leaves that arise near the base of a solid flowering stem.

IV. BROADLEAF PLANTS

A. Aizoaceae

Carpetweed (Color Plate 1-35)
Mollugo verticillata L.
Prostrate summer annual with numerous smooth, branched stems. Leaves light green in color, smooth, spoon-shaped, and arranged in whorls of five to six at each node. Flowers, white, arranged in clusters of two to five on slender stalks from leaf axils, petals five. Reproduces by tiny, reddish seeds. Usually a problem only during turfgrass establishment. Found throughout most of the USA. Also found in Canada, through Mexico into Central and South America, Africa, and Asia.

B. Amaranthaceae

Tumbleweed (Prostrate Amaranth) (Color Plate 1-36)
Amaranthus albus L. [*A. blitoides* S. Wats.; *A. graecizans* of American authors]
Annual herb from taproots; stems stout, often purplish, usually prostrate, branched at base, forming mats. Leaves usually crowded, with white margins. Infrequent to locally common in dry prairies, in waste places, pastures, fields, roadsides, stream valleys. Reproduces by seeds. Throughout North America. Introduced into Europe, Africa, Asia, and South America.

C. Caryophyllaceae

Mouse-ear Chickweed (Color Plate 1-37)
Cerastium fontanum Baumg. ssp. *triviale* (Link) Jalas, [*C. holosteoides* Fries; *C. vulgatum* L.]
Perennial, hairy with regular and sticky hairs; stems purplish, single or branched from the base. Leaves obovate to spatulate. Roadsides, pastures, meadows, prairies and open woods, often weedy lawns. Reproduces by seeds. Throughout most of North America except Florida. Native to Eurasia. Also introduced into Australia.

Bird's-eye Pearlwort (Color Plate 1-38)
Sagina procumbens L.
Matted, procumbent perennial with a dense central rosette and often with similar rosettes borne on the branches; rosette leaves bristle-tipped. Flowers small, white, 4-merous. Reproduces by seeds. Found in damp open areas.

Southeastern Canada, south to West Virginia, west to Ohio, and Minnesota. Throughout Europe.

Knawel (Color Plate 1-39)
Scleranthus annuus L.
Freely-branched winter annual with a prostrate habit. Leaves, opposite, very narrow, linear in shape, sharply pointed and generally bent downward. Small green flowers, that lack petals, found in clusters in the leaf axils. Reproduces by seeds. Found in the Eastern half of the USA, north to Canada, west to California and Pacific Coast, and Europe.

Common Chickweed (Color Plate 1-40)
Stellaria media (L.) Cyrillo
Mat-forming winter annual with numerous branched stems. Leaves opposite, smooth, oval to broadly elliptic in shape. Upper leaves without petiole; lower leaves with sparsely hairy long petiole. Stems with vertical lines of hairs. Flowers in small clusters at ends of stems, white, with five deeply notched petals. Reproduces by seeds. Located throughout North America except for the Rocky Mountains. Also found in Mexico, Central and South America, Hawaii, Asia, Africa, and Europe.

D. Chenopodiaceae

Common Lamb's-quarters (Color Plate 1-41)
Chenopodium album L.
Summer annual, stem solitary. Leaves white mealy underneath, blades variable, edges toothed. Flowers small, green without petals, borne at branch ends and leaf axils. Seeds shiny black with gray hull. Reproduces by seeds. Found in open, disturbed areas. Almost cosmopolitan.

E. Compositae

Common Yarrow (Color Plate 1-42)
Achillea millefolium L.
Aromatic perennial, wooly hairy. Stems simple or few-branched, from a fibrous-rooted, weakly spreading rhizome. Leaves equally distributed along the stem, but the lower and middle cauline leaves numerous and largest. Blades smooth to loosely hairy, bipinnately parted and dissected into fine segments. Reproduces by seeds. Found in disturbed areas. Throughout the USA except southern Texas and peninsula Florida. Throughout the northern part of the world (circumboreal).

Common Ragweed (Color Plate 1-43)
Ambrosia artemisiifolia L.
Taprooted summer annual with branched stems. Leaves hairy, deeply twice dissected. Male and female flowers separate, green. Reproduces by seeds. Fields, pastures, roadsides, and waste places. Occurs in the north-

western and southeastern USA. Also found in Canada, Central and South America, the West Indies, South Pacific, and Australia. Native to the USA. ·

Mugwort (Color Plate 1-44)
Artemisia vulgaris L.

Creeping perennial from long rhizomes. Stems hairy, round in cross section. Leaves alternate, dissected, each segment linear to elliptic in shape. Upper leaf surface dark green, smooth to slightly hairy; lower leaf surface whitish to grayish, densely wooly. Reproduces by rhizomes, not believed to produce viable seeds. Vegetatively resembles and has same characteristic odor of the garden chrysanthemum. Found in the Eastern half of the USA, west to Texas. Occurs also in the West Indies, Canada, Europe, Asia, and Hawaii.

English Daisy (Color Plate 1-45)
Bellis perennis L.

Perennial, with loosely clustered, hairy stems, arising from creeping, fibrous rootstocks. Leaves clustered toward the base, spatulate to obovate. Heads solitary at the ends of naked scapes. Flowers white to pink. Reproduces by seeds and division of rootstocks. Southern Canada and northern USA, south to Virginia, North Carolina, and west to California. Native to Europe. Also found in Australia, western Asia, and South America.

Spotted Knapweed (Color Plate 1-46)
Centaurea maculosa Lam.

Semierect freely-branched perennial to 1 m tall. Leaves alternate, deeply divided into narrow segments, hairy. Stems hairy. Flowers pink to purple, in terminal and axillary heads. Floral bracts, dark-tipped, with fringe of bristly hairs. Reproduces by seeds. Southeastern states north to Ontario, British Columbia, and Quebec, west to Missouri and Kansas, California, and Europe.

Oxeye Daisy (Color Plate 1-47)
Chrysanthemum leucanthemum L. [*Leucanthemum vulgare* L.]

Erect perennial, from rhizomes, nearly smooth. Most leaves basal, broadest at tip, with long stalks. Leaf margins toothed to lobed or parted. Flowers white, in solitary heads. Reproduces by seeds and rhizomes. Throughout the temperate areas of the USA. Native to Eurasia. Also in China, Australia, New Zealand, the Middle East, and South America.

Chicory (Color Plate 1-48)
Cichorium intybus L.

Freely-branched taprooted perennial, initially from a rosette. Leaves coarsely toothed, upper surface rough to the touch. Basal leaves usually absent at flowering. Stem leaves alternate, clasping and hairy. Stems smooth, with a milky juice. Flowers bright blue. Reproduces by seeds. Scattered throughout the USA with the exception of Florida. Native to North Africa, Europe, and Western Asia.

Bull Thistle (Color Plate 1-49)
Cirsium vulgare (Savi) Tenore
Biennial with erect, robust stems from a fleshy taproot. Leaves deeply lobed with sharp, stout spines at the leaf tip of each lobe. Upper leaf surface dark green with short, stiff hairs; lower leaf surface covered with wooly gray hairs. Flowers purple, in heads on ends of branches. Reproduces by seeds. Usually found only in low maintenance turfgrasses. Occurs in pastures, roadsides, and waste places. Southern Canada south to Georgia and Mississippi, west to Nebraska. Also in California and Oregon. Native to Eurasia.

Horseweed (Color Plate 1-50)
Conyza canadensis (L.) Cronq.
Tall-growing summer or winter annual with bristly hairy stems. Leaves alternate, lack petioles, linear to oblanceolate. Leaf margins often toothed; lower margins with long hairs. Flowers in numerous, small heads on branches in the upper portion of the plant. Reproduces by seeds. Found throughout the USA. Also occurs in Quebec, Ontario, Mexico, Central and South America, and Europe.

Dogfennel (Color Plate 1-51)
Eupatorium capillifolium (Lam.) Small
Tall-growing perennial with one to several densely, hairy stems from a woody crown. Leaves deeply cut into linear segments. Lower leaves opposite, upper leaves alternate. Leaves strongly aromatic when crushed. Reproduces by seeds and regrowth from woody base. Found from New Jersey to south Florida, and west to Texas and Arkansas. Also occurs in the West Indies and Guatemala.

Purple Cudweed (Color Plate 1-52)
Gnaphalium purpureum L.
Annual or biennial developing a basal rosette of leaves. Stems highly branched from base of plant. Stem and underside of leaves with soft velvet-like hairs. Upper leaf surface dull green. Rosette and lower stem leaves spatula-shaped with blunt tips, upper leaves reduced in size. Flowers tannish-white in clusters at upper leaf axils. Bracts surrounding flower clusters pink or purple in color. Reproduces by seeds. Found throughout the continental USA except for North and South Dakota. Also found in Saskatchewan, Manitoba, and Europe.

Mouse-ear (Photo not available)
Hieracium pilosella L.
Perennial herbs, dwarf, forming carpets, from many long stolons and a long slender rhizome. Stems with blackish hairs. Leaves in a basal rosette, spatulate, setose on both surfaces, green above, whitened beneath when young with close star-shaped hairs. Flowers yellow, in solitary heads. Reproduces by seeds. Found in pastures and fields. Southeastern Canada and Minnesota, south to New England, Long Island, North Carolina, Ohio, and Tennessee. Native to Europe.

Catsear Dandelion (Color Plate 1–54)
Hypochoeris radicata L.

Perennial with densely hairy leaves arranged in a basal rosette. Leaf margins, coarsely toothed, divisions or lobes with blunt to slightly pointed tips. Flower stalk with two to seven flowers, bright yellow, similar in appearance to dandelion flowers. Leaves and flower stalks exude a milky juice when broken. Reproduces by seeds. Found from New Jersey south into panhandle Florida and west to Mississippi. Also found in Ontario and North Africa. Native to Eurasia.

Lawn Burweed (Spurweed) (Color Plate 1–55)
Soliva pterosperma (Juss.) Less.

Low-growing, freely branched winter annual. Leaves opposite, sparsely hairy and twice divided into narrow segments or lobes. Flowers small and inconspicuous. Fruits clustered in leaf axils and having sharp spines that can cause injury to humans. Reproduces by seeds. Generally found in the Coastal Plain and Piedmont Regions of most southern states, North Carolina south into Florida, and west to Texas. Also occurs in South America and Europe.

Spiny Sowthistle (Color Plate 1–56)
Sonchus asper (L.) Hill

Winter annual. Leaves, alternate, deeply lobed with spiny margins. Leaf base rounded and clasps the stem. Stems smooth on the lower portion but with stalked, glandular hairs on the upper portion. Yellow flowers in clusters at top of plant. Leaves and stems exude a milky juice when broken. Reproduces by seeds. Found throughout the USA, north into Alaska and the Yukon. Also found in the West Indies, South America, Eurasia, Africa, and Hawaii. Annual sowthistle (*Sonchus oleraceus* L.) is similar but with a sharply-pointed, clasping leaf base.

Dandelion (Color Plate 1–57)
Taraxacum officinale Weber

Deeply taprooted, stemless perennial. Leaves, basal, slightly to deeply cut, with lobes that point back towards base. Single yellow flowers at end of each long, smooth hollow stalk. Leaves and flower stalks exude a milky juice when broken. Seeds brown, long stalked with a parachute of hairs forming a globe. Reproduces by seeds and can form new plants from fragments of broken taproots. Found throughout the USA, Alaska, and Hawaii. Also found in the West Indies, Mexico, Central and South America, Africa, Europe, and Asia.

F. Convolvulaceae

Field Bindweed (Color Plate 1–58)
Convolvulus arvensis L.

Perennial, herbaceous, trailing or twining and climbing vine. The roots branched and deep. Leaves variable, triangular to oblong. Flowers solitary, white to pink, funnelform, about 2 cm long. Reproduces by seeds and broken fragments of the roots. Throughout the USA. Native to Eurasia. Cosmopolitan.

Dichondra (Carolina Dichondra, Ponyfoot) (Color Plate 1–59)
Dichondra carolinensis Michx.
Creeping, prostrate perennial that roots at the nodes. Leaves alternate, sparsely-hairy, kidney-shaped to nearly round resembling a pony's foot. Flowers inconspicuous, white. Reproduces by seeds and stolons. Used in southern California as a lawn ground cover. Found from Virginia to Texas. Also found in the West Indies, Central and South America, Africa, Asia, Australia, and Hawaii.

G. Cruciferae

Yellow Rocket (Color Plate 1–60)
Barbarea vulgaris R.Br.
Smooth, erect biennial or perennial with angled stems. Lower leaves petiolate, lyrate with 1 to 4 pairs of small, rounded lateral lobes and a large, rounded terminal one; stem leaves progressively reduced, generally the uppermost entire or merely toothed. Petals yellow, 5 to 5.5 mm long. Fruit 2 to 2.5 cm long. Reproduces by seeds. A weed in moist to wet meadows, fields, roadsides, and cultivated areas. Scattered throughout the USA excluding the southern states from Florida west to Arizona. Native to Eurasia. Introduced into Canada and New Zealand.

Wild Mustard (Color Plate 1–61)
Brassica kaber (DC.) Wheeler [*Sinapis arvensis* L.]
Annual. Stems smooth to hairy with stiff hairs. Lower leaves with stiff hairy leaf stalks and lyre-shape blades. Upper leaves sparsely soft hairy with rounded or oblong blades. Petals yellow, 5.8 to 8.5 mm long. Fruit 2.1 to 2.4 cm long. Reproduces by seeds. Throughout the USA. Native to Mediterranean region. Introduced into most temperate areas of the world.

Shepherdspurse (Color Plate 1–62)
Capsella bursa-pastoris (L.) Medic.
Winter annual from a rosette of variously toothed or lobed leaves. Stem leaves few in number, arrow-shaped with the basal lobes extending past the stem. Flowers white, in clusters at end of stems, petals four, small. Fruit triangular or wedge-shaped. Reproduces by seeds. Found throughout North America except Arizona. Also found in Hawaii, South America, Europe, North Africa, and Asia.

Hairy Bittercress (Color Plate 1–63)
Cardamine hirsuta L.
Winter annual from a rosette of dark green, dissected leaves. Leaf segments rounded to wedge-shaped, lower petioles hairy near the base. Flowers

white, in dense clusters at end of stems, petals four. Fruit a flattened capsule, more than 10 times longer than broad. Reproduces by seeds. Found from Maine into Florida and west to Nebraska, Texas, and Washington. Also found in Hawaii, Canada, Europe, Asia, North Africa, and Australia.

Field Pepperweed (Color Plate 1–64)
Lepidium campestre (L.) R.Br.
Tap rooted winter annual from a basal rosette. Stems hairy. Basal leaves lobed, toothed or dissected; frequently absent at flowering and fruiting. Stem leaves elongate, often toothed and clasp the stem. Flowers white, small, four-parted. Seedpod oval, flat, with a flange of papery tissue at the top. Reproduces by seeds. Found in disturbed areas. Occurs throughout the South, and from Canada and Michigan southwards through Kansas, west to Texas, Wyoming, the Pacific Coast, Europe, Australia, and New Zealand.

Virginia Pepperweed (Color Plate 1–65)
Lepidium virginicum L.
Winter annual from a rosette of leaves. Stems smooth, erect, and freely branched. Basal and stem leaves serrated, lobed, or deeply notched. Basal leaves lacking on mature plants. Stem leaves reduced in size, more serrated and lobed toward the apex of the plant. Produces spike-like clusters of tiny white flowers at end of branches. Seedpod round, flat with notch at tip. Fruit with distinctive mustard taste. Reproduces by seeds. Found throughout the USA except for Arizona and New Mexico. Also occurs in Saskatchewan and Manitoba.

Field Pennycress (Color Plate 1–66)
Thlaspi arvense L.
Smooth, erect annual with a bad smell. Stems solitary, often branched above. Basal leaves spatulate, apex rounded or obtuse, margins smooth or irregularly toothed. Upper leaves oblong to lanceolate, apex obtuse to acute, margins sinuate to coarsely toothed, base with ears or clasping. Petals white, 3 to 4 mm long. Fruits 10 to 18 mm long, split at the tip. Reproduces by seeds. Found on roadsides, in disturbed areas, fields and pastures. Throughout North America. Native to Eurasia. Introduced into most temperate areas of the world.

H. Euphorbiaceae

Spotted Spurge (Prostrate Spurge) (Color Plate 1–67)
Chamaesyce maculata (L.) Small [*Euphorbia maculata* L.]
Summer annual with freely branched prostrate stems that do not root at the nodes. Stems smooth or hairy, with milky sap. Leaves opposite, usually with a reddish spot, not symmetrical. Occurring in any disturbed area. Found in the eastern USA, west to North Dakota and Texas and into California and Oregon. Also occurs in Canada, Mexico, Central America, South America, Japan, New Zealand, and Lebanon. Prostrate spurge [*Chamaesyce*

humistrata (Engelm. ex Gray)] is similar but roots at the nodes. Both species reproduce by seeds.

I. Geraniaceae

Redstem Filaree (Color Plate 1–68)
Erodium cicutarium (L.) L'Her. ex Ait.
   Prostrate to semierect winter annual with numerous branches that radiate from the crown. Leaves hairy, dissected into numerous segments, opposite on upper portion of stem, alternate below. Flowers pinkish-purple, in clusters of six to nine on long stalks. Fruit a five-parted capsule that forms a characteristic stork's bill up to 5 cm (2 in.) long. Reproduces by seeds. Found in most of the USA, Alaska, and Hawaii. Also occurs in Canada, Greenland, Mexico, Central and South America, Europe, South Africa, and Australia.

Carolina Geranium (Wild Geranium; Crane's-bill; Stork's-bill)
(Color Plate 1–69)
Geranium carolinianum L.
   Diffusely-branched semierect winter annual. Stems greenish-pink to red, densely hairy. Leaves with long petioles, hairy, dissected into variously divided segments, margins blunt toothed. Flowers pink to purplish with five petals. Fruit a five-parted capsule that forms a stork's bill up to 1.2 cm (0.5 in.) long. Reproduces by seeds. Found throughout the continental USA and Hawaii. Also occurs in Canada, the West Indies, Mexico, Central and South America, and Australia.

J. Labiatae

Ground Ivy (Color Plate 1–70)
Glechoma hederacea L.
   Prostrate, creeping perennial with four-sided, hairy stems. Leaves, opposite, kidney-shaped to rounded, prominently veined and with scalloped margins. Readily roots at stem nodes. Flowers, bluish to purplish with red speckles, arranged in groups of three to seven at stem ends or leaf axils. Reproduces by seeds and creeping stems. More common in shaded than full sunlight areas. Found in the eastern USA, extending south to the Piedmont region of the southern states; Georgia to Kansas, Oklahoma, Missouri, California, the Pacific Northwest, and Alaska. Also occurs in Canada, Europe, and Asia.

Henbit (Color Plate 1–71)
Lamium amplexicaule L.
   Sparsely-hairy winter annual with greenish to purplish, tender, four-sided stems. Similar in appearance to purple deadnettle but upper leaves lack petioles. Leaves opposite, broadly egg-shaped with bluntly toothed margins, and prominent veins on underside. Flowers, reddish-purple with darker coloring

in spots on lower petal, arranged in whorls. Reproduces by seeds. Found throughout most of North America. Also occurs in the West Indies, South America, Europe, Africa, Asia, and Australia.

Purple Deadnettle (Color Plate 1–72)
Lamium purpureum L.
Sparsely-hairy winter annual with greenish to purplish, tender, four-sided stems. Leaves opposite, broadly egg-shaped with bluntly toothed margins. Lower leaves on long petioles, upper leaves on short petioles (as opposed to petioles on upper leaves of henbit). Leaves often reddish or purplish tinged. Flowers, reddish purple with darker coloring in spots on lower petal, arranged in whorls. Reproduces by seeds. Found in most of the USA except for the Rocky Mountains. Also found in Canada, Greenland, Europe, and Asia.

Healall (Color Plate 1–73)
Prunella vulgaris L.
Perennial branched herb with upright to reclining growth habit. Numerous, opposite elliptic to lance-shaped leaves on square stems. Leaves and stems hairy. Lower leaves with long petioles, upper leaves sessile. Dense clusters of pale violet to purple trumpet-shaped flowers at the end of branches. Reproduces by seeds. Found in the continental USA and Hawaii. Also found in Canada, Central America, Europe, Asia, and Australia.

Florida Betony (Rattlesnake Weed) (Color Plate 1–74)
Stachys florida Shuttlew.
Smooth or hairy, delicate, freely branched perennial, from slender underground stems with segmented white tubers resembling a rattlesnake's rattle. Leaves opposite, long stalked, lance-shaped, usually with a nearly flat base. Stems square. Flowers white to pink with purple spots. Reproduces primarily by tubers. Turf, roadsides, thickets, and shrub borders. Native to Florida until it escaped in the 1940s or 1950s. Now found from North Carolina to Texas. Thought to be moved with nursery stock and ornamental plants.

K. Leguminosae

Common Lespedeza (Annual Lespedeza; Japanese Clover) (Color Plate 1–75)
Lespedeza striata (Thunb.) H. & A.
Wiry, prostrate, freely-branched summer annual. Leaves with three obovate to oblong, smooth leaflets. Leaflets with prominent midvein and many parallel veins that are nearly perpendicular to the midvein. Single flowers, pink to purple, in leaf axils. Reproduces by seeds. Common in the southern USA, north to Pennsylvania, west to Texas, Kansas, and Missouri.

Black Medic (Color Plate 1–76)
Medicago lupulina L.
Dark green taprooted annual with a spreading, prostrate growth habit. Leaves alternate, composed of three leaflets on square stems. Leaflets wedge-

shaped, as long as broad, toothed near tip, and with a small spur at tip. Produces tight, compressed cluster of bright yellow flowers (10 to 50) at the leaf axils. At maturity, each flower forms a tightly coiled black seed pod. Reproduces by seeds. Found throughout the continental USA and Hawaii. Also occurs in Canada, the West Indies, Central and South America, Europe, Asia, and Australia.

Bur-Clover (Color Plate 1–77)
Medicago polymorpha L.
    Prostrate or mat-forming, smooth annual. The three leaflets lacking stalks, oblong or broader at the tip, tip with a v and teeth on the margin. Flowers yellow. Fruit coiled, spiny. Reproduces by seeds. Occurs in fields, woods, and along roadsides. Virginia, south to Florida, west to Texas, Arizona, and Missouri; California to Washington. Native to Europe and Asia. Introduced into all warm temperate regions of the world.

Large Hop Clover (Photo not available)
Trifolium aureum Poll. [*T. agrarium* L., sensu American authors]
    Erect, smoothish annual or biennial. Leaves short-stalked, leaflets three, lacking stalks, oblong or broader at the tip, tip with v. Flower heads above leaves, dense, cylindric. Flowers bright yellow to orange-yellow. Reproduces by seeds. Roadsides, disturbed areas and old fields. Eastern USA, south to Georgia, west to Iowa, north to southeastern Canada. Native to Eurasia and Asia Minor.

Crimson Clover (Color Plate 1–79)
Trifolium incarnatum L.
    Erect, hairy annual. Lower and medium leaves with very long stalks. The three leaflets broader at the tip to almost round, toothed in upper half. Elongate, cylindrical heads on stalks. Flowers crimson. Reproduces by seeds. A cultivated forage plant, spreading to disturbed areas, roadsides and fields. Maine, south to Florida, west to Texas, north to North Dakota; California to Washington and Idaho, Hawaii. Infrequent in colder climates. Native to Europe. Introduced into China and Australia.

White Clover (Color Plate 1–80)
Trifolium repens L.
    Low-growing perennial with creeping stems that root at the nodes. Stems smooth to sparsely covered with hairs. Leaves with three elliptic to oval shaped leaflets. Leaflets with small marginal teeth. Flowers white, often with pink tinge, arranged in round heads. Reproduces by seeds. Found throughout the continental USA and Hawaii. Also found in Canada, Mexico, the West Indies, Central and South America, Europe, Asia, and Australia.

L. Malvaceae

Roundleaf Mallow (Color Plate 1–81)
Malva rotundifolia L. [*M. pusilla* Sm.]
    Long-lived annual, almost smooth, low spreading. Leaves long-stalked;

blades rounded, 5- to 7-lobed; margins with shallow teeth. Petals light purple to white. Fruit 8- to 13-parted, attached to a central disk. Reproduces by seeds. Established in disturbed areas, roadsides, cultivated fields. Florida to Texas, Michigan and Indiana, west to Washington, south to California. Native to Europe. Introduced into Canada, the Middle East, Australia, and Central and South America.

M. Onagraceae

Cutleaf Evening Primrose (Color Plate 1–82)
Oenothera laciniata Hill
Winter annual from a fibrous root system. Stems hairy, reclining, branched from base. Leaves alternate, elliptic to lance-shaped, margins irregularly notched or lobed. Single, five-petaled, yellow to reddish, tubular flowers borne in leaf axils. Fruit a cylindrical, four-ribbed seed pod. Both flowers and seed pods present at same time. Reproduces by seeds. Found in the continental USA except for the Pacific Northwest and Southwest. Also found in Quebec, Ontario, Central and South America, and Europe.

N. Oxalidaceae

Yellow Woodsorrel (Color Plate 1–83)
Oxalis stricta L. [*O. dillenii* Jacq.]
Upright, herbaceous perennial with hairy stems. Leaves, alternate, divided into three, partly-folded, deeply cut, heart-shaped lobes. Foliage with sour, acrid taste. Flowers, bright yellow, with five petals, on stalks bent below the fruit and attached to a common point. Fruit a narrow okra-like capsule. Found in most of the eastern and central USA. Also occurs in Canada, Europe, Africa, Asia, Japan, and New Zealand. Creeping woodsorrel (*Oxalis corniculata* L.), has a more prostrate growth habit than yellow woodsorrel. Stolons readily root at the nodes. Leaves similar to yellow woodsorrel but may be green to reddish purplish. Florida yellow woodsorrel (*Oxalis florida* Salisb.) is similar in appearance to yellow woodsorrel, but has slender stems and a smooth to sparingly hairy smaller capsule. All species reproduce by seeds.

O. Plantaginaceae

Buckhorn Plantain (Color Plate 1–84)
Plantago lanceolata L.
Perennial with a distinctive rosette of leaves and a slender, fibrous root system. Leaves narrowly elliptic to lance-shaped, often twisted or curled, with ribbed veins on lower leaf surface. Erect, leafless, hairy stalk terminated by dense, tapered, white to tannish flower spike. Reproduces by seeds. Found throughout the continental USA. Also found in Canada, the West Indies, Central and South America, Europe, and Asia.

Broadleaf Plantain (Color Plate 1–85)
Plantago major L.

Perennial with a distinctive rosette of leaves, and slender, fibrous root system. Leaves broad, egg-shaped, with several main veins. Erect, leafless stems terminate in dense, flower spikes. Found in all of North America except the northeastern USA. Also found in the West Indies, Central and South America, Europe, Asia, Australia, and Hawaii. Blackseed plantain (*Plantago rugellii* Dcne.) is similar except stems and petioles longer and leaves somewhat larger. Both species reproduce by seeds.

P. Polygonaceae

Prostrate Knotweed (Color Plate 1–86)
Polygonoum aviculare L.

Prostrate, mat-forming, blue-green colored summer annual. Leaves, alternate, smooth, oblong to linear, short-petioled, joined to stem by a sheathing membrane. Inconspicuous white flowers are formed in the leaf axils. Reproduces by seeds. Common on infertile and compacted soils. One of the first summer annuals to germinate in the spring. Found throughout the USA. Also occurs in Canada, Central and South America, Europe, Asia, Australia, and Hawaii.

Red Sorrel (Sheep Sorrel; Sourgrass) (Color Plate 1–87)
Rumex acetosella L.

Perennial with smooth, erect, four-sided stems. Produces large yellow taproot and spreads from sprouts from numerous rhizomes and roots. Leaves mostly basal, distinctively arrow- or lance-shaped. Flowers borne in clusters at end of stems. Flowers green to red at maturity. Reproduces by seeds and rhizomes. Found in the continental USA, except Florida, and in Alaska and Hawaii. Also found in Central and South America, Australia, Indonesia, Iceland, Africa, and Asia. Native to Europe. Heartwing sorrel (*Rumex hastatulus* Baldw. ex Ell.), a winter annual, is similar, but lacks rhizomes and produces larger red masses of flowers and fruits at maturity and only reproduces by seeds.

Curly Dock (Color Plate 1–88)
Rumex crispus L.

Taprooted perennial with mostly basal leaves. Stem leaves alternate, with wavy to curled margins, tapered at the base. Leaf petiole joined to stem by a membranous sheath. Greenish flowers on long terminal spikes. Fruit reddish-brown with three wing-like projections. Reproduces by seeds. Found throughout the USA. Also found in the West Indies, Mexico and Central America, Europe, Asia, and Australia. Broadleaf dock (*Rumex obtusifolius* L.) is similar but has leaves that are wide, heart-shaped at the base and lack wavy margins.

Q. Portulacaceae

Common Purslane (Color Plate 1-89)
Portulaca oleracea L.
    Prostrate, succulent summer annual. Leaves alternate or nearly oppo-
site, fleshy, somewhat spoon-shaped. Stems smooth, usually purplish-red.
Flowers yellow, solitary in leaf axils or clustered on ends of stems. Fruit a
round capsule, splitting open around the middle. Reproduces by seeds. Found
throughout the USA, more common in Northwest USA, less common in the
Pacific Northwest. Also found in Canada, the West Indies, Central and South
America, Europe, Africa, Asia, Oceania, and Hawaii.

R. Ranunculaceae

Creeping Buttercup (Color Plate 1-90)
Ranunculus repens L.
    Perennial with thick fibrous roots and prostrate, spreading branches
(stolons); flowering stems ascending. Leaves dark green, often mottled with
white; the lower divided into three leaflets that are lobed, the terminal leaflet
often 3-parted or divided; upper leaves less divided. Reproduces by seeds
and stolons. Found in moist to wet, open, disturbed areas, ditches, and fields.
Northeastern USA, south to North Carolina above the Coastal Plain, west
to Texas, Missouri and Michigan, California to Washington, Alaska. Native to Europe. Introduced into most cool temperate areas of the world.

S. Rosaceae

Parsley-piert (Color Plate 1-91)
Alchemilla arvensis (L.) Scop.
    Freely-branched, low-growing winter annual. Leaves, alternate, three-
lobed with each lobe again three- to four-lobed. Inconspicuous flowers in
leaf axils. Reproduces by seeds. Found from Maryland through Tennessee
into Georgia. Also found in Europe, Asia, and Australia.

Indian Mockstrawberry (Color Plate 1-92)
Duchesnea indica (Andr.) Focke
    Low-growing perennial with long stolons. Leaves with three leaflets and
toothed margins as opposed to the five leaflets found on Oldfield Cinquefoil.
Single flowers, on long stalks, five yellow petals. Fruit red, spongy, round,
and strawberry-like, not poisonous but not palatable. Reproduces by seeds
and stolons. Common in shaded areas. Found in the southeast USA, west
to Oklahoma, Texas, California and the Pacific Northwest, north into Pennsylvania and New York. Also occurs in the West Indies, Central and South
America, Asia, and Europe.

Woodland Strawberry (Photo not available)
Fragaria vesca L.
    Perennial with thick rootstock and aboveground runners. Plants form-

ing rosettes. Leaves with three leaflets. Leaflet blade round or broader at
the tip, margins with prominent teeth. Petals white, five. Fruit round, red,
fleshy. Reproduces by seeds and stolons. Occurs along roadsides, on hill-
sides and in moist disturbed areas. Northeastern USA, south to North Carolina and Georgia, west to Indiana, South Dakota and Montana, New Mexico,
Wyoming, Colorado, California north to Washington, Hawaii. Native to
both the USA and Europe. Some forms introduced from Europe. Canada.
Introduced into Japan.

Common Cinquefoil (Photo not available)
Pontentilla canadensis L.
   Perennial from a short, underground runner, prostrate; stem thin, softly
hairy. Leaves long-stalked, blades deeply five-parted, margins toothed.
Flowering from lowest leaf axil, one flower per stalk, petals yellow. Fruit
head-like. Reproduces by seeds and rhizomes. Found in open, grassy and
disturbed areas. Maine, south to Georgia and Tennessee, west to Missouri.
Canada.

T. Rubiaceae

Poorjoe (Color Plate 1-95)
Diodia teres Walt.
   Freely-branched, spreading to semierect summer annual. Stem often
reddish-purplish with lines of hairs. Leaves opposite, linear, usually light green
in color. Leaf bases joined by membrane with several hair-like projections.
Flowers tubular, white to pinkish white, in leaf axils. Reproduces by seeds.
Common on infertile soils in the southeast USA, north to Connecticut, Illinois
and Montana, and west to Texas and Arizona. Also found in Mexico, the
West Indies, Central America, and South America.

Virginia Buttonweed (Color Plate 1-96)
Diodia virginiana L.
   Spreading perennial herb with hairy branched stems. Leaves opposite,
elliptic to lance-shaped, sessile, joined across stem by membrane. Membrane
with a few hair-like projections. White tubular flowers with four lobes at
each leaf axil along the stem. Flower usually with only two sepals. Fruit green,
elliptically shaped, hairy, ridged and at each leaf axil. Reproduces by seeds,
roots, and stem fragments. Favors moist to wet sites. Found from New Jersey west to Missouri, south into the Gulf Coast States.

Florida Pusley (Color Plate 1-97)
Richardia scabra L.
   Prostrate and spreading summer annual with branched hairy stems.
Leaves opposite, oval-shaped, and somewhat thickened. Tubular flowers,
white, clustered at the ends of branches. Distinguished from Brazil pusley
(*Richardia brasiliensis* [Moq.] Gomez) by presence of fruit with small bump-

like projections and lack of thickened rootstock. Reproduces by seeds. Found in the southeast, northeast, and midwest USA. Also occurs in Mexico and Central and South America.

U. Scrophulariaceae

Oldfield Toadflax (Color Plate 1–98)
Linaria canadensis (L.) Dumont
Winter annual or biennial; when biennial often forming a dense basal cluster of prostrate stems. Leaves, linear, those in the basal cluster opposite or whorled; those of the main erect stem usually alternate. Flowers, blue to purple, with finger-like projection. Reproduces by seeds. Occurring in pastures, old fields, and along roadsides. Found throughout the USA. Also found in southern Canada, Mexico, and South America.

Corn Speedwell (Color Plate 1–99)
Veronica arvensis L.
Low-growing, freely-branched winter annual. Lower leaves round- to egg-shaped, toothed on the margins, with prominent veins. Upper leaves linear in shape. Leaves and stems with fine hairs. Flowers, light blue, nearly stalk-less. Seed capsules heart-shaped with a line of hairs on the outer edge. Reproduces by seeds. Found throughout most of the USA except for the Rocky Mountains. Also occurs in Central and South America, South Africa, Australia, and Hawaii. Native to Europe and Asia.

Creeping Speedwell (Color Plate 1–100)
Veronica filiformis Sm.
Procumbent or mat-forming perennial with slender, hairy stems that root at the nodes. Leaves stalked, alternate and opposite; blades kidney-shaped; margins with small, blunt teeth. Flowers solitary from leaf axils, long-stalked, pale purple-blue. Fruit a 2-lobed capsule. Reproduces by seeds and stolons. Occurs in lawns. Local in northeastern USA, Pennsylvania, New York. Native to Eurasia.

Purslane Speedwell (Neckweed) (Color Plate 1–101)
Veronica peregrina L.
Low-growing, freely-branched winter annual with smooth to somewhat fleshy leaves and stems. Leaves, opposite, longer than broad, coarsely toothed on the margins. Flowers, white, in the upper axils. Fruit a smooth heart-shaped capsule. Reproduces by seeds. Found throughout North America. Also found in the West Indies, Mexico, Central and South America, Europe, Asia, and Australia.

V. Umbelliferae

Wild Carrot (Queen Anne's Lace) (Color Plate 1–102)
Daucus carota L.
Slender, branched biennial with a white fleshy taproot shaped like a carrot. First year, develops only a rosette of finely divided leaves. Mature plant

with hollow stems and carrot-like odor. Leaves alternate, pinnately divided into small linear segments. Petiole sheath-like, clasping the stem. Small, white flowers in dense, flat or concave clusters at ends of stems or branches. Center flower in cluster, maroon to black in color. Fruit bristled, in clusters. Reproduces by seeds. Found from southern Canada south into northern Florida and west to Texas, Oklahoma, Kansas, and California. Also found in Mexico, Central and South America, Australia, Europe, Asia, and Hawaii.

Pennywort (Dollarweed) (Color Plate 1-103)
Hydrocotyle spp.
Coastal Plain Pennywort
H. bonariensis Comm. ex Lam.
Water Pennywort
H. umbellata L.
Whorled Pennywort
H. verticillata Thunb.

Perennials from rhizomes, occasionally with tubers. Erect long-stalked leaves with scalloped margins. Petiole in center of leaf, umbrella-like. Flowers in elongated spikes or rounded umbels at top of long stalk. Fruit greenish, rounded and somewhat flattened. Reproduces from seeds, rhizomes, and tubers. Found in moist to wet sites or anywhere moisture is in excess. Occurs from Maine south into Florida, and west to Minnesota and Texas, Utah, Arizona, and California. Also found in Nova Scotia, British Columbia, the West Indies, Mexico, Central and South America, southern Europe, and Tropical Africa.

W. Verbenaceae

Mat Lippia (Matchweed) (Color Plate 1-104)
Phyla nodiflora (L.) Green [*Lippia nodiflora* (L.) Michx.]

Mat-forming perennial with prostrate hairy stems. Stems freely branched, rooting at nodes. Leaves opposite with a few large teeth toward the tip. Flowers rose-purple or white, in a head at the tip of a long stalk, resembling the head of a match. Reproduces by seeds and stolons. Occurs in low moist areas in open woods and turf, common along the coastal beaches and marshes, preferring open sandy areas often with limestone outcrops. Occurs from Pennsylvania to Florida, Arkansas, Oklahoma, Texas, and in California. Also found in Hawaii, Mexico, Central and South America, the West Indies, Japan, and India.

X. Violaceae

Violet (Color Plate 1-105)
Viola spp.

Diverse group composed of winter annuals and perennials. Perennials from rhizomes or long stolons. Many with heart-shaped leaves on long petioles. Other species with linear leaves or leaves palmately lobed. Flowers range from purple to white to pink to yellow. Reproduces by seeds and, when produced, by rhizomes. Found throughout the continental USA except for the states of the High Plains. Also found in Canada, the West Indies, Mexico, Central and South America, Asia, Europe, Africa, Australia, and Hawaii.

REFERENCES

1. Bell, C.R., and B.J. Taylor. 1982. Florida wild flowers. Laurel Hill Press, Chapel Hill, NC.
2. Correll, D.S., and M.C. Johnston. 1979. Manual of the vascular plants of Texas. Univ. of Texas, Richardson.
3. Cronquist, A. 1988. The evolution and classification of flowering plants. The New York Botanical Garden, New York.
4. Davis, P.H., and V.H. Heywood. 1963. Principals of Angiosperm Taxonomy. D. Van Nostrand Company, New York.
5. Fernald, L.M. 1950. Gray's manual of botany. 8th ed. American Book Company, New York.
6. Lawrence, G.H.M. 1951. Taxonomy of vascular plants. Macmillan Company, New York.
7. Mayr, E. 1969. Principles of systematic zoology. McGraw-Hill, New York.
8. McCarty, L.B., and D.W. Hall. 1990. Weed identification and control. p. 18–31. *In* L.B. McCarty (ed.) 1990 University of Florida's Pest Control Recommendations for Turfgrass Managers. Cooperative Extension Service, Institute of Food and Agricultural Science, Univ. of Florida, Gainesville.
9. Munz, P.A., and D.D. Keck. 1959. A California flora. Univ. of California Press, Berkeley, CA.
10. Redford, A.E., H.E. Ahles, and C.R. Bell. 1974. Manual of the vascular flora of the Carolinas. Univ. of North Carolina Press, Chapel Hill.
11. Stace, C.A. 1980. Plant taxonomy and biosystematics. Univ. Park Press, Baltimore, MD.
12. Takhtajan, A. 1969. Flowering plants: Origin and dispersal. Oliver & Boyd, Edinburgh, Scotland.

Chapter 2

Ecology of Turfgrass Weeds

T. L. WATSCHKE, *The Pennsylvania State University,*
University Park, Pennsylvania

R. E. ENGEL, *Rutgers University, New Brunswick, New Jersey*

Ecology is the study of the reciprocal relations between organisms and their environment. In *Principles of Plant and Animal Pest Control* (2) it is stated that weeds possess many growth characteristics and adaptations that enable them to exploit successfully the numerous ecological niches left unoccupied, exposed, or only partially filled by crop cultures.

Interactions among turfgrasses, their management, and the environment are complex and dynamic with any ecological discussion concerning turfgrass communities strongly influenced by these interactions. Environments are dictated largely by climate, edaphic, and geographic factors; however, unlike naturally occurring climax vegetation, turfgrasses persist only in settings managed by humans. Human input is an intrinsic part of the turfgrass ecosystem. Without being managed by humans, most turfgrass species would succumb to the next plant succession. In early times, grass communities evolved when humans cleared forests and woody plant regrowth was prevented due to grazing by domesticated animals. These grasses were adapted to defoliation and persisted due to low growth habit. These forage species also had excellent regrowth capacity when defoliation pressure was removed. Turfgrass occurs in grass communities that are not grazed by animals (forage) or grown as annuals (grain production). Turfgrass communities exist as a result of management practices that manipulate many of their natural growth tendencies to increase their ecological fitness in the sward. Turfgrass management practices provide the foundation for turfgrass weed control strategies by minimizing opportunities for development of ecological niches necessary for weed encroachment.

Since turfgrass management may be defined as the creation of environmental conditions that favor the competitive nature of the desired species over all others, weeds are excluded from consideration as a permanent component in most turfgrass ecosystems. Such a management definition places an important emphasis on the reciprocal relations between turfgrasses and their environment and is uniquely suited to encompass all aspects of weed control strategies.

J.P. Grime (1) concluded that where the objective of turf management is to maintain a uniform monoculture, e.g., lawns, bowling greens, cricket patches, it is desirable to restrict the frequency of vegetation gaps to a minimum and to encourage the growth of grasses that produce a dense, rapidly-repairing, leaf canopy close to the ground surface. If the objective of turf management is to maintain a genetically diverse plant community, e.g., picnic areas, roadsides, parkland, nature reserves, it may be helpful to disturb the established vegetation by occasionally grazing, mowing, or harrowing in order to create gaps into which regeneration of the component species can take place.

Coring or any other management practice, pest, or site use that causes voids in the turf stand are considered to be ecological trigger factors. Management of turf creates a holocoenotic environment that responds dramatically to a trigger factor (the ecological change resulting from the void will cause another site change, which will cause another, and so on). Therefore, in almost all instances, proper turfgrass management minimizes voids in the stand. Most of the time, well maintained turf should be dense enough to prevent any view of the soil surface. When conditions exist that necessitate core cultivation (compacting and low infiltration rates), timing of the coring must be precise enough so that the void created in the stand does not provide an opportunity for weed encroachment. Coring during the spring can stimulate summer annual emergence and fall coring can increase winter annual emergence. When coring cannot be done at more opportune times of the year, the use of preemergence herbicides following or in conjunction with the coring may be desirable.

Within the context of the definition of turfgrass management, it is also important to provide turfgrass communities with the best combination of aesthetic quality and function. Such an integration occurs when there is concensus about the ecological purpose of the turfgrass area on which the management system is imposed. Usually, the purpose of the turfgrass community is to stabilize soil, provide a ground cover for the landscape, support recreational activity, reduce mud and dust, or improve overall aesthetic quality. Regardless of the purpose, quality turfgrass communities are the result of management strategies that best reflect the manager's ability to achieve compromise between aesthetics and function, manipulate plant competition through cultural practices, and correctly anticipate plant responses to changing environments.

I. CLIMATIC INFLUENCES

The most important climatic factors that affect persistence and competitiveness of plants are light, temperature, moisture, and the seasonal variations of these factors. Moisture, nutrients, and light are the major environmental factors that may become limiting due to plant competition.

Light density, quality, and duration are important as they are the controlling factors for growth, reproduction, and, in some cases, the geographic distribution of weeds. Photoperiod governs flowering and determines timing of seed maturation, and therefore, can influence latitudinal distribution. Shade tolerance is often of particular importance in developing weed control strategies in turfgrass culture as a result of reduced growth rate of many species and increased disease incidence.

Soil and ambient air temperature determine the latitudinal and elevational distribution of turfgrass weeds. Soil temperature influences time of germination, dormancy, and sometimes the survivability of vegetative propagules.

Water, in the form of precipitation or irrigation affects persistence and competitiveness of many weed species. Soil moisture level may vary from essentially none to saturated. The total water available to any given plant is a function of the original supply and losses associated with percolation, runoff, and evapotranspiration. Seasonal variation in water supply can also influence plant competition, particularly if moisture level is critical at some stage of plant growth (e.g., seedling establishment, flowering).

Wind velocity and direction can cause conditions that favor weed competitiveness. Generally, such effects are localized, but may well be the cause of more troublesome and chronic weed problems. Wind also influences distribution of weed seed, disease spores, and perhaps insects, all of which can result in weed infestation.

II. EDAPHIC INFLUENCES

Edaphic factors influencing weed persistence and competitiveness include soil texture, pH, fertility level, infiltration and percolation rate, aeration, temperature, and the effects of various management practices on the soil.

Weeds such as sedges (*Cyperus* spp.) and rushes (*Scirpus* spp.) thrive in nearly waterlogged conditions, while annual bluegrass (*Poa annua* L.) and bentgrasses (*Agrostis* spp.) do well in poorly drained, but not waterlogged conditions. Red sorrel (*Rumex acetosella* L.) is very tolerant of acidic conditions, while prostrate knotweed (*Polygonam auiculare* L.) is tolerant of pHs ranging from 5.6 to 8.4. Most turfgrass species are most competitive at soil pHs of 6.0 to 7.0. Turfgrasses generally do not grow well in compacted soils with low O_2 diffusion rates, but goosegrass [*Eluesine indica* (L.) Gaerth.] and knotweed are quite tolerant. Legumes of the *Trifolium* spp. and *Medicago* spp. are more competitive under conditions of low N nutrition, while most turfgrasses are not competitive when N availability is low.

Soil temperature can play a significant role in the encroachment of weeds. High soil temperature can enforce seed dormancy on some species (annual bluegrass), while cold soil temperatures can enforce dormancy of others (*Digitaria* spp.). Conversely, cooler soil temperatures break dormancy and favor germination of winter annual weeds such as annual bluegrass, while warm soil temperatures break the dormancy and promote germination of summer annual weed species (*Digitaria* spp).

Cool soil conditions favor the development of the root system in cool season turfgrass species, while elevated soil temperatures cause losses in root length and volume. Warm soil conditions are also conducive to the vegetative growth of warm season weed species; hence, they are more competitive during the summer months. In the lower latitudes, winter annual species are competitive and persist in the winter months when warm season turfgrass species are semidormant or dormant. Both ambient air and soil temperatures are important in determining the survivability and competitive advantage between species within a plant community.

III. SURVIVAL MECHANISMS

Persistent and competitive weeds are those that either have unique dormancy mechanisms (summer annual grasses), have adequate reserve supplies of seed (annual bluegrass), or have vegetative propagules from which new plants can form when the opportunity arises (bulbs, nutlets, and tap rooted and rhizomatous perennials). In addition, weeds that compete well under conditions of proper turfgrass culture do so by virtue of having physical characteristics and growth habits similar to the turfgrass species adapted to a given site. Such weeds are generally of three distinct types: grasses; those that produce a short stem or crown with a rosette of leaves that remains close to the soil surface; and those that produce rhizomes or stolons. Each of these three types have one thing in common, their growing points are close to the soil surface allowing them to withstand the selective pressure resulting from mowing (even as close as 3.2 mm or one eighth of an inch for some species).

The survivability of weeds involves four major processes: seed production, dormancy, dissemination, germination, and vegetative (asexual) reproduction. Although some weed control has been accomplished by preventing seed production and dissemination (collecting annual bluegrass clippings), most successful control of annual weeds is the result of producing high turf density, particularly when weed germination is occurring. In addition to high turf density minimizing space for weed development, shading of emerged seedlings is particularly effective in reducing the establishment of summer annual grass species that have a high light intensity requirement for growth and development. The use of preemergence herbicides is also a very effective measure for controlling of weeds during the germination stage of plant development. Control of weeds that spread by vegetative propagules (stolons, rhizomes, nutlets, or bulbs) has long been effectively accomplished via the use of translocatable herbicides. More recently, paclobutrazol and flurprimidol (plant growth regulators that reduce cell elongation by limiting the synthesis of gibberelin) have been found to differentially suppress the competitive ability of certain species. For example, application of either paclobutrazol or flurprimidol to a mixed stand or annual bluegrass and creep-ping bentgrass (*A. stolonifera* L.) favors the growth of the bentgrass due to its unaffected stolon development compared with the bluegrass.

A. Seed Production

Most annual weeds are capable of producing abundant amounts of seed, which is their principal means of perpetuation. Survivability is dependent upon the production of a sufficient amount of seed for the species to withstand environmental hazards. Seed production may also coincide with cultural practices that improve survivability (coring and vertical mowing during annual bluegrass seedhead production).

Mowing is the maintenance practice that provides the most selective management pressure in turfgrass systems. Many of the weed species found in conventional crop production systems do not persist in turf because frequent, low clipping reduces competitiveness. Turfgrasses are managed as a perennial ground cover that is generally undisturbed and is commonly mowed at a height of cut that precludes seed production by most annual weed species. Therefore, the seed production potential for many weeds is a mute point and mowing is the only control required; however, certain decumbent weeds (annual bluegrass, goosegrass, and crabgrass) can produce significant seed in a mowed situation.

B. Seed Dissemination

Weed seed is disseminated by wind, water, birds, and most of all by man in turfgrass systems. Because turfgrass is almost exclusively managed as a perennial crop, weed dissemination mechanisms that most directly introduce the seed to the potential site are the most effective. Humans, through the use of equipment, mulches, soils, seed, sod, nursery stock, and their own footwear are one of the most effective weed seed disseminators in the turfgrass ecosystem.

When weed seeds are disseminated by natural agents (dandelions by the wind), cultural control can only be afforded by maintaining dense turfgrass swards. Since humans may be the principal dissemination agent in turfgrass systems, however, control of weeds at the dissemination point is an obvious component of the overall weed control strategy. Management practices that minimize weed dissemination, e.g., equipment sanitation, the use of weed free mulch, certified seed and sod, and weed free nursery stock, fundamentally address weed control on a preventative basis.

C. Seed Dormancy

Seed dormancy is that characteristic that allows certain plant species to survive adverse environmental conditions and enables them to maintain the potential for encroachment for many years. In higher latitudes, dormancy is the survival mechanism that prevents the germination of those species that are frost sensitive or that are not winter hardy. Weed scientists have determined the causes of dormancy for a few species and a convenient classification system has been developed. This system recognizes three categories of dormancy: innate, induced, and enforced. The system was based on the observed behavior of seeds, not on the processes that bring about dormancy. Seed from some species may possess one or more types of dormancy and may exhibit all three during a period of time.

Innate dormancy is an inherent property of the seed and is present at the time the seed shatters from the parent plant. After-ripening is required before an innately dormant seed can germinate. After-ripening processes include: alternating freezing and thawing, leaching of germination inhibitors, and wetting and drying cycles. It has been determined that the causes of innate seed dormancy may be grouped into five broad categories which include: rudimentary embryos, physiologically immature embryos resulting from inactive enzyme systems, mechanically restrictive seedcoats, impermeable seed coats, and the presence of germination inhibitors.

Induced and enforced dormancy are influenced by the seed and environment interaction. Induced dormancy can develop when a nondormant seed becomes dormant as a result of some environmental condition. Such conditions may include high soil temperatures and elevated CO_2 levels. In most situations, induced dormancy persists for a time after the inducing mechanism is removed.

Enforced dormancy results when the seed habitat does not provide the necessary conditions required for germination of a particular species. Once the restrictive mechanism is removed, germination occurs freely and usually without delay. A common cause of enforced dormancy is seed being buried to a soil depth that precludes germination. Once the soil is disturbed by tillage, core cultivation, or other practices, and the seed is brought to the surface, germination will occur.

Weed control, as part of turfgrass culture, utilizes the knowledge of dormancy mechanisms to provide tactics that take advantage of weed seed dormancy. For example, since annual bluegrass seed remains dormant at elevated soil temperature, overseeding of more desired species can be accomplished during the summer months. In lower latitudes, timing of fall overseeding of cool season grasses is intended to reduce the competition from winter annuals that have not yet germinated due to dormancy associated with elevated soil temperatures.

D. Seed Germination

In some situations, the highly developed specialization found in the germination process provides a parallel to, and can extend the effects of, dormancy mechanisms. Although the termination of innate and induced dormancy is necessary before germination can occur, such seeds may still exist in a condition of enforced dormancy. Germination will result only when all environmental conditions are favorable.

Germination and seedling vigor are determining factors in the ability of a weed to invade a site. Once environmental conditions conducive to germination are present and germination occurs, a space must be available for occupancy by the weed seedling, and the developing weed must be able to compete with existing plants for encroachment to be successful. In crop situations, those weed seeds that germinate at the same time as the desired crop are the most persistent and successful. In turfgrass culture, knowledge of the germination requirements of various weeds (soil temperature and soil disturbance) can facilitate their control.

Repeated tillage and fallowing of areas that are to be established can reduce future weed competition. Such an approach encourages germination of annuals that can then be readily controlled by subsequent tillage before they produce viable seed.

Timing of fertilizer applications is important to insure that available nutrients are utilized by desired species rather than by weeds that may be germinating concurrently. Many homeowners fertilize only during spring coincident with crabgrass germination. As a result, if a lawn of cool season grasses is weakened or thinned, typically by diseases, the germinating crabgrass finds a niche available and at the same time benefits from the fertilizer application. It is a principle of plant competition, however, that the first plants to occupy a space have an advantage over subsequent plants. Usually in turfgrass culture, weeds that emerge after the turf is established do not pose a significant competitive threat provided no ecological niche is exposed for an extended period.

E. Allelopathic Effects

There is increasing evidence that plants can adversely influence one another by means other than simple competition for nutrients, light, and water. One such means is by allelopathy, the production of exudates by one plant that suppress the competitiveness of another. Allelopathic compounds may affect the germination process or plant growth in general. In some cases, decaying roots can release more toxic substances than living roots; and some plants contribute allelopathic compounds from all plant parts, not just roots.

Several studies have shown that extracts of quackgrass roots and mixtures of quackgrass roots and soil can inhibit plant growth or prevent germination of numerous plants. The exact role of allelopathy in turf and weed competition is not well understood nor very well documented. As these interactions become more comprehensively researched, such knowledge will be extremely valuable and can be integrated into various weed control strategies.

IV. WEED ECOLOGY AND MANAGEMENT

Knowledge of weed and turfgrass ecology and the population dynamics of turfgrass communities is fundamental to the development of successful weed control programs. By applying sound agronomic principles and concepts to turfgrass culture, controlling weeds is made significantly easier by understanding why and how the weed was able to establish itself in the first place. By recognizing that a niche existed for the weed and by determining the cause of that niche, a weed control program can be implemented that will minimize the need for herbicides.

In other chapters, specific attention is given to the various weed control programs available, the technology of existing herbicide delivery systems and other important information necessary for the turfgrass manager to successfully combat weed problems. An understanding of weed ecology, however, provides the foundation upon which this other information must build to develop a weed control strategy in which a determination is made of the ecological basis for the weed incidence rather than using strictly reactive measures for control.

REFERENCES

1. Grimes, I.P. 1980. An ecological approach to management. p. 13–35. *In* I.H. Rorison and R. Hunt (ed.) Amenity grasslands: An ecological perspective. John Wiley & Sons, New York.
2. National Academy of Sciences. 1969. Weed control. p. 22. *In* Principles of plant and animal pest control. Vol. 2. National Academy of Sciences, Washington, DC.

Chapter 3

Herbicide Action and Metabolism

DONALD PENNER, *Michigan State University, East Lansing, Michigan*

Research on herbicide action is extensive and the subject of several books (12, 26, 78). Structure–function relationships, herbicide resistant weeds, and the desire to discover herbicides that act only on pathways unique to plants have created considerable research interest on herbicide action. Research directed at developing herbicide resistant crops has also enhanced both interest and research on herbicide action. Early interest in herbicide metabolism was fueled by the necessity of determining herbicide residues in plants for the establishment of regulatory tolerances. More recently, there has been a realization of the value of herbicide metabolism research to more fully understand pesticide interactions, the action of chemical protectants or antidotes, and herbicide dissipation in plant tissues. The metabolism of herbicides in higher plants has been reviewed (42), but much remains unknown about herbicide metabolism in specific plant species. The diversity of metabolism across plant species appears much greater than the diversity in plant species with respect to herbicide action.

I. DEFINITIONS

The terms herbicide mode, mechanism, and site of action have at times been used interchangeably; however, they can have distinctly different meanings. For greater clarification, the following definition of these terms will be used in this chapter.

Mode of Action: Refers to the action of a herbicide on a physiological system such as photosynthesis.

Mechanism of Action: Refers to the mechanism whereby the herbicide exerts its action such as binding to the 32 kd protein also known as the D_1 protein in the electron transport chain and inhibiting electron flow in photosynthesis.

Site of Action: Refers to the locus of herbicide action whether it is a plant organ, tissue, cellular organelle, or chemical group of an enzyme.

Prefacing these terms with the adjective primary indicates that it is the first action detected in time or at the lowest concentration of the herbicide eliciting a response. The lethal mode of action is that mode of action that results in death of the plant. It is not necessarily the primary mode of action. Herbicides may have multiple modes of actions. Furthermore, they may be concentration dependent with the primary mode not necessarily the lethal mode of action.

Since differential herbicide metabolism and available sites of action as well as differential herbicide absorption and translocation are key physiological factors determining herbicide selectivity several additional relevant terms will be defined for use throughout this chapter.

Herbicide tolerance: Survival of the normal population of a plant species following an herbicide dosage lethal to other species.

Herbicide resistance: Survival of a segment of the population of a plant species following an herbicide dosage lethal to the normal population.

Herbicide susceptibility: Death or injury to plants following herbicide application.

Recent trends in postemergence herbicide use frequently result in the application of a combination of herbicides or the combination of herbicides with other pesticides or with fertilizer solutions. Combination of a fast-acting herbicide (bentazon [3-(1-methylethyl)-(1*H*)-2,1,3-benzothiadiazin-4(3*H*)-one 2,2-dioxide]) with a slow-acting herbicide (glyphosate [*N*-(phosphonomethyl) glycine) can result in less than the desired amount of action by the slow-acting herbicide resulting in antagonism. Terms relevant to herbicide interactions are antagonism, synergism, and additive action. These have been defined as follows (43).

Synergism: Cooperative action of two agrochemicals such that the observed response of a test organism to their joint application appears to be greater than the response predicted to occur by an appropriate reference model.

Antagonism: A type of joint action of two agrochemicals such that the observed response of a test organism to their combined application appears to be less than the response predicted to occur by an appropriate reference model.

Additive action: Cooperative action of two agrochemicals such that the observed response of a test organism to their joint application is equal to the response predicted to occur by an appropriate reference model.

II. FUNDAMENTAL PRINCIPLES

The herbicide must move to the site of action to be effective. Implicit in observed herbicide activity is the penetration of the herbicide into the cell protoplast. For example, a photosynthesis inhibitor must penetrate the chloroplast to be active.

Herbicide activity is a function of the concentration of free active herbicide at the site of action. The concentration of herbicide present at the site of action is a function of the herbicide dosage, the rate of herbicide absorption and movement to the site of action, and the rate of herbicide inactivation or immobilization. The plant must have, however, a site sensitive to the herbicide for the herbicide to be effective. In some plant species products of herbicide metabolism such as partially dealkylated atrazine may also show some herbicidal activity (93).

Certain herbicides require activation to become phytotoxic. Esters of 2,4-D [(2,4-dichlorophenoxy)acetic acid] are hydrolyzed to release 2,4-D, which is the active moiety. Paraquat (1,1'-dimethyl-4,4'-bipyridinium ion), a cation, is reduced by accepting an electron from Photosystem I in the electron transport chain of photosynthesis. The reduced form is autooxidized to initiate a chain of reaction involving free radicals eventually resulting in the peroxidation of lipid double bonds in membranes.

Herbicides may exhibit a bimodel response dependent on herbicide concentration. Low application dosage or soil residue levels of the triazine herbicides increase stomatal aperture; however, following application of higher rates or dosages, the stomatal apertures are nearly closed (60). Growth regulators are well known to exhibit bimodal responses (106). The Schultz–Arndt Law of 1888 states that toxicants can become stimulants at low concentrations.

Herbicides may have multiple modes or sites of action. The phenoxy and benzoic acid herbicides are generally considered to affect several metabolic systems in plants. Bentazon has been shown to inhibit photosynthetic electron transport at two sites (105). Repetitive use of herbicides with a single mode of action enhances the chances for the appearance of weeds resistant to that particular herbicide. Triazine resistant weeds exemplify the concept. Thus, the use of herbicides with multiple modes of action is less likely to be plagued with the appearance of weeds resistant to the herbicide. Consistent with this concept, the development of turfgrass resistant to various herbicides by genetic engineering would be very difficult with herbicides that have multiple modes of action unless the focus of the genetic engineering was to enhance the metabolism of the herbicide in the turfgrass.

Observed herbicide symptoms may be the consequence of secondary reactions. Although the triazines block photosynthesis, the symptoms of plants dying from triazine action are not those of starvation for carbohydrate. When the triazines block photosynthesis, the electron flow is blocked and the energy captured in the chloroplasts dissipated in another manner. Fluorescence and the generation of free radicals occur. The latter eventually may result in tissue damage and the observed herbicide injury symptoms (6).

Herbicide action usually requires the binding of the herbicide to a site of action for a sufficient time to disrupt normal plant processes. If the binding is reversible, metabolism of the herbicide may result in recovery of the plant. Herbicides can inhibit specific enzymes even though they may bind to sites on the enzyme other than the active center of the enzyme. The binding of imazaquin [2-[4,5-dihydro-4-methyl-4-(1-methylethyl)-5-oxo-1H-imidazol-2-yl]-3-quinoline carboxylic acid] to the acetalactate synthase (ALS) enzyme is an example of this type of binding (90).

Herbicides are generally metabolized in plants by endogenous metabolism systems already functional in the plant at the time of herbicide entry. Conjugation with glutathione or glucose are naturally occurring plant processes that plants can effectively use to inactivate xenobiotics (i.e., chemicals foreign to the plant).

III. HERBICIDES REGISTERED FOR TURFGRASS USE

The common names of herbicides, the trade names of herbicide products, their use, and the structures of the herbicides used in turfgrass are given in Table 3-1. The herbicides included in the list are those registered for use on turfgrass for 1991 (71). Trade names presented may not be all inclusive and are not the endorsement of any specific name or product.

A. Chemical Classification of Turfgrass Herbicides

The herbicides listed in Table 3-1 were placed in groups based on their chemical structure for discussion of their action and metabolism. This classification is given in Table 3-2.

B. Turfgrass Herbicide Action and Metabolism by Chemical Group

1. Arsenicals

Action. The action of the arsenicals generally results in leaf chlorosis and growth cessation followed by browning of the tissue and death (114). Since arsenate can substitute for P in certain reactions, it has been proposed that arsenicals participate in certain enzyme reactions to form a labile arsenate analog of the normal P containing compound. The arsenate containing product of the reaction is readily hydrolyzed, the bond energy lost, and the arsenate regenerated. Methanearsonate can act as an oxidant in the Hill reaction and the product arsenomethane, reacts with SH groups on enzymes such as the malic enzyme in johnsongrass [*Sorghum halepense* (L.) Pers.] resulting with the accumulation of malate. Since the C4 johnsongrass transport C to the bundle sheath as malate, blocking CO_2 release from malate normally catalyzed by the malic enzyme, deprives the johnsongrass from its C source (59).

Metabolism. The metabolism of organoarsenical herbicides by plants is limited and the carbonarsenate bond generally remains intact (114). Metabolites are usually associated with a ninhydrin-positive reaction indicating the formation of a possible complex with an amino acid.

Table 3-1. Herbicides registered for turfgrass use (compiled by Steve Keeley).

Common name	Trade name(s)	Use	Category†	Structure
AMA	Super Dal-E-Rad AMA	Post-grass and broad-leaf control	c	
AMA + 2,4-D	Super Dal-E-Rad-2	Post-grass and broad-leaf control	c	Octyl-dodecylammonium salt
Asulam	Asulox	Post-annual grass on St. Augustine and Tifway 419 bermudagrass	c	
Atrazine	Aatrex 4L Aatrex 80W Aatrex Nine-0	Pre-weed control on warm season grasses	c, e	
Benefin	Balan 2.5G	Pre-annual grass control	c	
Bensulide	Betasan Bensumec	Pre-annual weed control	c	

(continued on next page)

Table 3–1. Continued.

Common name	Trade name(s)	Use	Category†	Structure
Bentazon	Basagran	Post-yellow nutsedge and broadleaf control	c	
Bromoxynil	Buctril 2EC	Post-broadleaf control	e	
Cacodylic acid	Montar Weed Ender	Non-selective	c	
CMA	Calar	Post-broadleaf and grass control	c	
Dazomet	Basamid granular	Pre-plant (before establishment)	a	
DCPA	Dacthal	Pre-annual grass and broadleaf control Post-creeping speed-well control	b, c	

Dicamba	Banvel	c	Post-broadleaf control
Diclofop	Illoxan	c	Post-goosegrass control in bermudagrass
Diquat	Valent Diquat Herbicide H/A	c	Weed control in dormant bermudagrass
Dithiopyr	Dimension	c	Pre- or early post-emergence
Diuron	Direx 4L or 80W Drexel Diuron 4L or 80W	d	Pre-weed control

Methyl ester

(continued on next page)

Table 3-1. Continued.

Common name	Trade name(s)	Use	Category†	Structure
DSMA	DSMA liquid Drexel DSMA liquid or slurry Helena liquid DSMA Inter-Ag DSMA 81% Methar 30	Post-annual grass control	c	
Endothal	Endothal Turf Herbicide	Post-broadleaf and grass control	c	
Ethofumesate	Progress 1.5EC	Pre- and early post-annual weed control	c	
Fenoxaprop	Acclaim 1EC Horizon 1EC	Post-annual grass control	c, e(Acclaim) d(Horizon)	 Ethyl ester
Fluazifop	Ornamec	Post-grass control	c	
Glyphosate	Roundup Rattler	Nonselective weed control	a, c, d, e	

Imazaquin	Image 1.5LC	Post- and pre-grass, sedge and broadleaf control in warm season grasses	c
Isoxaben	Gallery	Pre-broadleaf control	c
MCPA	Rhonox	Post-broadleaf control	c
MCPP	Cleary's MCPP Mecomec 2.5 Mecomex 4	Post-broadleaf control	c
Metribuzin	Sencor 75 Turf Herbicide	Goosegrass control in bermudagrass	c, e

(continued on next page)

Table 3-1. Continued.

Common name	Trade name(s)	Use	Category†	Structure
MSMA	Ansar 6.6 Daconate 6 Bueno 6 Drexel MSMA 6.6 Drexel MSMA 6 Plus or 4 Plus Drexar 530 Dal-E-Rad 70 and 120 Helena MSMA Plus H.C. Inter-Ag MSMA 600 Monterey Weed-Hoe Weed-Hoe 108 Weed-Hoe 2X	Post-annual grass control	c	
Oryzalin	Surflan	Pre-annual grass control	c	
Oxadiazon	Chipco Ronstar G	Pre-annual weed control	c	

Pendimethalin	Pre-M	Pre-annual weed control	c	
Prodiamine	Barricade	Pre-annual weed control	c	
Pronamide	Kerb 50W	Pre- and post-annual bluegrass control	c, d, e	
Siduron	Tupersan	Pre-annual grass control in new seedings	b, c	
Simazine	Princep Caliber 90	Pre-weed control in warm season grasses	c, e	

(continued on next page)

Table 3-1. Continued.

Common name	Trade name(s)	Use	Category[†]	Structure
Triclopyr	Turflon Amine Turflon Ester	Post-broadleaf control	c	
2,4-D amine	Dacamine Formula 40 Weed Rhap A-42 Weedar 64 and 64A Weeder Emulsamine E-3	Post-broadleaf control	c d (Hi-Dep only)	
2,4-D ester	Hi-Dep Esteron 99 concentrate Salvo SEE 2,4-D Weed Rhap LV-4D Weedone LV-4			Dichlorprop
		Herbicide combinations		
2,4-D + dichlorprop 2,4-D ester + dichlorprop ester 2,4-D + MCPP + dicamba + MSMA 2,4-D + 2,4-DP + dicamba 2,4-D + MCPP + dicamba 2,4-D amine + triclopyr amine 2,4-D ester + triclopyr ester 2,4-D amine + MCPP	Cleary's Weedone DPC Weedone DPC amine Weedone DPC ester Weedone HG quadmec Trimec Plus Super Trimec Trimec Classic Trimec Weeder Granules Trimec Southern Turflon II Turflon D 2 plus 2	Post-broadleaf control (Quadmec Trimec Plus also has post- annual grass activity	c	

MCPA + MCPP + dicamba	Trimec Encore	Post-broadleaf control	c
Benefin + oryzalin	XL 2G	Pre-annual grass control	c
Benefin + trifluralin	Team 2G	Pre-annual grass control	c
Triclopyr + clopyralid	Confront	Post-broadleaf control	c

Trifluralin

Clopyralid

† Letters in this column indicate registration status: a—lawn and turf seedbeds (prior to establishment); b—newly sprigged or seeded turf; c—established lawns and turf; d—established grasses for lawn seed production; e—turfgrasses for sod production.

Table 3-2. Chemical classification of turfgrass herbicides.

Chemical class	Turfgrass herbicide (common name)
Arsenicals	AMA
	Cacodylic acid
	CMA
	DSMA
	MSMA
Aryloxyphenoxypropionates	Diclofop
	Fenoxaprop
	Fluazifop
Benzamides	Isoxaben
	Pronamide
Benzoic acid	Dicamba
Benzonitrile	Bromoxynil
Benzothiadiazole	Bentazon
Bipyridylium	Diquat
Carbamate	Asulam
Dinitroanilines	Benefin
	Oryzalin
	Pendimethalin
	Prodiamine
	Trifluralin
Imidazolinone	Imazaquin
Organophosphates	Bensulide
	Glyphosate
Phenylurea	Siduron
Phenoxys	2,4-D
	2,4-DP (Dichlorprop)
	MCPA
	MCPP (Mecoprop)
Pyridines	Clopyralid
	Triclopyr
Triazines	Atrazine
	Metribuzin
	Simazine
Miscellaneous	Dazomet
	DCPA
	Dithiopyr
	Endothall
	Ethofumesate
	Oxadiazon

2. Aryloxyphenoxypropionates

Action. Herbicides in the chemical group that may be used on turfgrass are diclofop-methyl [(±)-2-[4-(2,4-dichlorophenoxy)phenoxy]propanoic acid], fenoxaprop-methyl [(±)-2-[4-[(6-chloro-2-benzoxazolyl)oxy]phenoxy] propanoic acid], and fluazifop-butyl [(±)-2-[4-[[5-(trifluoromethyl)-2-pyridinyl]oxy]phenoxy]propanoic acid]. In other chemical classification systems, these have also been grouped under the polycyclic alkanonic acids and oxyphenoxy alkanoic acids (30). These herbicides are generally considered postemergence, foliarly applied herbicides although small amounts can be absorbed by plant roots. In sensitive plants a portion of the applied esters of these herbicides are hydrolyzed to the acids usually considered the active form; however, both the ester and the acid may contribute to the activity of the herbicide (50).

This chemical class of herbicides may have multiple modes of action. The observed physiological effects of herbicides in this class include inhibition of fatty acid synthesis, disruption of membranes, disruption of auxin action, and inhibition of meristematic growth (30). The inhibition of fatty acid synthesis has been measured by the inhibition of ^{14}C-acetate incorporation into lipids (50). The target enzyme with respect to this inhibition is acetyl CoA carboxylase (ACCase). This enzyme catalyzes the following reaction.

$$\text{Acetyl CoA} + \text{HCO}_3^- + \text{ATP} \xrightarrow{\text{ACCase}} \text{Malonyl CoA} + \text{ADP} + \text{Pi}$$

In higher plant fatty acid synthesis in the chloroplast the malonyl CoA then enters a cyclic process of condensations with units of acetyl CoA to generate intermediate fatty acid chains.

Shimabukuro and Hoffer (95) proposed a dual mechanism to explain the action of diclofop-methyl. They proposed a biophysical mechanism that results in pertubation of the transmembrane proton gradient as measured by membrane depolarization. They also proposed a biochemical mechanism which is the inhibition of the ACCase. The very active R+ enantiomer affects both mechanisms whereas the less active S-enantiomers affects only the biophysical mechanisms. Since the racemic mixture is as active as the R+ enantiomers by itself there is indication of an interaction between the action of the R+ and the S− enantiomers. Observed antagonism of 2,4-D with diclofop-methyl can be explained with antagonism of the biophysical mechanism. Observed plant chlorosis is due to the action on the biochemical mechanism. DiTomaso et al. (25) concluded from their research with low levels of diclofop-methyl that the effect of this herbicide on membrane potentials of susceptible species was probably unrelated to the inhibitory effect of this herbicide on plant growth.

Walker et al. (112) concluded that fluazifop-butyl acts by inhibiting ACCase, the same biochemical mechanism proposed for diclofop-methyl. The inhibition of ACCase is also proposed as the mode of action for the cyclohexanedione herbicides, such as sethoxydim [2-[1-(ethoxyimino)butyl]-5-[2-(ethylthio)propyl]-3-hydroxy-2-cyclohexen-1-one] (15).

Selectivity of the aryloxyphenoxypropionates is associated with differences in the site of action between the sensitive and tolerant plants and not metabolism. This class of herbicides are generally formulated as short-chain esters.

Metabolism. Following foliar absorption of the aryloxyphenoxypropionate esters they are hydrolyzed in the plant to the parent acids (30). It has been assumed that this reaction is catalyzed by the carboxylesterase, however the catalysis does not represent a loss of herbicide activity.

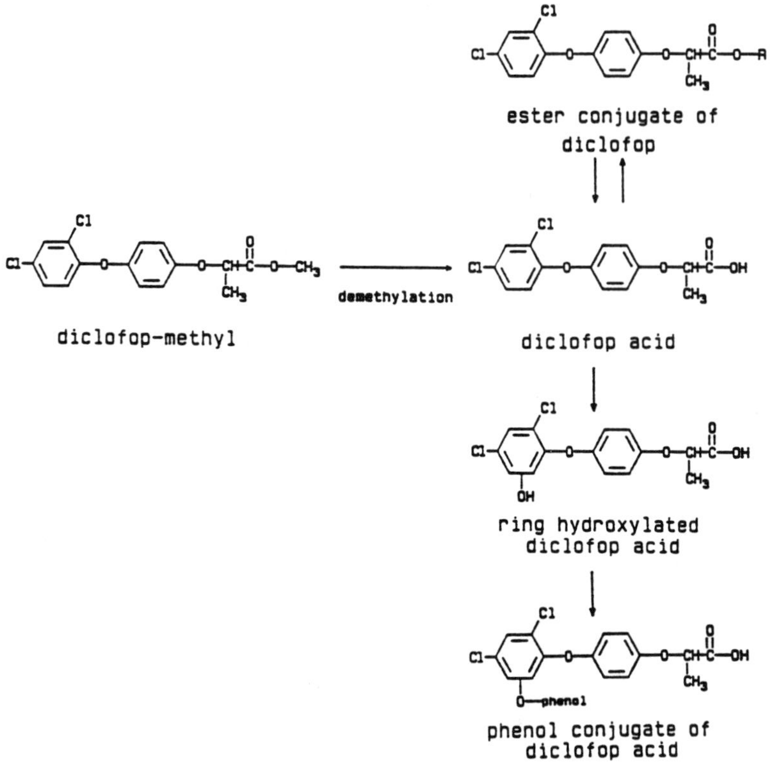

ester conjugate of
diclofop

diclofop-methyl   demethylation   diclofop acid

ring hydroxylated
diclofop acid

phenol conjugate of
diclofop acid

Fig. 3-1. Metabolism of diclofop-methyl after Jacobson and Shimabukuro (52) and Shimabukuro (94).

The proposed pathway for the metabolism of diclofop-methyl in plants is shown in Fig. 3-1. The information on the metabolism products formed from fluazifop-butyl and fenoxaprop-methyl is sparse. Conversion to the parent acid and subsequent conjugation has been reported (23).

3. Benzamides

Action. Benzamides used for turfgrass weed control are isoxaben [N-[3-(1-ethyl-1-methylpropyl)-5-isoxazolyl]-2,6-dimethoxybenzamide] and pronamide [3,5-dichloro(N-1,1-dimethyl-2-propynyl)benzamide]. Pronamide rapidly disrupts the mitotic sequence and produces symptoms similar to colchicine or dinitroaniline herbicide (18). Apparently pronamide does not cause a total loss of microtubules but causes a shortening of the microtubules, interfering with their function (107).

Although some morphological responses to isoxaben resemble those of pronamide they have been characterized as more closely resembling those of dichlobenil considered to be a cellulose biosynthesis inhibiting herbicide (86). Heim et al. (45) concluded that isoxaben is a powerful and specific inhibitor of cell wall biosynthesis.

Metabolism. Pronamide metabolism in alfalfa (*Medicago sativa* L.) plants was slow and involved alterations to the aliphatic side chain, and ultimately resulted in derivatives of dichlorobenzoic acids bound to insoluble residues (115). Isoxaben is more readily metabolized and in grass species the alkyl side chain is readily hydroxylated (113).

4. Benzoics

Action. Dicamba (3,6-dichlorobenzonitrile) applied alone or in combination with phenoxy herbicides has provided control of numerous hard-to-kill broadleaf weeds in turf. Injury symptoms of dicamba closely resemble those of the phenoxy herbicides. Dicamba is readily absorbed through both foliage and roots and is considered to have multiple modes of action. Dicamba may have a direct effect on the binding of histones to DNA (3, 20, 85) and act as an auxin agonist. Furthermore, dicamba appears to enhance ethylene production (102). The increased levels of ethylene may then affect protein synthesis, epinasty, and membrane permeability resulting in numerous physiological effects.

Metabolism. Dicamba metabolism in plants varies with the species. For example, in purple nutsedge (*Cyperus rotundus* L.) no metabolism of dicamba was observed in 10 d (66) whereas in a grass species such as wheat (*Triticum aestivum* L.), metabolism may be complete in 18 d (13). Differential metabolism appears to contribute to the observed selectivity of dicamba. Metabolites vary with plant species as well. In Kentucky bluegrass (*Poa pratensis* L.) the major metabolite appears to be a glucose conjugate of dicamba that yields 5-hydroxy-2-methoxy-3,6-dichlorobenzoic acid on hydrolysis (13).

5. Benzonitriles

Action. The benzonitrile herbicide used for turf applications is bromoxynil (3,5-dibromo-4-hydroxybenzonitrile). Bromoxynil action is rapid and resembles contact action. The most sensitive sites affected by bromoxynil are the uncoupling oxidative and photosynthetic phosphorylation (77). Less sensitive reactions inhibited by bromoxynil include electron transport, hormonal regulation of proteolytic and amylolytic enzymes in germinating seeds, and essential biosynthetic pathways such as RNA, protein, and lipid synthesis (32).

Metabolism. The metabolism of bromoxynil octanoate ester applied to wheat appears to proceed to hydrolysis of the ester to yield the free bromoxynil (14). This is followed by hydrolysis of the $C \equiv N$ group to form the amide, then the carboxylic acid, and finally the decarboxylation of the carboxylic acid group (14). The fate of the remainder of the molecule appears unknown.

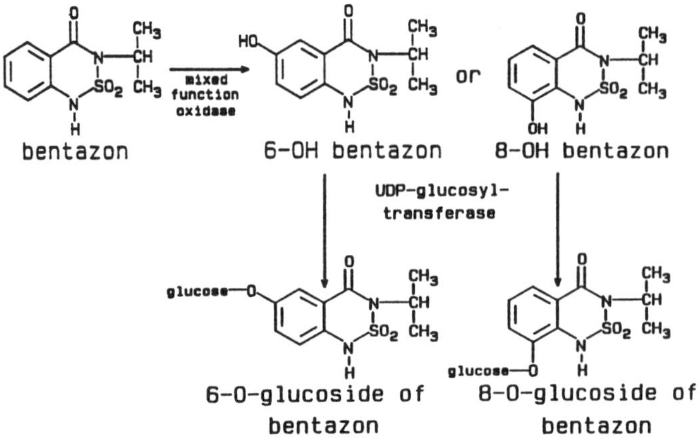

Fig. 3-2. Hydroxylation and glucose conjugation of bentazon in plants.

6. Benzothiadiazoles

Action. Bentazon is a fast acting postemergence herbicide that is effective on numerous broadleaf weeds as well as sedges. Bentazon is a potent inhibitor of photosynthesis (83). The primary site appears to be the electron transport chain on the reducing side of Photosystem II, competing with plastoquinone for binding on the D_1 protein (105). This site is similar to that proposed for the s-triazine and the substituted urea herbicides. Bentazon at higher concentrations may also inhibit electron transport in the oxidizing side of Photosystem II, thus having at least two sites of action (105). The lack of cross-resistance of triazine resistant weeds to bentazon (35) supports the conclusion that bentazon acts at more than a single site of action.

Metabolism. Bentazon was readily metabolized by tolerant species (68, 83) with metabolism differences among species readily apparent and as many as four bentazon conjugates formed in tolerant species (67). In tolerant soybean [*Glycine max* (L.) Merr.] the glucosyl conjugate of 6- and 8-hydroxybentazon were identified (81), but in rice (*Oryza sativa* L.) only the glucosyl conjugate of 6-hydroxybentazon was found (73).

The metabolism of bentazon appears to proceed through a monooxygenase catalyzed hydroxylation of the aromatic ring of bentazon at the 6 or 8 position as mixed function oxidase inhibitors enhance bentazon activity inhibiting bentazon detoxication (64). This is followed by glucosylation of the 6- or 8-hydroxybentazon by a glucosyltransferase as shown in Fig. 3-2 (42). In rice, the bound bentazon residue is associated with lignin in the straw and starch in the grain, whereas in soybean it is associated with lignin and lignocellulose in the vegetative parts and the globulin protein in the seed (81).

7. Bipyridyliums

Action. Diquat [6,7-dihydrodipyrido[1,2-α:2',1'-c]pyrazinediium ion] is a fast acting contact herbicide in this class. Injury symptoms may be ap-

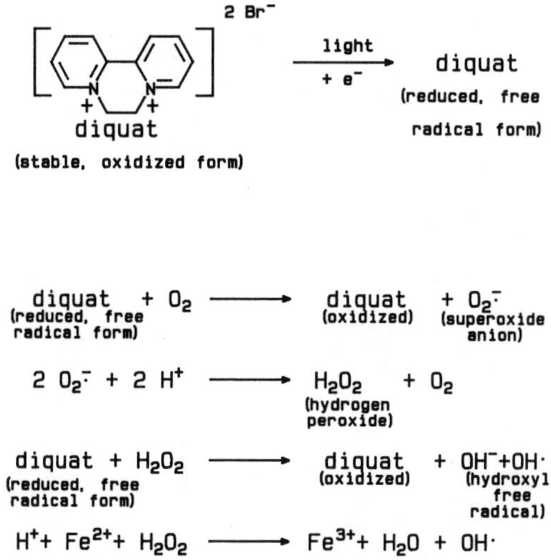

Fig. 3-3. Reactions involved in the formation of the highly phytotoxic hydroxyl free radical.

parent in several hours. The activity of the bipyridylium herbicides is closely related to their redox potential and has been reviewed by Ashton and Crafts (7, p. 164–179) and Calderbank and Slade (17). Diquat as applied is an oxidized cation. In the presence of light, diquat captures an electron from the excited chlorophyl in Photosystem I of the electron transport chain, instead of NADP reduction diquat is reduced. This may be considered a diquat activation step. Diquat is subsequently autooxidized to the oxidized form to repeat the cycle, O_2 and H_2O are involved in the autooxidation step resulting in the formation of O_2^- (singlet oxygen free radical) and OH^- (hydroxyl free radical) as shown in Fig. 3-3. The latter appears to be the primary toxicant reacting readily with unsaturated lipids resulting in membrane lipid peroxidation. The resulting membrane leakage produces the observed herbicide symptoms.

Metabolism. Diquat does not appear to be metabolized in plants; however, diquat can readily be phototransformed on grass surfaces with the loss of 75% in 4 d in June (16).

8. Carbamates

Action. Asulum [methyl[(4-aminophenyl)sulfonyl]carbamate] like other carbamates has been shown to be a mitotic inhibitor (104). The responsible mechanism for the observed blocking of mitosis has not been reported. There is evidence that asulum may inhibit RNA and protein synthesis (110). Folic acid is an important coenzyme in C_1 metabolism in plants. Asulam has been shown to interfere with folic acid synthesis by inhibiting the enzyme, 7,8-dihydrofolate reductase (111). This competitive inhibition affects 7,8-dihydropteroate synthesis and can be reversed by the addition of p-

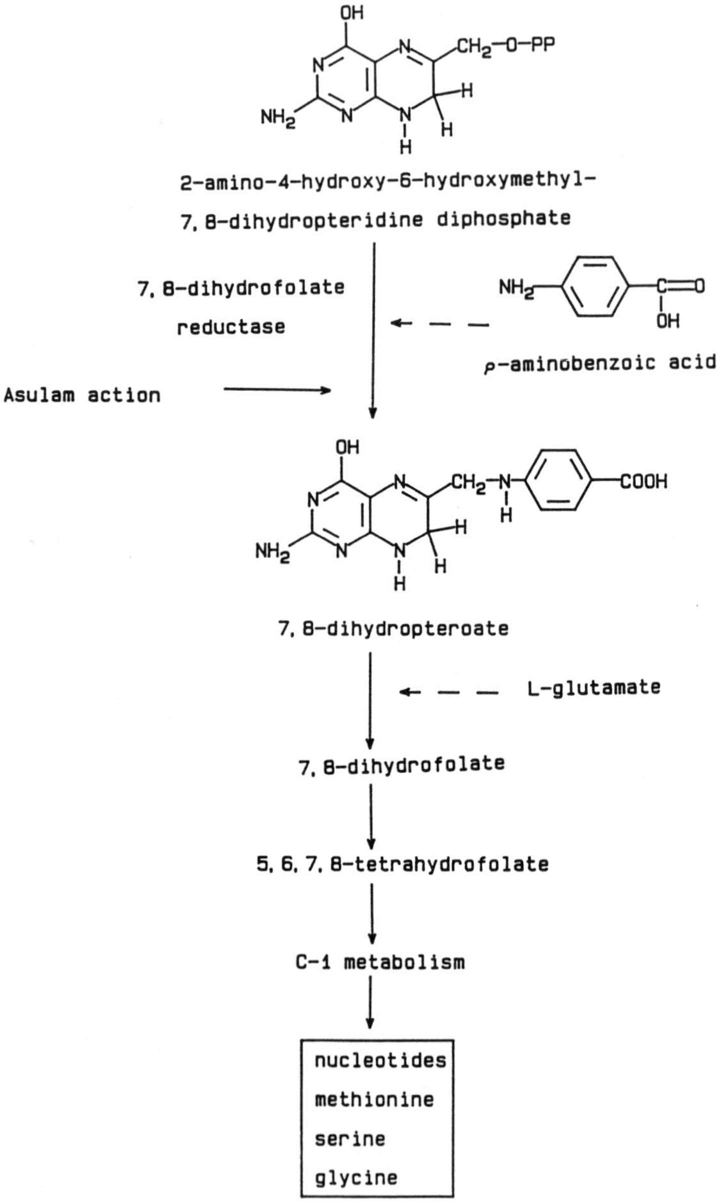

2-amino-4-hydroxy-6-hydroxymethyl-

7, 8-dihydropteridine diphosphate

7, 8-dihydrofolate

reductase

p-aminobenzoic acid

Asulam action

7, 8-dihydropteroate

L-glutamate

7, 8-dihydrofolate

5, 6, 7, 8-tetrahydrofolate

C-1 metabolism

nucleotides

methionine

serine

glycine

Fig. 3-4. Inhibitory action of asulam on folate synthesis.

aminobenzoic acid (58). Thus, asulam action would ultimately affect nucleotide synthesis (Fig. 3-4).

Metabolism. Data on asulum metabolism in plants are not plentiful. Based on the metabolism of other carbamates in plants one would expect to find ring hydroxylation by mixed function oxidase activity followed by conjugation to form polar metabolites.

9. Dinitroanilines

Action. Substituted dinitroaniline herbicides of utility for weed control in turf include benefin [*N*-butyl-*N*-ethyl-2,6-dinitro-4-(trifluoromethyl)benzenamine], oryzalin [4-(dipropylamino)-3,5-dinitrobenzenesulfonamide], pendimethalin [*N*-(1-ethylpropyl)-3,4-dimethyl-2,6-dinitrobenzenamine], prodiamine [N^3,N^3,-di-n-propyl-2,4-dinitro-6-(trifluoromethyl)-m-phenylenediamine], and trifluralin [2,6-dinitro-*N,N*-dipropyl-4-(trifluoromethyl)benzenamine]. Injury symptoms involve severe stunting of shoot growth, failure of grass leaves to unfurl early during development, decreased numbers of roots, greatly shortened lateral roots with characteristic swelling near the tips and swollen stem at the ground line. Not all symptoms are evident in all plant species. The symptoms largely result from dinitroaniline herbicide disrupted mitosis. The behavior of dinitroaniline herbicides has been reviewed recently by Appleby and Valverde (2). The disruption of cell division has been related to dinitroaniline herbicide binding to the protein dimer, tubulin, in cells and this binding results in blocking of spindle microtubule formation (9, 46). In normal cells tubulin is assembled into filametous spindle or cortical microtubules. The spindle microtubules are involved in cell division and the cortical microtubules in cellulose microfibril deposition and thus cell wall formation. Studies on a dinitroaniline resistant goosegrass [*Eleusine indica* (L.) Gaertn.] observed normal formation of microtubules (108). The resistant biotype appears to have an altered beta tubulin not affected by dinitroaniline binding (109). Whenever the action of the substituted dinitroaniline herbicide is evident by restricted or reduced root development, the injured plants are more vulnerable to drought injury and the negative impacts of soil compaction (87).

Metabolism. Metabolism of trifluralin in plants is relatively slow. *N*-Dealkylation involving mixed function oxidase of one and ultimately both of the alkyl chains occurs. Similar reduction of one or of both of the nitro groups to form amines also occurs. Cyclization results in the formation of the benzimidazole (38, 42, 70).

Metabolism of pendimethalin also involves oxidation of the 4-methyl group on the benzene ring. The importance of this metabolic step is illustrated by the studies of Moss (79) with slender foxtail (*Alopecurus myosuroides* Huds.) resistant to several herbicides including pendimethalin but not trifluralin. The basis for the observed resistance of the slender foxtail involves enhanced ability to degrade herbicide by *N*-dealkylation and ring-alkyl oxidation, the latter involved in pendimethalin but not trifluralin metabolism in plants (55).

10. Imidazolinones

Action. The imidazolinone herbicide of current use for turfgrass weed control is imazaquin. This class of herbicides is slow-acting, inhibits plant

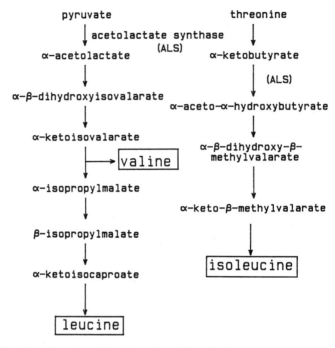

Fig. 3–5. Role of acetolactate synthase in amino acid synthesis.

growth, reduces root development and eventually causes weed necrosis. The mode of action of the imidazolinones is similar to the sulfonylurea herbicides. Both inhibit the action of acetolactate synthase (ALS) also known as acetohydroxy acid synthase (AHAS) (74). This enzyme is essential in the synthesis of three branched-chain amino acids, isoleucine, leucine, and valine as shown in Fig. 3–5. The consequent reduction in synthesis of these amino acids caused by the action of the imidazolinone herbicides disrupts protein synthesis and causes the observed symptomology (8, p. 234–240). It appears the imidazolinone and sulfonylurea herbicides have only a single site of action, namely the ALS enzyme (19). However, the uncompetitive binding of imazaquin to this enzyme with respect to pyruvate versus mixed competitive binding for sulfometuron indicates that there may be different binding sites for the various herbicides (90).

Metabolism. Crop plants are tolerant to the imadazolinone herbicides because they can metabolically inactivate or metabolize the herbicide very rapidly (92). Plants resistant to the imidazolinone herbicides have an altered ALS enzyme that is less sensitive to the herbicide (74).

Metabolism of imazaquin can proceed by two routes, destruction of the imidazolinone ring or side-chain hydroxylation of the alkyl groups (61).

11. Organophosphates

Action. The two herbicides in this class, bensulide [*O,O*-bis(1-methylethyl) *S*-[2-[(phenylsulfonyl)amino]ethyl]phosphorodithioate] and glyphosate, are very different in use, action, and metabolism and will be treated separately. Bensulide inhibits root growth (5, 11) and has an inhibitory effect on cell division (24).

The literature on the organophosphate herbicide, glyphosate, has been reviewed in the book edited by Grossbard and Atkinson (39). The mode of action literature has been reviewed by Cole (22). Initial mode of action studies by Jaworski (53) on duckweed (*Lemna gibba* L.) and *Rhizobium japonica* showed that mixtures of the amino acids, phenylalanine, tyrosine, and tryptophan could alleviate glyphosate injury to these species, implicating the shikimic acid pathway as a site of action. However, only rarely can feeding these amino acids alleviate all of the glyphosate injury in higher plants (22). The enzyme in the shikimic acid pathway affected by the lowest level of glyphosate is 5-enolpyruvylshikimic acid-3-phosphate (EPSP) synthase (103). The inhibition is competitive and causes an accumulation of shikimic acid. In 1978, Duke and Hoagland (28) hypothesized that glyphosate could be stimulating phenylalanine ammonia-lyase (PAL) and that this would explain the symptomology. More recently they consider the action on PAL as marginally or indirectly involved in glyphosate action (29).

Glyphosate readily forms chelates with numerous metal ions. The interaction between glyphosate and metals essential for plant growth have been reviewed (80); however, the exact contribution of these interactions to the mode of glyphosate action remains undetermined.

There is evidence thus far indicating that glyphosate has multiple modes of action. Inhibition of EPSP synthase may be the primary mode of action, the one that occurs at the lowest glyphosate application rate, but most likely is not solely responsible for the symptoms. Evidence to support this conclusion include failure of exogenously supplied phenylalanine, tyrosine, and tryptophan to always overcome glyphosate injury on higher plants, lack of appearance of glyphosate-resistant weeds, and the difficulty despite considerable effort to develop glyphosate-resistant crop plants than can withstand the recommended herbicidal application rates of glyphosate. Other proposed modes of glyphosate action include a rapid direct effect on stomatal conductance (91) and inhibition of 3-deoxy-D-arabino-heptulosonate 7-phosphate (DAHP) synthase (88) and other enzymes in the shikimic acid pathway as shown in Fig. 3–6.

Metabolism. Metabolism studies using lettuce (*Lactuca sativa* L.) found rapid metabolism of bensulide in the leaves with the evolution of $^{14}CO_2$ from ^{14}C-bensulide (113).

Glyphosate is a nonselective postemergence herbicide. Variability in efficacy appears associated with differences in absorption and translocation, not metabolism of glyphosate (89). In certain plant species very limited metabolism of glyphosate to aminomethylphosphonic acid may occur (89).

12. Phenylureas

Action. The substituted phenylurea herbicide of significance for weed control in turfgrasses is siduron [*N*-(2-methylcyclohexyl)-*N*)-phenylurea). Sid-

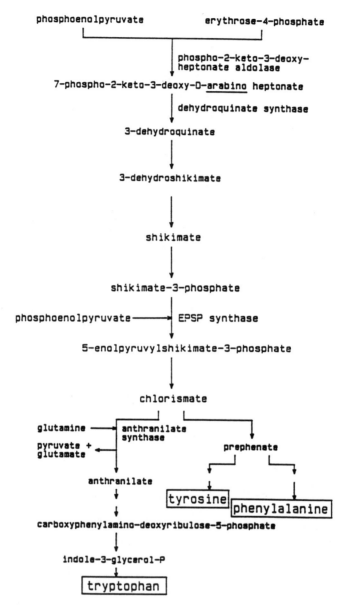

Fig. 3-6. Enzymes inhibited by glyphosate.

uron unlike the other commercial substituted phenylurea herbicides is not a potent inhibitor of photosynthesis. Instead, siduron inhibits root growth (101) apparently by inhibiting mitosis (100).

Metabolism. Little is known about the metabolism of siduron. Splitt-stoesser and Hopen (99) did not observe any metabolism of siduron on barley (*Hordeum vulgare* L.) plants 8 d after treatment.

13. Phenoxys

Action. The phenoxy herbicides used for weed control in turf include 2,4-D, MCPA [(±)-2-(2,4-dichlorophenoxy)propanoic acid] and mecoprop [(±)-2-(4-chloro-2-methylphenoxy)propanoic acid] both having a propanoic side chain. These phenoxy herbicides differ in their selectivity due to differences in absorption and metabolism but not in their mode of action.

The action of the phenoxy herbicide results in very characteristic symptoms such as epinasty, distorted and feathered leaves in broadleaf plants, stunting, twisting of plants, and distorted roots in grasses. The effects are most obvious in meristematic tissue. There may even be a reversion to meristematic activity in some plant tissues. The stimulated cell division may play a role in the lethal action of the phenoxys (41). The phenoxys like benzoics appear to be auxin agonists. A multitude of biochemical and metabolic changes may occur in treated plants and have been reviewed by Penner and Ashton (84).

The critical action of the phenoxys appears to involve a stimulation of nucleic acid metabolism, probably in RNA, which in turn affects protein synthesis (56, 57). The action of the phenoxy herbicides in nucleic acid metabolism could in part explain the herbicide effect on cell wall loosening associated with the cell elongation symptom of herbicide action. The action of the phenoxys has been extensively reviewed by Loos (65).

Metabolism. Plant metabolism of the phenoxys plays an important role in the tolerance of grass species to this class of herbicides (42). Known metabolism reactions in higher plants as shown in Fig. 3–7 involve side chain oxidation, amino acid conjugation, glucose ester formation, ring hydroxylation, and glucose conjugation.

14. Pyridines

Action. Clopyralid (3,6-dichloro-2-pyridinecarboxylic acid) and triclopyr [[(3,5,6-trichloro-2-pyridinyl)oxy]acetic acid] are the members of the class of herbicides that are registered for weed control in turfgrass. These herbicides like the phenoxys are especially effective on dicotyledoneous weed species. They elicit the typical auxin type response characteristic of the phenoxy herbicides. The detailed mode of action of these herbicides has not yet been documented.

Metabolism. Little is known regarding the metabolism of clopyralid and triclopyr. Based on the research of Zollinger (116), metabolism in sensitive species is either slow or negligible as slow absorption and translocation of very low dosages were sufficient to kill the sensitive plants.

15. Triazines

Action. The primary mode of action of triazine herbicides as defined by the mode of action affecting the plants at the lowest concentration or first in time does not appear related to the lethal mode of action for these

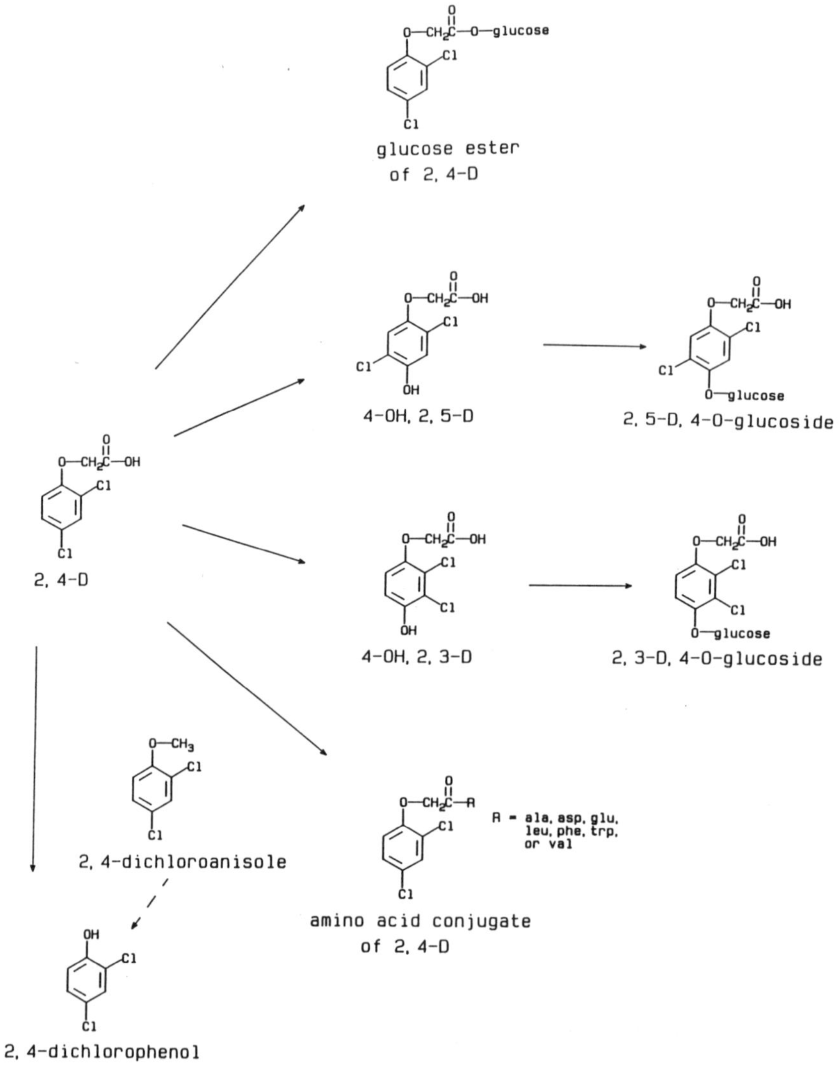

Fig. 3-7. Plant metabolism of 2,4-D after Chkanikov et al. (21), Feung et al. (31), and Loos (65).

herbicides. Low dosages of the triazine herbicide increase stomatal apera-
ture (60). This action can affect the subsequent root absorption of other herbicides, the triazines themselves, or passively absorbed ions such as NO_3.
Increased absorption of the latter explains the darker green color sometimes
observed from the presence of very low levels of the triazine herbicides. At
higher dosages of the triazines the stomatal apertures are reduced, thus
demonstrating a bimodal response to the triazine herbicides (60).

Soil-applied triazine herbicides can also affect early seedling development in the dark (82). Again this inhibition of growth does not appear to
be related to the lethal action of the triazine.

Both foliar-applied and soil-applied triazine are potent inhibitors of the Hill reaction in photosynthesis (72, 76). The inhibition involves the binding of the triazine molecules to a 32 kd protein in the electron transport chain known as the D_1 protein (4). This results in competition for the normal binding site of plastoquinone. Triazine-resistant biotypes have a glycine amino acid moiety substituted for a serine moiety in this protein that appears related to the inability of the triazine to bind to the protein and block photosynthesis (48).

Blocking carbohydrate production by blocking photosynthesis can be accomplished by putting plants in the dark; however, the subsequent plant injury is vastly different from that observed from triazine herbicide application. Ashton et al. (6) postulated that the action involved the interaction of light, chlorophyll, and the herbicide to produce secondary phytotoxic substances. When the electron transport chain is blocked, energy accumulates as excited chlorophyll, that which cannot be quenched by the carotenoids, is dissipated as fluorescence or in the production of free radicals such as singlet O_2 (37). The latter attack membranes, possibly through peroxidation of the unsaturated lipids resulting in leaf desiccation and the observed injury response.

Metabolism. The metabolism of the symmetrical chloro-triazines, atrazine [6-chloro-N-ethyl-N'-(1-methylethyl)-1,3,5-triazine-2,4-diamine], and simazine (6-chloro-N,N'-diethyl-1,3,5-triazine-2,4-diamine), are very similar; however, the metabolism of the asymmetrical traizine, metribuzin [4-amino-6-(1,1-dimethylethyl)-3-(methylthio)-1,2,4-triazin-5(4H)-one], is different and has been reviewed by Hatzios and Penner (42, 43).

N-Dealkylation of one and ultimately both alkyl side chains of atrazine and simazine is catalyzed by a mixed function oxidase (93). In a transfer reaction by glutathione s-transferase, atrazine and simazine can be conjugated with glutathione (62, 97). The glutathione can undergo subsequent metabolism to a lanthionine derivative (96). In corn (*Zea mays* L.) roots the cyclohexamic acid, DIMBOA, nonenzymatically catalyzes the hydroxylation of both simazine and atrazine (40). These reactions are illustrated in Fig. 3–8.

Metribuzin metabolism involves initial deamination or demethylthiolation to form the deaminated diketo metribuzin (98), sulfoxidation and conjugation with homoglutathione (34), conjugation of the diketo metabolite with malonic acid (34) conjugation of the deaminated metribuzin with glucose and subsequent conjugation of this metabolite with malonic acid (33, 34) is shown in Fig. 3–9.

The metabolism of metribuzin has been reviewed by Hatzios and Penner (42). Metabolism plays a key role in the observed selectivity of the triazine of various crops tolerant to the triazines.

16. Miscellaneous

Dazomet. Dazomet (tetrahydro-3,5-dimethyl-2H-1,3,5-triadiazine-2-thione) is a soil fumigant used prior to seeding. Within 10 to 15 min following application to warm moist soil it chemically degrades to form methyliso-

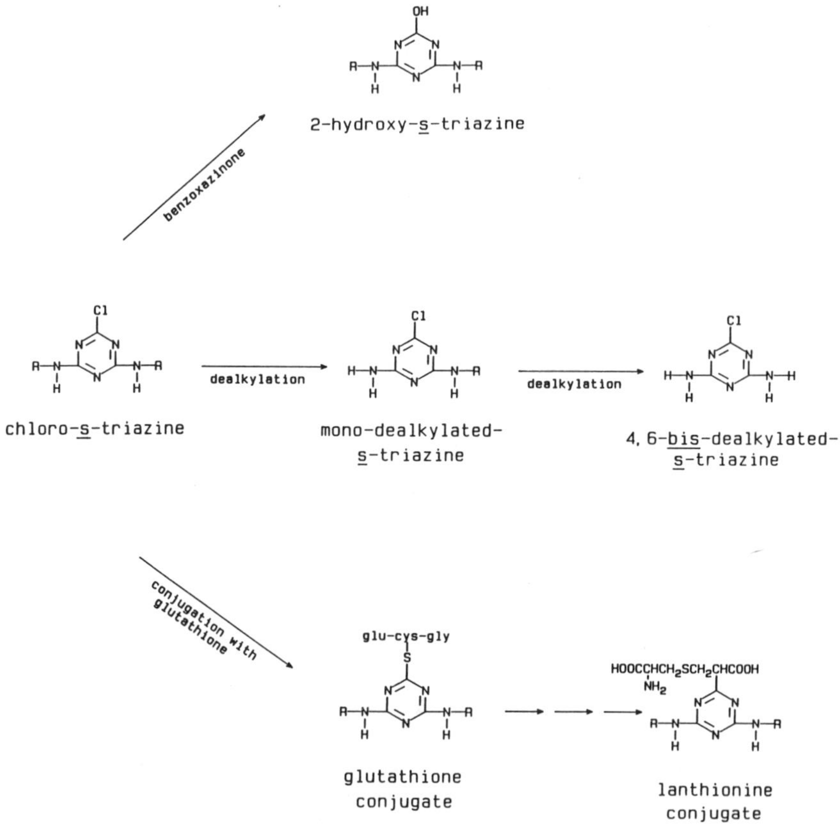

Fig. 3-8. Metabolism of chloro-*s*-triazines in plants after Shimabukuro et al. (96).

thiocyamate, formaldehyde, hydrogen sulfide, and monomethylamine. These interact to produce the desired fumigant action (113).

DCPA. This herbicide acts by inhibiting growth of germinating seeds, most likely by interfering with cell division (10). Mitosis in oat (*Avena sativa* L.) was disrupted after prophase as were other processes involving organized microtubules (49). Published data on the metabolism of DCPA in plants is limited. Mono- and di-demethylation has been reported (36).

Dithiopyr. Dithiopyr [*S,S*-dimethyl 2-(difluoromethyl)-4-(2-methylpropyl-6-(trifluoromethyl)-3,5-pyridinedicarbothioate] might be classified as a pyridine derivative. It inhibits mitosis arresting cell division at prometaphase (75). The research of Molin et al. (75) suggests that dithiopyr binds to a specific protein involved in regulation of tubulin polymerization.

Endothall. Endothall (7-oxabicyclo[2-2-1]heptane-2,3-dicarboxylic acid) rapidly desiccates plant foliage. Promotion of ethylene synthesis has been observed (1). Mann and Pu (69) reported that endothall caused a modest

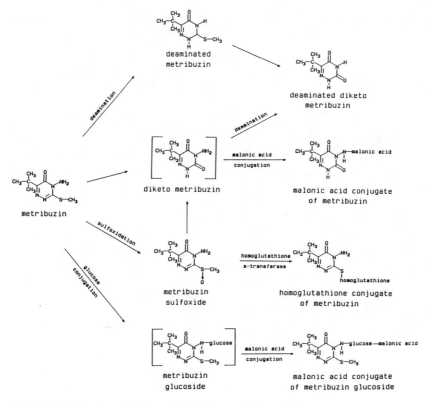

Fig. 3-9. Metribuzin metabolism after Hatzios and Penner (44).

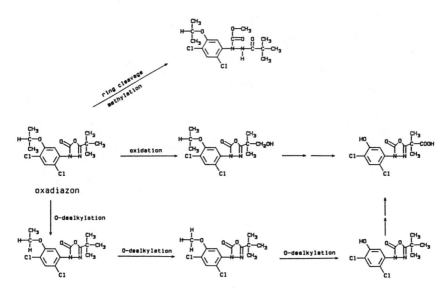

Fig. 3-10. Oxadiazon metabolism in rice after Hirata and Ishizuka (47) and Ishizuka et al. (51).

inhibition of lipid synthesis. α-Amylase induction in barley half seeds is severely inhibited by relatively high concentrations (5×10^{-4}M) of endothall (54). Little is known about endothall metabolism in plants.

Ethofumesate. Inhibition of epicuticular wax formation and deposition of ethofumesate [($\pm$)-2-ethoxy-2,3-dihydro-3,3-dimethyl-5-benzofuranyl methanesulfonate] has been reported (63). This is indicative of a more basic interference with lipid synthesis. Tolerant species readily metabolize ethofumesate to two metabolites that are subsequently conjugated (113).

Oxadiazon. Oxadiazon [3-[2,4-dichloro-5-(1-methylethoxy)phenyl]-5-(1,1-dimethylethyl)-1,3,4-oxadiazol-2-(3H)-one] causes rapid loss of plant pigment or bleaching and desiccation. Duke et al. (27) found marked accumulation of Protoporphyrin IX following oxadiazon treatment. The massive accumulation was interpreted by Duke et al. (27) as indicative of oxadiazon inhibition of the transformation of Protoporphyrin IX to magnesium protoporphyrin. The accumulation of the former could act as a singlet O_2 generator eliciting the observed rapid desiccation from membrane peroxidation. Furthermore, chlorophyll synthesis would be blocked.

The metabolism of oxadiazon in plants involves o-dealkylation, oxidation, and ring cleavage methylation reaction (47, 51). The metabolism pathway is shown in Fig. 3-10.

REFERENCES

1. Abeles, A.L., and F.B. Abeles. 1972. Biochemical pathway of stress induced ethylene. Plant Physiol. 50:496-498.
2. Appleby, A.P., and B.E. Valverde. 1989. Behavior of dinitroaniline herbicides in plants. Weed Technol. 3:198-206.
3. Arnold, W.E., and J.D. Nalewaja. 1971. Effect of dicamba on RNA and protein. Weed Sci. 19:301-305.
4. Arntzen, C.J., K. Pfister, and K.E. Steinbeck. 1982. The mechanism of chloroplast triazine resistance: Alterations in the rate of herbicide action. p. 185-214. In H.M. LeBaron and J. Gressel (ed.) Herbicide resistance in plants. John Wiley & Sons, New York.
5. Ashton, F.M., D. Penner, and S. Hoffman. 1968. Effect of several herbicides on proteolytic activity of squash seedlings. Weed Sci. 16:169-171.
6. Ashton, F.M., E.M. Gifford, and T. Bisulputra. 1963. Structural changes in *Phaseolus vulgaris* induced by atrazine: 2. Effects on fine structure of chloroplasts. Bot. Gaz. 124:336-343.
7. Ashton, F.M., and A.S. Crafts. 1981. Mode of action of herbicides. 2nd ed. John Wiley & Sons, New York.
8. Ashton, F.M., and T.J. Monaco. 1991. Weed science principles and practices. 3rd ed. John Wiley & Sons, New York.
9. Bartels, P.G., and J.L. Hilton. 1973. Comparison of trifluralin, oryzalin, pronamide, propham and colchicine treatments on microtubules. Pestic. Biochem. Physiol. 3:462-472.
10. Bingham, S.W. 1968. Effect of DCPA on anatomy and cytology of roots. Weed Sci. 16:449-452.
11. Bingham, S.W., and R.E. Schmidt. 1967. Residue of bensulide in turfgrass soil following annual treatments for crabgrass control. Agron. J. 59:327-329.
12. Boger, P., and G. Sandmann (ed.). 1989. Target sites of herbicide action. CRC Press. Boca Raton, FL.
13. Broadhurst, N.A., M.L. Montgomery, and V.A. Freed. 1966. Metabolism of 2-methoxy-3,6-dichlorobenzoic acid (dicamba) by wheat and bluegrass plants. J. Agric. Food Chem. 14:585-588.

14. Buckland, J.L., R.F. Collins, and E.M. Pullin. 1973. Metabolism of bromoxynil octanoate in growing wheat. Pestic. Sci. 4:149–162.

15. Burton, J.D., J.W. Gronwald, D.A. Somers, J.A. Connelly, B.G. Gengenbach, and D.L. Wyse. 1987. Inhibition of plant acetyl-coenzyme A carboxylase by the herbicides sethoxydim and haloxyfop. Biochem. Biophys. Res. Commun. 148:1039–1044.

16. Calderbank, A. 1968. The bipyridylium herbicides. Adv. Pestic. Control Res. 8:127–235.

17. Calderbank, A., and P. Slade. 1977. Diquat and paraquat. p. 501–540. In P.C. Kearney and D.D. Kaufman (ed.) Herbicides chemistry, degradation, and mode of action. Vol. 2. Marcel Dekker, New York.

18. Carlson, W.C., E.M. Lignowski, and H.J. Hopen. 1975. The mode of action of pronamide. Weed Sci. 23:155–161.

19. Chaleff, R.S., and T.B. Ray. 1984. Herbicide resistant mutants from tobacco cell cultures. Science (Washington, DC) 223:1481–1151.

20. Chen, L.G., A. Ali, R.A. Fletcher, C.M. Switzer, and G.R. Stephenson. 1973. Effects of auxin-like herbicides on nucleohistones in cucumber and wheat roots. Weed Sci. 21:181–184.

21. Chkanikov, D.I., N.N. Pavlova, A.M. Makeev, T.A. Nazarova, and A.Y. Makoveichuk. 1977. Paths of detoxification and immobilization of 2,4-D in cucumber plants. Soviet Plant Physiol. 24:457–463.

22. Cole, D.J. 1985. Mode of action of glyphosate—a literature analysis. p. 48–74. In E. Grossbard and D. Atkinson (ed.) The herbicide glyphosate. Butterworths, London.

23. Coupland, D. 1985. The influence of environmental factors on the metabolic fate of ^{14}C-fluazifop-butylin Elymus repens. p. 317–324. In Proc. of the British Crop Protection Conference, Brighton, England. 18–21 Nov. 1985. British Crop Protection Council, Croyden, England.

24. Cutter, E.G., F.M. Ashton, and D. Huffstutter. 1968. The effect of bensulide on the growth, morphology, and anatomy of oat roots. Weed Res. 8:346–352.

25. DiTomaso, J.M., P.H. Brown, A.E. Stowe, D.L. Linscott, and L.V. Kochian. 1991. Effects of diclofop and diclofop-methyl on membrane potentials in roots of intact oat, maize, and pea seedlings. Plant Physiol. 95:1063–1069.

26. Duke, S.O. (ed.). 1985. Weed physiology. Vol. II. CRC Press, Boca Raton, FL.

27. Duke, S.O., J. Lydon, and R.N. Paul. 1989. Oxadiazon activity is similar to that of p-nitrodiphenyl ether herbicides. Weed Sci. 37:152–160.

28. Duke, S.O., and R.E. Hoagland. 1978. Effects of glyphosate on metabolism of phenolic compounds: I. Induction of phenylalanine ammonia-lyase activity in dark-grown maize roots. Plant Sci. Letters 11:185–190.

29. Duke, S.O., and R.E. Hoagland. 1985. Effects of glyphosate on metabolism of phenolic compounds. p. 75–91. In E. Grossbard and D. Atkinson (ed.) The herbicide glyphosate. Butterworths, London.

30. Duke, S.O., and W.H. Kenyon. 1988. Polycyclic alkanoic acids. p. 71–116. In P.C. Kearney and D.D. Kaufman (ed.) Herbicides chemistry, degradation, and mode of action. Vol. 3. Marcel Dekker, New York.

31. Feung, C.S., S.L. Loerch, R.H. Hamilton, and R.O. Mumma. 1978. Comparative metabolic fate of 2,4-dichlorophenoxyacetic acid in plants and plant cultures. J. Agric. Food Chem. 26:1064–1067.

32. Frear, D.S. 1976. The benzoic acid herbicides. p. 541–607. In P.C. Kearney and D.D. Kaufman (ed.) Herbicides, chemistry, degradation, and mode of action. Marcel Dekker, New York.

33. Frear, D.S., E.R. Mansager, H.R. Swanson, and F.S. Tanaka. 1983. Metribuzin metabolism in tomato: isolation and identification of N-glucoside conjugates. Pestic. Biochem. Physiol. 19:270–281.

34. Frear, D.S., H.R. Swanson, and E.R. Mansager. 1985. Alternate pathways of metribuzin metabolism in soybean: formation of N-glucoside and homoglutathione conjugate. Pestic. Biochem. Physiol. 23:56–65.

35. Fuerst, E.P., C.J. Arntzen, K. Pfister, and D. Penner. 1986. Herbicide cross-resistance in triazine-resistant biotypes of four species. Weed Sci. 34:344–353.

36. Gershon, H., and G.W. McClure, Jr. 1966. Approach to the study of the degradation of dimethyl tetrachloroterephthalate. Contrib. Boyce Thompson Inst. 23:291–294.

37. Giannopolitis, C.N., and G.S. Ayers. 1978. Enhancement of chloroplast photooxidations with photosynthesis including herbicide and protection with NADH or NADPH. Weed Sci. 26:440–443.

38. Golab, T., R.J. Herberg, S.J. Parker, and J.B. Tepe. 1967. Metabolism of carbon-14 trifluralin in carrots. J. Agric. Food Chem. 15:638–641.
39. Grossbard, E., and D. Atkinson (ed.). 1985. The herbicide glyphosate. Butterworths, London.
40. Hamilton, R.H. 1964. Tolerance of several grass species to 2-chloro-s-triazine herbicides in relation to degradation and content of benzoxazinone derivatives. J. Agric. Food Chem. 12:14–17.
41. Hanson, I.B., and F.W. Slife. 1969. Role of RNA metabolism in the action of auxin-herbicides. Residue Rev. 25:59–67.
42. Hatzios, K.K., and D. Penner. 1982. Metabolism of herbicides in higher plants. Burgess Publ. Co., Minneapolis.
43. Hatzios, K.K., and D. Penner. 1985. Interactions of herbicides with other agrochemicals in higher plants. Rev. Weed Sci. 1:1–63.
44. Hatzios, K.K., and D. Penner. 1988. Metribuzin. p. 191–243. In P.C. Kearney and D.D. Kaufman (ed.) Herbicides chemistry, degradation, and mode of action. Vol. 3. Marcel Dekker, New York.
45. Heim, D.R., J.R. Skomp, E.E. Tschabold, and I.M. Larrinua. 1990. Isoxaben inhibits the synthesis of acid insoluble cell wall materials in Arabidopsis thaliana. Plant Physiol. 93:695–700.
46. Hess, D., and D. Bayer. 1974. The effect of trifluralin on the ultrastructure of dividing cells of the root meristem of cotton (Gossypium hirsutum). J. Cell Sci. 15:429–441.
47. Hirata, H., and K. Ishkizuka. 1975. Identification of the metabolite (M-1) of 2-tert-butyl-4-(2,4-dichloro-5-isopropoxyphenyl)-Δ^2-1,3,4-oxidiazolin-5-one (oxadiazon) in rice plants. Agric. Biol. Chem. 39:1447–1454.
48. Hirschberg, H., and L. McIntosh. 1983. Molecular basis of herbicide resistance in Amaranthus hydridus. Science (Washington, DC) 222:1346–1347.
49. Holmsen, V.D., and F.D. Hess. 1984. Growth inhibition and disruption of mitosis by DCPA in oat (Avena sativa) roots. Weed Sci. 32:732–738.
50. Hoppe, M.M., and M. Zacher. 1985. Inhibition of fatty acid biosynthesis in isolated bean and maize chloroplasts by herbicidal phenoxy-phenoxypropionic acid derivatives and structurally related compounds. Pestic. Biochem. Physiol. 24:298–305.
51. Ishizuka, K., H. Hirata, and K. Fukunaga. 1975. Absorption, translocation, and metabolism of 2-tert-butyl-4-(2,4-dichloro-5-isopropoxyphenyl)-Δ^2-1,3,4-oxidiazolin-5-one (oxadiazon) in rice plants. Agric. Biol. Chem. 39:1431–1446.
52. Jacobson, A., and R.H. Shimabukuro. 1984. Metabolism of diclofop-methyl in root-treated wheat and oat seedlings. J. Agric. Food Chem. 32:742–746.
53. Jaworski, E.G. 1972. Mode of action of N-phosphonomethyl-glycine: Inhibition of aromatic amino acid biosynthesis. J. Agric. Food Chem. 20:1195–1198.
54. Jones, D.W., and C.L. Foy. 1971. Herbicide inhibition of GA-induced synthesis of α-amylase. Weed Sci. 19:595–597.
55. Kemp, M.S., S.R. Moss, and T.H. Thomas. 1990. Herbicide resistance in Alspecurus myosuroides. p. 376–393. In M.B. Green, H.M. LeBaron, and W.K. Moberg (ed.) Managing resistance to agrochemicals: From fundamental research to practical strategies. Am. Chem. Soc., Washington, DC.
56. Key, J.L. 1966. Effect of purine and pyrimidine analogues on growth and RNA metabolism in the soybean hypocotyl—the selective action of 5-fluoruacil. Plant Physiol. 41:1257–1264.
57. Key, J.L., and J. Ingle. 1964. Requirement for the synthesis of DNA-like RNA for growth of excised plant tissue. Proc. Natl. Acad. Sci. 52:1382–1388.
58. Killmer, J.L., J.M. Widholm, and F.W. Slife. 1980. Antagonistic effect of p-aminobenzoate or folate on asulam [methyl(4-aminobenzensulphonyl carbamate)] inhibition of carrot suspension cultures. Plant Sci. Letters 19:203–208.
59. Knowles, F.C., and A.A. Benson. 1983. Mode of action of a herbicide johnsongrass and methanearsonic acid. Plant Physiol. 71:235–240.
60. Ladlie, J.S., W.F. Meggitt, and D. Penner. 1977. Effect of atrazine on soybean tolerance to metribuzin. Weed Sci. 25:115–121.
61. Ladner, D.W. 1990. Structure-activity relationships among the imidazolinone herbicides. Pestic. Sci. 29:317–333.
62. Lamoureux, G.L., L.E. Stafford, R.H. Shimabukuro, and R.G. Zaylskie. 1973. Atrazine metabolism in sorghum: Catabolism of the glutathione conjugates of atrazine. J. Agric. Food Chem. 21:1020–1030.
63. Leavitt, J.R.C., D.N. Duncan, D. Penner, and W.F. Meggitt. 1978. Inhibition of epicuticular wax deposition in cabbage by ethofumesate. Plant Physiol. 61:1034–1036.

64. Leavitt, J.R.C., B. Rubin, and D. Penner. 1978. Increasing herbicide activity with antioxidants. Proc. North Cent. Weed Control Conf. 33:115.

65. Loos, M.A. 1975. Phenoxyalkanoic acids. p. 1–28. *In* P.C. Kearney and D.D. Kaufman (ed.) Herbicides chemistry, degradation and mode of action. Marcel Dekker, New York.

66. Magalhaes, A.C., F.M. Ashton, and C.L. Foy. 1968. Translocation and fate of dicamba in purple nutsedge. Weed Sci. 16:240–245.

67. Mahoney, M.D., and D. Penner. 1975. Bentazon translocation and metabolism in soybean and navy bean. Weed Sci. 23:265–271.

68. Mahoney, M.D., and D. Penner. 1975. The basis for bentazon selectivity in navy bean, cocklebur, and black nightshade. Weed Sci. 23:272–276.

69. Mann, J.D., and M. Pu. 1968. Inhibition of lipid synthesis by certain herbicides. Weed Sci. 16:197–198.

70. Marquis, L.Y., R.H. Shimabukuro, G.E. Stolzenberg, V.J. Feil, and R.G. Zaylskie. 1979. Metabolism and selectivity of fluchloralin in soybean roots. J. Agric. Food Chem. 27:1148–1156.

71. Meister Publishing. 1991. Weed control manual. Meister Publ. Co., Willoughby, OH.

72. Mets, L., and A. Thiel. 1989. Biochemistry and genetic control of the Photosystem II herbicide target site. p. 1–24. *In* P. Boger and G. Sandmann (ed.) Target sites of herbicide action. CRC Press, Boca Raton, FL.

73. Mine, M., M. Miyakado, and S. Matsunaka. 1975. The mechanism of bentazon selectivity. Pestic. Biochem. Physiol. 5:566–574.

74. Mobery, W.K., and B. Cross. 1990. Herbicides inhibiting branched-chain amino acid biosynthesis. Pestic. Sci. 29:241–246.

75. Molin, W.T., T.C. Lee, and M.W. Bugg. 1988. Purification of a protein which binds MON 7200. Plant Physiol. 86(4) suppl.:31.

76. Moreland, D.E., W.A. Gentner, J.L. Hilton, and K.L. Hill. 1959. Studies on the mechanism of herbicidal action of 2-chloro-4,6-bis(ethylamino)-*s*-triazine. Plant Physiol. 34:432–435.

77. Moreland, D.E., and W.I. Blackmon. 1970. Effects of 3,5-dibromo-4-hydroxybenzaldehyde *O*-(2,4-dinitrophenyl) oxime on reactions of mitochondria and chloroplasts. Weed Sci. 18:419–426.

78. Moreland, D.E., J.B. St. John, and F.D. Hess (ed.). 1982. Biochemical responses induced by herbicides. Am. Chem. Soc., Washington, DC.

79. Moss, S.R. 1990. Herbicide cross-resistance in slender foxtail (*Alopecurus myosuroides*). Weed Sci. 38:492–496.

80. Nilsson, G. 1985. Interactions between glyphosate and metals essential for plant growth. p. 35–47. *In* E. Grossbard and D. Atkinson (ed.) The herbicide glyphosate. Butterworths, London.

81. Otto, S., P. Beutel, M. Decker, and R. Huber. 1978. Investigations into the degradation of bentazon in plant and soil. Adv. Pestic. Sci. 3:551–556.

82. Penner, D. 1970. Herbicide and inorganic phosphate influence on phytase in seedlings. Weed Sci. 18:360–364.

83. Penner, D. 1975. Bentazon selectivity between soybean and Canada thistle. Weed Res. 15:259–262.

84. Penner, D., and F.M. Ashton. 1966. Biochemical and metabolic changes in plants induced by chlorophenoxyherbicides. Residue Rev. 14:39–113.

85. Quimby, P.C. 1967. Studies relating to the selectivity of dicamba for wild buckwheat (*Polygonum convolvulus* L.) vs. Selkirk wheat (*Triticum aestivum* L.) and a possible mode of action. Ph.D. thesis. North Dakota State Univ., Fargo (Diss. Abstr. 67-16495).

86. Roberts, J.L. 1991. Morphological responses of susceptible plants to the herbicide isoxaben. p. 78. *In* Weed Sci. Soc. Am. Abstr., Weed Sci. Soc. Am., Champaign, IL.

87. Roggenbuck, F., and D. Penner. 1983. Evaluation of corn tolerance to several dinitroaniline herbicide residues in soils with varying levels of compaction. Proc. North Cent. Weed Control Conf. 38:105–106.

88. Rubin, J.L., C.G. Gaines, and R.A. Jensen. 1982. Enzymological basis for herbicidal action of glyphosate. Plant Physiol. 70:833–839.

89. Sandberg, C.L., W.F. Meggitt, and D. Penner. 1980. Absorption, translocation, and metabolism of ^{14}C-glyphosate in several weed species. Weed Res. 20:195–200.

90. Schloss, J.V. 1990. Acetolactate synthase, mechanism of action and its herbicide-binding site. Pestic. Sci. 29:283–292.

91. Shaner, D.L., and J.L. Lyons. 1979. Stomatal cycling in *Phaseolus vulgaris* L. in response to glyphosate. Plant Sci. Letters 15:83–87.

92. Shaner, D.L., and P.A. Robson. 1985. Absorption, translocation, and metabolism of AC 252 214 soybean (*Glycine max*), common cocklebur (*Xanthium strumarium*), and velvetleaf (*Abutilon theophrasti*). Weed Sci. 33:469–471.

93. Shimabukuro, R.H. 1967. Significance of atrazine dealkylation in root and shoot of pea plants. J. Agric. Food Chem. 14:392–395.

94. Shimabukuro, R.H. 1985. Detoxication of herbicides. p. 215–240. *In* S.O. Duke (ed.) Weed physiology. Vol. II. CRC Press, Boca Raton, FL.

95. Shimabukuro, R.H., and B.L. Hoffer. 1991. The dual mechanism hypothesis for dichlofopmethyl as indicated by the action of its enantiomers. p. 54. *In* Weed Sci. Soc. Am. Abstrs. Weed Sci. Soc. Am., Champaign, IL.

96. Shimabukuro, R.H., G.L. Lamoureauxx, and D.S. Frear. 1978. Glutathione conjugation: A mechanism for herbicide detoxification and selectivity in plants. p. 133–149. *In* F.M. Pallos and J.E. Casida (ed.) Chemistry and action of herbicide antidotes. Academic Press, New York.

97. Shimabukuro, R.H., H.R. Swanson, and W.C. Walsh. 1970. Glutathione conjugation: Atrazine detoxication mechanism in corn. Plant Physiol. 46:103–107.

98. Smith, A.E., and R.E. Wilkinson. 1974. Differential absorption, translocation, and metabolism of metribuzin 4-amino-6-tert-butyl-3-(methythio) *as*-triazin-5(4*H*)-one by soybean cultivars. Physiol. Plant. 32:253–257.

99. Splittstoesser, W.E., and H.J. Hopen. 1968. Metabolism of siduron by barley and crabgrass. Weed Sci. 16:305–308.

100. Splittstoesser, W.E., and H.J. Hopen. 1970. Root growth inhibition by siduron and its relief by kinetin. Physiol. Plant 23:964–970.

101. Splittstoesser, W.E., and H.J. Hopen. 1967. Response of bentgrass to siduron. Weeds 15:81–83.

102. Stacewicz-Sapuncakis, M., H.V. Marsh, Jr., J. Vengris, P.H. Jennings, and T. Robinson. 1973. Response of common purslane to dicamba. Weed Sci. 21:385–388.

103. Steinrucken, H.C., and N. Amrhein. 1980. The herbicide glyphosate is a potent inhibitor of 5-enolpyruvylshikimic acid-3-phosphate synthase. Biochem. Biophys. Res. Commun. 94:1207–1212.

104. Sterrett, R.B., and T.A. Fritz. 1975. Asulum-induced mitotic irregularities in onion root tips. HortScience 10:161–162.

105. Suwanketnikom, R., K.K. Hatzios, D. Penner, and D. Bell. 1982. The site of electron transport inhibition by bentazon (3-isopropyl-1H-2,1,3-benzothiadiazin-(4)BH-one 2,2-dioxide) in isolated chloroplasts. Can. J. Bot. 60:409–412.

106. Thiman, K.V. 1956. Promotion and inhibition: twin themes of physiology. The Am. Nat. 90:145–162.

107. Vaughan, M.A., and K.C. Vaughn. 1987. Cytological effects of pronamide indicate that it disrupts mitosis in a unique manner. Pestic. Biochem. Physiol. 28:182–193.

108. Vaughn, K.C. 1986a. Cytological studies of dinitroaniline-resistant *Eleusine*. Pestic. Biochem. Physiol. 20:66–74.

109. Vaughn, K.C. 1986b. Dinitroaniline resistance in goosegrass [*Eleusine indica* (L.) Gaertn.] is due to an altered tubulin. p. 77. *In* Weed Sci. Soc. Am. Abstr. Weed Sci. Soc. Am., Champaign, IL.

110. Veerasekaran, P., R.C. Kirkwood, and W.W. Fletcher. 1977. Studies on the mode of action of asulum in bracken (*Pteriduim aquilinum* (L.) Kuhn). 2. Biochemical activity in the rhizome buds. Weed Res. 17:85–92.

111. Veerasekaran, P., R.C. Kirkwood, and E.W. Parnell. 1981. Studies of the mechanism of action of asulam in plants: II. Effect of asulam on the biosynthesis of folic acid. Pestic. Sci. 12:330–338.

112. Walker, K.A., S.M. Ridley, T. Lewis, and J.L. Harwood. 1989. Action of aryloxyphenoxy carboxylic acids on lipid metabolism. Rev. Weed Sci. 4:71–84.

113. Weed Sci. Soc. Am. 1989. Herbicide handbook. Weed Sci. Soc. Am., Champaign, IL.

114. Woolson, E.A. 1976. Organoarsenical herbicides. p. 741–776. *In* P.C. Kearney and D.D. Kaufman (ed.) Herbicides chemistry, degradation, and mode of action. Marcel Dekkar, New York.

115. Yih, R.Y., and C. Swithenbank. 1971. Identification of metabolites of N-(1,1-dimethylpropynyl)-3,5-dichlorobenzamide in soil and alfalfa. J. Agric. Food Chem. 19:314–319.

116. Zollinger, R.K. 1989. Perennial sowthistle (*Sonchus arvensis* L.) distribution, biology, and control in Michigan. Ph.D. thesis. Michigan State Univ., E. Lansing (Diss. Abstr. DA 90118771).

Chapter 4

Turfgrass Phytotoxicity from Preemergence Herbicides

L. M. CALLAHAN, *University of Tennessee, Knoxville, Tennessee*

I. INTRODUCTION

Preemergence herbicides are soil-applied chemicals that are effective against most germinating weeds but are targeted mainly toward annual grasses. The principle site for absorption of preemergence herbicides is the root tip; however, a few of these herbicides may be absorbed by newly forming shoots prior to their emergence from the soil (48). Germination of annual weeds generally requires the seed to be located within several millimeters of the soil surface. Preemergence herbicides are most effective when applied shortly before germination of the target weed and irrigated into the soil surface to set up a chemical barrier (17, 19, 25). The herbicide is either dissolved in the soil solution or present in the vapor phase (48). Emerging, highly sensitive root tips of the germinating weed seed penetrate this chemical barrier and absorb the herbicide.

Movement of preemergence herbicides within plants varies considerably (113). Some herbicides are translocated in the xylem and thus move apoplastically, some move symplastically through the phloem, and others are contact herbicides that affect the immediate point of entry. The activity of herbicides within the plant also varies considerably, and includes: inhibition of mitosis, metabolism, photosynthesis, chlorophyll formation, or root and shoot development; disruption of cell growth or membrane permeability; and abnormal plant growth or adverse hormonal effects.

The type and extent of cellular responses induced in root meristems of selected turfgrasses in sand or solution culture are well documented (6, 9, 13, 22, 52, 69, 115). Root injury elicited by these herbicides also has been found under controlled conditions in the field (7, 18, 20, 21, 24, 25, 27, 28, 49, 58, 87, 104, 121, 122, 123, 131, 132). A confounding aspect emerges when herbicides found to be severely phytotoxic in field test plots often result in little or no visual turf loss on golf courses, athletic fields, and home lawns (25). The level of phytotoxicity of an herbicide under field conditions ap-

parently is influenced by several factors, including: volatilization and pho-
todeactivation, herbicide solubility in the soil solution, timing of treatment
as related to the turfgrass root or shoot growth cycle, thatch thickness and
composition, soil texture and organic matter (OM) percentage, soil pH, soil
porosity, infiltration and percolation rate, herbicide chemistry and metabolism, soil organisms, temperature, rainfall, and turfgrass species.

The effectiveness of preemergence herbicides varies with herbicide formulation, geographic region, elevation, rainfall, temperature, soil type, application timing, and from year to year (11, 12, 18, 20, 21, 24, 25, 26, 27,
28, 30, 32, 37, 53, 65, 67, 80, 84, 86, 88, 89, 90, 100, 111, 121, 130, 131,
134, 136). Herbicides exhibiting severe phytotoxicity to bentgrass (*Agrostis*
spp.) and bermudagrass (*Cynodon* spp.) maintained on golf greens on a clay
loam soil (18, 20) often exhibited little visual injury when the same treatments were applied to greens maintained on United States Golf Association
(USGA) specification (64) high-porosity rootzones (21, 28). The reported
differences in herbicide phytotoxicity to turfgrasses are related to widely varying environmental conditions present in the field. Turfgrass responses to root-
absorbed herbicides applied to natural soils varies considerably due to wide
variations in the content of silt, clay, sand and OM. The type of clay and
its cation-exchange capacity (CEC), the proportions of the different fractions of sand, and the type of OM affect herbicide retention and activity
within the soil. The populations of microorganisms in the soil also directly
influence herbicide activity. Results obtained under artificial environments
are only indicators of the potential level of turfgrass phytotoxicity from herbicides. The confounding effects that natural soils have on herbicide activity
are not present in studies conducted in solution culture; however, the effect
that an herbicide produces in a plant grown in solution culture corresponds
much more accurately to the concentration of the herbicide active ingredient
than effects produced under natural soil conditions. Studies in solution culture do have their counterpart to some degree under field conditions as
represented by artificial rootzones, such as high sand content golf greens.
The USGA specification golf greens are minimally 90% sand by weight (64);
however, even with the accuracy of plant response to herbicide rate, as
achieved in solution culture, studies under these conditions are still used only
as indicators of the kinds of effects that can occur in the field.

II. HERBICIDE PHYTOTOXICITY

Very few herbicides were used prior to 1940. The first major advancement in selective weed control came with the development of 2,4-D [(2,4-
dichlorophenoxy)acetic acid] reported by Pokarny in 1941 (108). Although
herbicide injury to the foliage of some economic plants was obvious, the
general view was that selective herbicides caused little or no injury to turfgrass roots. This view persisted for more than two decades until the first published accounts of herbicide-induced, root-meristem abnormalities in bent-

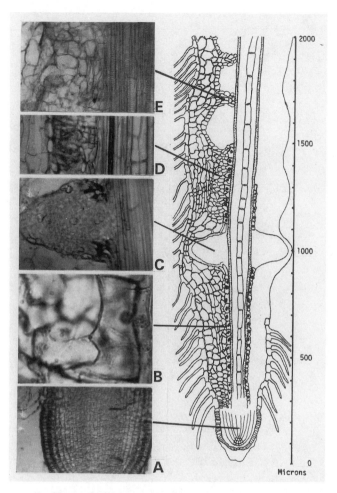

Fig. 4–1. A median longitudinal section of the apical 2000 μm of a 2,4,5-TP treated colonial bentgrass root after 4 wk in nutrient culture. Drawing at 100x, photomicrographs A, C, D, and E at 300x and B at 1290x (22).

grass following a foliar application of 2,4,5-TP [2-(2,4,5-trichlorophen-oxy)propionic acid] (Fig. 4–1) (22).

Root-meristem abnormalities were found to occur commonly in colonial bentgrass (*A. capillaris* L.) (Fig. 4–1), creeping bentgrass (*A. palustris* Huds.), Kentucky bluegrass (*Poa pratensis* L.), red fescue (*Festuca rubra* L.), and common bermudagrass [*C. dactylon* (L.) Pers.] following treatment with 2,4-D, 2,4,5-TP, and 2,4-DB [4-(2,4-dichlorophenoxy)butanoic acid] (22). A comparison of a normal 2000-μm root tip of colonial bentgrass is shown in Fig. 4–2. The 2,4,5-TP affected root tip shows the abnormal occurrence of root hairs (Fig. 4–1A) within 200 μm, and lateral root formations (Fig. 4–1C) within 850 μm of the tip (Fig. 4–1). Cortical cells were very disorganized with some swollen to at least 24 times normal size. Although

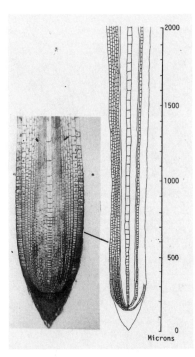

Fig. 4-2. Diagram of a median longitudinal section of the apical 2000 μm of a normal, healthy
Penncross creeping bentgrass root after 8 wk in nutrient culture. Drawing at 75x and photomicrograph at 132x (69).

the 200-μm meristematic tip showed well defined epidermal, cortical, and
stelar cells (Fig. 4-1A), they did not exhibit the normal cell arrangement and
size corresponding to cells in a healthy root tip (Fig. 4-2). Other cellular abnormalities following treatment with 2,4,5-TP (Fig. 4-1) were greatly enlarged
pericyle cells and their nuclei (Fig. 4-1B), a massive proliferation of pericy-
clic cells (Fig. 4-1D) occurring within 1100 μm of the tip, and massed lateral
root formations (Fig. 4-1E), with accompanying hypertrophic cortical cells,
conspicuous at 1500 μm from the tip.

The discovery that turfgrasses were not immune to adverse effects of
selective herbicides stimulated a new wave of research. Chemical weed control research since 1941 also has included studies to determine the relative
phytotoxicity of new herbicides developed for turfgrasses. When postemergence herbicides produced phytotoxic effects, the visual injury symptoms were
easy to associate with the chemical applied. Turfgrass injury following use
of preemergence herbicides, however, is more subtle. As a consequence, injury is often attributed to disease-inciting agents, insects or environmental
stresses rather than the preemergence herbicide applied weeks or months earlier. The presence of disease-inciting agents in affected plants tends to sub-
stantiate this conclusion (17, 19).

Although many studies demonstrated that preemergence herbicides can
significantly injure turfgrasses and often result in extensive turf loss, this con-

sequence of herbicide use was still ignored. Researchers tended to attribute the cause of turf loss to preemergence herbicide injury to turfgrass roots; however, many individuals contended that turfgrass roots were perennial in nature and persisted well below the herbicide barrier and thus were protected from injury; therefore, turf loss had to be due to some other cause. Eventually research results were presented supporting the contention of herbicide-induced turf loss from root injury. Several studies reported turfgrass foliar injury and progressive turf loss with multiyear preemergence herbicide treatments (11, 15, 18, 20, 21, 25, 27, 28, 33, 37, 53, 56, 68, 80, 83, 84, 85, 86, 90, 92, 93, 94, 107, 111, 120, 121, 122). Some showed impaired regrowth of bermudagrass in the spring following fall or winter herbicide treatment (15, 32, 53). There also were many reports of actual reduction in turfgrass root mass following treatment with preemergence herbicides (7, 18, 20, 25, 58, 87, 117, 121, 128, 130, 131, 132). Several studies demonstrated that soil residues of preemergence herbicides were phytotoxic to turfgrass roots (9, 18, 20, 49, 104, 121, 122, 123). Some investigations documented the type of cell damage herbicides can induce in root meristems (6, 13, 22, 52, 69, 115). There was strong evidence to show that preemergence herbicides could injure turfgrass roots and cause turf loss; however, research had not clearly revealed how these herbicides were coming into contact with deeper roots under field soil conditions.

Before 1980, the prevailing view was that turfgrass roots were perennial, dying only when attacked by pathogens, insects, nematodes, or from extended exposure to waterlogged soil or drought. This theory persisted despite indirect evidence supporting the contention that the turfgrass root system was annual in nature. The perennial nature of the turfgrass root system was supported in some early text books; however, more recent texts began correcting this assumption (129). These were challenged in 1980 following rhizotron investigations with warm season turfgrasses conducted at Texas A&M University by DiPaola and Beard (46), and their results were supported by subsequent studies (5, 47, 119). According to these studies, roots of warm season turfgrasses may rapidly senesce and die with the advent of spring green-up. New root initiation occurs ≈ 1 d later from crowns and from nodes of lateral stems. New roots can reach 30 cm (12 in.) in ≈ 20 d. This phenomenon has been termed spring root decline (SRD) and is triggered by a shoot canopy temperature higher than 28 °C (82 °F) after spring shoot green-up and/or when a soil temperature at a 10-cm (4-in.) depth rises to 18 °C (64 °F). Warm season turfgrasses were thus shown to have an annual root-growth cycle.

During SRD and the subsequent regrowth period, warm season turfgrasses become especially susceptible to root inhibition, or root pruning, from preemergence herbicides applied for annual weed control (17, 19). This explained turf loss in warm season turfgrasses (15, 20). Further evidence was provided in 1990 by a study that showed that herbicide injury to 'Tifgreen' bermudagrass [C. dactylon (L.) Pers. × C. transvaalensis Burtt-Davy] roots grown under lawn conditions during SRD does occur under practical field conditions. The closer bermudagrass spring green-up occurred to the herbicide treatment date, the more severe the turf loss (25).

Although herbicides cause numerous changes in the growth of target weeds, the physiology and morphology of turfgrass plants may also be altered (1, 3, 6, 13, 22, 29, 40, 52, 69, 97, 101, 113, 115). Some of the effects reported on turfgrasses are inhibition of root growth (7, 18, 20, 25, 28, 49, 87, 117, 121, 123), and cellular abnormalities in roots (6, 7, 13, 22, 52, 69, 115) and shoots (15, 18, 20, 21, 24, 25, 27, 28, 32, 33, 34, 37, 55, 56, 68, 79, 80, 83, 85, 86, 89, 90, 92, 94, 111, 121, 122, 128, 130, 131). Root cellular abnormalities were shown to be extensive; the types of abnormalities reported were as follows: proliferations of the pericycle, hypertrophic cortical cells; massed lateral root and root hair formations abnormally close to root tips; and compressed epidermal and cortical cells (6, 13, 22, 52, 69, 115). Biochemical changes also generally precede cell structural changes in plant growth (1, 3, 38, 40, 51, 70, 97, 101, 113, 127).

The following anatomical and morphological determinations were the result of studies conducted at the University of Tennessee under highly controlled conditions in the greenhouse with histological determinations conducted in the laboratory. These studies utilized healthy plants of 'Penncross' bentgrass and Tifgreen bermudagrass growing in nutrient solution culture. Turfgrass plants ≈ 12 wk of age were maintained in culture jars that were part of a continuous flow, constant-level solution culture renewal system (23) containing modified Hoagland nutrient solution (71). Crowns of the seedlings were suspended at or just above the level of solution in the jars.

Just prior to herbicide treatment, the roots of all seedlings were excised back to 5 cm below the crown, leaving sufficient root stubs to absorb water as new roots were initiating. Herbicides were applied to the 123-cm^2 surfaces of the solutions in the culture jars at rates equivalent to those used in the field. However, since the automatic renewal system in the greenhouse completely changed the solution every 3 d, a repeat treatment of herbicide was made every 4 d during the 28-d experimental period. Herbicide concentrations in the solution cultures were never found to be above the high label rate for any of the chemicals employed in the studies. At the end of 28-d herbicide-treatment periods, root tips were collected for histological processing. Then, a culture jar of herbicide-free nutrient solution was attached to the lid holding turfgrass seedlings and the plants allowed to grow in clean, continuously renewing nutrient solution for an additional 28 d. Root growth in the clean nutrient solution determined the degree of recovery from herbicide injury. At the end of the 28-d recovery period, root tips were again collected for histological processing. For herbicides causing very rapid root damage within a few days of initial treatments, root tips were collected at that time. Root tips were handled and processed by a modification of procedures from several sources (61, 77, 78, 95, 114, 135).

Healthy, 2000-μm root meristems of Penncross bentgrass exhibited good cortical cell columnar arrangement and absence of root hairs after 4 wk in nutrient culture (Fig. 4-2) (13, 22, 48, 52, 69, 115). Root caps were large, ≈ 200 μm in length, and healthy in appearance. Meristematic cell initials,

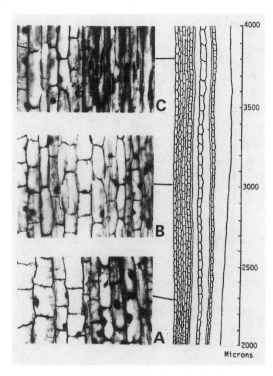

Fig. 4-3. Diagram of a median longitudinal section of the subapical 2000 μm of a normal, healthy Penncross creeping bentgrass root after 8 wk in nutrient culture. Drawing at 97.5x and photomicrographs A B, and C at 347x (69).

at 200 μm, were typically rounded, then differentiated into column-type rows of epidermal, cortical and stelar square shaped cells, and then into rectangular-shaped cells progressing back from the tip. Rectangular-shaped cells were fully apparent at ≈ 1000 μm. Stelar cells at 1000 μm were normally arranged and the pericycle, xylem, and phloem were well defined. Root tips were straight allowing for a continuous median longitudinal section. The subapical 2000-μm region exhibited healthy appearing columnar rows of cells characteristically elongated and well differentiated with a general absence of root hairs and lateral root initials (Fig. 4-3A, 4-3B, and 4-3C) (13, 22, 48, 52, 69, 115). Bentgrass root tips generally appeared thinner than bermudagrass roots. Apical and subapical sections of untreated Penncross bentgrass roots showed no changes in cellular formation or arrangement after 8 wk of growth in nutrient culture.

The cellular organization of the apical and subapical 2000-μm region of healthy Tifgreen bermudagrass roots after 8 wk in nutrient culture are shown in Fig. 4-4 and Fig. 4-5 (13, 22, 48, 52, 69, 115). Root caps were normally developed and ≈ 250 μm in length (Fig. 4-4A). Meristematic cell initials were round in shape and differentiated into square-shaped, then into rectangular-shaped epidermal, cortical, and stelar cells uniformly arranged in columns back from the tip (Fig. 4-4A and 4-4B). Stelar elements were

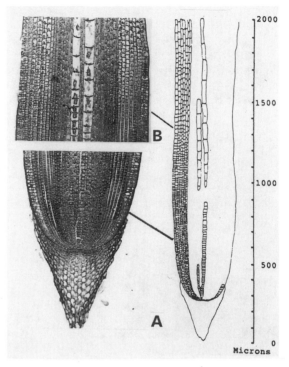

Fig. 4-4. Diagram of a median longitudinal section of the apical 2000 μm of a normal, healthy
    Tifgreen bermudagrass root after 8 wk in nutrient culture. Drawing at 80x, photomicrographs
    A and B at 175x (13).

well defined within 50 μm from the tip and throughout this region. The subapical 2000-μm region was characterized by columnar rows of rectangular
shaped cells (Fig. 4–5A, 4–5B, and 4–5C). Healthy appearing epidermal cells
were evident along the entire length of this region and with a general absence of root hairs (13, 22, 48, 52, 69, 115). Stelar cell definition was excellent. From one to three lateral root initials were commonly observed in the
subapical 2000-μm region (Fig. 4–5C). Harper (69) reported that the presence
of a few lateral root initials in the subapical 2000-μm region for bermudagrass
appeared normal. These findings were also supported by observations of other
researchers (13, 48, 52, 115). The thickness of bermudagrass root tips were
almost twice that of bentgrass.

A. Benzofurans

1. Ethofumesate

Ethofumesate [(±)-2-ethoxy-2,3-dihydro-3,3-dimethyl-5-benzofuranyl
methanesulfonate] currently is the only chemical in the benzofuran group
being used as an herbicide in turfgrass. Ethofumesate is a selective herbicide
used both as a preemergence and as a postemergence treatment in turfgrass-

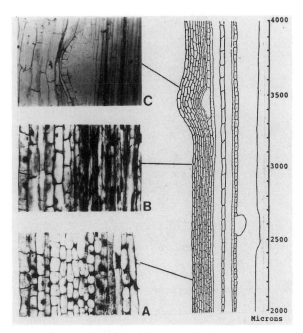

Fig. 4-5. Diagram of a median longitudinal section of the subapical 2000 μm of a normal, healthy Tifgreen bermudagrass root after 8 wk in nutrient culture. Drawing at 97.5x and photomicrographs A and B at 347x and C at 113x (13).

es for selective control of annual grasses and a few broadleaf weeds (73, 113). Label directions for this chemical stress timing. Specific labeling is for preemergence or postemergence control of annual bluegrass (*P. annua* L.) and common chickweed (*Stellaria media* L.) in dormant bermudagrass overseeded with perennial ryegrass (*Lolium perenne* L.). Late applications, however, may temporarily delay resumption of active growth of bermudagrass in the spring (45). It may also cause premature onset of dormancy or injury to bermudagrass that was not fully dormant (45). For postemergence control of annual weedy grasses and broadleaf weeds, ethofumesate should be applied at the earliest possible growth stage of the target species (92, 105).

Emerging shoots and roots of susceptible plants readily absorb ethofumesate, but it is not easily absorbed by leaves after the plant has generated a mature cuticle (73). It is translocated to the foliage following uptake by roots and emerging shoots, but it is not translocated out of treated leaves. Ethofumesate caused some tissue abnormalities in root tips of Penncross bentgrass grown in solution culture with what appeared to be a general overall weakening and thinness of cells making it easy for them to shatter when histologically processed (Fig. 4-6) (69). Root caps were ≈ 100 μm in length. Other types of injury and growth modification observed were slight disruptions of columnar organization of cortical cells, enlarged cortical cells, and the sparse occurrence of root hairs. General plant responses were light green leaves, sparse shoot growth and a 50% reduction in root mass. A general weaken-

Fig. 4-6. Photomicrograph (113x) of a median longitudinal section of the apical 1400 μm of an ethofumesate-treated Penncross creeping bentgrass root after 4 wk in nutrient cuture. (69).

ing of cells remained evident in the subapical 2000-μm root tip region of bentgrass (69). An abnormal occurrence of small lateral root initials also was noted in the subapical region. During a 4-wk recovery period evidence persisted of weakened cells which shattered easily accompanied by enlarged cortical cells. In the absence of ethofumesate, however, newly developing root tips appeared stronger than those directly exposed to this chemical. A few lateral root initials were still observed in the subapical region. McLean (105) reported no significant damage to swards of browntop bentgrass (*A. capillaris* L.), Penncross bentgrass, and Chewing's fescue (*F. rubra* var. *commutata* Gaud.) from repeated applications of ethofumesate at 0.25 kg ha^{-1}. However, single treatments of 1 kg ha^{-1} did appear more damaging to the turfgrasses. Callahan (21) found no significant turf loss of Penncross bentgrass, maintained on a USGA rootzone green, following ethofumesate first-year treatments of 1.1 and 2.2 kg ha^{-1} and three consecutive annual treatments in the same plots at 0.6 and 1.1 kg ha^{-1}.

Four weeks after treatments in solution culture with ethofumesate, Tifgreen bermudagrass plants exhibited ≈ 25% necrotic leaves, stunted shoot growth, and very little root growth (69). Following a 4-wk recovery period green leaves declined to 50% and only a few new roots developed. Tissue abnormalities were extensive in the apical 2000-μm region of roots of Tifgreen bermudagrass after a 4-wk treatment period (Fig. 4-7) (69). Massive lateral roots developed abnormally close (1700 μm) to root tips. Roots were abnormally enlarged and a few root hairs were observed. Root caps were greatly reduced in length; however, cortical cells retained their columnar arrangement and root tips appeared to be functional. After a 4-wk recovery period newly developed root tips showed very few abnormalities except that

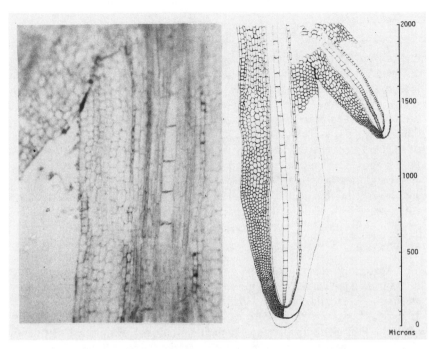

Fig. 4-7. Diagram of a median longitudinal section of the apical 2000 μm of an ethofumesate-treated Tifgreen bermudagrass root after 4 wk in nutrient culture. Drawing at 75x and photomicrograph 113x. Drawing and scale reduced 61% (69).

the tips remained abnormally enlarged. The columnar organization of cells in the apical region was maintained but enlarged cortical cells persisted. Stelar elements were well defined and no lateral roots or root hairs were observed. In the subapical 2000-μm root region of Tifgreen bermudagrass extensive lateral root formations occurred with greatly enlarged cortical cells (69); however, the turfgrass readily recovered from the effects of ethofumesate when contact with the chemical was halted.

B. Diamino-s-Triazines

Herbicides in this group include both foliar- and soil-applied types ranging from being photosynthetic and meristem inhibitors to causing contact phytotoxicity (73, 113). The triazines most commonly used in turfgrasses are soil-applied, readily absorbed by roots, and apoplastically translocated causing inhibition of photosynthesis. They provide effective control of annual grasses and some broadleaf weeds. Even though root absorbed, phytotoxicity is expressed more commonly in shoot tissue than in root meristems. Plant species show selective sensitivity to these herbicides due to differential metabolism in altering the herbicide within the plant.

1. Simazine

Simazine (6-chloro-N,N'-diethyl-1,3,5-trazine-2,4-diamine) is recommended only for established warm season turfgrasses such as bermudagrass, centipedegrass [*Eremochloa ophiuroides* (Munro.) Hack.], St. Augustinegrass [*Stenotaphrum secundatum* (Walt.) Kuntze] and *Zoysia* (73, 113). Simazine is absorbed by roots with little or no foliage activity. Following root absorption, it is translocated acropetally in the xylem, accumulating in apical meristems. It is a photosynthetic inhibitor. In studies to aid establishment of selected *Zoysia* cultivars, simazine severely damaged sprigs of 'Midwest' (50), it caused severe injury to plugs of 'Emerald' (122), and severely reduced root weight and length of 'Belair' (54). Treatments to common bermudagrass significantly inhibited stolon spread (128), and severely thinned an established stand after 8 yr of annual applications (27).

2. Atrazine

Atrazine [6-chloro-N-ethyl-N'-(1-methylethyl)-1,3,5-trazine-2,4-diamine] is recommended for use only in well established warm season (C_4) turfgrasses such as bermudagrass, centipedegrass, St. Augustinegrass, and *Zoysia*. It is absorbed through both roots and foliage, although foliar absorption is small. Following absorption through roots it is translocated acropetally in the xylem and accumulates in apical meristems and leaves. It is a photosynthetic inhibitor. In atrazine treatments to aid establishment of selected *Zoysia* cultivars, stolons of Midwest were severely damaged (50), and plugs of Emerald were moderately injured (122). Treatments in established centipedegrass severely reduced sod strength (133). Engel et al. (50) reported that atrazine was more phytotoxic to 'Meyer' and Midwest *Zoysia* than simazine.

3. Metribuzin

Metribuzin [4-amino-6-(1,1-dimethyl)-3-(methylthio)-1,2,4-triazin-5(4H)-one] is an asymmetrical triazine that is both foliar and soil applied in turfgrass. It is primarily used as a preemergence or early postemergence herbicide for weeds in bermudagrass, but is fatal to cool season (C_3) turfgrasses (73, 113). Although it can be foliar absorbed, it is mainly absorbed through roots. Following root absorption, it translocates upward in the xylem. It moves distally when applied at the base of leaves. When foliar absorbed, it does not move downward in the plant. It is a photosynthetic inhibitor, highly soluble in water (1.9 deciSiemens or 1200 ppm), and mobile in soils. Metribuzin-treated Penncross bentgrass roots and shoots in solution culture died during 4 wk of chemical exposure (69). Root meristem tissue was collected within 2 wk of metribuzin exposure but cells were still deteriorating and did not survive paraffin imbedding. Cell malformations could not be determined due to rapid death of the meristematic region. Metribuzin-treated Tifgreen bermudagrass plants in solution culture exhibited green leaves but with reduced shoot density after 4 wk of treatments (69). Roots were stunt-

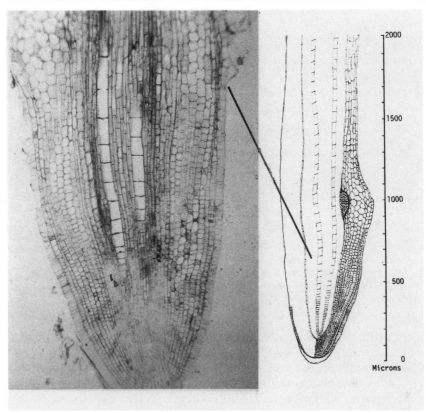

Fig. 4–8. Diagram of a median longitudinal section of the apical 2000 μm of a metribuzin-treated Tifgreen bermudagrass root after 4 wk in nutrient culture. Drawing at 75x and photomicrograph at 113x. Drawing and scale reduced 61% (69).

ed and brown. Following a 4-wk recovery period, approximately one-fourth of the foliage was green and roots still were stunted and brown. Effects of metribuzin in the apical 2000-μm root region of Tifgreen bermudagrass after 4 wk of exposure were observed as hypertrophic cortical cells accompanied by lateral root proliferations abnormally close (900 μm) to tips (Fig. 4–8). Epidermal cells were compressed close to tips. Many root hairs also occurred abnormally close to tips (800 μm) and the length of root caps was greatly reduced. Root sections of Tifgreen bermudagrass from the subapical 2000-μm region exhibited typical elongated cells with good columnar organization and well defined stelar elements (Fig. 4–9) (69). Lateral root initials were observed in this region and were more numerous than found in untreated plants. Numerous root hairs also occurred in this region, which is abnormal. After a 4-wk recovery period, the bermudagrass apical region still showed enlarged cortical cells and compressed epidermal cells close to the tips (69). Root hairs continued to occur abnormally in this region and the general shape and form of roots were distorted. Cellular structure in the subapical region remained inconsistent with untreated plants. Cortical cells were enlarged and

Fig. 4-9. Photomicrograph (113x) of a median longitudinal section of the apical 900 μm section from the subapical 2000-μm region of a metribuzin-treated Tifgreen bermudagrass root after 4 wk in nutrient culture. (69).

uncharacteristically elongated. Epidermal and cortical cells appeared weak and degenerated easily. Root hairs occurred abnormally in this region but a normal compliment of lateral roots was observed. Previously, Johnson (86) noted moderate foliar injury to Tifgreen, 'Tifdwarf', 'Tifway' and 'Ormond' bermudagrass, but only slight injury to 'Floraturf' bermudagrass, with a single treatment of metribuzin. Metribuzin was also reported to significantly reduce the density of Belair and Meyer *Zoysia* (54), and caused severe root injury to 'Midiron' and 'Vamont' bermudagrass (8). However, it took two consecutive annual applications at 0.3 kg ha^{-1} to significantly reduce the density of Penncross bentgrass maintained on a USGA specification green (21).

C. Dinitroanilines

Herbicides in the dinitroaniline group generally are soil-applied preemergence chemicals that effectively control germinating annual grasses (113). Some provide control of a few broadleaf weeds. These herbicides are almost strictly root absorbed, but with little or no apoplastic translocation (113). The principle effects on roots are interference with mitosis and prevention of normal cell formation and development. Affected root meristems tend to swell and lateral root formation is inhibited. Severe phytotoxicity to root meristems can eventually result in death of the entire plant due to interference with nutrient uptake and translocation. There are apparent differences among turfgrass in their sensitivity to the dinitroanilines. When root inhibition is slight to moderate some turfgrass species appear able to recover from root injury and eventually develop normally. Fast growing turfgrasses that

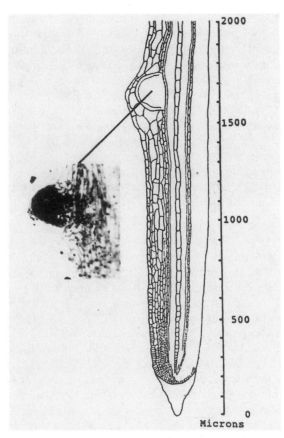

Fig. 4–10. Diagram of a median longitudinal section of the apical 2000 μm of a benefin-treated Penncross creeping bentgrass root after 4 wk in nutrient culture. Drawing at 97.5x and photomicrograph at 113x (115).

are highly efficient in their use of energy, such as bermudagrass, tend to be most successful in recovery from injury caused by herbicides in this group.

1. Benefin

Benefin [N-butyl-N-ethyl-2,6-dinitro-4-(trifluoromethyl)benzenamine] caused extensive cellular disruptions and malformations in root meristems of Penncross bentgrass in solution culture studies (Fig. 4–10) (115). Epidermal cells showed compression within 500 μm of the root tip and extensive irregularities in size and shape of cells. Cortical cells showed columnar disruption with cells greatly enlarged. Lateral roots occurred abnormally close (1600 μm) to the root tip with enlarged epidermal and cortical cells that easily ruptured. Root hairs were not observed in this region. Root mass was also greatly reduced. Results supported findings by other investigators that benefin readily injures bentgrass (18, 19). Tissue abnormalities were only slight in benefin-affected Tifgreen bermudagrass root tips in solution culture (115).

Cellular maturation and elongation was only slightly affected compared with untreated plants. Neither lateral roots nor root hairs were observed in this zone. Root numbers were only slightly reduced in the benefin-treated plants as compared to untreated plants. Benefin has also been reported to cause root injury to common, Floraturf, 'No Mow', Tifdwarf, Tifgreen and Tifway bermudagrass and to Kentucky bluegrass in field studies (33, 74, 79, 110, 121, 122, 128). Benefin also significantly reduced the density of Meyer *Zoysia*, 'Kenblue' and 'Merion' Kentucky bluegrass, 'Pennlawn' red fescue, a mixed stand of cool-season grasses overseeded on a bermudagrass green, and Penncross bentgrass and Tifgreen bermudagrass greens (4, 18, 20, 34, 82, 130). Delayed spring greenup also resulted following late winter treatments with benefin in Tifgreen bermudagrass under green conditions and a Tifway bermudagrass lawn (15, 32, 53).

2. Oryzalin

Tissue abnormalities were extensive in root meristems of Penncross bentgrass in solution culture studies following 4 wk of exposure to oryzalin [4-(dipropylamino)-3,5-dinitrobenzenesulfonamide] (52). An overall weakening and thinness of cells in root meristems resulted in shattering and disintegration of cells during histological processing; thus, no photographs could be made. Meristematic cell injury was indicated within 1 wk during the herbicide-treatment period. All of the roots and shoots of bentgrass were dead before the end of a 4-wk recovery period. Damage to Tifgreen bermudagrass root meristems following oryzalin treatments in solution culture was extensive, but less severe than that which occurred with bentgrass (Fig. 4-11) (52). By the end of a 4-wk oryzalin treatment period, Tifgreen bermudagrass roots appeared dead. All of the test plants were dead by the end of a 4-wk recovery period. Root injury was apparent by the second week

Fig. 4-11. Photomicrograph (113x) of a median longitudinal section of the apical 1300 μm of a oryzalin-treated Tifgreen bermudagrass root after 4 wk in nutrient culture. (52).

of oryzalin treatments but a few root meristems were collected for histological processing. Types of damage appeared as enlarged epidermal and cortical cells close to the tip (300 μm) with columnar arrangement of cells beginning to distort. The abnormal occurrence of several lateral root initials, beginning at 1300 μm, were evident in the apical region and marked curvature of the root had begun.

Oryzalin is labeled for use in mature bermudagrass turf, and other warm season turfgrasses, which are well established in field soils and that are not in a weakened condition. It is not labeled for use on golf greens, on newly sprigged turfgrasses, or on cool season turfgrasses. Lewis et al. (102) reported a 60% reduction in rooting and reduced sod strength for centipedegrass, Tifway bermudagrass, Meyer *Zoysia*, and three tall fescue (*F. arundinacea* Schreb.) cultivars treated in field soils with oryzalin.

3. Pendimethalin

Foliar absorption of pendimethalin [*N*-(1-ethylpropyl)-3,4-dimethyl-2,6-dinitrobenzenamine] is limited and very little is taken up by plants from the soil (73). Penncross bentgrass grown in solution culture was very sensitive to root exposures of pendimentalin (Fig. 4–12) (52). Although shoots were not killed following root exposures, shoot and root weights were greatly reduced and roots were brown. Microscopic observations of root tips following root treatments with pendimethalin revealed extensive cellular malformations and proliferations beginning as new cells emerged. Root caps were almost nonexistent and epidermal and cortical cells were greatly enlarged with the columnar organization of cells disrupted. Several well developed lateral roots were abnormally present (at 800, 1000, and 1300 μm) in the apical region. Subapical root sections of pendimethalin-treated Penncross bentgrass

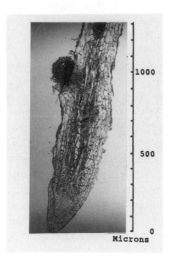

Fig. 4–12. Photomicrograph (113x) of a median longitudinal section of the apical 1300 μm of an pendimethalin-treated Penncross creeping bentgrass root after 4 wk in nutrient culture (52).

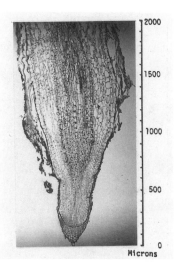

Fig. 4-13. Photomicrograph (113x) of a median longitudinal section of the apical 2000 μm of a pendimethalin-treated Tifgreen bermudagrass root after 4 wk in nutrient culture (52).

exhibited numerous well developed abnormally occurring lateral roots (52). Root hairs were not observed, which is normal, and cortical cells tended to retain some columnar organization. Cellular abnormalities tended to diminish during a 4-wk recovery period in nutrient solution. Shoots and roots were also still alive at the end of the 4-wk recovery period. Pendimethalin treatments in field studies have been reported to reduce rooting of Kentucky bluegrass (36, 102, 109, 110), three cultivars of tall fescue (102), perennial ryegrass (44), Penncross bentgrass under green conditions (42), and centipedegrass, Meyer *Zoysia*, and 'Raleigh' St. Augustinegrass (102, 126).

Visual observations of Tifgreen bermudagrass root and shoot growth in solution culture suggested only slight to moderate injury from pendimethalin (52); however, microscopic examination of bermudagrass root meristems following 4 wk of pendimethalin exposure revealed extensive root abnormalities (Fig. 4-13). Epidermal and cortical cells were greatly enlarged near the tip. A tremendous enlargement of cortical cell development began 600 μm from the tip and more than doubled the width of the tip (at 1200 μm) compared with an untreated healthy bermudagrass root tip. Columnar organization of cells was also greatly distorted. Although no root hairs were observed in the apical region, there was an abnormal presence of lateral root initials in many root sections. Root cells were brittle and tissue was difficult to handle. After a 4-wk recovery period in nutrient solution, the apical root region of Tifgreen bermudagrass still showed signs of damage (52). Epidermal and cortical cells were still enlarged close to root tips, although root meristems appeared to function and roots appeared alive. Shoots also remained alive. Pendimethalin has been reported to reduce rooting of Tifway bermudagrass (102, 126), centipedegrass, Meyer *Zoysia*, and Raleigh St. Augustinegrass (102, 126).

4. Prodiamine

Prodiamine [N^3,N^3-di-n-propyl-2,4-dinitro-6-(trifluoromethyl)-m-phenylenediamine] accumulates slightly in roots with very little translocation to leaves, stems, and seed (73). When translocation occurs it is mainly as degradation products and metabolites. It is metabolized and rapidly degraded by plants. Several researchers have reported that prodiamine caused reduced rooting of Kentucky bluegrass (72, 106, 110, 125). Both spring and fall applications of prodiamine significantly reduced germination of fall-seeded Kentucky bluegrass (66). Prodiamine also reduced rooting of three cultivars of tall fescue (102) and perennial ryegrass (44), and it significantly reduced rooting of nine cultivars of creeping bentgrass maintained on golf greens (42, 98). Rooting was also significantly reduced in centipedegrass and Meyer *Zoysia* (102), Raleigh St. Augustinegrass (126), and in Tifway bermudagrass (102, 126).

5. Trifluralin

Trifluralin [2,6-dinitro-*N,N*-dipropyl-4-(trifluoromethyl)benzenamine] severely inhibits root development by affecting physiological growth processes during seed germination (73, 113). It has little or no foliar activity. Trifluralin has been reported to reduce rhizome and tiller numbers and length in Kentucky bluegrass. Applications at or just prior to seeding severely reduced stands of Kentucky bluegrass, colonial bentgrass, and red fescue (120). Soil residues taken about 10 mo following a trifluralin treatment indicated that it readily leached in a clay loam soil resulting in much greater inhibition of root regrowth of Kentucky bluegrass sod-plugs grown over residues taken from the 5- to 10-cm soil depth compared with 0- to 5-cm soil depths (123). Trifluralin also caused moderate to severe injury to Emerald *Zoysia* sod-plugs when treated at the date of plugging (122).

D. Inorganic Arsenicals

Arsenicals (As) have long been used as pesticides (113). When used for weed control, they act primarily as contact herbicides with symplastic movement in susceptible plants. Although As can be effective herbicides for annual grass control, they also have the potential to be phytotoxic to turfgrasses (18, 20, 28, 30, 35, 76, 113, 130, 131, 132). The chances for phytotoxicity are great when As are applied as annual preemergence treatments at a single, very high rate. Thus, determining the proper rate, timing, and frequency of treatments becomes very important for safety to the turfgrass (41, 99).

Arsenic has many properties similar to P and can substitute for P in biochemical reactions within the plant (113). It can seriously disrupt the metabolic process in plants resulting in wilting and yellowing of leaf tissue, cessation of growth, desiccation, and eventual defoliation and death. Reports vary on the influence of P on herbicide activity of As and their phytotoxicity to turfgrasses. Arsenic, like P, is tightly bound to soil and resists leaching by water (113). Elemental As does not break down, so there is potential for its accumulation as residues in soil if used repeatedly. Some reports state that when soil-solution P is high, As is less toxic (138). Other researchers have found that increased As levels decreased turfgrass growth regardless of P levels in soil, and that P rates as high as 4 kg 100 m^{-2} had little or no effect on As toxicity (29, 30). Early recommendations were that, in order to increase As uptake for effective annual weed control in turfgrasses, soil pH should be maintained between 6.0 and 7.8, and P should be reduced so it does not compete for As uptake (99, 113). One researcher reported increased phytotoxicity to turfgrasses and a 50% reduction in annual bluegrass with 582 kg ha^{-1} of calcium arsenate in a loam soil with high P and K levels and a pH of 5.5 (93). Other researchers reported that 209 kg ha^{-1} of calcium arsenate significantly reduced turfgrass root numbers and controlled crabgrass (*Digitaria* spp.) when applied to a soil high in P, medium in K, and with a pH of 6.0 (68). Still another researcher reported effective control of annual bluegrass and crabgrass, and no visible phytotoxicity to creeping bentgrass, with repeated low-rate applications of tricalcium arsenate totaling 136 kg ha^{-1}, and that soil P and pH did not increase or diminish As toxicity (28).

1. Tricalcium Arsenate

Tricalcium arsenate [Ca$_3$ (AsO$_4$)$_2$] has often been used in turfgrass culture as a preemergence selective herbicide primarily for annual grass control (113). Label recommendations advocate repeated applications at low rates to achieve a buildup of soil As levels sufficient to control target species of annual grasses. Continued control is maintained by subsequent applications to sustain soil As at sufficient levels. Symptoms are expressed in plants as yellowing and then browning leaves followed by plant death. Penncross bentgrass and Tifgreen bermudagrass root meristems treated with tricalcium arsenate in solution culture showed little difference in cellular organization and development as compared with untreated root tips (69). Low-rate treatments (33 kg ha^{-1}) of tricalcium arsenate actually produced higher bentgrass and bermudagrass root dry weights than those measured from untreated plants. Color and appearance of bentgrass and bermudagrass roots were similar to untreated roots. Field studies in a Penncross bentgrass soil-based green with tricalcium arsenate at individual high rates of 224, 336, and 448 kg ha^{-1} resulted in slight shoot discoloration to severe browning, from low to high rates, respectively (18). Although root mass was reduced moderately with frequent, low-rate applications gradually building up to 272 kg ha^{-1}, little direct injury occurred to roots or shoots of Penncross bentgrass maintained on a USGA rootzone green (28). A Tifgreen bermudagrass soil-based green treated annually with 224 and 448 kg ha^{-1} of tricalcium arsenate exhibited only slight injury to shoots or roots after 3 yr (20).

E. Oxadiazoles

1. Oxadiazon

Oxadiazon [3-[2,4-dichloro-5-(1-methylethoxy)phenyl]-5-(1,1-dimethylethyl)-1,3,4-oxadiazol-2-(3H)-one] is the only member of the oxadiazoles used as a preemergence herbicide on turf. The activity of this chemical is similar to that of diphenyl ethers. Oxadiazon is labeled for use in turfgrass as a soil-applied preemergence herbicide effectively controlling annual grasses and some broadleaf weeds as they germinate. Shoots are affected as they grow through the treated soil zone (113), but there are indications that the chemical is root absorbed and is apoplastically translocated (21, 69). Light is required for herbicide activity but it is reported that photosynthesis is not involved (113). Postemergence activity has been reported on young seedlings.

Oxadiazon-treated Penncross bentgrass exhibited yellow-green leaves, including a few bleached leaves, but with good foliar growth following 4 wk of herbicide root exposure in solution culture (69). Root growth was very good and roots were white. Following a 4-wk recovery period, shoots appeared stressed and were beginning to wilt. Approximately two-thirds of the leaves were yellow-green with remaining leaves appearing bleached. Root growth remained abundant, but roots appeared whitish-brown. Hurto and Turgeon (74) also noted initial oxadiazon injury as bleaching of leaf tips. Other researchers noted a temporary leaf discoloration (42, 91). No apparent abnormalities were noted in the apical 2000-μm root region of Penncross bentgrass following 4 wk of oxadiazon root exposure in solution culture (69). Root caps were well developed and meristematic cell development and differentiation appeared similar to untreated plants. No lateral roots or root hairs were observed; however, in the 2000-μm subapical region, lateral root formations and root hairs were noted that were not characteristic of untreated plants. Cells were more elongated and enlarged than normal. Root tissue collected after a 4-wk recovery period revealed enlarged epidermal and cortical cells abnormally close to apical tips of oxadiazon-treated Penncross bentgrass plants (69). In the subapical 2000-μm root tip region, lateral root development was in advanced stages and root hairs remained prominent following a 4-wk recovery period (Fig. 4–14). It appeared that oxadiazon was absorbed by roots during the 4-wk period of exposure to the herbicide, but extensive cellular effects were manifested only during the subsequent 4-wk recovery period. Researchers have reported that oxadiazon can cause moderate to severe injury to bentgrass both on golf greens and on turf maintained at higher mowing heights (42, 98, 118). This chemical has also caused reduced rooting (10) and stand thinning (83) in perennial ryegrass. Reduced rooting has also been caused in several cultivars of Kentucky bluegrass (31, 37) and a large number of red fescue cultivars (37).

Oxadiazon-treated Tifgreen bermudagrass plants, after 4 wk of exposure to the herbicide in solution culture, exhibited medium green leaves and good foliar growth (69). Root growth was comparable to untreated plants and new roots were white. Shoot and root growth improved progressively during the 4-wk recovery period. Apical 2000-μm root tips of oxadiazon-treated Tifgreen bermudagrass appeared similar to untreated plants (69). Subapical root sections generally appeared similar to untreated plants, except that cortical cells were square instead of elongated in shape. After a 4-wk recovery period oxadiazon-treated Tifgreen bermudagrass apical and subapical root tips showed no apparent tissue abnormalities and appeared similar to untreated

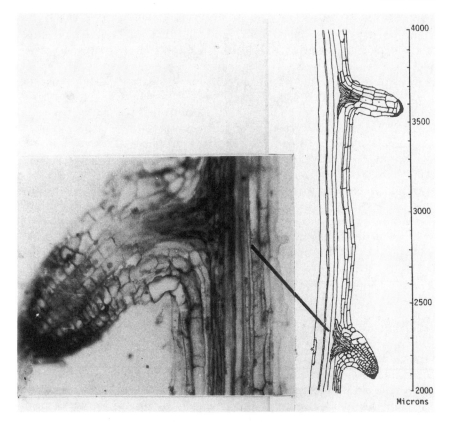

Fig. 4-14. Diagram of a median longitudinal section of the apical 2000 μm of a oxadiazon-treated Penncross creeping bentgrass root after 4 wk in nutrient culture. Drawing at 75x and photomicrograph at 150x. Drawing and scale reduced 61% (69).

plants. Oxadiazon has been reported to cause reduced rooting in several bermudagrass cultivars, such as Midiron (8, 10), Tifway (10, 15, 90), and 'Tufcote' (10). Reduced turf quality or thinned stand density was noted in Tifdwarf (89, 90), Tifgreen (25, 90), and Ormond (90) bermudagrass cultivars, and the spreading ability of common bermudagrass was inhibited (128).

F. Phthalic Acids

1. DCPA

The only member of this group used for preemergence weed control in turfgrass is DCPA (dimethyl 2,3,5,6-tetrachloro-1,4-benzenedicarboxylate). It is labeled for use in turfgrass as a soil-applied preemergence herbicide for controlling germinating annual grasses and some broadleaf weeds following root absorption. It is a mitotic disrupter and inhibits the growth of root tips but it is neither translocated nor shoot absorbed (73, 113). The effects of DCPA in Penncross bentgrass grown in solution culture were manifested as

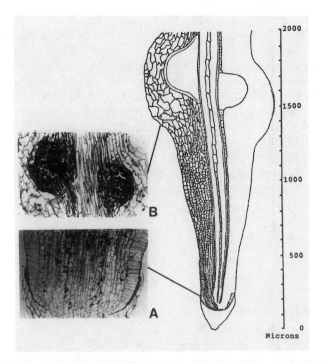

Fig. 4–15. Diagram of a median longitudinal section of the apical 2000 μm of a DCPA-treated
Tifgreen bermudagrass root after 4 wk in nutrient culture. Drawing at 97.5x and photomicrographs A at 281x and B at 113x (115).

compressed epidermal and cortical cells within 700 μm of the tip, cortical
cells abnormally enlarged progressing back from the tip, but only slight disruption of cell columnar arrangement (115). DCPA caused abnormally enlarged bentgrass roots >1.5 times thicker than healthy, untreated roots;
however, as is normally the case, lateral roots and root hairs were absent
in this region. Compared with untreated plants, fewer roots developed in
solution cultures containing DCPA. Results support findings by others that
DCPA causes slight to moderate injury to bentgrass (18, 19, 43, 57, 62, 63,
75, 107, 111). Injury reported to other cool season grasses by DCPA included: reduced rooting of Kentucky bluegrass (58, 110), reduction in stand density of Kentucky bluegrass (37, 49), rough bluegrass and annual ryegrass (*L.
multiflorum* Lam.) (34), reduced quality of Pennlawn red fescue (130), and
injury to roots during regrowth of Kentucky bluegrass sod plugs grown in
soils containing DCPA residues from both the 0- to 5-cm and the 5- to 10-cm
soil depths (123). Some of the most extensive root abnormalities observed
occurred following DCPA treatments of Tifgreen bermudagrass in solution
culture (Fig. 4–15) (115). Root tips showed abnormal narrowing with epidermal cells greatly compressed beginning at 150 μm from the tip (Fig. 4–15A).
Cell columns were seriously disrupted with epidermal and cortical cells greatly
enlarged beginning at 500 μm from the tip (Fig. 4–15A). Lateral roots prolifer-
ated abnormally close (1500 μm) to the tip accompanied by massive hyper-

trophic cortical cells (Fig. 4–15B). Many enlarged epidermal and cortical cells ruptured easily; however, root hairs were not observed in this region. The number of roots oberved in solution culture in greenhouse experiments were considerably fewer than in untreated plants. These results support findings by other researchers that DCPA can cause severe injury to Tifgreen and Tifdwarf bermudagrass (6, 7, 20, 25, 32, 33, 34, 56). DCPA also caused root injury and delayed dormancy break of Tifway bermudagrass during spring regrowth following dormant and postdormant treatment (15, 53). DCPA thinned the stand (27), reduced rooting (33), and inhibited spread and pegging (128) of common bermudagrass. It inhibited rooting of Tifway and No Mow bermudagrass (33), retarded stolon, rhizome and root development of several cultivars of bermudagrass, and Emerald *Zoysia* and manilagrass [*Z. matrella* (L.) Merr.] (55). It also caused significant injury to centipedegrass, Emerald *Zoysia*, and Tifway and Floraturf bermudagrass at sprigging (79), and caused moderate loss of Emerald *Zoysia* plugs when treated at planting time (122).

G. Pyridines

1. Dithiopyr

Dithiopyr [S,S-dimethyl 2-(difluoromethyl)-4-(2-methylpropyl)-6-(trifluoromethyl)-3,5-pyridinedicarbothioate] is the first of a new class of pyridine herbicides (96). It provides excellent preemergence and early postemergence control of crabgrass. Its postemergence effects on seedling crabgrass are probably due to the vapor saturated air resulting in growth cessation. Dithiopyr is a mitotic inhibitor similar to dinitroanilines and it has a low use rate of 0.28 to 0.84 kg ha^{-1} (96). In studies with wheat (*Triticum aestivum* L. 'Chris'), dithiopyr caused cessation of root elongation and swelling of root tips (2). The mitotic index of root tips increased from 2.5 to 12% with mitotic cells arresting in late prometaphase within a 6-h treatment period; however, it did not alter processes regulating the entry of cells into mitosis. The mode of action may be to alter microtubule polymerization and stability by interacting with microtubule associated proteins or microtubule organizing centers rather than interaction directly with tubulin. Reports of phytotoxicity to turfgrasses have been few. Bermudagrass treated at 0.84 to 1.12 kg ha^{-1} exhibited good tolerance to dithiopyr (16), with Tifway bermudagrass and Raleigh St. Augustinegrass exhibiting little reduction in root length (126). No observable injury was noted to a bentgrass green at one to three times the recommended rate (118). Other researchers have reported, however, that dithiopyr reduced total root weight in creeping bentgrass grown on a modified sandy soil green (43), and it caused thinning of stands, a darkening of foliage, and inhibition of root development of bentgrass (14).

H. Substituted amides

This is a diverse group of soil applied preemergence herbicides that provide control of germinating annual grasses and some broadleaf weeds (113).

They include metolachlor, which affects both shoots and roots of germinating seedlings inhibiting meristematic activity. Included also are bensulide and napropamide that primarily affect root growth disrupting cell division and cell enlargement. Another member of this group is pronamide, which inhibits photosynthesis and causes rapid burning of foliage.

1. Bensulide

Bensulide [O,O-bis(1-methylethyl) S-[2-[(phenylsulfonyl)amino]ethyl] phosphorodithioate] is labeled for use in turfgrass as a soil-applied preemergence herbicide affecting only root meristems of germinating seed where it disrupts cell division and inhibits cell enlargement (113). It is adsorbed onto root surfaces and some is absorbed by the root, but little or none is translocated upward to leaves (73, 113). Epidermal cells in Penncross bentgrass root meristems were greatly compressed over a distance of 1300 μm from the tip following exposure to bensulide in solution culture (115). Cell columnar arrangement showed slightly irregular development. Lateral roots and root hairs were not observed in the apical 2000-μm region. Numbers of roots produced in solution culture were slightly fewer compared with untreated plants. Other researchers have reported bensulide causing reduced rooting and stand density of several cultivars of Kentucky bluegrass (31, 68, 120, 130, 131), and a severe reduction of roots and shoot injury of Kentucky bluegrass sod plugs grown on 10-mo, 0- to 5-cm soil residues (49). Slight to moderate injury has occurred to red fescue cultivars and colonial bentgrass (39, 130, 131), and severely reduced rooting or stand loss has been reported in colonial and creeping bentgrass on greens, and to several cultivars of tall fescue (18, 43, 102, 107, 120). A severe reduction in stand density also occurred in red fescue overseedings with treatment shortly prior to or at seeding time (68, 120).

The effects of bensulide on Tifgreen bermudagrass root meristems in solution culture resulted in compressed epidermal cells close to root tips, but only slight cortical cell columnar disruption (115). Cortical cells, however, appeared abnormally enlarged progressing back from tips. Lateral roots and root hairs were not found in this region. Numbers of roots observed in solution culture were fewer in number compared with untreated plants. Investigators have reported that bensulide causes significant root reduction (7, 25, 33), stand loss (20), and delayed spring green-up (32, 53) of Tifgreen bermudagrass. Other adverse effects on bermudagrasses included: severe sod thinning (27), root inhibition (36), and prevention of spreading (99) of common bermudagrass; and root injury or sod thinning of Tifdwarf (33), Tifway (33, 55, 79, 102), Floraturf (79), No Mow (33), and several other cultivars (55). Severe root injury or sod thinning has also been reported for centipedegrass (79, 102), and for the *Zoysia* cultivars Belair, Meyer and Emerald and for manilagrass (54, 55, 79, 102, 122).

2. Isoxaben

Isoxaben [N-[3-(1-ethyl-1-methylpropyl)-5-isoxazolyl]-2,6-dimethoxybenzamide] is a soil-applied preemergence selective herbicide used in turfgrass for the control of certain annual grasses and many broadleaf weeds (113). It requires rainfall or irrigation for activation and is root absorbed by germinating seed and translocates to stem and leaf tissues. It has no activity when foliar applied. Root and shoot development are disrupted following root absorption. New seedlings appear unable to take up water and susceptible plants do not normally emerge. It also severely retards root and stem development. It is recommended for use in all well established perennial cool- and warm-season turfgrasses. Isoxaben applied to Kentucky bluegrass and tall fescue cultivars at 2, 4, and 6 wk after seeding in field studies inhibited establishment of both species (60). Rooting of Kentucky bluegrass was inhibited following all three treatment dates and rooting of tall fescue was inhibited following the 2- and 4-wk treatment dates.

3. Metolachlor

Metolachlor [2-chloro-*N*-(2-ethyl-6-methylphenyl)-*N*-(2-methoxy-1-methylethyl)acetamide] is recommended for use primarily as a selective preemergence herbicide for annual grass and broadleaf weed control (73, 113). Metolachlor can enter seedlings through shoots or roots but translocates very little. Most of the absorption by grasses appears to occur through emerging shoots just above the seed, while in dicots absorption is through both shoots and roots. Metolachlor appears to be a general growth inhibitor, especially of root elongation. It appears to be involved in disrupting the integrity of cell membranes resulting in leakage of certain key constituents.

4. Napropamide

Napropamide [*N,N*-diethyl-2-(1-naphthalenyloxy)propanamide] is labeled as a preemergence herbicide for controlling germinating annual grasses and some broadleaf weeds (73, 113). It is absorbed by emerging root meristems, disrupts cell division and enlargement, and may translocate upward to shoots. It is resistant to leaching in most mineral soils. After 4 wk of treatments with napropamide in solution culture, Penncross bentgrass leaves appeared mostly brown with a few dark green leaves (69). Roots were brown and appeared in a state of senescence. Following a 4-wk recovery period plants appeared dead. Plants were regrown, roots again exposed to napropamide, and root apical 2000-μm segments collected at 2 wk for histological processing. Root tips collected exhibited early stages of senescence (Fig. 4–16). Root caps were greatly reduced and beginning to disorganize. Lateral root initials were developing abnormally close to root tips ($\approx 800\ \mu$m). Roots showed marked distortion and twisting with enlarged cortical cells. Epidermal and cortical cells were very fragile and already in early stages of disintegration. Loss of columnar arrangements of cells was extensive. In the bentgrass subapical 2000-μm region, epidermal and cortical cells were sloughing off. Cortical cells showed some disruption and a few abnormally occurring lateral root initials were observed. Root tissue collected after the 4-wk treatment period was dead. Napropamide was reported to have caused only slight injury to colonial bentgrass and red fescue in previous research by

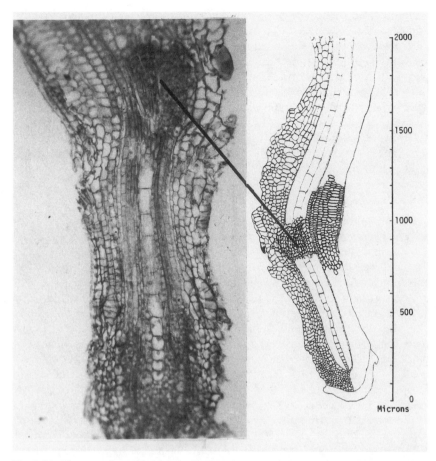

Fig. 4-16.   Diagram of a median longitudinal section of the apical 2000 μm of a napropamide-
treated Penncross creeping bentgrass root after 2 wk in nutrient culture. Drawing at 75x and
photomicrograph at 94x. Drawing and scale reduced 61% (69).

Coville and Jagschitz (39); however, napropamide severely reduced rooting
of Penncross bentgrass grown on a sandy loam soil green (44), and caused
moderate to severe stand loss of Penncross bentgrass maintained on a loam
soil green (21).

Following napropamide treatments in solution culture, Tifgreen bermudagrass plants exhibited ≈ 50% green foliage and stunted, brown roots
(69). After a 4-wk recovery period, foliage was 90% brown and what roots
had developed where whitish-brown and stunted. Napropamide-treated plants
had no viable root tissue available for sampling following the 4-wk herbicide treatment period; thus, no histological results were available for this
period. New roots did develop, however, during a 4-wk recovery period and
histological sections revealed no severe herbicide-induced abnormalities.
Although root caps were reduced in length, cells in the meristematic zone
showed normal cell differentiation into column-type rows of square-shaped

epidermal and cortical cells. Further back from tips, cells characteristically elongated, stelar elements were well defined, and no lateral roots or root hairs were observed. In the subapical region of Tifgreen bermudagrass root tips following solution culture treatments, columnar arrangement of cells was slightly disrupted and cortical cells were slightly enlarged and lacked typical elongation (69). Epidermal cells showed a tendency to degenerate but occurrence of lateral root initials appeared normal. Napropamide has been reported to interfere with rooting of Midiron and Tufcote (12), and reduce rooting of Tifdwarf, Tifgreen, and Tifway (87) bermudagrass. Reduced rooting (87) and reduced stand density (85) have also been reported for Emerald and Meyer *Zoysia*, and manilagrass.

5. Pronamide

Pronamide [3,5-dichloro (*N*-1,1-dimethyl-2-propynyl)benzamide] is labeled for selective weed control in turfgrass and exhibits both preemergence and postemergence herbicide activity (73, 113). It controls both germinating seed and well-developed seedlings. To be most effective it must be moved into the rootzone for root absorption. It can translocate upward and distribute throughout shoots. Some activity results from foliar absorption. It disrupts cell division in root meristems and inhibits growth.

In solution culture studies, pronamide treatments quickly killed all Penncross bentgrass plants during the herbicide exposure period (13). During the short time shoots remained alive, no new root tissue was formed. Pronamide-treated Tifgreen bermudagrass roots in solution culture exhibited newly formed root apices in advanced stages of senescence by the end of a 4-wk treatment period (Fig. 4–17). The root apices were very fragile and tended to shatter easily during histological processing. Lateral root proliferations occurred abnormally close (500 μm) to root tips and hypertrophic cortical cells evolved with no distinct columnar arrangement. Stelar elements were poorly defined and severe root curvature made it impossible to cut median longitudinal sections. Roots were abnormally enlarged as compared with untreated plants. The Tifgreen bermudagrass subapical region continued the abnormal cell development observed in the apical region. An abnormal number of lateral root initials were present with cortical cells enlarged, fragile, and easily shattering during histological processing. Tifgreen bermudagrass plants exposed to pronamide for 4 wk died during the subsequent 4-wk recovery period. Other researchers have reported that pronamide severely reduced stand density of overseeded perennial ryegrass following a spring treatment to aid regrowth of a bermudagrass green (81). Severe injury has also been reported to Floraturf bermudagrass when treated at time of sprigging (79). Pronamide has also caused significant injury to shoot and root growth of Tifdwarf, Tifgreen, and Tifway bermudagrass (121).

I. Substituted Ureas

Most of the herbicides in this group are soil applied (73, 113). These are root absorbed and some are apoplastically translocated to shoots;

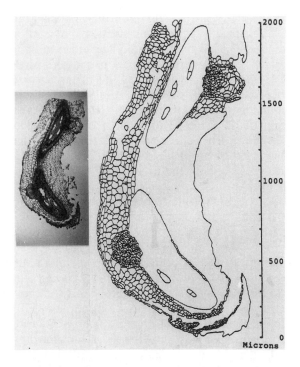

Fig. 4-17. Diagram of an intermittent median longitudinal section of the apical 2000 μm of a pronamide-treated Tifgreen bermudagrass root after 4 wk in nutrient culture. Drawing at 80x, photomicrograph at 25x (13).

however, those used in turf have not demonstrated apoplastic movement, but affect only root growth and development. The substituted ureas are readily decomposed by soil microorganisms. Sensitivity of turfgrasses to the substituted ureas varies widely, probably due to the considerable variation in the mode of action of chemicals in this group (113). Some turfgrasses have shown a tendency to recover and eventually grow normally following what initially appeared to be severe root phytotoxicity. Growth rate and energy efficiency do not appear to influence turfgrass resistance to certain chemicals in this group.

1. Siduron

Siduron [N-(2-methylcyclohexyl)-N'-phenylurea] is labeled for use in turfgrass as a soil-applied preemergence herbicide providing selective control of a few annual grasses (73, 113). This chemical is root absorbed, but does not apoplastically translocate. It also tends to cause much greater phytotoxicity in warm season (C_4) grasses than in cool season (C_3) grasses; thus, control of crabgrass, a C_4 plant, has been very good but phytotoxicity to bermudagrass, also a C_4 plant, has been severe. Because certain cool-season turfgrasses have exhibited very good tolerance, siduron is labeled for use in newly seeded and established stands of selected cool-season turfgrasses mainly for crabgrass control (124). Siduron is readily absorbed by roots but less readily absorbed by foliage and stems. Its mode of action seems to be confined to affecting cell division and cell enlargement in root meristems.

The effects of siduron were only slight in root tips of Penncross bentgrass under solution culture conditions (115). Tissue abnormalities appeared as compressed epidermal cells within 1000 μm of the root tip showing slight cortical cell columnar disruption; however, no lateral roots or root hairs occurred in this region. Penncross bentgrass produced a large number of roots in siduron-treated nutrient culture and appeared to show tolerance to this chemical. Other investigators reported slight to moderate sod injury to Penncross bentgrass growing on a soil-based green (18), and reduced new root growth of 'IaGreen' bentgrass (124). Injury to other cool season grasses was reported as: reduced root growth of Kentucky bluegrass cultivars (117, 130, 131), increased wilting and drought injury of Kentucky bluegrass (117), reduced root growth and clipping yields of Pennlawn red fescue (130, 131), and reduced root weights and stand density of tall fescue (116).

Compared with Penncross bentgrass, cellular abnormalities were extensive in root meristems of Tifgreen bermudagrass following siduron treatments in nutrient culture (Fig. 4–18) (115). Affected roots showed epidermal cells moderately compressed close to the tips and cortical cell differentiation showed disruption and columnar disorganization. Lateral root proliferations occurred abnormally close (1500 μm) to tips accompanied by severe hypertrophic cortical cell development. Many cortical cells ruptured easily. No root hairs were found in the apical region but root development was greatly reduced in siduron-treated solution culture compared with untreated plants. Other investigators have also reported that siduron severely inhibits rooting or kills Tifgreen bermudagrass (7, 20, 25, 103). Injury to other warm season turfgrasses include: severe root inhibition of Midiron, Tifway, and Tufcote bermudagrass (10), severe sod thinning of common bermudagrass (27), and severe injury at seeding time of common bermudagrass, centipedegrass, and carpetgrass (*Axonopus affinis* Chase) (103).

J. Sulfonyl Ureas

This new class of herbicides is biologically active at extremely low rates of application (0.16–0.3 kg ha^{-1}) (73, 113). They are effective when applied either preemergence of postemergence. Sulfonyl ureas are taken up by roots and shoots and are readily translocated in plants. They inhibit cell division in the shoot and in root meristems. A slow decline in plant vigor occurs with developing symptoms of distinctive reddish-purple leaves to chlorosis and necrosis.

1. Chlorsulfuron

Chlorsulfuron [2-chloro-*N*-[[(4-methoxy-6-methyl-1,3,5-triazin-2-yl)amino]carbonyl]benzenesulfonamide] is recommended for use in turfgrass as both a preemergence and an early postemergence herbicide for selective con-

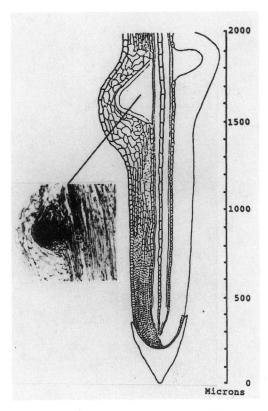

Fig. 4-18. Diagram of a median longitudinal section of the apical 2000 μm of a siduron-treated Tifgreen bermudagrass root after 4 wk in nutrient culture. Drawing at 97.5x and photomicrograph at 113x (115).

trol of a few annual grasses, and as a preemergence and postemergence treatment for effective control of several broadleaf weeds (73, 113). Foliar absorption is rapid and it is systemic after absorption by either the foliage or roots. Growth inhibitory effects are slow to develop, taking ≈ 1 to 3 wk.

Apical root meristems of Penncross bentgrass treated with chlorsulfuron in solution culture showed evidence of moderate tissue abnormalities (52). Root meristematic cells appeared to differentiate normally from rounded to rectangular shaped cells, but with slight columnar disorganization. In the subapical region several advanced stage lateral root initials (two shown at 2200 and 2700 μm) were present that is abnormal for Penncross bentgrass (Fig. 4-19). Root weights of chlorsulfuron-treated bentgrass were greatly reduced and roots were brown compared with white untreated roots. Gual and Christians (59) found chlorsulfuron to be phytotoxic, especially to shoots of creeping bentgrass. Root tips of Tifgreen bermudagrass exposed to chlorsulfuron in solution culture showed little difference in meristematic cell development compared with root tips of untreated plants (52). By the end of a 4-wk chlorsulfuron treatment period, stelar elements were well defined

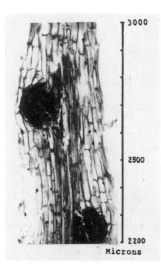

Fig. 4-19. Photomicrograph (175x) of a median longitudinal 800-μm section of the subapical 2000 μm of a chlorsulfuron-treated Penncross creeping bentgrass root after 4 wk in nutrient culture (52).

and columnar arrangement of epidermal, cortical, and stelar cells appeared normal. No root hairs or lateral roots were present in the apical 2000-μm region. The subapical region appeared similar to this same region in untreated Tifgreen bermudagrass.

2. Sulfometuron

Sulfometuron [2-[[[[(4,6-dimethyl-2-pyrimidinyl)amino]carbonyl]amino]sulfonyl]benzoic acid] is much less selective in its herbicide activity than chlorsulfuron (113). It is labeled for use in turfgrass as a preemergence or postemergence treatment on unimproved industrial sites, highway roadsides, and noncropland areas of well established common bermudagrass and bahiagrass (*Paspalun notatum* Flugge). It effectively controls a large number of annual and perennial grasses and broadleaf weeds. It is absorbed by both roots and foliage giving visual symptoms progressing from growth inhibition to reddish-purple leaves, then chlorosis, necrosis, vein discoloration, and death. Initial effects are seen in 2 or 3 wk following application with death in 4 wk. Wilcut et al. (137) reported that bahiagrass and centipedegrass absorbed sulfometuron by both roots and leaves. Apoplasmic and symplasmic translocation of the chemical was evident in both species. Centipedegrass metabolized 72% of foliar applied and 68% of root-applied sulfometuron by 72 h after application. Bahiagrass metabolized 35% of foliar- and 28% of root-applied sulfometuron. Centipedegrass tolerance to the herbicide appeared to be related to its ability to rapidly metabolize the chemical.

All plants of Penncross bentgrass treated with sulfometuron in nutrient solution were dead by the end of 8 wk; this included 4 wk of herbicide treatment followed by a 4-wk recovery period (52). Root weights were very low and roots were brown until they died. Root tissue was collected early during the herbicide-treatment period but meristematic cells had still degenerated to the extent that root tips did not survive histological processing. Sulfometuron treatments of Tifgreen bermudagrass in nutrient solution killed the roots by the end of 4 wk. Root meristem tissue was too fragile to successfully process histologically. Rogers and King (112) reported that sulfometuron caused delayed greenup of common bermudagrass.

REFERENCES

1. Anderson, W.P. 1983. Weed science principles. West Publ. Co., St. Paul, MN.
2. Armbruster, B.L., W.T. Molin, and M.W. Bugg. 1991. Effects of the herbicide dithiopyr on cell division in wheat root tips. Pestic. Biochem. Physiol. 39:110–120.
3. Ashton, F.M., and A.S. Crafts. 1981. Mode of action of herbicides. John Wiley & Sons, New York.
4. Bailey, G.W., and J.L. White. 1970. Factors affecting the adsorption, desorption, and movement of pesticides in soil. Residue Rev. 32:29–92.
5. Beard, J.B. 1986. Spring root decline of warm season grasses. Grounds Maint. 21:91–94, 138–139.
6. Bingham, S.W. 1968. Effect of DCPA on anatomy and cytology of roots. Weed Sci. 16:449–452.
7. Bingham, S.W. 1967. Influence of herbicides on root development of bermudagrass. Weed Sci. 15:363–365.
8. Bingham, S.W., and J.R. Hall. 1985. Effects of herbicides on bermudagrass (*Cynodon* spp.) spring establishment. Weed Sci. 33:253–257.
9. Bingham, S.W., and R.E. Schmidt. 1967. Residue of bensulide in turfgrass soil following annual treatments for crabgrass control. Agron. J. 59:327–329.
10. Bingham, S.W., and R.E. Schmidt. 1983. Turfgrass establishment after application of preemergence herbicides. Agron. J. 75:923–926.
11. Bingham, S.W., and R.L. Shaver. 1979. Effectiveness of herbicide programs for annual bluegrass (*Poa annua*) control in bermudagrass (*Cynodon dactylon*). Weed Sci. 27:367–370.
12. Bingham, S.W., and R.L. Shaver. 1991. Goosegrass (*Eleusine indica*) control during bermudagrass (*Cynodon dactylon*) establishment. Weed Sci. 29:11–16.
13. Bogert, J.M. 1988. Cellular response of two turfgrass cultivars to selected herbicides. M.S. thesis. University of Tennessee, Knoxville.
14. Brauen, S.E., R. Crockett, S.K. Parrish, and R.L. Goss. 1988. Efficacy of MON 15100 on annual bluegrass control in mixed colonial and creeping bentgrass turf. p. 148. *In* Agronomy Abstracts. ASA, Madison, WI.
15. Breuminger, J.M., and R.E. Schmidt. 1981. Post-dormancy growth of bermudagrass as influenced by low temperatures and selected preemergence herbicides. Agron. J. 73:945–949.
16. Bundschuh, S.H., T.E. Dutt, N.E. Jackson, and J.M. Higgins. 1990. Winter weed control in turf with dithiopyr. p. 170. *In* Agronomy Abstracts. ASA, Madison, WI.
17. Callahan, L.M. 1970. Are diseases really to blame? Weeds/Today. 1:19–21.
18. Callahan, L.M. 1972. Phytotoxicity of herbicides to a Penncross bentgrass green. Weed Sci. 20:387–391.
19. Callahan, L.M. 1972. The real culprit behind turf diseases. Golf Superintendent. 40:12–16.
20. Callahan, L.M. 1976. Phytotoxicity of herbicides to a Tifgreen bermudagrass green. Weed Sci. 24:92–98.
21. Callahan, L.M. 1986. Crabgrass and goosegrass control in a bentgrass green in the transition zone. Agron. J. 78:625–628.
22. Callahan, L.M., and R.E. Engel. 1965. Tissue abnormalities induced in roots of colonial bentgrass by phenoxyalkylcarboxylic acid herbicides. Weed Sci. 13:336–338.
23. Callahan, L.M., and R.E. Engel. 1986. A compact continuous flow and constant level solution culture renewal system. Agron. J. 78:547–549.
24. Callahan, L.M., R.E. Engel, and R.D. Ilnicki. 1968. Environmental influence on bentgrass treated with silvex. Weed Sci. 16:193–196.

25. Callahan, L.M., and J.W. High, Jr. 1990. Herbicide effects on bermudagrass lawn recovery and crabgrass control during spring root decline in the north–south transition zone. J. Am. Soc. Hortic. Sci. 115:597–601.

26. Callahan, L.M., and E.R. McDonald. 1992. Effectiveness of bensulide in controlling two annual bluegrass (Poa annua) subspecies. Weed Tech. 6:97–103.

27. Callahan, L.M., J.R. Overton, and W.L. Sanders. 1983. Initial and residual herbicide control of crabgrass (Digitaria spp.) in bermudagrass (Cynodon dactylon) turf. Weed Sci. 31:619–622.

28. Callahan, L.M., and D.P. Shepard. 1991. Control of annual weedy grasses and phytotoxicity in a bentgrass green with treatment programs of tri-calcium arsenate. J. Am. Soc. Hortic. Sci. 116:30–35.

29. Carrow, R.N., and P.E. Rieke. 1977. Effect of tricalcium arsenate formulations on control of annual bluegrass (Poa annua L.). Weed Sci. 25:364–367.

30. Carrow, R.N., P.E. Rieke, and B.G. Ellis. 1975. Growth of turfgrasses as affected by soil phosphorus and arsenic. Soil Sci. Soc. Am. Proc. 39:1121–1124.

31. Christians, N.E. 1982. Preemergence herbicide effects on four Kentucky bluegrass cultivars. HortScience 17:911–912.

32. Coats, G.E., W.E. Fleeman, III, and C.Y. Ward. 1974. Influence of preemergence herbicides on spring transition of Tifgreen bermudagrass. p. 21. In Weed Sci. Soc. of Am. Abstr. WSSA, Champaign, IL.

33. Coats, G.E., and C.Y. Ward. 1972. Response of bermudagrass cultivars to preemergence herbicides. Proc. South. Weed Conf. 25:193.

34. Coats, G.E., C.Y. Ward, and E.L. McWhirter. 1973. Effect of benefin and DCPA on overseeded grasses maintained as putting greens. Weed Sci. 21:528–531.

35. Cole, M.A., and A.J. Turgeon. 1978. Microbial activity in soil and litter underlying bandane and calcium arsenate treated turfgrass. Soil Biol. Biochem. 10:181–186.

36. Cooper, R.J., P.C. Bhowmik, and L.A. Spokas. 1990. Root and rhizome growth of Kentucky bluegrass following application of pendimethalin. HortScience. 25:84–86.

37. Cooper, R.J., and J.A. Jagschitz. 1980. Crabgrass control and turfgrass injury resulting from pre and postemergence herbicides. Proc. Northeast. Weed Sci. Soc. 34:344–352.

38. Corbett, J.R., K. Wright, and A.C. Baillie. 1984. The biochemical mode of action of pesticides. Academic Press, Orlando.

39. Coville, C.M., and J.A. Jagschitz. 1976. Herbicides for preemergence crabgrass and goosegrass control in turfgrass. Proc. Northeast. Weed Sci. Soc. 30:367–371.

40. Crafts, A.S. 1975. Modern weed control. Univ. of California Press, Berkeley.

41. Daniel, W.H. 1955. Poa annua control with arsenic materials. Golf Course Rep. 23:5–8.

42. Dernoeden, P.H. 1987. Phytotoxic effects of some herbicides applied to bentgrass. Proc. Northeast Weed Sci. Soc. 41:224–228.

43. Dernoeden, P.H., N.E. Christians, J.M. Krouse, and R.G. Roe. 1993. Creeping bentgrass rooting as influenced by dithiopyr. Agron. J. 85:560–563.

44. Dernoeden, P.H., D.B. Davis, and J.D. Fry. 1988. Rooting and cover of three turf species as influenced by preemergence herbicides. Proc. Northeast. Weed Sci. Soc. 42:169–173.

45. Dickens, R. 1979. Control of annual bluegrass (Poa annua) in overseeded bermudagrass (Cynodon spp.) golf greens. Weed Sci. 27:642–644.

46. DiPaola, J.M., and J.B. Beard. 1980. Spring root dieback of warm season turfgrasses. USGA Green Sec. Rec. 18:6–9.

47. DiPaola, J.M., J.B. Beard, and H. Brawand. 1982. Key events in the seasonal root growth of bermudagrass and St. Augustinegrass. HortScience 17:829–831.

48. Dukes, S.O. 1985. Weed physiology: Herbicide physiology. Volume II. CRC Press, Baca Raton, FL.

49. Engel, R.E., and L.M. Callahan. 1967. Merion Kentucky bluegrass response to soil residue of preemergence herbicides. Weeds 15:128–130.

50. Engel, R.E., C.R. Funk, and D.A. Kinney. 1968. Effect of varied rates of atrazine and simazine on the establishment of several Zoysia strains. Agron. J. 60:261–262.

51. Fedtke, C. 1982. Biochemistry and physiology of herbicide action. Springer-Verlag, New York.

52. Finney, S.B. 1991. Cellular responses of bentgrass and bermudagrass to selected preemergence herbicides. M.S. thesis. Univ. of Tennessee, Knoxville.

53. Fleeman, W.E., III, G.E. Coats, and J.A. Spencer. 1975. Effect of preemergence herbicides on bermudagrass transition. Proc. South. Weed Conf. 28.45.

54. Fry, J.D., P.H. Dernoeden, and J.J. Murray. 1986. Establishment and rooting of zoy-siagrass (*Zoysia japonica*) as affected by preemergence herbicides. Weed Sci. 34:413–418.
55. Fullerton, T.M., A.M. Davis, and R.E. Frans. 1967. The effect of selected preemergence herbicides and fertilizer levels on the establishment of several turfgrasses. Proc. South. Weed Conf. 20:69–74.
56. Fullerton, T.M., C.L. Murdock, A.E. Spooner, and R.E. Frans. 1970. Effects of DCPA on winter injury of recently established bermudagrass. Weed Sci. 18:711–714.
57. Gallagher, J.E. 1962. Preemergence crabgrass control. Golf Course Rep. 30:10–17.
58. Gaskin, T.A. 1964. Effect of preemergence crabgrass herbicides on rhizome development in Kentucky bluegrass. Agron. J. 56:340–342.
59. Gaul, M.C., and N.E. Christians. 1985. The use of fenarimol and chlorsulfuron for *Poa annua* control in cool-season turfgrasses. p. 116. *In* Agronomy Abstracts. ASA, Madison, WI.
60. Gaussoin, R.E. 1990. Isoxaben effects on root growth of seedling Kentucky bluegrass and tall fescue. p. 73. *In* Agronomy Abstracts. ASA, Madison, WI.
61. Gill, G.W., J.K. Frost, and K.A. Miller. 1974. A new formula for a half-oxidized hematox-ylin solution that neither overstains nor requires differentiation. Acta Cytol. 18:300–311.
62. Goss, R.L. 1965. preemergence control of annual bluegrass. Agron. J. 56:479–481.
63. Goss, R.L. 1965. Preemergence control of annual bluegrass (*Poa annua* L.). Golf Course Rep. 33:24–30.
64. Green Section Staff. 1973. Refining the green section specifications for putting green con-struction. USGA Green Sec. Rec. 11:1–8.
65. Guenzi, W.D. (ed.) Pesticides in soil and water. SSSA, Madison, WI.
66. Haley, J.E., and T.W. Fremanian. 1990. Prodiamine, a new preemergence herbicide for turf. p. 174. *In* Agronomy Abstracts. ASA, Madison, WI.
67. Hance, R.J. (ed.) Interactions between herbicides and the soil. Academic Press, New York.
68. Hall, J.R., E.E. Deal, and A.J. Powell. 1974. Seven years of smooth crabgrass control in turfgrass with registered and experimental herbicides. Proc. Northeast Weed Sci. Soc. 28:399–405.
69. Harper, C.A. 1982. Root histology of two turfgrass cultivars in response to selected her-bicides. M.S. thesis. Univ. of Tennessee, Knoxville.
70. Hatzios, K.K., and D. Penner. 1982. Metabolism of herbicides in higher plants. Burgess Publ. Co., Minneapolis, MN.
71. Hewitt, E.J. 1966. Sand and water culture methods used in the study of plant nutrition. 2nd ed. Commonwealth Bur. Hortic. Plant. Crops (GB) Tech. Commun. no. 22, Com-monwealth Bur. of Hortic. Plant. Crops, East Malling, England.
72. Hummel, N.W., Jr., M.C. Fowler, and J.C. Neal. 1990. Prodiamine effects on quality and rooting of Kentucky bluegrass turf. Crop Sci. 30:976–979.
73. Humburg, N.E. et al. (ed.). 1989. Herbicide Handbook of the Weed Science Society of America. 6th ed. WSSA, Champaign, IL.
74. Hurto, K.A., and A.J. Turgeon. 1979. Influence of thatch on preemergence herbicide ac-tivity in Kentucky bluegrass (*Poa pratensis*) turf. Weed Sci. 27:141–146.
75. Jagschitz, J.A., and C.R. Skogley. 1965. Turfgrass response to dacthal and nitrogen. Agron. J. 57:35–38.
76. Jansen, I.J., and A.J. Turgeon. 1977. Indirect effects of a thatch-inducing herbicide on soil physical properties under turf. Agron. J. 69:67–70.
77. Jenson, W.A. 1962. Botanical histochemistry. W.J. Freeman Co., San Francisco.
78. Johansen, D.A. 1940. Plant microtechnique. McGraw-Hill Book Co. New York.
79. Johnson, B.J. 1975. Minimal herbicide treatments on the establishment of four turfgrass-es. Agron. J. 67:786–789.
80. Johnson, B.J. 1976. Bermudagrass tolerance to consecutive butralin and oxadiazon treat-ments. Weed Sci. 24:302–305.
81. Johnson, B.J. 1976. Transition from overseeded cool-season grass to warm season grass with pronamide. Weed Sci. 24:309–311.
82. Johnson, B.J. 1977. Difference in tolerance of bermudagrass and zoysiagrass cultivars to herbicides. p. 217–225. *In* J.B. Beard (ed.) Proc. Third Int. Turfgrass Conf., Munich, Germany.
83. Johnson, B.J. 1977. Effect of herbicide treatment on overseeded putting greens turf. Weed Sci. 25:343–347.

84. Johnson, B.J. 1978. Multiple herbicide treatments for grassy weed control in turf. Weed Sci. 26:650–653.

85. Johnson, B.J. 1978. Response of zoysia (*Zoysia* spp.) and bermudagrass (*Cynodon dactylon*) cultivars to herbicide treatments. Weed Sci. 26:493–497.

86. Johnson, B.J. 1978. Tolerance of five bermudagrass cultivars to herbicide treatment. Georgia Agric. Res. Rep., Athens. 282:316.

87. Johnson, B.J. 1980. Root growth of southern turf cultivars as affected by herbicides. Weed Sci. 28:526–528.

88. Johnson, B.J. 1982. Frequency of herbicide treatments for summer and winter weed control in turfgrass. Weed Sci. 30:116–124.

89. Johnson, B.J. 1983. Tolerance of bermudagrass (*Cynodon dactylon*) putting greens to herbicide treatments. Weed Sci. 31:415–418.

90. Johnson, B.J. 1985. Response of four bermudagrass (*Cynodon dactylon*) cultivars to dates of oxadiazon treatments. Weed Sci. 33:371–375.

91. Johnson, B.J. 1987. Tolerance of bentgrass to dates and frequency of preemergence herbicide treatment. Agron. J. 79:992–996.

92. Jukes, A.M., and P.M. Goode. 1981. Observations on the effect of postemergence application of ethofumesate on the shoot growth of *Poa annua* and *Lolium perenne* seedlings. Grass Forage Sci. 36:231–235.

93. Juska, F.V. 1961. Preemergence herbicides for crabgrass control and their effects on germination of turfgrass species. Weeds. 9:137–144.

94. Juska, F.V., A.A. Hanson, and A.W. Hovin. 1970. Phytotoxicity of preemergence herbicides. USGA Green Sec. Rec. 8:2–6.

95. Karnovsky, M.J. 1965. A formaldehyde-glutaraldehyde fixative of high osmolality for use in electron microscopy. J. Cell. Biol. 27:137A.

96. Kaufman, J.E. 1990. Influence of physical and chemical properties of dithiopyr behavior in the turf environment. p. 176. *In* Agronomy Abstracts. ASA, Madison, WI.

97. Kearney, P.C., and D.D. Kaufman, (ed.). 1975 and 1976 Herbicides, chemistry, degradation, and mode of action. Vol. I and II. Marcel Dekker, New York.

98. Kenna, M.P., J.F. Barber, and A.D. Brede. 1988. Phytotoxicity of five pesticides on creeping bentgrass. p. 152. *In* Agronomy Abstracts. ASA, Madison, WI.

99. Kerr, C.F. 1969. Program for gradual removal of *Poa annua*. The Golf Supt. 37:28–29.

100. King, J.W., and E.M. Miller. 1982. Preemergence control of crabgrass and goosegrass in common bermudagrass turf. Proc. South. Weed Sci. Soc. 35:89.

101. Klingman, G.C., and F.M. Ashton. 1982. Weed science. John Wiley & Sons, New York.

102. Lewis, W.M., J.M. DiPaola, and A.H. Bruneau. 1988. Preemergence herbicide effects on turf rooting. p. 153. *In* Agronomy Abstracts. ASA, Madison, WI.

103. Lewis, W.M., and W.B. Gilbert. 1966. The effect of siduron on crabgrass and goosegrass control on the establishment of five warm-season and three cool-season turfgrasses. Proc. South. Weed Conf. 19:150–154.

104. Mazur, A.R., J.A. Jagschitz, and C.R. Skogley. 1969. Bioassays for bensulide, DCPA, and siduron in turfgrass. Weed Sci. 17:31–34.

105. McLean, J.R.F. 1978. Control of *Poa annua* in fine turf using ethofumesate. Proc. New Zealand Weed and Pest Control Conf. 31:192–194.

106. Neal, J.C., N.W. Hummel Jr., and M. Fowler. 1986. Effect of preemergence herbicides on growth and morphology of *Poa pratensis* L. turf. p. 137. *In* Agronomy Abstracts. ASA, Madison, WI.

107. Neidlinger, T.J., W.R. Furtick, and N.R. Goetze. 1968. Susceptibility of annual bluegrass and turfgrass to bensulide and three uracil herbicides. Weed Sci. 16:16–18.

108. Pokarny, R. 1941. New compounds. J. Am. Chem. Soc. 63:1768.

109. Reicher, Z.J., and N.E. Christians. 1986. Effect of preemergence herbicides on rooting of *Poa pratensis*. p. 137. *In* Agronomy Abstracts. ASA, Madison, WI.

110. Reicher, Z.J., and N.E. Christians. 1988. Herbicide effect on rooting of Kentucky bluegrass. p. 155. *In* Agronomy Abstracts. ASA, Madison, WI.

111. Roberts, E.C., and D.R. Brockshus. 1966. Kind and extent of injury to greens from preemergence herbicides. Golf Supt. 34:13–36.

112. Rogers, J.N., III, and J.W. King. 1985. Sulfometuron methyl on dormant bermudagrass turf. p. 120. *In* Agronomy Abstracts. ASA, Madison, WI.

113. Ross, M.A., and C.A. Lembi. 1985. Applied weed science. Burgess Publ. Co., Minneapolis, MN.

114. Sass, J.E. 1958. Botanical Microtechnique. 3rd ed. Iowa State Univ. Press, Ames.

115. Seagle, E.D. 1978. Cellular responses in roots of bentgrass and bermudagrass to selected herbicides. M.S. thesis, Univ. of Tennessee, Knoxville.

116. Shearman, R.C., E.J. Kimbacher, and K.A. Reierson. 1980. Siduron effects on tall fescue (*Festuca arundinacea*) emergence, growth, and high temperature injury. Weed Sci. 28:194–196.

117. Shearman, R.C., E.J. Kinbacher, and D.H. Steinnegger. 1979. Herbicide effects on sod transplant rooting of three Kentucky bluegrass cultivars. HortScience 14:282–283.

118. Shim, S.R., and B.J. Johnson. 1990. Tolerance of creeping bentgrass to spring applied preemergence herbicides. p. 182. *In* Agronomy Abstracts. ASA, Madison, WI.

119. Sifers, S.I., J.B. Beard, and J.M. DiPaola. 1985. Spring root decline: Discovery, description and causes. Sect. 6:777–788. *In* F. Lonnaire (ed.) Proc. Fifth Int. Turf Res. Conf., Avignon, France. INRA Publications, Paris.

120. Skogley, C.R., and J.A. Jagschitz. 1964. The effect of various crabgrass herbicides on turfgrass seed and seedlings. Proc. Northeast Weed Contr. Conf. 18:523–529.

121. Smith, G.S., and M. Ayer. 1971. Effects of several herbicides effective against *Poa annua* on top and root growth of Tifdwarf, Tifgreen and Tifway bermudagrass. p. 50. *In* Agronomy Abstracts. ASA, Madison, WI.

122. Smith, G.S., and L.M. Callahan. 1968. Herbicidal phytotoxicity to Emerald Zoysia during establishment. Weeds 6:312–315.

123. Smith, G.S., and L.M. Callahan. 1969. The response of Kentucky bluegrass to soil residues to preemergence herbicides. Weed Sci. 17:13–15.

124. Splittoesser, W.E., and H.J. Hopen. 1967. Response of bentgrass to siduron. Weed Sci. 15:82–83.

125. Stahnke, G.K., R.C. Shearman, P.J. Shea, and R.N. Stougaard. 1988. Preemergence herbicide effects on Kentucky bluegrass rooting. p. 156. *In* Agronomy Abstracts. ASA, Madison, WI.

126. Tillman, P.H., J.B. Beard, and W.G. Menn. 1990. The effects of six preemergence herbicides on root systems of *Stenotaphrum secundatum* and *Cynodon dactylon* × *C. transvaalensis*. p. 183. *In* Agronomy abstracts. ASA, Madison, WI.

127. Torrey, J.G., and D.T. Clarkson (ed.). 1975. The development and function of roots. Academic Press, New York.

128. Troutman, B.C., J.W. King, and R.E. Frans. 1976. Effects of herbicides on establishment of bermudagrass turf. Proc. South. Weed Sci. Soc. 29:66.

129. Turgeon, A.J. 1980. Turfgrass management. Reston Publ. Co., Reston, VA.

130. Turgeon, A.J., J.B. Beard, D.P. Martin, and W.F. Meggitt. 1973. Effects of repeated applications of six preemergence herbicides on three turfgrasses. Weed Sci. Soc. of Am. Abstr. p. 23–24.

131. Turgeon, A.J., J.B. Beard, D.P. Martin, and W.F. Meggitt. 1974. Effects of successive applications of preemergence herbicides on turf. Weed Sci. 22:349–352.

132. Turgeon, A.J., R.P. Freeborg, and W.N. Bruce. 1975. Thatch development and other effects of preemergence herbicides in Kentucky bluegrass turf. Agron. J. 67:563–565.

133. Turner, D.L., and R. Dickens. 1983. Centipedegrass sod strength as affected by atrazine. p. 130. *In* Agronomy Abstracts. ASA, Madison, WI.

134. Upchurch, R.P. 1966. Behavior of herbicides in soil. Residue Rev. 16:46–85.

135. Warmke, H.E., and J. Sheu-Ling Lee. 1976. Improved staining procedures for semithin epoxy sections of plant tissues. Stain Technol. 51:179–185.

136. Weber, J.B., T.J. Monaco, and A.D. Worsham. 1973. What happens to herbicides in the environment? Weeds Today. 4:16–17.

137. Wilcut, J.W., J.H. Baird, G.R. Wehtje, and R. Dickens. 1987. Behavior of sulfometuron methyl in centipedegrass and bahiagrass. p. 140. *In* Agronomy Abstracts. ASA, Madison, WI.

138. Woolson, E.A., J.H. Axley, and P.C. Kearney. 1973. The chemistry and phytotoxicity of arsenic in soils: II. Effects of time and phosphorus. Soil Sci. Soc. Am. Proc. 37:254–259.

Chapter 5

Herbicide Fate in Turf

B. E. BRANHAM, *Michigan State University, East Lansing, Michigan*

In order to understand the fate of an applied herbicide (more generally an organic chemical) one must have a solid understanding of the nature and properties of soils and an appreciation for the chemistry underlying the interactions between organic molecules and the soil constituents. Once an herbicide has been applied to soil or turf, many competing processes begin that result in the dissipation of the herbicide over time. These processes are soil sorption, plant uptake, leaching, chemical decomposition, biological decomposition, photochemical decomposition, and volatilization. Each of these processes are controlled by underlying physical or chemical processes that can be quite complex and are beyond the scope of this chapter. The discussions below are more qualitative in nature and designed to give the reader an overview and understanding of the processes that affect herbicide fate.

I. HERBICIDE FATE PROCESSES

A. Herbicide Sorption

Sorption plays the controlling role in herbicide fate in soils. The strength and extent of sorption greatly impacts the amount of leaching and volatilization and will also influence plant uptake and chemical, biological, and photochemical decomposition.

During the last 10 yr, much has been written concerning the nature of sorption in soils and sediments. The field has become increasingly important with the concern about groundwater contamination by pesticides and industrial chemicals. During that time, the term sorption has largely replaced adsorption since it is more general and inclusive of the various processes that can result in the removal of organic chemicals from the soil water solution. There are many reviews of herbicide sorption in soil (20, 56, 59, 62) and the interested reader should consult these references for a detailed description of the mechanisms of sorption. Herbicide sorption is predominantly controlled by the colloidial organic matter and clay fractions of the soil. Most of the early studies of sorption of pesticides concerned their interactions with clay surfaces, however, in soils the sorbing surface is the more complicated clay–organic matter complex.

The mechanisms of interaction between herbicides and clays or organic matter are merely applications of the general principles of sorption between sorbents (organic matter and clay) and adsorbates (organic and inorganic molecules and ions). These mechanisms have been described by many authors with one of the more thorough descriptions found in Hamaker and Thompson (56). They list the following sorption mechanisms: van der Waals' forces, hydrophobic bonding, charge transfer, hydrogen bonding, ligand exchange, ion exchange, direct and induced ion–dipole and dipole–dipole interactions, and chemisorption.

Van der Waals' forces are relatively weak interactions between individual atoms in the sorbent and adsorbate. They arise from variations in electron distribution caused by the movement of electrons in their orbitals. These momentary variations in charge can induce dipole–dipole interactions resulting in a net electrostatic attraction between atoms and molecules. The energy of these interactions is small, usually on the order of 1 to 2 kcal mol^{-1}, however, in larger molecules these interactions between atoms can become additive yielding significant energies of sorption.

Charge transfer is the general term used to describe the formation of a charge-transfer complex where electrons from an electronegative atom or molecule are shared by an electropositive species. Hydrogen bonding is a very important special case of the charge transfer mechanism. In general, two types of electron-donor compounds participate in charge transfer bonding. One group contains electronegative functional groups possessing an unshared pair of electrons that can include alcohols, amines, thiols, and ethers. A second group of electron donors are those molecules having an electron-rich π cloud (bonding electrons), examples would include alkenes, alkynes, and aromatics. These two classes of electron donating sources could charge transfer with either electron-deficient π cloud molecules (examples could include heteroaromatics with strongly electronegative substituents) or weakly acidic hydrogens from a wide range of compounds that are sufficiently electronegative to deshield the H nucleus. Clays and organic matter are rich in these types of functional groups and charge transfer and H bonding, in particular, are important mechanisms of sorption in soils.

Ligand exchange refers to the ability of an herbicide or other organic compound to chelate to transition metals, and in the process, exchange or replace the ligand that had occupied the chelating site. This process has frequently been postulated as important in the binding of triazines in soils (20).

Ion exchange can occur between charged organic molecules or those organic molecules in which a charge can be induced. Cation exchange predominates in soils because of the net negative charge resulting from isomorphous substitution in clays. Anion exchange occurs much less frequently but can occur when highly charged cations such as Al^{3+} or Fe^{3+} form the counterions to clays.

The importance of dipole–dipole interactions in pesticide sorption have not been well studied. A dipole results from asymmetric distribution of charge in a molecule. Thus, two dipoles can align the charges of opposite sign and a slight attraction will result although the energies are generally small and on the order of 2 kcal mol^{-1} or less. A molecule with a permanent dipole can also induce a dipole in molecules which do not have an appreciable dipole, again forming the basis for electrostatic attraction.

Chemisorption involves the actual formation of a chemical bond with concommitantly much higher levels of energy generally in the range of 30 to 50 kcal mol^{-1}. Once chemisorption has taken place it is unlikely that the molecule would be released back into the soil solution unaltered.

All of the above mechanisms are electrostatic in nature. The last mechanism to discuss is termed hydrophobic bonding that is thought to be driven by entropy generation (56). Briefly, hydrophobic bonding concerns the adsorption of an organic molecule onto a nonpolar (i.e., soil organic matter) surface. When a nonpolar organic molecule is dissolved in water, an energetically unfavorable interaction occurs between water and the organic molecule resulting in a decrease in the entropy of the system that is thermodynamically undesirable. If the organic molecule is sorbed onto another organic surface, the attraction between the two organic substances is usually of the weak van der Waals' type but the increase in entropy when the organic molecule is removed from solution is what drives the sorption mechanism. This mechanism has been termed hydrophobic bonding.

A different mechanism than hydrophobic bonding has been postulated by Chiou and coworkers (25, 26). They propose that organic molecules (e.g., herbicides) are not adsorbed on the surface of the organic matter but rather are partitioned (or absorbed) into the organic matter. In effect, they propose that soil is a two-phase system with an aqueous phase, the soil water solution, and an organic phase, the soil organic matter. Chiou (25) presents experimental evidence that supports his theory that partitioning, not hydrophobic bonding, is the mechanism for sorption of nonpolar organic molecules by soil organic matter. Points that support this view are that numerous authors have shown that the extent of sorption of a variety of organic components is directly related to the organic matter content of soils (56, 77, 79, 112) and that in multiple solute systems competitive reductions in binding are not observed at normal concentrations (37). The issue of the mechanism of sorption of nonpolar organics by soil organic matter has not been resolved and the debate will probably settle somewhere in the middle with both mechanisms having applicability under certain conditions. Regardless of which mechanism is operating, the sorption of nonpolar organic materials is directly related to and controlled by the organic matter fraction of the soil.

The sorbent for herbicides is the soil, but equally important is the nature of the adsorbate (herbicide) in determining the extent and mechanism of sorption. Organic herbicides fall into two general classes, nonionizable and those molecules that either carry a charge or are capable of being charged (ionized) under the proper conditions. The latter group contains such herbicides as paraquat (1,1'-dimethyl-4,4'-bipyridinium ion) and diquat [6,7-dihydrodipyrido[1,2-α:2',1'-c]pyrazinediium ion] that are organic cations and always carry a positive charge or ionizable herbicides such as the phenoxy acids and the triazines.

Paraquat and diquat are unusual cases in that they are true organic cations and always carry a positive charge in solution. Because of their charge and polarity, these herbicides are very water soluble and only very slightly soluble in organic solvents. Therefore, while these are organic compounds they will not partition into soil organic matter. Instead clays will be the preferred site for paraquat or diquat sorption. Weber and Weed (148) studied the sorption of paraquat by Na-montmorillonite and Na-kaolinite. They found that paraquat was sorbed to near the CEC for both clays. Using a 1 M BaCl$_2$ solution to desorb paraquat removed 80% of the sorbed paraquat from kaolinite, but only 5% from the montmorillonite. The authors postulated that paraquat was held in the interlayers of montmorillonite by a combination of electrostatic and van der Waals' forces, while the paraquat sorbed on the external surface of kaolinite was held by electrostatic forces only and could be replaced by smaller cations with higher charge/volume ratios.

Herbicides that are ionizable can be sorbed through ion exchange mechanisms with the charged species. The ability of a molecule to undergo ion exchange is determined by the pK_a or pK_b of the herbicide. The pK_a is the negative log of the ionization constant of the acid (K_a) and for the dissociation of typical weak acid (HA) is determined by the following equilibrium.

$$\text{HA} + \text{H}_2\text{O} \overset{K_a}{\rightleftharpoons} \text{H}_3\text{O}^+ + \text{A}^- \qquad [1]$$

$$K_a = [\text{HA}]/[\text{A}^-][\text{H}_3\text{O}^+]$$

For 2,4-D [(2,4-dichlorophenoxy)acetic acid], K_a equals 1.6×10^{-3} and pK_a = 2.8. Thus, 2,4-D is a moderately strong organic acid. Note that at a pH of 2.8 the concentration of the dissociated and associated species are exactly equal (i.e., [HA] = [A$^-$]), at pHs above 2.8 the equilibrium will shift towards the dissociated species. At normal soil pHs of 6 to 7.5, almost all of the 2,4-D would exist as the dissociated, charged species. Due to the overall negative charge on soil colloids, 2,4-D is actually repulsed from most sites of sorption making this herbicide very mobile in most soils (148).

From these two examples, it is clear that herbicides carrying a positive charge will be strongly sorbed in soils, while those possessing a negative charge will have very little sorption in most soils. Herbicides that can accept a proton would be considered weak bases and the protonated species would be readily sorbed in soils. The s-triazines are weak bases with pK_bs of 12.3 for atrazine [6-chloro-N-ethyl-N'-(1-methylethyl)-1,3,5-triazine-2,4-diamine] and simazine (6-chloro-N,N'-diethyl-1,3,5-triazine-2,4-diamine). Only if soil pH were to approach 12 would these herbicides carry a positive charge and cationic sorption of these pesticides is unlikely. Some s-triazines have pK_bs of

9.7 to 10.0 (e.g., terbutryn [*N*-(1,1-dimethylethyl)-*N'*-ethyl-6-(methylthio)-1,3,5-triazine-2,4-diamine] or prometryn [*N,N'*-bis(1-methylethyl)-6-(methylthio)-1,3,5-triazine-2,4-diamine] and under basic soil conditions cation-exchange could be a sorption mechanism for these herbicides.

The largest number of herbicides used in turf, however, would be those that are nonionic organics. Sorption of these noncharged species would depend upon polarity of the molecules. Polarity results from an asymmetric distribution of charge within the molecule. The more polar an organic herbicide the more likely it is to be water soluble and to bind by H bonding. These polar organics are sorbed by dry soil, presumably by the clay fraction, but in wet soils water displaces these materials from the site of adsorption. These materials will tend to leach because of their greater water solubility and lack of a significant retention mechanism. More nonpolar organics, which tend to have very low water solubilities, e.g. 0.5 to 30 mg L^{-1}, tend to sorb through partitioning (or hydrophobic bonding) into the organic matter of the soil. This tendency of nonwater soluble compounds to sorb to organic matter makes these materials fairly resistant to leaching.

Throughout this discussion, qualitative terms such as strong or weak have been used to describe herbicide sorption. To more quantitatively assess herbicide sorption, distribution coefficients, K, between soil and water have been experimentally determined. The most commonly used approach employs the empirical Fruendlich equation to describe sorption.

$$C_s = K_d \, C_L \hspace{3cm} [2]$$

where C_s is the concentration of adsorbate in the solid phase (M M^{-1}), C_L is the equilibrium solution concentration (M L^{-3}), and K_d is the ratio of these experimentally determined values ($L^3 \, M^{-1}$). As stated earlier, the extent of herbicide sorption is largely determined by the organic matter content of a soil (62). In Eq. [3], K_d is experimentally determined for an individual soil and converted to K_{oc} by dividing K_d by the percent organic C of that soil.

$$K_{oc} = K_d / \%\text{o.c.} \times 100 \hspace{2.5cm} [3]$$

Thus, K_{oc} should be relatively independent of soil type and can estimate the distribution of an organic compound between the soil solution and the soil organic matter. For an organic compound, the larger the K_{oc} value, the more strongly it will be sorbed to soils. Table 5–1 shows the K_{oc} values for some commonly used turf herbicides. Note that the preemergence herbicides, which must stay at or near the soil surface to be effective, tend to have K_{oc} values >1000.

Because K_{oc} values measure the distribution between water and a solid organic matter phase, it has been hypothesized that K_{oc} can be predicted based upon water solubility and other chemical data. Karickhoff et al. (79) estimated K_{oc} values from water solubility and melting point data according to the following formula.

Table 5-1. Soil sorption coefficients, K_{oc}, for selected herbicides used in turf.†

Herbicide	K_{oc}
	mL g^{-1}
dicamba salt	2
clopyralid amine	6
MCPP dimethylamine salt	20 (E)
MCPA dimethylamine salt	20 (E)
triclopyr amine	20 (E)
2,4-D ester	100 (E)
atrazine	100
ethofumesate	340
siduron	420
triclopyr ester	780
bensulide	1 000 (E)
pendimethalin	5 000
DCPA	5 000
trifluralin	8 000
benefin	9 000
fenoxaprop-ethyl	9 490
glyphosate isopropyl amine salt	24 000 (E)
E = values are estimates	

† Data from Wauchope et al. (146).

$$\log K_{oc} = -0.921 \log X_{sol} - 0.00953 \,(MP - 25) - 1.405 \qquad [4]$$

In this formula X_{sol} is the water solubility and MP is the melting point of the herbicide. In addition, Wauchope et al. (146) used linear regression to develop the relationship

$$K_{oc} = 3000/\sqrt{s} \qquad [5]$$

where s is the water solubility. These K_{oc} values derived from solubility data can serve as a check on experimentally determined values especially in light of the problems with determining K_{oc} values experimentally (50). Due to the wide variance of K_{oc} values reported in the literature, the values reported in the SCS/ARS/CES pesticide properties database (146) will be used in this text.

B. Herbicide Leaching

During the past decade the most important issue related to pesticide use is leaching to groundwater. As public and legislative concern has grown concerning the issue of pesticide leaching, the fallout has been widespread, dramatically impacting the turfgrass industry. This is due to a number of factors including the prominence of turf in urban areas, the view by some that it is totally an aesthetic crop with little functional value, and the perception, perhaps justified in some cases by the activities of the lawn care and golf course industries, that pesticides are overused on turf areas.

Golf courses and other development projects using turf have had to spend many dollars convincing local, state, and national regulatory agencies that pesticides used on turf do not represent a threat to groundwater resources. Very little experimental data have been collected on leaching from turf treated with pesticides although that is changing rapidly as university investigators respond to the need to develop this kind of information.

The leaching of organic chemicals through soil is a complex process due to the variability and complexity of soil. A mathematical treatment of transport of organics in soil has been developed and is necessary for computer-simulation models of pesticide leaching in soils (109, 139, 140). Pesticide movement in soils is considered the result of two processes that can occur in either the gas or liquid phase. The first is diffusion of the herbicide in response to a concentration gradient. The second process is the convective transport of the herbicide in bulk water or air. This process is also called mass flow and can be in either direction for liquid and gaseous phases. Fick's first law of diffusion is used as the basis for the contribution from diffusive interactions, while Darcy's law governing water flow is used to describe mass flow in soils. These two contributions to pesticide flux in the soil can be combined into a single equation to describe or predict pesticide movement in soils (109, 139). The diffusion contribution is more than just molecular diffusion resulting from concentration gradients. Because of the nonuniformity of pores within the soil, downward flowing water has different pore velocities resulting in a dispersal of the herbicide across a larger volume of soil than would be predicted under ideal conditions. The term *hydrodynamic dispersion* is used to describe the dispersion of the herbicide under the combined effects of molecular diffusion, dispersion between pores of different water velocities, and the diffusion that will occur between pores of different herbicide concentration. The hydrodynamic dispersion coefficient is the sum of the diffusion coefficients of each of these processes.

Despite the complexity of the equations developed to describe herbicide leaching, comparison of predicted versus observed levels of leaching usually find more movement in the field than predicted. This increased depth of leaching has been attributed to the effects of macropore flow or preferential flow (75, 108). Macropores are cracks, earthworm channels, or root channels, creating very large pores that during saturated flow may transport the bulk of downward flowing water. Some researchers have attempted to include the effects of macropores in models for water movement (12, 13, 115). The above discussion focused on the physical description of leaching; however, a qualitative understanding of leaching is important in assessing the likelihood of groundwater contamination from the use of an herbicide.

Two parameters that tend to control leaching are sorption and persistence. Sorption, which was discussed above, can be described by the coefficient K_{oc}. Presistence is best described by the half-life, $t_{1/2}$, which is an experimentally determined value that is highly dependent on application conditions, temperature, and moisture. Nonpersistent herbicides, those with $t_{1/2}$ values of 30 d or less are less likely to leach to groundwater regardless of strength of adsorption because of their short residence time in soils. The tendency of more persistent herbicides to leach will be controlled by their sorption coefficients. Those with large K_{oc} values (>500) will be unlikely to leach unless their $t_{1/2}$ values are quite large (>100 d). Problems can develop with moderately persistent herbicides that are only moderately sorbed. A prime example is atrazine that is a frequent contaminant of groundwater. With an estimated $t_{1/2}$ of 60 d, atrazine is moderately persistent and combined with a K_{oc} value of 100, which indicates moderate sorption, small but significant amounts of atrazine can reach groundwater.

C. Herbicide Volatilization

Volatilization is a complex process that can dramatically affect the persistence and performance of pesticide compounds. Volatilization is also a concern because of the potential to cause economic losses when herbicide vapors are absorbed by nontarget plants. For an excellent discussion of factors influencing volatilization see Spencer and Cliath (128) or Spencer et al. (129).

A solid or liquid will have an average energy determined by the temperature of the compound. A fraction of the molecules of this compound will have enough energy to escape into the vapor phase. The fraction of molecules having sufficient energy to vaporize is proportional to the Boltzman factor, $e^{-E/kt}$, where E is the amount of energy needed for vaporization to occur and k is the Boltzman constant. Thus, the larger E is, the smaller will be the fraction of molecules having sufficient energy to vaporize. If E is large enough, the herbicide will be essentially nonvolatile.

If a liquid or solid is introduced into a closed vessel, evaporation will continue until equilibrium is reached at which point the rate of volatilization will equal the rate of condensation. The gas phase is then saturated and at equilibrium and there will be no net change in the content of either phase. The pressure exerted by the gas phase is its vapor pressure at the temperature of the vessel. Vapor pressure is highly dependent upon temperature and a 10 °C increase in temperature will typically raise the vapor pressure three- to four-fold.

Vapor pressure is determined in the absence of any other material and is a good yardstick to determine relative volatility. Volatility of an herbicide in the field generally takes place while dissolved in water and is determined by Henry's law (Eq. [6]). Henry's law is used to describe the solubility of gases in water and also relates the vapor pressure of any substance in solution as long as the concentration is dilute. As solutions become more concentrated, deviations from Henry's law can occur.

$$P_a = K_h C_a \qquad [6]$$

where P_a is the partial vapor pressure of the herbicide in the vapor phase, C_a is the concentration of the herbicide in the soil solution, and K_h is the dimensionless proportionality constant referred to as the Henry's law con-

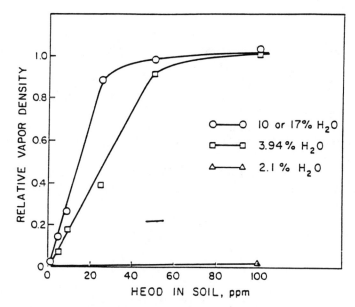

Fig. 5–1. Relative vapor density of dieldrin (HEOD) vs. concentration in Gila silt loam as affected by soil water content. Spencer et al. (129).

stant. It is important to realize that C_a is the solution concentration; sorbed herbicide is nonvolatile.

Water plays two very important roles in herbicide volatility. First, water competes very effectively for adsorption sites on soil colloids. Figure 5–1 displays data from Spencer et al. (129) on the relative vapor density of dieldrin (1,2,3,4,10,10-hexachloro-1R,4S,4aS,5R,6R,7S,8S,8aR-octahydro-6,7-epoxy-1,4:5,8-dimethanonaphthalene) vs. concentration in a soil at different water contents. Relative vapor density is the ratio of measured vapor density to the saturated vapor density of pure dieldrin. In very dry soils, practically no dieldrin volatilization is observed. In wetter soils, i.e., soils with approximately one molecular layer of water, which is still quite dry by plant needs, dieldrin volatilization increases towards a maximum rate as concentration in soil increases. Nonpolar organics such as dieldrin would be expected to partition into organic matter but concentrations at the soil surface will exceed the capacity of the organic matter to sorb the compound. Thus, more polar sites on clay minerals will sorb the nonpolar organic materials by van der Waals' forces when water is absent; however, small quantities of water will displace the nonpolar organics from these sorption sites. The mechanism of sorption at ultra-low water concentrations will not be important in turf since the turfgrass will not survive at the low moisture levels needed to realize significant soil adsorption of pesticides by mineral sites.

The second role water plays in influencing volatilization is in moving the pesticide to the soil surface where volatilization can take place. In traditional row crop agricultural, pesticides may be incorporated to reduce volatility. As the soil dries out, however, upward moving water can carry the pesticide to the surface where it can volatilize (128). This has been shown to be an important mechanism for volatilization of persistent, slightly volatile pesticides under field crop conditions. In turf, however, where irrigation is frequent and evaporation from the soil limited, it is doubtful that this mechanism is very important.

Relative humidity can influence pesticide volatility due to its effects on soil and plant surface drying. A moist soil subjected to air with very little moisture, or low relative humidity, will quickly dry out at the surface level thus reducing herbicide volatilization since the herbicide can then be adsorbed onto the soil. A herbicide applied to turfgrass may volatilize for a longer period of time under high relative humidity conditions because the herbicide droplets will not evaporate as quickly. Under low relative humidity conditions, volatilization may cease at an earlier time as the water from the spray droplets quickly evaporates leaving the herbicide sorbed on the cuticle of the plant, or in the thatch layer.

D. Photolysis

Photolysis occurs when a compound absorbs light energy causing an irreversible change in structure, usually resulting in an alteration or loss of biological activity. All compounds absorb some form of light energy; however, photolysis occurs when the light energy absorption leads to a rearrangement or dissociation of molecular bonds. These changes involve absorption of light energy causing excitation of the electronic structure of the molecule. Less energetic wavelengths of light cause excitation of rotational or vibrational energy levels of the molecule that do not lead to molecular rearrangement or dissociation.

The energy available to cause photolysis is dependent upon the wavelength of the incoming radiation. The energy of a particular wavelength of light, can be calculated using Eq. [7].

$$E = hc/\lambda \qquad\qquad [7]$$

where h is Planck's constant, c is the speed of light in a vacuum, and λ is the wavelength of the light, commonly expressed in nanometers (nm). From Eq. [7], the energy of light is inversely related to the wavelength and, therefore, the shorter the wavelength the more energetic the light.

The amount and energy of light reaching the earth's surface is affected by the earth's atmosphere. Ozone very efficiently absorbs ultraviolet light at wavelengths < 290 nm. Thus, the light energy available to cause photolysis of a molecule lies > 290 nm. This is more than enough energy to disrupt many types of bonds found in common organic molecules.

Photolysis of pesticides is an area that has received sporadic study. Studies are routinely carried out on glass surfaces or in water but infrequently on leaf tissue or soil. Studies on glass surfaces may give information on potential pathways of photolysis but contribute little to our understanding of the impact of photolysis in the overall dissipation of a pesticide.

In a turfgrass ecosystem the major site for photolysis is the leaf surface, with the soil playing a negligible role. Leaf surfaces are the most important site for pesticide photolysis in turf since pesticide sprays are generally deposited on turfgrass leaves. Effects of leaf surfaces on photolytic processes have received little investigation. Articles by Takade et al. (133) and Makary et al. (86) showed no qualitative changes in the kinds of photoproducts produced on the surface of leaves as compared with glass or other surfaces.

Photolysis in turf is likely to occur on the leaf tissue or in solution during the time the spray droplets dry, or during rewetting from irrigation or rainfall. The following discussion centers on photochemistry in the aqueous phase and attempts to show the complexity of the process.

The solvent in which a pesticide is dissolved can have a significant effect on the photolysis of the pesticide. If a solvent can participate in H bonding, the absorption spectra of the pesticide can be shifted to a lower energy (higher wavelength). This can then affect the photolysis of the herbicide if the shift happens to overlap with the energetic portion of the sun's spectra. Water can serve strictly as a solvent with no participation in the photolysis reaction; however, it is probably more common for the water to actively participate in the photoreaction.

The photolysis of 2,4-D involves the active participation of water in the reaction. Crosby and Tutass (34) examined the photolytic degradation of 2,4-D in aqueous solution. They found that hydroxyl ions participated in the photonucleophilic displacement of Cl^- ions from the phenyl ring of the 2,4-D molecule. Thus, water can serve as a reactant as well as a solvent by providing OH^- ions for photonucleophilic reactions. In addition, natural waters, i.e., irrigation waters, contain relatively small quantities of dissolved organics, amino acids, and fatty acids that can serve as photoreactants and sources of reduced H for photoreductions.

Photosensitizers are molecules that can absorb light energy and pass the energy to other molecules, possibly causing the photolysis of those molecules. An herbicide having no ultraviolet absorption spectra can be degraded by accepting the energy from an electronically excited photosensitizer. There are many types of photosensitizers including plant pigments, dyes, small organic molecules, and surfactants. Burkhard and Guth (16) examined the photolysis of several triazine herbicides, including atrazine, with and without acetone. They found that the additions of 1% acetone to the herbicide solution caused a five-fold decrease in the half-life of atrazine.

One area receiving interest is the effect of surfactants on the photolysis process. Surfactants are used in formulating most herbicides and can have a significant effect on herbicide photolysis. Tanaka et al. (134) examined the effect of two surfactants, Triton X-100 and Tergitol TMN-10 (Sigma Chemicals, St. Louis, MO), on the photolysis of some herbicides. TMN-10 has no ultraviolet absorption spectra, while Triton X-100 (photosensitizer) does. They found that surfactants can cause an increased rate of degradation of herbicides that have low water solubilities, chloro substituents, and triplet energies lower then the added photosensitizer (surfactant). Further, they postulated that surfactants can cause photolysis by two mechanisms. First, the micelles that solubilize the herbicide also form a C rich environment around the herbicide with C–H bond energies that are lower than H–O–H bond energies. This creates an environment with a greater chance of production of photoreactive species, such as free radicals and hydride ions. Secondly, surfactants having an aryl substituent, such as Triton X-100, can act as photosensitizers absorbing light energy and passing that energy to the herbicide molecule. Surfactants can also enhance the rate of photolysis reactions by concentrating the reactants. A study by Hautala and Letsinger (63) examined the nucleophilic substitution by CN^- of 4-methoxy-1-nitronapthlene. They found that, in the presence of a cationic surfactant, the quantum yield was increased by a factor of 6800 compared with when no surfactant was present. The cationic surfactant attracted the CN^- ions so that their concentration in the surfactant micelle was much greater than in the bulk solution, accounting for the increased quantum yield.

The above discussion concerns photolysis in water; however, in normal use situations photolysis on the leaf surface or on the soil surface would be most likely to occur.

Hebert and Miller (64) examined the depth of photolysis in field soils and found that direct photolysis depths were ≈ 1 mm. Indirect photolysis, i.e., the production of singlet O at the soil surface, was found to occur at depths of 2 mm. While these depths of penetration are slight, it could be an important loss mechanism since pesticides in soil are often moved to the surface by evaporating water. Unfortunately, similar studies on the extent of photolysis on leaf surfaces are lacking.

E. Herbicide Persistence

All the processes described above act in concert to reduce the level of the herbicide in the soil. Soil persistence is the term used to describe the length of time residues last in the soil. The most accepted means of reporting herbicide persistence is the soil half-life, $t_{1/2}$. The mathematical expression relating degradation to soil half-life is given in Eq. [8].

$$dC/dt = \mu C^n \qquad [8]$$

where C represents pesticide concentration, μ is the dissipation rate constant and n is the reaction rate order. Pesticide degradation is usually approximated by a first order rate process ($n = 1$). If $n = 1$ then integration of eight with respect to time yields

$$C_t = C_o e^{-\mu t} \qquad [9]$$

where C_t equals the pesticide concentration at some time t after application and C_o is the initial pesticide concentration. Solving for $t_{1/2}$ ($C_t = 1/2\ C_o$) yields

$$t_{1/2} = 0.693/\mu \qquad [10]$$

Thus, if the $t_{1/2}$ value is experimentally determined in the field or lab, estimates of μ, in units of per day, can be made. Nash (93) has compiled a listing of dissipation rate constants for a wide range of herbicides. The rate constants determined by this approach do not necessarily have a wide application since they may be specific to the site and conditions under which the $t_{1/2}$ value was determined. As an example, a rate constant determined under warm, moist soil conditions would not be applicable to predict degradation under cold, dry conditions. Thus, rate constants or $t_{1/2}$ values can be used as yardsticks to give estimations of degradation rates, but can vary widely based on site conditions, environmental conditions, and whether the studies are conducted in the field or laboratory. Laboratory studies tend to yield longer $t_{1/2}$ values since usually only one or two modes of pesticide dissipation are operative in laboratory settings.

F. The Turfgrass Ecosystem

Compared with traditional agriculture, turf is an unique cropping system in that it is a perennial crop and, except at establishment, pesticides and fertilizers are not applied to soil but instead to the plants themselves. That portion of the spray or granules that is not intercepted by the foliage is deposited in the thatch, which is a layer of living and dead roots, stems, and leaves in various states of decomposition. Thus, the soil underlying a turfgrass community may receive only a small fraction of the original dose of the applied pesticide.

Turfgrass researchers (69, 70) have recognized the role of thatch as a buffer to the soil and that thatch will retain or retard the movement of most pesticides. However, most researchers have ignored the role of the plant community in considering pesticide fate. The importance of the plant community was illustrated in a recent article by Stahnke et al. (130) on the persistence of pendimethalin [N-(1-ethylpropyl)-3,4-dimethyl-2,6-dinitrobenzenamine]. At application, nearly 95% of the applied pendimethalin was sorbed by the plants. Very little reached the thatch and none was detected in the soil. The effect of plant community and thatch will be largest for those pesticides with large K_{oc} coefficients that would be expected to partition readily into organic matter.

Studies comparing the volatility and photolysis of pesticides from turf are limited. Cooper et al. (32) reported on the volatility of pendimethalin from turf and Glotfelty and coworkers (46) have examined the volatility of herbicides used in turf from fallow soil but there has been only one study comparing volatility of the same herbicide from turf vs. bare soil. Nash and Hill (95) studied the volatilization of trifluralin [2,6-dinitro-N,N-dipropyl-4-(trifluoromethyl)benzenamine] and dieldrin from a weedy turf and fallow soil in enclosed chambers. Both pesticides were more volatile from turf than from bare soil. The flux of trifluralin was much higher during the first day after application from turf than from fallow soil. Nash and Hill (95) attributed the higher flux from turf to its larger surface area and they believed that air circulation and transfer would be greater for turf than bare soil.

More research is needed to examine the role of turf as it affects pesticide fate. Losses due to volatility, photolysis, and microbial decomposition will be impacted by the plant community. The magnitude of these differences will be important to quantify and will help develop a theoretical understanding of the impact of turf on pesticide fate. As we understand the effects of turf on pesticide fate, this knowledge can be incorporated into computer models that are currently being used to predict the fate of pesticides in row crop agriculture. This knowledge should create a bridge allowing researchers to transfer information developed in row crops to turf situations.

II. FATE OF HERBICIDES IN TURF

A. Preemergence Grass Herbicides

Preemergence herbicides are widely used to control large crabgrass [*Digitaria sanguinalis* (L.) Scop.], goosegrass [*Eleusine indica* (L.) Gaertn.], and other annual grasses. Some generalizations can be made concerning the fate of these herbicides in turf. Because preemergence herbicides are applied months before weed seed germination ceases, the herbicide must remain at the soil surface in sufficient concentration to provide effective weed control. Thus, by necessity, preemergence herbicides are relatively immobile in soil. Leaching losses of preemergence herbicides are generally insignificant. Preemergence herbicides are characterized by low water solubility, limited leaching potential, and $t_{1/2} > 30$ d.

Preemergence herbicides act by forming a chemical barrier to the weed. As weed seeds germinate, the developing shoot and root systems contact and absorb the herbicide resulting in death of the seedling, usually through inhibition of root growth. Thus, it is important to uniformly cover the turf with the herbicide in order to achieve satisfactory weed control.

Because of the low water solubility and limited leaching of the preemergence herbicides, soil types have a minor effect on the depth of leaching. Specially constructed turf areas, such as golf course greens or athletic fields, whose soil type is sand or modified sand, may still show little leaching of these herbicides.

Preemergence herbicides are applied at rates that yield an effective concentration at the soil surface that is substantially higher than the critical concentration needed for weed control. As time progresses, however, the herbicide concentration is reduced by processes such as photolysis, microbial decomposition, volatilization, and leaching. Ideally, the herbicide concentration remains above the minimum for weed control to provide season-long weed control. If the concentration should fall below the minimum, a second application would be needed to extend the weed control period throughout the summer, or a postemergence herbicide could be used.

Table 5-2. Selected chemical properties of preemergence grass herbicides†.

Herbicide	Solubility	Half-life	K_{oc}	Vapor pressure
	mg L^{-1}	d	mL g^{-1}	mm Hg
benefin	0.1	40	9000	6.6×10^{-5}
trifluralin	0.3	60	8000	1.1×10^{-4}
pendimethalin	0.275	90	5000	9.4×10^{-6}
DCPA	0.5	100	5000	2.5×10^{-6}
bensulide	5.6	120	1000	8.0×10^{-7}
oxadiazon	0.7	60	3200	1×10^{-6}
siduron	18	90	420	4.0×10^{-9}
linuron	75	60	400	1.7×10^{-5}
ethofumesate	50	30	340	4.9×10^{-6}
pronamide	15	60	800	8.5×10^{-5}

† From Wauchope et al. (146).

The following sections will discuss the fate of each of the preemergence herbicides currently used in turf. Most research on these herbicides was conducted under field crop management and these sources will be used to describe the fate of the herbicide. Limited research exists as to how a turfgrass ecosystem affects pesticide fate; this information, where it exists, will be included. Chemical properties of the preemergence herbicides used in turf are shown in Table 5-2.

1. Benefin

Dinitroaniline herbicides such as benefin [N-butyl-N-ethyl-2,6-dinitro-4-(trifluoromethyl)benzenamine] are strongly sorbed to soil. Various authors have determined K_d and K_{oc} values for the dinitroaniline herbicides (71, 114) and Weber (147) has recently reviewed dinitroaniline behavior in soils. These values vary widely, for example Jacques and Harvey (71) report an average K_{oc} value of 410 for benefin, while Scott and Phillips (114) report a K_d value of 62.5, which can be converted to a K_{oc} value of 1520. Wauchope et al. (146) have compiled a pesticide properties database and they report a K_{oc} value of 9000 for benefin, which indicates that benefin is strongly sorbed by soil (Table 5-2). Hurto and Turgeon (70) used a procedure similar to that of Scott and Phillips (114) to examine the effect of turfgrass thatch on the binding of benefin, bensulide [O,O-bis(1-methylethyl) S-[2-[(phenylsulfonyl)amino]ethyl]phosphorodithioate], and DCPA (dimethyl 2,3,5,6-tetrachloro-1,4-benzenedicarboxylate). Hurto and Turgeon (70) did not calculate K_d values, but reported the percent sorbed over time. They found that sorption in soil, from highest to lowest, was in the order of bensulide, DCPA, and benefin. When these herbicides were equilibrated with ground thatch, all three herbicides were sorbed to a greater extent by thatch than by soil, on a weight basis.

Due to the strong soil adsorption of benefin, leaching losses would be expected to be minimal. Anderson et al. (6) examined the leaching of benefin, trifluralin, and nitralin in soils columns. They found that nitralin was the most easily leached, while benefin was the least mobile. Bioassays with jungle rice [*Echinochloa colonum* (L.) Link] showed that benefin was leached in small quantities into the 6 cm (2.5-in.) layer whereas trifluralin was found in the 9 cm (3.5-in.) layer.

Golab et al. (48) examined the rate of degradation of benefin in flooded (anaerobic) and moist (aerobic) soils. Degradation occurred much faster under anaerobic than aerobic conditions. Under anaerobic conditions only 4.6% benefin remained after 16 d whereas under aerobic conditions 47.4% remained after 28 d. Additionally, after this 28-d period, the loss rate slowed considerably so that after 260 d, 20% of the benefin still remained in the aerobic soil. The authors attributed this rapid initial loss under aerobic conditions to volatilization.

Several studies have examined the photolysis of benefin. Parochetti and Dec (100), in studying the photolysis of eleven dinitroaniline herbicides, applied the benefin to dry, thin-layer soil plates and exposed the plates to sunlight. During a 7-d period, 17.1% of the benefin was lost due to photolysis. This was a moderate loss rate for the dinitroaniline herbicides tested.

Parochetti et al. (101) studied the volatility of 11 dinitroaniline herbicides from a Lakeland sand (thermic, coated Typic Quartzipsamment) at soil temperatures of 30, 40, and 50 °C and 7% soil moisture. Benefin losses at 30, 40 and 50 °C were 2.4, 11.5, and 25.0%, respectively. Parochetti and Hein (102) found that trifluralin was more volatile than benefin under similar conditions. At 50 °C and 8% soil moisture on a Lakeland sand, $\approx 25\%$ of the trifluralin and 12.5% of the benefin were lost to volatilization during a 3-h period. The authors also compared the effects of spray vs. granular applications of benefin and trifluralin on the volatility of these two herbicides. A trend was found towards less volatilization from a granular formulation, but it was not significant. Harvey (61) examined volatility effects on 12 dinitroaniline herbicides and found benefin to be among six of the herbicides, including trifluralin, that were the most volatile.

The bottom line for any preemergence herbicide is persistence. Again, much variability will be expected from the data. The herbicide handbook of the Weed Science Society of America (150) states that benefin provides season-long weed control. Burnside et al. (17) in studies conducted in south Georgia on peanut (*Arachis hypogaea* L.) found no accumulation of benefin residues after 3 yr of successive applications. In all years, <10% of the benefin remained in the soil 1 yr after treatment. Miller et al. (91) studied soil persistence of trifluralin and benefin using two times the rates for weed control in cotton (*Gossypium hirsutum* L.) and found that benefin and trifluralin behaved similarly with respect to persistence. Both were present in sufficient quantities to injure grain sorghum [*Sorghum bicolor* (L.) Moench.] 15 mo after the final application. After 30 mo, residue levels were at the limit of chromatographic detection and did not injure grain sorghum. Hurto et al. (69) examined the fate of benefin when incubated in ground soil or thatch during a 16-wk period. In soil, $\approx 90\%$ of the benefin remained unchanged after 16 wk. Zimdahl and Gwynn (155) examined benefin degradation in two soil types, an Ascalon sandy loam (fine-loamy, mixed, mesic

Aridic Argiustoll) and Weld loam (fine, montmorillonitic, mesic Aridic Paleustoll); at 30 °C, the half-lives were 6 and 3 wk, respectively.

Benefin is a relatively long lived herbicide in the soil with an expected $t_{1/2}$ of 40 d (146). Soil type, organic matter content, soil moisture content, soil temperature and other edaphic factors will cause variability in the $t_{1/2}$ of benefin.

2. Trifluralin

Trifluralin behaves very similarly to benefin. It is strongly sorbed in soils, although not quite as strongly as benefin (Table 5-2). Grover (52) examined the adsorption of trifluralin by different adsorbents and found that it was strongly adsorbed by activated charcoal and peat moss, and weakly adsorbed by kaolinite and montmorillonite clays. Harvey (61) observed that trifluralin was moderately adsorbed by a Plano silt loam soil (fine-silty, mesic Typic Argiudoll) when compared with 11 other dinitroaniline herbicides.

Trifluralin is similar in leaching potential to benefin. Anderson et al. (6) found that trifluralin was slightly more leachable than benefin. Their experiments with soil showed some inhibition of jungle rice growth to depth of 9 cm (3.5 in.) with trifluralin vs. 6 cm (2.5 in.) with benefin; however, with sorghum as a bioassay plant, growth reductions were only seen to a 6 cm (2-in.) depth with trifluralin. Harris (60) examined the mobility of 28 herbicides in soil columns and found that benefin and trifluralin were among the least mobile of the herbicides tested.

Trifluralin is rapidly lost from anaerobic soils (103, 106, 110, 152), much in the same manner as benefin. Probst et al. (106) found that trifluralin degraded at essentially the same rate in nonautoclaved soil as in autoclaved soil at 24 °C. At 3 °C, the nonautoclaved soil caused trifluralin to degrade more rapidly than the autoclaved soil. Savage (110) measured $t_{1/2}$ values for trifluralin. Under aerobic conditions, $t_{1/2}$ for trifluralin was 55 d whereas, under anaerobic conditions, $t_{1/2}$ was 6 d. Willis et al. (152) showed two distinct rates of trifluralin degradation under different redox potentials and anaerobic conditions. At higher redox potentials, a slower rate of trifluralin degradation was observed with 60% of the trifluralin remaining at 20 days after treatment (DAT). However, more-reduced, lower E_h systems had no trifluralin remaining at 8 DAT. Parr and Smith (103) studied trifluralin degradation under anaerobic conditions. They demonstrated that trifluralin degradation under anaerobic conditions was primarily a microbial process and required the addition of organic matter to proceed. These results may explain the results of Willis et al. (152) since organic matter additions to an anaerobic system would lead to more-reduced, or lower, E_h systems. Trifluralin is rapidly decomposed under anaerobic conditions; however, degradation under aerobic conditions proceeds much more slowly. Carter and Camper (23) were able to isolate two members of the genus *Pseudomonas* capable of utilizing trifluralin as a sole source of C.

Trifluralin is susceptible to photolysis. Parachetti and Dec (100) exposed soil plates uniformly treated with trifluralin to sunlight for 7 d and found that 18.4% was lost due to photolysis during this time period.

Trifluralin is considered quite volatile and in most field crops the herbicide is incorporated after application to minimize volatility and photolysis losses. Parochetti et al. (101) examined the volatility of 11 dinitroaniline herbicides and found that trifluralin was very volatile with >20% lost in 3 h from a Lakeland sand at 7% soil moisture and 50 °C. Trifluralin loss was also measured from two soils maintained at field moisture capacity and 50 °C. Almost 35% trifluralin was lost from a Hagerstown clay loam (fine, mixed, mesic Typic Hapludalf) as compared with 17% from a Littleton silt loam (fine-silty, mixed, mesic Cumulic Hapludoll). The silt loam soil had an organic matter content of 5.2 vs. 1.9% for the clay loam soil. The higher adsorptive capacity of organic matter for trifluralin as shown by Grover (52) may explain the difference in volatility. Ketchersid et al. (80) studied trifluralin volatilization from a commercial sand and a Miller clay (fine, mixed, thermic Vertic Haplustoll), each soil at either 75% of field capacity or air dry when treated. More than 50% of the trifluralin was lost from the wet sand during a 24-h period, while the wet clay lost ≈45% during the same time period. When the soils were oven dry, only 11% was lost from each soil type. Water, therefore, will compete with the dinitroanilines for adsorption sites on the soil, and wet soils or foliage will lose much more of the herbicide than dry soils. The best data on trifluralin volatility comes from a field scale study of volatility losses of trifluralin from fallow soil (46). Where the soil surface was moist and trifluralin was not incorporated, 50% of the applied trifluralin was volatilized in 7.5 h with 90% lost after 7 d. Where the soil surface was dry, between 2 and 25% of the trifluralin was volatilized in 50 h. These data, coupled with a higher trifluralin flux rate from turf than from fallow soil (95), indicate that volatilization losses could be substantial for trifluralin applied to turf.

The resulting persistence of the herbicide in turf is difficult to pinpoint. In soils where trifluralin is incorporated, residues equal to 10 to 15% of the amount applied can usually be found 1 yr after application, but residues do not accumulate with repeated applications. In turf, trifluralin is applied as a granular product and the effects of volatility and photolysis are not clear. The work of Parochetti and Hein (102) would indicate that granules tend to exhibit less volatility than sprayable products. It would seem to be especially important to ensure that either rainfall or irrigation follow an application of benefin or trifluralin to move the herbicide into the thatch to reduce volatility and photolysis losses.

3. Pendimethalin

Pendimethalin is a relatively new herbicide for use in turf, but it has been the subject of much research in row crops. A review of the literature found no data detailing the strength of adsorption of pendimethalin in soils. Harvey (61) examined strength of adsorption of 12 dinitroaniline herbicides (pendimethalin was omitted) and found that they were all strongly adsorbed by a Plano silt loam soil. A K_{oc} value of 5000 (146; Table 5–2) indicates that pendimethalin is tightly sorbed by soils.

Due to the strong adsorption by most soils the leaching potential of pendimethalin is slight. Berayon and Mercado (11) found very little leaching out of the 0- to 5-cm layer of soil. This agrees with the findings for other dinitroaniline herbicides that show minimal leaching (6, 91).

Evidence for microbial degradation points to the same pattern as seen for benefin and trifluralin; dinitroanilines are susceptible to microbial decomposition and are degraded much more rapidly in anaerobic soil than in aerobic soil. Savage (110) calculated a $t_{1/2}$ of 7 d for pendimethalin degradation in flooded soils and 82 d for aerobic soils.

The photolysis of pendimethalin has been studied by several authors. Parochetti and Dec (100) reported the photolysis of 11 dinitroaniline herbicides and found that 10% of the pendimethalin had photodecomposed during a 7-d exposure to natural sunlight. Of the dinitroaniline herbicides examined by Parochetti and Dec (100), pendimethalin was one of the least susceptible to photolysis. Savage and Jordon (111) examined the persistence of pendimethalin applied to bare soil. To determine the effect of direct sunlight on herbicide loss rates, treatments consisted of shaded vs. unshaded plots. The rate of loss of pendimethalin was much lower under shaded conditions where no loss was detected until after 3 d. Where pendimethalin was exposed to direct sunlight on the soil surface, however, 56% remained after 3 d. Some of the losses under nonshaded conditions could have resulted from increased volatility due to the soil surface temperature differences between shaded and nonshaded plots. Recent studies on pendimethalin photolysis (36, 98) have examined the pathway of pendimethalin photolysis. Dureja and Walia (36) studied the photolysis of pendimethalin on soil but used a low pressure Hg lamp for the light source instead of sunlight. They recovered 78% of the pendimethalin after 48 h of irradiation. Photolysis losses from leaf surfaces have not been studied.

Volatility has also been studied by several authors. Parochetti et al. (101) reported data on the volatility of 11 dinitroaniline herbicides. They found pendimethalin to be moderately volatile losing about 4% in a 3-h period at 50 °C and 7% soil moisture. Benefin and trifluralin lost 24 and 22%, respectively, under the same conditions. Oliver (96) studied the volatility of trifluralin and pendimethalin from a Matapeake loam soil (fine-loamy, mixed, mesic Typic Hapludult). The experiment was conducted during a 28-d period and the importance of using time periods longer than the 3-h period used by other authors was shown. Trifluralin volatilized much more rapidly initially than did pendimethalin; however, pendimethalin continued to volatilize at a steady rate during the course of the experiment, while trifluralin leveled off after ≈ 10 d. Thus, during the 28-d period, trifluralin losses were near 20%, while pendimethalin losses were at 11%.

Cooper et al. (32) reported results on the volatilization of pendimethalin when applied to a Kentucky bluegrass (*Poa pratensis* L.) turf. The study was conducted in the field using glass chambers to quantitatively assess volatilization. The authors observed a diphasic pattern of loss with a more rapid rate of loss during the first 5 d following application and then a much slower, linear rate of loss until the end of the 15-d sampling period. Losses due to volatility, expressed as the percentage of the initially applied dose, were 4.8, 6.1, and 13% at 1, 2, and 5 d after application, respectively.

The persistence of pendimethalin in soils has been extensively studied. Walker and Bond (143) examined the degradation of pendimethalin in seven soils and found $t_{1/2}$ values ranging from 72 to 172 d. The $t_{1/2}$ values tended to increase with increasing soil organic matter. In a Sheeps Pen soil, the $t_{1/2}$ values were 98, 122, 168, 265, and 409 d when the soil temperatures were constant at 30, 25, 20, 15, or 10 °C, respectively. In field experiments where pendimethalin was incorporated into the soil, nearly 80% could be recovered 20 wk after application whereas only 25% could be recovered if pendimethalin was not incorporated. Zimdahl et al. (154) found shorter $t_{1/2}$ than did Walker and Bond (143). Zimdahl et al. (154) found $t_{1/2}$ ranging from 42 to 54 d for three soil types at 30 °C and 75% of field capacity and also showed that $t_{1/2}$ will increase as soil moisture content decreases.

Persistence studies in turf have recently been reported (130). This study was important because the authors examined the leaf tissue for pendimethalin residues. Perhaps as the result of agronomic training, residue studies conducted in turf traditionally examined the soil, while discarding the thatch and leaf tissue. The work of Hurto and Turgeon (70) pointed out the impact of thatch on the fate of pesticides applied to turf, but these investigators did not examine the leaf tissue. Stahnke et al. (130) found that, at application, >95% of the applied pendimethalin was sorbed to the leaf surface. The leaf fraction still contained 44% of the recovered pendimethalin at 20 DAT with an additional 53% in the thatch layer. Very little pendimethalin ever reached the underlying soil. The highest amount of pendimethalin in the soil was 22% of the recovered pendimethalin at 84 DAT. The total amount of pendimethalin remaining at 84 DAT was <1% of the original dose; thus, the actual amount in the soil at 84 DAT was quite small.

Pendimethalin is a relatively persistent herbicide (Table 5-2). Primary loss mechanisms are volatility, photodecomposition, and microbial degradation. It would seem to be very important, therefore, to use irrigation to move the dinitroaniline herbicides into the thatch in order to prevent excessive losses of the herbicide. The dinitroanilines are persistent if not exposed to direct sunlight and if the surface concentration is reduced by postapplication irrigation.

4. DCPA

DCPA is widely used on many ornamental and vegetable crops, but not on any of the major field crops. Consequently, very little data exist on the strength or extent of sorption of DCPA to soils. Hurto and Turgeon (70) compared the sorption of DCPA in soil and thatch with the herbicides benefin and bensulide. They found that DCPA was most strongly sorbed to thatch while, in soil, the order was bensulide > DCPA > benefin. The K_{oc} values reported in Table 5-2 would indicate that benefin is more strongly sorbed to organic matter than DCPA.

Because of the strong adsorption of DCPA, leaching of the parent herbicide is not a concern with this herbicide. Hurto et al. (69) examined the mobility of DCPA in soil and thatch columns. They found increased mobility of all herbicides studied in thatch compared with soil. Very little DCPA moved from the 0- to 1-cm layer of a soil profile; however, >20% of the applied DCPA was found in the 1- to 2-cm thatch layer. This amount of movement is still insignificant with respect to the soil profile. Miller et al. (91) compared the movement of 10 herbicides used in cotton plantings; they classed DCPA as having the lowest mobility of the herbicides studied and equal to that of benefin and trifluralin. While DCPA itself is immobile in soils, the degradation products of DCPA, tetrachloro-1,4-benzene dicarboxylic acid and tetrachloro monomethyl ester -1,4-benzene dicarboxylic acid, are organic acids that are very mobile and very persistent in soils. The mobility and persistence of these metabolites were convincingly determined in the recently completed well-water survey conducted by the USEPA (137); metabolites of DCPA were the most frequently detected pesticide product found in wells in the USA with more detections of these metabolites than all other pesticides combined (137). The biological activities of the metabolites have not been documented but the continued use of this product in light of the many competing herbicides available for use in turf must be questioned.

Tweedy et al. (136) showed an enhanced rate of growth of actinomycetes when exposed to high concentrations of DCPA. At normal field concentrations, however, stimulatory effects from DCPA on soil microorganisms were observed. Since the two major metabolites of DCPA degradation were the half acid and diacid, there was very little C available for microorganisms to utilize and the degradation of DCPA by microorganisms would surely be considered a cometabolic process.

Photolysis of DCPA has not been studied in a field situation. Chen et al. (24) examined the photolysis of DCPA by exposing thin films of DCPA to a ultraviolet light source. They found very rapid photolysis with >50% lost after 5-h exposure. They also detected a product, tetrachlorobenzene, that has not previously been observed in studies of DCPA degradation (38, 45). Chen et al. (24) used a light source at 254 mm, which is much more energetic than sunlight. The increased energy could be responsible for the rate and extent of degradation observed.

Volatilization of DCPA has been studied by several researchers. Branham (15) did not detect any volatilization of DCPA during a 2-mo period when using a microecosystem to determine the fate of DPCA. Glotfelty et al. (46) studied the volatilization of DCPA when applied to fallow soil using air sampling methods to determine volatility losses. When comparing DCPA and trifluralin, Glotfelty et al. (46) saw 2% DCPA volatilized during a 34-h period, whereas 50% of the trifluralin was lost in 7.5 h. Volatilization losses of DCPA appear to be minimal.

DCPA is a fairly persistent preemergence herbicide. Walker (142) determined the $t_{1/2}$ of DCPA under a variety of conditions and calculated values from 295 d at 5 °C and 3.7% moisture to 13 d at 30 °C and 9.5% moisture, respectively. Of the eight herbicides studied by Walker (142), he found DCPA to be the most dependent on soil temperature. A change from 30 to 10 °C at constant soil moisture resulted in a 17.9-fold increase in $t_{1/2}$.

Choi et al. (27) conducted a study similar to that of Walker (142) by following the degradation of DCPA in a silt loam under various soil temperature and soil moisture regimes. They found that $t_{1/2}$ ranged from 11 d under optimal conditions (25–30 °C, 20% soil moisture) to 105 d under conditions of 10 °C soil temperature and 10% soil moisture. Regression analysis indicated that soil temperature was more important than soil moisture on DCPA degradation. A study by Branham (15) was conducted using model ecosystsems under controlled conditions to examine the degradation of DCPA applied to a turf. Half lives in this study were much higher than those found in the Choi et al. (27) or Walker (142) studies. Only one treatment had more than 50% DCPA degradation when the study was terminated at 56 DAT.

5. Bensulide

Bensulide is an organophosphorus herbicide used to control annual grasses in turf. No studies on the extent of adsorption of bensulide were found in the literature. Values of K_{oc} have been estimated based on water solubility data, although these estimates show wide variance (e.g., 740 to 46 000) (146); an estimated value of 1000 (Table 5–2) indicates that bensulide is strongly sorbed in soils, though not to the same degree as the dinitroanilines. It has a tendency to leach to a somewhat greater depth than the other preemergence herbicides. For a preemergence herbicide, it has a relatively high water solubility of 26 mg L^{-1}. Miller et al. (91) examined the persistence and movement of 10 herbicides including bensulide. Bensulide was detected at depths of 90 to 120 cm (35–47 in.) in this study. Concentrations as high as 0.8 mg kg^{-1} were detected in the 15- to 30-cm (6–12 in.) layer, which is directly underneath the zone of incorporation. While bensulide was detected at fairly deep soil depths, the concentration found was low and in the range of 0.15 to 0.01 mg kg^{-1}. Menges and Tamez (90) found some movement of bensulide out of the zone of incorporation and into lower soil depths, but attributed this to deep plowing of the carrot beds. An earlier study by Menges and Hubbard (89) saw movement of bensulide below the zone of incorporation, with $\approx 40\%$ of the bensulide found in this lower layer. Bensulide has more leaching potential than other turf preemergence herbicides, but the amount of leaching is likely to be slight.

Ahrens (1) applied bensulide at 22.4 kg ha^{-1} (20 lb acre^{-1}) in early May of 1965 and 1966. Soil samples in May of 1967, 1 yr after the second application, found the equivalent of 7.8 kg ha^{-1} (7 lb acre^{-1}) in the upper 15 cm (6 in.) of soil. This would indicate that two successive applications at high rates (label recommendations call for 14 kg ha^{-1} [12.5 lb acre^{-1}]) could leave enough residual activity to yield some crabgrass control the following season. Bingham and Schmidt (14) also examined bensulide residues about 11 mo after four consecutive yearly applications of 16.8 kg ha^{-1} (15 lb acre^{-1}). They found that residues of the emulsifiable concentrate formulation could not be detected with the bioassay technique employed, which could detect concentrations > 8 mg kg^{-1} in the soil surface layer. However, 27 mg kg^{-1} concentrations were found in the surface 2.5-cm (1 in.) layer from granular applications of bensulide. Menges and Tamez (90) found considerable herbicidal activity 6 mo after application but very little 12 mo after application when using an Italian millet [*Setaria italica* (L.) P. Beauv.] bioassay. There seems to be some belief within the turfgrass industry that, after several years of repeated applications, enough residual herbicide will remain to provide effective grass control for another season. This may have resulted from the work of Ahrens (1). However, Millet et al. (91) observed a tendency for increased breakdown of bensulide and DCPA residues after 3 yr of successive applications. Their study included 6 yr of successive treatments and they observed less residues in the last 3 yr of their study than in the first 3 yr.

Very little research has been reported in the literature on the photolysis, volatilization or microbial decomposition of bensulide. The Weed Science Society Handbook (150) states that bensulide is not susceptible to volatilization, is photodecomposed to a limited extent, and is slowly degraded by microorganisms.

6. Oxadiazon

Oxadiazon [3-[2,4-dichloro-5-(1-methylethoxy)phenyl]-5-(1,1-dimethylethyl)-1,3,4-oxadiazol-2-(3H)-one] was introduced in 1969 as a specialty use herbicide and has not been the subject of extensive research on its environmental fate. What is known concerning the environmental fate of oxadiazon comes from other cropping systems; the fate of oxadiazon in a turfgrass ecosystem has not been examined.

The water solubility of oxadiazon is very low (0.7 mg L^{-1}) (Table 5–2) and, like most other preemergence herbicides, it is strongly sorbed onto soil. Carringer et al. (22) studied the adsorption and desorption of oxadiazon and found it to be strongly adsorbed to organic matter but not appreciably sorbed by montmorillonite clay. Thus, soil organic matter is the controlling factor in determining the extent of sorption of oxadiazon in soils.

Leaching of oxadiazon in five soils was determined by Ambrosi and Helling (4). They used a soil thin-layer chromatographic procedure to study leaching. Oxadiazon was found to be relatively immobile in four of the soils but did move somewhat in a Lakeland sandy loam soil. With the exception of the Lakeland soil, the higher the organic matter content, the less mobile was oxadiazon.

There is a lack of information concerning microbial degradation. An article by Ambrosi et al. (5) examined the metabolism of phenyl-^{14}C oxadiazon in two soils maintained in an aerobic or anaerobic state. They found very little ^{14}CO$_2$ production, indicating very little microbial degradation of the phenyl ring of oxadiazon. There are several other sites on the oxadiazon molecule that may be susceptible to microbial degradation; this study did not document whether microbes attack these sites on the oxadiazon molecule. No information could be found in the literature concerning the photolysis of oxadiazon.

Ambrosi et al. (5) monitored volatility losses in their studies and found only 1.1% of the applied oxadiazon had been volatilized during a 25-wk period. The soil was formulated so as to simulate incorporation; therefore, surface applications may be subject to greater volatility losses than where incorporated.

Ambrosi et al. (5) found >80% of the applied oxadiazon 25 wk after application. Flooding the soils slowed the rate of oxadiazon decomposition. Barrett and Lavy (7) studied the effects of soil water content on oxadiazon dissipation in upland and flooded rice (*Oryza sativa* L.) cropping systems. Under laboratory conditions, they found that soil water content had little effect on the rate of oxadiazon dissipation and an average of 59% of the applied oxadiazon remained 20 wk after application. In field experiments, however, observed rates of dissipation were much more rapid, with $t_{1/2}$ of 6 to 11 d under a flush irrigation followed by flooding and 15 to 17 d under irrigated, nonflooded conditions. The authors postulated that oxadiazon undergoes a two-phase pseudo-first order degradation rate that includes an initial rapid loss of oxidation in the first 10 to 40 d, followed by a second phase that resulted in a much slower rate of oxadiazon dissipation. The rate of dissipation during the second phase was similar to that observed in laboratory studies. The authors reasoned that sorbed oxadiazon degrades more slowly than nonsorbed oxadiazon and that the field applications, which were surface applied, result in an initial concentration of nonsorbed oxadiazon, which is more rapidly degraded, resulting in the observed rapid initial loss in the field. Other avenues of dissipation could be operating in the field, particularly photolysis, that could also be responsible for the rapid initial loss of oxadiazon. Laboratory studies such as those discussed above can give false impressions of herbicide persistence, since applications of oxadiazon in the field would not be expected to have 80% of their original activity 6 mo after application. Burnside and Schultz (19) applied oxadiazon to soybean [*Glycine max* (L.) Merr.] planted 13 May and performed bioassays on 1 August for three consecutive years. They saw no injury to winter wheat (*Triticum aestivum* L.) from oxadiazon applications made 12 wk earlier. Nash and Dernoeden (94) found that waiting 20 wk after spring application of oxadiazon provided the best establishment of perennial ryegrass (*Lolium perenne* L.). Establishment at 15 wk was poor, but so were environmental conditions for germination. In light of the results of Burnside and Schultz (19), it would appear the residual activity of oxadiazon would be in the range of 8 to 15 wk. The $t_{1/2}$ value of 120 d in Table 5-2 from Wauchope et al. (146) would probably be high for most use conditions.

7. Linuron

Linuron [N'-(3,4-dichlorophenyl)-N-methoxy-N-methylurea] has been used on a wide array of crops and has received much investigation. Linuron is strongly sorbed by organic matter (57, 85). McNamara and Toth (85) found up to 80% linuron adsorption by humic acid. Hance (57) decreased the K value from 30.3 to 6.2 by removing the organic matter from the soil with H_2O_2 oxidation. This treatment also increased the half-life from 87 to 220 d. Thus, organic matter binds linuron more strongly than other soil constituents and also provides the energy substrates for the microbial populations that ultimately degrade linuron. The microbial degradation of linuron has been described as a cometabolic process by Torstensson (135) and microbes have long been thought to be the major pathway for linuron disappearance (43).

Linuron is not very mobile in most soils. Harris (60) studied the movement of 28 herbicides in soil columns with two different soil types. Linuron was less mobile than all the substituted urea herbicides tested, the triazine herbicides, and the organic acid herbicides. Linuron was more mobile than the dinitroanilines tested.

Very little information could be found on the photolysis of linuron. An article by Tanaka et al. (134) examined the effect of surfactants on herbicide photolysis. They found 67% photolysis of linuron in water. When photolyzed in the presence of 0.2 percent Triton X-100 surfactant, photolysis increased to 75%. The Triton X-100 can act as a photosensitizer and increase the rate of linuron photolysis. No informaiton could be found concerning the amount of photolysis of linuron when applied to soil; however, the Weed Science Society of America handbook (150) reports negligible photolysis losses under normal use conditions.

The $t_{1/2}$ values for linuron vary with soil type, temperature, and moisture status. Walker and Thompson (144) studied the degradation of linuron in 18 different soils. They found the half-life for linuron to vary from 22 to 86 d with soils incubated at 25 °C. They also determined that linuron decomposition was correlated to microbial respiration, clay and organic matter content, and the amount of linuron adsorption. Kempson-Jones and Hance (76) determined $t_{1/2}$ of linuron in two different soils at various moisture levels and depths to vary between 20 and 147 d when incubated at 22 °C. Clearly, there is a wide variance in linuron half-life. Most researchers place the half-life of linuron in soils between 8 and 12 wk (Table 5-2).

8. Siduron

Not much information exists concerning the fate of siduron [N-(2-methylcyclohexyl)-N'-phenylurea] in the soil. Weed et al. (149) reported that siduron was resistant to leaching, volatilization, and photolysis. Helling (65), in reporting the relative mobilities of 34 herbicides, found siduron to be classed as a low mobility herbicide, but slightly more mobile than linuron.

The only other information available on siduron comes from a study by Belasco and Langsdorf (10). The soil degradation of siduron was followed in the field using a Keyport silt loam soil (clayey, mixed, mesic Aquic Hapludult). Analysis of soil samples at 1, 2, 6, and 12 mo after application indicated a half-life of between 16 and 20 wk. Very little movement of the radiolabeled siduron was detected below the 2.5-cm soil depth. One year after application, 18.1% of the applied radioactivity remained as the parent herbicide. Soil microbiological studies indicated two bacteria and one fungal species capable of degrading siduron. Microbial degradation was implicated as the primary loss mechanism for siduron.

9. Ethofumesate

Ethofumesate [(±)-2-ethoxy-2,3-dihydro-3,3-dimethyl-5-benzofuranyl methanesulfonate] is a preemergence herbicide labeled to control annual bluegrass (*P. annua* L.) in perennial ryegrass, Kentucky bluegrass, creeping bentgrass (*Agrostis stolonifera* L.), and bermudagrass [*Cynodon dactylon* (L.) Pers.]. Ethofumesate is an unusual herbicide in that it appears to function as both a preemergence and a postemergent herbicide when controlling annual bluegrass. More research is needed to determine optimum conditions for ethofumesate activity, but this herbicide appears to hold promise as a means of controlling annual bluegrass.

The adsorption of ethofumesate by soil was discussed in a study by Van Hoogstraten et al. (138) who reported a K_d value of 6.5. Diuron was included as a standard compound and yielded a higher K_d value of 22. Therefore, it would appear that ethofumesate is only moderately sorbed by most soils (Table 5–2).

Leaching studies with ethofumesate (138) had indicated that leaching was not likely to cause ethofumesate to move beyond a depth of 10 cm (4 in.). While the results of Van Hoogstraten et al. (138) suggested slight leaching potential. Helling (65) placed ethofumesate in Mobility Class 4, which is moderately high soil mobility. Class 5 is the highest mobility classification and contains only organic acid herbicides such as dicamba (3,6-dichloro-2-methoxybenzoic acid) and chloramben (3-amino-2,5-dichlorobenzoic acid). Based on the moderate soil adsorption and moderately long $t_{1/2}$ values, ethofumesate would appear to be a likely groundwater contaminant, especially on sensitive sites. Under turf conditions, however, applications are made to organic matter that will sorb ethofumesate more strongly than soil.

Decomposition by microorganisms is thought to be the major pathway for ethofumesate disappearance. Van Hoogstraten et al. (138) showed a much reduced rate of ethofumesate disappearance when soils were sterilized before incubation with ethofumesate; however, McAuliffe and Appleby (87) demonstrated a nonbiological decomposition process when ethofumesate was applied to dry soil. Under dry soil conditions they postulated that either ethofumesate was more strongly adsorbed by dry soil, or that significantly lower pH on the clay colloids catalyzed the degradation of ethofumesate. Based on the low vapor pressure of ethofumesate, volatility has not been implicated in the loss of this material.

Persistence studies have been conducted by several authors. Schweizer (113) determined half lives in a sandy loam and a loam soil and calculated values of 7.7 and 12.6 wk, respectively. Haggar and Passman (54) determined a $t_{1/2}$ of just over 8 wk when ethofumesate was applied to sandy loam soil in September in Great Britain. They also determined that with a 2-kg ha^{-1} (1.8 lb acre^{-1}) rate, enough residual ethofumesate remained in the soil 7 mo after the September application date to provide a 50% reduction in annual bluegrass emergence.

10. Pronamide

Pronamide [3,5-dichloro(N-1,1-dimethyl-2-propynyl)benzamide] is used in warm season turf for controlling annual bluegrass. Carlson et al. (21) reported sorption data but did not determine K_d or K_{oc} values. Assuming 58% organic C in organic matter, K_{oc} values of 135 to 215 for six different soils could be calculated. The values are considerably lower than that reported by Wauchope et al. (146) (Table 5-2). Leistra et al. (83) studied leaching of pronamide and found no significant leaching below the 2.5 to 5 cm (1–2 in.) layer. Little information is available on the volatility of pronamide. The vapor pressure of pronamide is between that of benefin and trifluralin. Thus, under proper conditions (surface application, wet soils) volatilization would be expected to be a significant loss mechanism.

The method of degradation in soil appears to be a combination of both chemical and microbial processes. Yih et al. (153) proposed a cyclization of the amide side chain by acid, base, or increased temperature. Fisher (39) evaluated the decomposition of pronamide in sterilized and unsterilized soils and found very little $^{14}CO_2$ evolution from sterilized soils; while his results showed that microbial organisms are capable of transforming pronamide, they did not determine which process, chemical cyclization or microbial decomposition, is responsible for the loss of activity in soils.

The half-life of pronamide in soil has been investigated by several workers. Walker (142) examined the degradation of pronamide in a sandy loam soil under different temperature and moisture regimes. The $t_{1/2}$ values varied from 16 d at 30°C and 9.5% soil moisture, to 373 d at 5°C and 3.7% soil moisture. From this study, he concluded that pronamide degradation rate was greatly affected by temperature. In another study, Walker (141) showed that pronamide degradation was more sensitive to changes in soil temperature than in soil moisture. A rise in soil temperature of 10°C caused a 2.2-fold increase in the degradation rate of pronamide. A reduction in soil moisture from field capacity to air dried decreased the rate of pronamide degradation by a factor of three. Walker and Thompson (144) studied degradation of pronamide in 18 different soils and found $t_{1/2}$ varying from 10 to 32 d when incubated at 25°C. Various soil properties such as pH, organic matter, clay, and sorption were correlated with the degradation rates of pronamide; however, no significant correlation was found between pronamide degradation and any of the soil properties measured. Their findings were not in agreement with those of Hance (58) who studied the effect of soil pH on pronamide degradation. Hance (58) saw an increased rate of degradation as soil pH became more alkaline. Leistra et al. (83) also studied pronamide degradation in the field and found $t_{1/2}$ ranging from 33 to 75 d in five different soils; this range seems to adequately describe the persistence of pronamide in soil.

B. Postemergence Herbicides

1. Dicamba

Dicamba is a herbicide with the same auxin-like mode of action as the phenoxy herbicides. Dicamba has a broad spectrum of control and is superior to 2,4-D on many weed species. The chief drawbacks to its use are the potential for injury from volatility and leaching. Dicamba is quite mobile in the soil and is phytotoxic to many ornamentals, particularly *Juniper* and *Taxus*. Because of the leaching problem, dicamba is often a minor component in mixtures with 2,4-D or 2,4-D and mecoprop [(±)-2-(4-chloro-2-methylphenoxy)propanoic acid]. The use rate for dicamba in these mixtures is usually between 0.11 to 0.14 kg ha^{-1} (0.1–0.125 lb acre^{-1}). A synergistic effect from the addition of dicamba to mixtures has often been claimed by formulators. Evidence to support this claim is lacking. Instead, an additive effect is probably the result. An article by Colby (31), using data from Jagschitz and Skogley (72), calculated the expected response of two- and three-way combinations of 2,4-D, mecoprop, and dicamba from the response seen from each herbicide used alone. Colby's calculations showed antagonism from the three-way mixture of 2,4-D, mecoprop, and dicamba on dandelion (*Taraxacum officinale* Wigg.). Data on chickweed [*Stellaria media* (L.) Villaus] control showed either the expected response or a slight, but not significant, synergism. Thus, the effectiveness of mixtures seem to come from the additive effect of each herbicide's toxicity on a particular species.

Dicamba is very mobile in the soil. The pK$_a$ for dicamba is 1.91 (Table 5–3), which indicates that it will always be dissociated in soils. Carringer et al. (22) showed that dicamba was not sorbed by organic matter and weakly adsorbed by montmorillonite. Burnside and Lavy (18) determined dicamba adsorption on eight soils and three clays and found that only kaolinite adsorbed any of the dicamba. It was postulated by Carringer et al. (22) that

Table 5–3. Selected chemical properties of the postemergence broadleaf herbicides.†

Herbicide	Solubility	Half-life	K_{oc}	Vapor pressure	pK$_a$
	mg L^{-1}	d	mL g^{-1}	mm Hg	
dicamba, DMA salt	850 000	14	2	3.4×10^{-5} (Acid)	1.91
2,4-D Acid	890	10	20	8×10^{-6}	2.8
2,4-D DMA salt	796 000	10	20	0	2.8
2,4-D esters	100	10	100	–‡	2.8
2,4-DP ester	50	10	1000	3×10^{-6}	2.86
2,4-DP acid	710	10	170	$<10^{-7}$	2.86
MCPP, DMA salt	660 000	21	20 (E)	0	3.11
MCPP, acid	620	21	20	$<10^{-7}$	3.11
MCPA, DMA salt	866 000	25	20 (E)	0	3.12
triclopyr, amine salt	210 000	46	20 (E)	0	2.68
triclopyr acid	430	46	20	1.2×10^{-6}	2.68
clopyralid, amine salt	300 000 (E)	40	6	0	2.3

† Data from Wauchope et al. (146).
‡ Vapor pressure varies depending upon the ester; methyl ester is 2.3×10^{-3} mm Hg, while 3-butoxy propyl ester is 3×10^{-6} mm Hg.

the saturating ion on the clay may form a complex with the free acid of dicamba, providing a mechanism for adsorption on some clays. Helling (65) found dicamba to be among the most mobile of 40 pesticides tested; using a soil thin-layer chromatography procedure, dicamba essentially moved with the water front. Friesen (41) used a bioassay to show that dicamba was very mobile in two soils tested; he observed that dicamba readily moved with water added to the soil, and that the dicamba lagged only slightly behind the movements of the water front.

Dicamba has been recognized as a volatile compound. The free acid is very volatile and to reduce volatility, the herbicide is formulated as the dimethylamine (DMA) salt. The DMA salt of dicamba is very low in volatility. Several investigators, however, have shown volatility injury from the DMA salt of dicamba (9, 44). Behrens and Lueschen (9) also extensively studied dicamba volatility from sprayed field corn (*Zea mays* L.) with soybeans as a bioassay plant. They observed volatility injury up to 60 m (200 ft) downwind from corn treated with the DMA salt of dicamba. The salt used in the formulation of dicamba also had a large effect on dicamba volatility when measured in closed containers. Sodium, Li, and K salts of dicamba did not exhibit any volatility. The triethanolamine and diethanolamine salts exhibited low levels of volatility, while the methylamine and DMA forms caused significant volatility injury. Bauer et al. (8) studied volatility and photolysis losses of dicamba. The free acid of dicamba was quite volatile with 41% lost after 1 d at 30 °C. When they irradiated the free acid and the K salt of dicamba, they noted that the losses from the photolysis study were about the same as the losses from volatility in a study conducted under similar conditions. By subtraction, they concluded that dicamba may be resistant to long wavelength ultraviolet photolysis. Hahn et al. (55) exposed dicamba solutions to sunlight during a 16-d period, they saw a slight decrease in dicamba phytotoxicity, but were not sure whether photolysis or biological decomposition occurred.

Dicamba is relatively short-lived in the soil. Altom and Stritzke (3) found that initially dicamba disappeared rapidly from three different soil types but the rate slowed after the first 20 d, giving a significant quadratic response by regression analysis. They determined a $t_{1/2}$ of 17 to 32 d for the three soils tested. Smith (117) examined dicamba degradation at 25 °C at various moisture contents for three soils. Where moisture was adequate, dicamba degraded quite rapidly. A silty clay soil with 11.7% OM showed almost complete degradation 2 wk after application. A fine-textured clay soil showed a somewhat slower rate of breakdown and where soil moisture was low dicamba degradation was retarded. Stewart and Gaul (132) studied the dissipation of dicamba over time. They found that 5% dicamba remained 42 d after application of 1.1, 2.2, and 4.5 kg ha^{-1} (1, 2, and 4 lb a.i. acre^{-1}) to a silty loam soil. Dicamba dissipation in the soil is due to leaching and microbial degradation. Smith (117) could recover >90% of the original dicamba after incubation in sterile soils for 4 wk, indicating that microbial decomposition is the major pathway for dicamba degradation in soils. In a different study,

Smith (118) reported that after 9 wk in sterile soils, no dicamba degradation product could be identified and recovery of the parent herbicide was >90%.

Data from the literature indicate a $t_{1/2}$ for dicamba in soils in the range of 2 to 4 wk. Where conditions are favorable for dicamba degradation (i.e., moist soils and warm temperatures), degradation will be rapid; however, where soil moisture is low and temperatures are cool, dicamba may persist for several months.

3. 2,4-D and Related Phenoxy Acids

Adsorption–Leaching. The phenoxy acids tend to be very mobile in soils (65). Although they are applied as salts or esters, once in the soil solution they are rapidly converted to the free acid. With adequate soil moisture, phenoxy acid esters are converted to the corresponding acids within 24 h for iso-propyl and n-butyl esters and within 48 to 72 h for the isooctyl esters (116, 119). Thus, the free acid is available for leaching or adsorption.

Several studies on adsorption of phenoxy acids by soils have been reported (51, 92). Moreale and Van Bladel (92) characterized the adsorption of 2,4-D by 21 Belgian soils. They found that 2,4-D adsorption was controlled by soil organic matter and soil pH. The pK_a for 2,4-D is 2.8, so at low soil pHs adsorption of the uncharged form of 2,4-D is to be expected. All the soils in the study of Moreale and Van Bladel (92) were below pH 7.0. As soil pH increases, adsorption of phenoxy acid herbicides will decrease. Table 5–3 describes physicochemical data for the phenoxy acid herbicides including pK_a values. These play an important role in adsorption and leaching especially since clay colloids can be one to two pH units more acidic than the bulk soil solution pH. All of the pK_as of the phenoxy herbicides used in turf weed control are approximately three. Thus, only in very acid soils would sorption of the nonionic forms be appreciable. Moreale and Van Bladel (92) determined the Freundlich K_d values for the soils in their studies and found a range of 0.05 to 23.89. Approximately one-half the soils had K values of less than one, which indicates practically no adsorption.

Two studies have been conducted with turf that directly examine leaching of 2,4-D in the field. Gold et al. (49) studied the leaching of 2,4-D and dicamba from home lawns using suction lysimeters placed at a soil depth of 20 cm (8 in.). Standard rates of 2,4-D and dicamba, 1.1 and 0.1 kg ha^{-1} (1 and 0.1 lb a.i. acre^{-1}), respectively, were applied either once or three times per growing season during a 3-yr period. Additionally, two irrigation regimes were chosen: a minimal irrigation treatment and an overwatering treatment. The soil type was a sandy loam. The overwatered plots generated much more leachate than the minimal water plots (72.9 vs. 25.6 cm; 29 vs. 10.1 in.) during the 2-yr monitoring period of the study. While detectable concentrations of 2,4-D and dicamba had maximum values of 15 and 38 μg L^{-1}, respectively, 83 to 95% of the dicamba measurements and 54 to 90% of the 2,4-D measurements were <1 μg L^{-1}. For all rates and irrigation treatments, the seasonal cumulative mean values for 2,4-D and dicamba in the percolate were <1 μg L^{-1}. A second study was conducted by Cohen et al. (30) on golf courses in Cape Cod, MA. This study used 19 ground-water monitoring wells on four different golf courses to directly monitor movement of agrichemicals into groundwater. The wells were monitored for 1.5 y and 2,4-D was detected only at one sampling period from a sampling well beneath a green at a concentration of 0.1 μg L^{-1}.

Photolysis. Studies of photolysis of phenoxy acids in solution have indicated that relatively rapid decomposition can occur. Osman and Faust (97) studied the photolysis of the sodium salt, isopropyl ester, and butyl ester of 2,4-D in distilled water irradiated with a Hg discharge lamp. At pH 7.0 $t_{1/2}$s of 31 and 42 min were observed for the isopropyl and butyl esters, respectively. As solution pH was increased, the decomposition rate also increased, while more acidic solutions resulted in slightly lowered photolysis rates. Crosby and Tutass (34) showed that the pathway for 2,4-D photolysis involved replacement of Cl$^-$ by OH$^-$ to ultimately form 1,2,4 benzenetriol, which would then polmerize to a mixture of humic acids.

Crosby and Bowers (33) also studied the photolysis of the dimethylamine salt of MCPA [(4-chloro-2-methylphenoxy)acetic acid] spray solutions deposited on glass surfaces and exposed to natural sunlight. Approximately 30% of the MCPA photodegraded in 1 d and $t_{1/2}$ of 2 d was determined. The principal photolysis product was 4-chloro-2-methylphenol. An interesting sidelight of this study was a field experiment where MCPA dimethylamine salt was applied aerially to rice fields at rates of 0.84 and 0.96 kg ha^{-1} (0.75 and 0.85 lb a.i. acre^{-1}). Only 24 to 43% of the applied MCPA was recovered in the field immediately after application. Although variability in recovery should be expected, the results indicated that a significant amount of airborne photolysis may occur.

The phenoxy acids are readily decomposed by sunlight. It is quite difficult to determine the extent of photolysis that occurs in field situations. Since absorption of phenoxy acids into plants is relatively rapid, photolysis should not be expected to affect herbicide efficacy but may contribute to reducing residues of these herbicides. Studies on phenoxy photolysis on leaf surfaces have not been reported.

Volatilization. It is difficult to draw absolute numbers from volatility data that are collected during short time periods. Herbicide volatility will be at a maximum when the herbicide concentration at the soil surface is saturating. As the herbicide concentration falls below saturation, volatility rates will decrease. Thus, many situations can be conceived where Herbicide A may be more volatile initially than Herbicide B, but Herbicide B may volatilize during a longer period of time because its concentration at the surface remains saturated. During short time periods, Herbicide A may be more volatile but, in terms of total volatility losses, Herbicide B would be greatest. Thus, most volatility studies provide information on relative volatility only.

The discussion of phenoxy acid herbicide volatilization is complicated by the fact that the parent acids are rarely used in turf weed control; instead, either salt or ester derivatives are applied in the field. Salts most commonly used are various substituted amines, the most common being dimethyl amine and diethyl amine. As salts, these materials are essentially nonvolatile (53). Any volatility that occurs, would result from the volatilization of the free acid not the salt. Ester formulations are volatile. In the late 1940s and through the early 1950s, high volatile esters of 2,4-D such as methyl or butyl esters were used. These provided excellent weed control but the injury from volatility was often dramatic. Currently, low volatile esters such as the isooctyl or butoxy ethanol esters of 2,4-D are commonly used. As the names imply, these esters are less volatile than their shorter-chain predecessors; however, they are still volatile.

Volatility is best approximated by the vapor pressure of the various esters, which is shown in Table 5-3. Several environmental and application variables will affect the amount of volatilization that occurs when using these products. Temperature has the most dramatic impact on volatilization of these herbicides with higher temperatures, particularly when temperatures exceed 30 °C, causing high volatility and high potential for nontarget plant injury. Relative humidity is also important as it affects droplet drying time. Increasing time for droplets to reach dryness will result in greater volatilization.

Droplet size is a very important determinant of herbicide volatility. Que Hee and Sutherland (107) examined the volatilization and absorption of the isobutyl and butyl esters of 2,4-D by sunflower seedlings (*Helianthus annuus* L.). When mean droplet size was quite small (55 μ), 66% of the isobutyl ester of 2,4-D was volatilized within 10 h with 34% staying on or in the leaf. When the mean droplet diameter was increased to 225 μ, however, 64% of the herbicide stayed on or in the plant, while only 35% was volatilized after 10 h.

Thus, volatility of phenoxy acid esters can be quite large and can be an important avenue for transport of the herbicides and reduction of the quantity remaining in the soil. Because absorption of phenoxy acid ester herbicides into plants is relatively rapid, efficacy should not be affected unless conditions are very favorable for volatilization. A search of the literature failed to find any field-scale studies of phenoxy ester volatilization similar to those of Glotfelty et al. (47) on the long-term volatilization of DCPA and trifluralin. These field-scale studies tend to be conducted on more persistent herbicides that may volatilize slowly during a period of weeks or months. Field-scale studies with phenoxy acids would be of shorter duration but would be valuable from an overall understanding of the fate of these herbicides and the percentage losses to be expected in the field.

Microbial Degradation. The phenoxy acid herbicides are readily metabolized in soils by microorganisms (2, 81, 84, 99) and this is the principal pathway for phenoxy degradation in soils. The kinetics of microbial degradation of 2,4-D were studied by Parker and Doxtader (99) and they observed two phases of 2,4-D degradation in soils. The initial slow phase yielded a degradation rate of 0.23 μg 2,4-D g^{-1} (soil) d^{-1}, while the fast degradation phase had a degradation rate of 2.23 μg g^{-1} d^{-1}. These rates were determined at a temperature of 27 °C and 0.01 MPa soil moisture content that were optimum for 2,4-D degradation. At lower soil moisture contents, the fast phase of degradation was not observed.

The lag phase could result from not having a sufficient number of microorganisms present to degrade the applied dose of herbicide. A study by Fournier et al. (40) showed this to be true. At low 2,4-D concentrations in soil, 0.33 to 3.3 mg kg^{-1}, degradation was rapid and linear. The rate of degradation at concentrations of 33 and 330 mg kg^{-1} showed an initial lag phase followed by a more rapid degradation. These authors also showed that a pretreatment would reduce the initial lag phase resulting in faster degradation. Pretreatment was shown to dramatically increase the number of 2,4-D-metabolizing microorganisms but had relatively little impact on the population of 2,4-D cometabolizing microorganisms.

Cullimore (35) examined the population of 2,4-D degraders in soils of Saskatchewan. He isolated between 2.7 to 5.7 × 10^3 degraders in soils receiving annual 2,4-D applications over the previous 32 yr. Plots that had not received annual 2,4-D applications had 2.5 × 10^3 degraders indicating a moderate increase in degraders from previous applications. These data would indicate that multiple applications within a single growing season may result in an increased rate of breakdown due to the preceding applications, as has been suggested by the work of Gold et al. (49). Where one yearly application of 2,4-D is used, however, significant increases in the rate of 2,4-D degradation may not be observed.

Persistence in Soil. An excellent review of the degradation and persistence of phenoxy acid herbicides in soils was recently published by Smith (122). Due to the rapid metabolism of phenoxy herbicides in soil, and their susceptibility to volatilization, photolysis, and leaching; the half-life of these materials in soils is relatively short. Half-life data comes primarily laboratory studies using ^{14}C-labeled herbicides (3, 120, 125). Field studies on persistence of phenoxy acids in soils or turf are surprisingly difficult to find. Those that were conducted usually used a sampling protocol that was insufficient to develop $t_{1/2}$ values or did not report $t_{1/2}$ data (122). Representative soil $t_{1/2}$ values are shown in Table 5–3.

Therefore, even though these herbicides are relatively mobile in soils, their rapid metabolism makes it unlikely that they would pose much environmental concern. Only MCPA, a recent addition in turf weed control that is used as a replacement for 2,4-D, has a long enough $t_{1/2}$ value to cause concern (125).

3. Triclopyr

Triclopyr [(3,5,6-trichloro-2-pyridinyl)oxy]acetic acid] is a herbicide that has been used for turf weed control since 1984. It usually combined with 2,4-D but has excellent activity on some hard to control turf weeds, particularly wild violet (*Viola* spp.). It is widely used for brush control in forests, highway roadsides, and rights-of-way, and most of the information on fate comes from research on these uses.

The photolysis of triclopyr in water has been studied by several authors. McCall and Gavit (88) examined the photolysis of triclopyr in aqueous solutions under laboratory conditions. Triclopyr acid was shown to have a $t_{1/2}$ of 5.4 h in a pH 5.2 buffer with a light intensity of 1.16 mE L^{-1} h^{-1}. Triclopyr butoxyethanol ester had a photolysis $t_{1/2}$ of 26.8 h under these same conditions. It should be noted that triclopyr ester is rapidly converted to the free acid in water and soil. In soil, the half-life for conversion to the free acid is 3 h, while in water the rate of hydrolysis is pH dependent and varies from 84 d at pH 5 to 0.5 d at pH 9 (88). Photolysis can thus be a significant pathway for degradation, while triclopyr is in solution. Studies of the photolysis of triclopyr on leaf surfaces would be of interest.

Surprisingly little data exist on the persistence of triclopyr in soils. Lee et al. (82) examined the movement of triclopyr in quartz sand and loam soil. In the soil column, no movement of triclopyr or its metabolites below the top 2.5 cm (1 in.) of soil was observed following 68 cm (26.8 in.) of simulated rainfall. Stephenson et al. (131) studied the persistence and leaching of triclopyr in two soils in northern Ontario. In both soils studied, the $t_{1/2}$ for triclopyr degradation was 2 wk. Both soils had substantial surface organic deposits that retained >90% of the applied triclopyr, and 97% of the triclopyr recovered was in the top 15 cm (6 in.) of the soil core. Thus, these authors saw little evidence of any significant leaching from triclopyr applications. These findings are surprising since triclopyr is an organic acid that should be susceptible to leaching. The above data suggest that organic matter may reduce the leaching potential of triclopyr, an important point when triclopyr is used in turf.

4. Clopyralid

Clopyralid (3,6-dichloro-2-pyridinecarboxylic acid) is a herbicide for controlling broadleaf weeds in turf. It is only available in a mixture with triclopyr and its application rate in the mixture is low, 0.14 kg ha^{-1} (0.125 lb $acre^{-1}$). While this herbicide has been the subject of a wide variety of publications concerning its efficacy, fate studies are limited. Pik et al. (105) comprehensively studied the adsorption, persistence, and leaching of clopyralid in three Canadian soils. They reported low K_d values of 0.01 to 0.10 (equivalent to K_{oc} values of 1.5 to 3.1), which compare closely to that of Wauchope et al. (146) (Table 5-3). These low K values indicate little to no adsorption, as would be expected for an organic acid herbicide with a pK_a of 2.3.

Leaching of clopyralid would be expected to occur and was confirmed by the results of Pik et al. (105). After a 9-wk leaching period during which 119.0 mm (4.7 in.) of rainfall occurred, all three of the soils tested showed significant leaching with one soil, with an organic C content of only 0.68%, having a concentration pulse from 20 to 50 cm (7.9–19.7 in.) in depth with a maximum concentration at 30 cm below the soil surface. While these data represented a worst case situation, the high organic C content soil had a maximum concentration pulse at 7.5 cm (3 in.) with detectable residues at 30 cm (12 in.). This is a highly mobile herbicide that will leach in soils.

Pik et al. (105) also studied the degradation of clopyralid in sterile and nonsterile soils. Degradation in nonsterilized soils was rather slow with only 30, 38, and 55% of the applied dose degraded in three different soils after 9 wk of incubation. In sterilized soils, only 28% of the clopyralid was degraded after 57 wk. These studies were performed with soil placed in jars in the field, so the long degradation times should reflect the cooler climate of Canada where these tests were performed. Additionally, with respect to the sterile soil, the 57 wk included the winter season when no microbial degradation would be expected. Regardless, results from this study indicated that microbial degradation is primarily responsible for the degradation of clopyralid.

The persistence of clopyralid in soils was determined by Pik et al. (105) and by Smith and Aubin (123). The study by Pik et al. (105) was in Canada under field conditions with applications made in early July. In two of the soils tested, $t_{1/2}$ values were dosage-dependent being ≈ 2 wk for the high rate 1.9 kg ha^{-1} (1.71 lb acre^{-1}) of clopyralid and slightly longer for the lower rate 0.95 kg ha^{-1} (0.85 lb acre^{-1}) tested. Smith and Aubin (123) examined persistence in three soils at three temperatures. At 30 °C, $t_{1/2}$ values of 10, 26, and 29 d were reported for clay loam, sandy loam, and clay soils, respectively. At 10 °C, the $t_{1/2}$ values were 42, 44, and 47 d for the clay loam, sandy loam, and clay soils, respectively. Galoux et al. (42) did not report $t_{1/2}$ values, but did use rates more representative of those used in turf weed control. At 0.15 kg ha^{-1}, soil residues could not be detected by 21 DAT. By their sampling protocol and detection methods, however, residues at Day 0 were only four times above their limit of detection.

The above discussion indicates that clopyralid is a mobile herbicide with greater persistence than many of phenoxy herbicides or dicamba. Thus, while clopyralid may be a likely groundwater contaminant, its low use rate in turf, coupled with the fact that it is applied to a layer of organic matter (i.e., thatch and thatchlike derivatives) will greatly reduce its leaching to groundwater in significant quantities.

C. Miscellaneous Herbicides

1. Isoxaben

Isoxaben [N-[3-(1-ethyl-1-methylpropyl)-5-isoxazolyl]-2,6-dimethoxybenzamide] is a relatively new preemergence herbicide for broadleaf weed control in turf that features new chemistry with a selectivity that has not previously been available. Because isoxaben is a new product, little published data have been accumulated concerning its fate in soil or turf. A search of the literature revealed only three articles concerning the movement of isoxaben in soil. Jamet and Thoisy-Dur (74) assessed the movement of isoxaben in soil by soil thin-layer chromatography. The movement of isoxaben and four other pesticides was studied on seven different soil thin-layers. Isoxaben showed no mobility in any of the soils tested. These same authors examined

Table 5-4. Selected chemical properties of miscellaneous herbicides used in turf.[†]

Herbicide	Solubility	Half-life	K_{oc}	Vapor pressure
	mg L^{-1}	d	mL g^{-1}	mm Hg
fenoxaprop-ethyl	0.8	9[‡]	9490	3.2 × 10^{-8}
isoxaben	1.0	150	183[§]	<3.9 × 10^{-7}
atrazine	32	60	100	2.89 × 10^{-7}

[†] Data from Wauchope et al. (146).
[‡] Applied as ester readily converted to acid in <1 d, value is for degradation of the acid form.
[§] Estimated from K_{ow} of 434 and the formula of Karickhoff (78).

the adsorption of isoxaben on a single soil and determined Fruendlich K_d values for this system (73). However, the reported Freundich K_d values of 2.5 to 3.3 do not seem to match the low mobility observed by these authors. In contrast, Huggenberger and Ryan (68) estimated a K_{oc} value of 303. These data would indicate isoxaben is only moderately sorbed in soils that is unusual in light of its lower water solubility (Table 5-4). Mobility studies in the field indicated little leaching with most of the material in the top two cm, and a small fraction of the total material was measured at the 6-cm depth ≈ 5 mo following application.

Persistance data were developed from a field test at four different sites in France. Half-life values of 75 to 107 d were determined when isoxaben was applied to winter cereals. Spring applications of isoxaben would yield shorter $t_{1/2}$s. These same authors determined $t_{1/2}$s of 5 to 6 mo for fall applications of isoxaben in central Indiana (67).

2. Fenoxaprop-ethyl

Fenoxaprop-ethyl [(±)-ethyl-2-[4-[(6-chloro-2-benzoxazolyl)oxy]phenoxy]propanoate] is a postemergence herbicide for grass control that was commercially introduced in 1985. No information that has been published on the fate of this herbicide in the environment was found in the literature. Only studies on persistence of the herbicide in laboratory soils were available.

Fenoxaprop is a complex organic herbicide with the familiar phenoxy propanoate structure in common with some other postemergence grass herbicides. The herbicide is applied in an ester form but is rapidly hydrolyzed (<24 h) in moist soils to the free acid (121, 124). The free acid is phytotoxic and can provide some residual activity. Smith and Aubin (124) studied the degradation of fenoxaprop acid in three Saskatchewan soils. Observed half-life values were very temperature dependent ranging from 5 to 6 d at 30°C, 12 to 13 d at 20°C, and 30 to 42 d at 10°C, in the three soil types. Thus, under normal use conditions, fenoxaprop would not be expected to persist in the soil. Movement of fenoxaprop-ethyl in soil has been shown to be very slight (126). The free acid would be more mobile, although leaching should not be a concern because of the short soil $t_{1/2}$.

3. Triazines

Atrazine and other triazines, simazine and metribuzin [4-amino-6-(1,1-dimethylethyl)-3-(methylthio)-1,2,4-triazin-5(4H)-one], are used for preemergence and postemergence weed control on warm season turfgrass species. Atrazine is one of the most widely used herbicides in the USA and atrazine residues are being routinely detected in ground and surface water samples in areas where atrazine has been used extensively. There are no reported studies in the literature on the fate of atrazine applied to turf; however, extensive data exist on the persistence, volatilization, leaching and adsorption of atrazine applied to field crops.

The vapor pressure of atrazine is fairly low, 6.6×10^{-7} mm Hg, with a Henry's law constant of 2.5×10^{-7}, which indicates that volatilization will not be a significant loss mechanism. Field experiments bear this out; Glotfelty et al. (47) measured the volatilization of atrazine from a bare soil using a micrometeorological method. They reported that only 2.4% of the applied atrazine volatilized in 21 d following application. These researchers also noted that some volatilization occurred as the dust from the wettable powder formulation of atrazine would become airborne on dry, windy days. Indeed, research by Clendening et al. (28) indicated that only 0.16% of the applied atrazine volatilized during 17 d following application. Therefore, volatilization of atrazine is not a significant loss mechanism. Similarly, simazine, which has vapor pressure, 1.5×10^{-8} mm Hg, even lower than atrazine, would be expected to be less volatile than atrazine. Glotfelty et al. (47) measured a volatilization loss for simazine of 1.3% during a 21-d period.

The triazines vary greatly in terms of soil persistence. Half-lives for atrazine range from 44 to 74 d (125), 73 to 80 d for simazine (145), and 22 to 62 d for metribuzin (127). This information shows that triazines are moderately persistent herbicides that, in the case of atrazine and simazine, may persist in the soil for 1 yr. The propensity for detecting atrazine in groundwater is due to its persistence in the soil, moderate sorption onto soil organic matter ($K_{oc} = 100$), and a moderately low water solubility of 32 mg L^{-1}. The combination of these three factors makes atrazine susceptible to leaching, although the amount that reaches groundwater is usually <0.5% of the total applied (29). Studies in the field have verified these small but significant leaching events. Wehtje et al. (151) monitored the leaching of atrazine in a loamy sand planted to corn in Nebraska. Using suction lysimeters buried at a depth of 1.5 m, they found leaching of atrazine at amounts equivalent to 0.0068 and 0.0077% in the 2 yr they conducted the experiment. Other investigators have seen similar results. Clendening et al. (28) observed movement of atrazine to depths of 1 m (3.3 ft), although concentrations were quite low. Helling et al. (66) reported movement of atrazine to depths of 50 cm (19.7 in.), the lowest depth they sampled, at 124 DAT. At 124 DAT, the largest pulse of atrazine was found at the 5-10 cm (2-4 in.) depth and was approximately one-half the concentration found in the 0- to 5-cm (0–2 in.) layer at 14 DAT. This again indicates the potential for leaching from atrazine. Metribuzin is more mobile than atrazine but less persistent. Metribuzin is strongly sorbed by organic matter (104). The triazines represent a class of herbicides which, due to their persistence and water solubility characteristics, present a hazard to groundwater. This should be considered since many turf areas have high sand content rootzones with abundant irrigation, conditions that could lead to considerable leaching of triazines.

REFERENCES

1. Ahrens, J.F. 1969. Persistence and counteraction of bensulide in turf. Proc. Northeast. Weed Control Conf. 23:405.
2. Alexander, M., and M.I.H. Aleem. 1961. Effect of chemical structure on microbial decomposition of aromatic herbicides. J. Agric. Food Chem. 9:44–47.
3. Altom, J.D., and J.F. Stritzke. 1973. Degradaton of dicamba, picloram, and four phenoxy herbicides in soil. Weed Sci. 21:556–560.
4. Ambrosi, D., and C.S. Helling. 1977. Leaching of oxidiazon and phosalone in soils. J. Agric. Food Chem. 25:215–217.
5. Ambrosi, D., P.C. Kearney, and J.A. Macchia. 1977. Persistence and metabolism of oxadiazon in soils. J. Agric. Food Chem. 25:868–872.
6. Anderson, W.P., A.B. Richards, and J.W. Whitworth. 1968. Leaching of trifluralin, benefin, and nitralin in soil columns. Weed Sci. 16:165–169.
7. Barrett, M.R., and T.L. Lavy. 1984. Effects of soil water content on oxadiazon dissipation. Weed Sci. 32:697–701.
8. Baur, J.R., R.W. Bovey, and H.G. McCall. 1973. Thermal and ultraviolet loss of herbicides. Arch. Environ. Contam. Toxicol. 1:289–302.
9. Behrens, R., and W.E. Lueschen. 1979. Dicamba volatility. Weed Sci. 27:486–493.
10. Belasco, I.J., and W.P. Langsdorf. 1969. Synthesis of ^{14}C-labeled siduron and its fate in soil. J. Agric. Food Chem. 17:1004–1007
11. Berayon, B.F., and B.L. Mercado. 1983. Persistence of pendimethalin in the soil. Philipp. Agric. 66:367–378.
12. Beven, K.J., and R.T. Clarke. 1986. On the variation of infiltration into a homogeneous soil matrix containing a population of macropores. Water Resour. Res. 22:383–388.
13. Beven, K.J., and P. Germann. 1982. Macropores and water flow in soils. Water Resour. Res. 18:1311–1325.
14. Bingham, S.W., and R.E. Schmidt. 1967. Residue of bensulide in turfgrass. Agron. J. 59:327–329.
15. Branham, B.E. 1983. The fate of DCPA and diazinon in turf using model ecosystems. Ph.D. thesis.
16. Burkhard, N., and J.A. Guth. 1976. Photolysis of atrazine, atraton, and ametryne in aqueous solutions with acetone as a photosensitizer. Pestic. Sci. 7:65–71.
17. Burnside, K.R., D.A. Addison, R.B. Cooper, R.D. Hicks, and H.L. Webster. 1982. Benefin degradation rate and effect on subsequent rotation crops in the Southeast. Proc. South. Weed Sci. Soc. 35:56–63.
18. Burnside, O.C., and T.L. Lavy. 1966. Dissipation of dicamba. Weeds. 14:211–214.
19. Burnside, O.C., and M.E. Schultz. 1978. Soil persistence of herbicides for corn, sorghum, and soybeans during the year of application. Weed Sci. 26:108–115.
20. Calvert, R. 1980. Adsorption-desorption phenomena. p. 1–30. In R.J. Hance (ed.) Interactions between Herbicides and the Soil. Academic Press, London.
21. Carlson, W.C., E.M. Lignowski, and H.J. Hopen. 1975. Uptake, translocation, and adsorption of pronamide. Weed Sci. 23:148–154.
22. Carringer, R.D., J.B. Weber, and T.J. Monaco. 1975. Adsorption-desorption of selected pesticides by organic matter and montmorillonite. J. Agric. Food Chem. 23:568–572.
23. Carter, G.E., Jr., and D.N. Camper. 1975. Soil enrichment studies with trifluralin. Weed Sci. 23:71–74.
24. Chen, Y.L., C.H. Fang, L.J. Chen, and Y.S. Wang. 1976. Photolysis and some behavior of herbicides benthiocarb and DCPA in soils. J. Chin. Agric. Chem. Soc. 14:59–67.
25. Chiou, C.T. 1989. Theoretical considerations of the partition uptake of nonionic compounds by soil organic matter. p. 31–44. In B.C. Sawhney and K. Brown (ed.) Reactions and Movement of Organic Chemicals in Soils. SSSA Special Publ. 22. SSSA, Madison, WI.

26. Chiou, C.T., T.D. Shoup, and P.E. Porter. 1985. Mechanistic roles of soil humus and minerals in the sorption of nonionic organic compounds from aqueous and organic solutions. Org. Geochem. 8:9–14.

27. Choi, J.S., T.W. Fermanian, D.J. Wehner, and L.A. Spomer. 1988. Effect of temperature, moisture, and soil texture on DCPA degradation. Agron. J. 80:108–113.

28. Clendening, L.D., W.A. Jury, and F.F. Ernst. 1990. A field mass balance study of pesticide volatilization, leaching, and persistence. p. 47–60. *In* D.A. Kurtz (ed.) Long Range Transport of Pesticides. Lewis Publ., Chelsea, MI.

29. Cohen, S.Z., C. Eiden, and M.N. Lorber. 1986. Monitoring groundwater for pesticides. p. 170–196. *In* W.Y. Garner et al. (ed.) Evaluation of pesticides in groundwater. ACS Symp. Ser. 315. Am. Chem. Soc., Washington, DC.

30. Cohen, S.Z., S. Nickerson, R. Maxey, A. Dupuy, Jr., and J.A. Senita. 1990 A ground water monitoring study for pesticides and nitrates associated with golf courses on Cape Cod. Ground Water Monit. Rev. 10:160–173.

31. Colby, S.R. 1967. Calculating synergistic and antagonistic responses of herbicide combinations. Weeds. 15:20–22.

32. Cooper, R.J., J.J. Jenkins, and A.S. Curtis. 1990. Pendimethalin volatility following application to turfgrass. J. Environ. Qual. 19:508–513.

33. Crosby, D.G., and J.B. Bowers. 1985. Composition and photochemical reactions of a dimethylamine salt formulation of (4-chloro-2-methylphenoxy) acetic acid (MCPA). J. Agric. Food Chem. 33:569–573.

34. Crosby, D.G., and H.O. Tutass. 1966. Photolysis of 2,4-dichlorophenoxyacetic acid. J. Agric. Food Chem. 14:596–599.

35. Cullimore, D.R. 1981. The enumeration of 2,4-D degraders in Saskatchewan soils. Weed Sci. 29:440–443.

36. Dureja, P., and S. Walia. 1989. Photodecomposition of pendimethalin. Pestic. Sci. 25:105–114.

37. Everett, D.H. 1983. Adsorption from solution. p. 1–29. *In* R.H. Otteweil (ed.) Adsorption from solution. Academic Press, London.

38. Fields, M.L., R. Der, and D.D. Hemphill. 1967. Influence of DCPA on selected soil microorganisms. Weeds 15:195–197.

39. Fisher, J.D. 1974. Metabolism of the herbicide pronamide in soil. J. Agric. Food Chem. 22:606–608.

40. Fournier, J.C., P. Cadaccioni, and G. Soulas. 1981. Soil adaptation to 2,4-D degradation in relation to the application rates and the metabolic behavior of the degrading microflora. Chemosphere. 10:977–984.

41. Friesen, H.A. 1965. The movement and persistence of dicamba in soil. Weeds. 13:30–33.

42. Galoux, M.P., A.C. Bernes, and J.C. Van Damme. 1985. Gas chromatographic determination of 3,6-dichloropicolinic acid residues in soils and its application to the residue dissipation in a soil. J. Agric. Food Chem. 33:965–968.

43. Geissbuhler, H. 1970. The substituted ureas. p. 79–108. *In* P.C. Kearney and D.D. Kaufmann (ed.) Degradation of Herbicides. Marcel Dekker, New York.

44. Gentner, W.A. 1964. Herbicidal activity of vapors of 4-amino-3,5,6-trichloro-picolinic acid. Weeds. 12:239–240.

45. Gershon, H., and G.W. McClure, Jr. 1966. Approach to the study of the degradation of dimethyl tetrachloroterephthalate. Contrib. Boyce Thompson Inst. 23:291–294.

46. Glotfelty, D.E., A.W. Taylor, B.C. Turner, and W.H. Zoller. 1984. Volatilization of surface applied pesticides from fallow soil. J. Agric. Food Chem. 32:638–643.

47. Glotfelty, D.E., M.M. Leech, J. Jersey, and A.W. Taylor. 1989. Volatilization and wind erosion of soil surface applied atrazine, simazine, alachlor and toxaphene. J. Agric. Food Chem. 37:546–551.

48. Golab, T., R.H. Herberg, J.V. Gramlich, A.P. Raun, and G.W. Probst. 1970. Fate of benefin in soils, plants, artificial rumen fluid, and the ruminant animal. J. Agric. Food Chem. 18:838–844.

49. Gold, A.J., T.G. Morton, W.M. Sullivan, and J. McClory. 1988. Leaching of 2,4-D and dicamba from home lawns. Water Air Soil Pollu. 37:121–129.

50. Green, R.E., J.M. Davidson, and J.W. Biggar. 1980. An assessment of methods for determining adsorption-desorption of organic chemicals. p. 73–82. *In* A. Banin and U. Kafkafi (ed.) Agrochemicals in Soils. Pergamon, New York.

51. Grover, R. 1973. The adsorptive behavior of acid and ester forms of 2,4-D on soils. Weed Res. 13:51–58.

52. Grover, R. 1974. Adsorption and desorption of trifluralin, triallate, and diallate by various adsorbents. Weed Sci. 22:405–408.

53. Grover, R. 1976. Relative volatilities of ester and amine forms of 2,4-D. Weed Sci. 24:26–28.

54. Haggar, R.J. and A. Passman. 1981. Soil persistence and distribution of ethofumesate applied to autumn-sown perennial ryegrass for *Poa annua* control. Weed Res. 21:153–159.

55. Hahn, R.R., O.C. Burnside, and T.L. Lavy. 1969. Dissipation and phytotoxicity of dicamba. Weed Sci. 17:3–8.

56. Hamaker, J.W., and J.M. Thompson. 1972. Adsorption. p. 49–143. *In* C.A.I. Goring and J.W. Jamaker (ed.) Organic chemicals in the soil environment. Vol. 1. Dekker, New York.

57. Hance, R.J. 1974. Soil organic matter and the adsorption and decomposition of the herbicides atrazine and linuron. Soil Biol. Biochem. 6:39–42.

58. Hance, R.J. 1979. Effect of pH on the degradation of atrazine, dichloroprop, linuron and propyzamide in soil. Pestic. Sci. 10:83–86.

59. Hance, R.J. 1988. Adsorption and bioavailability. p. 1–19. *In* R. Grover (ed.) Environmental chemistry of herbicides. CRC Press, Boca Raton, FL.

60. Harris, C.I. 1967. Movement of herbicides in soil. Weeds. 15:214–216.

61. Harvey, R.G. 1974. Soil adsorption and volatility of dinitroaniline herbicides. Weed Sci. 22:120–124.

62. Hassett, J.J., and W.L. Banwart. 1989. The sorption of nonpolar organics by soils and sediments. p. 31–34. *In* B.L. Sawhney and K. Brown (ed.) Reactions and movement of organic chemicals in soils. SSSA Spec. Publ. 22, SSSA, Madison, WI.

63. Hautala, R.R., and R.L. Letsinger. 1971. Effects of micelles on the efficicney of photoinduced substitution reactions and fluorescence quenching. J. Org. Chem. 36:3762–3768.

64. Hebert, V.R., and G.C. Miller. 1990. Depth dependence of direct and indirect photolysis on soil surfaces. J. Agric. Food Chem. 38:913–918.

65. Helling, C.S. 1971. Pesticide mobility in soils: II. Applications of soil thin layer chromatography. Soil Sci. Soc. Am. Proc. 35:737–743.

66. Helling, C.S., W. Zhuang, T.J. Gish, C.B. Coffman, A.R. Isensee, P.C. Kearney, D.R. Hoagland, and M.D. Woodward. 1988. Persistence and leaching of atrazine, alachlor, and cyanazine under no-tillage conditions. Chemosphere. 17:175–187.

67. Huggenberger, F., E.A. Jennings, P.J. Ryan, and K.W. Burrow. 1982. EL-107 a new selective herbicide for use in cereals. p. 47–52. *In* Proc. 1982 British Crop Prot. Conf. Weeds Brighton, England 22–25 Nov. 1982. BCPC Publ., Croydon, England.

68. Huggenberger, F., and P.J. Ryan. 1985. The biological activity of EL-107 and its mobility and degradation in soil. Proc. Br. Crop Prot. Conf. Weeds 947–954.

69. Hurto, K.A., A.J. Turgeon, and M.A. Cole. 1979. Degradation of benefin and DCPA in thatch and soil from a Kentucky bluegras (*Poa pratensis*) turf. Weed Sci. 27:154–157.

70. Hurto, K.A., and A.J. Turgeon. 1979. Influence on thatch on preemergence activity in Kentucky bluegrass turf. Weed Sci. 27:141–146.

71. Jacques, G.L., and R.G. Harvey. 1979. Persistance of dinitroaniline herbicides in soils. Weed Sci. 27:450–455.

72. Jagschitz, J.A., and C.R. Skogley. 1966. Dicamba, mecoprop, and 2,4-D combinations for the control of clover, chickweed and dandelion in turfgrass. Proc. North. Weed Sci. Soc. 20:496–501.

73. Jamet, P., and D. Hoyoux-Roche. 1989. Quantitative study on the influence of the soil–water ratio on pesticide adsorption and desorption. p. 3–12. *In* P. Jamet (ed.) Methodological aspects of the study of pesticide behaviour in soil, Versailles, 16–17 June 1988. INRA, Paris.

74. Jamet, P., and J.C. Thoisy-Dur. 1988. Pesticide mobility in soils: Assessment of the movement of isoxaben by soil thin-layer chromatography. Bull. Environ. Contam. Toxicol. 41:135–142.

75. Jury, W.A., H. Elabd, and M. Resketo. 1986. Field study of napropamide movement through unsaturated soil. Water Resour. Res. 22:749–755.

76. Karickhoff, S.W. 1981. Semi-empirical estimates of sorption of hydrophobic pollutants on natural sediments and soils. Chemosphere 10:833–846.

77. Karickhoff, S.W., D.S. Brown, and T.A. Scott. 1979. Sorption of hydrophobic pollutants on natural sediments. Water Res. 13:241–248.

78. Kempson-Jones, G.F., and R.J. Hance. 1979. Kinetics of linuron and metribuzin degradation in soil. Pestic. Sci. 10:449–454.

Turf Weeds and Their Control

© 1994 ASA–CSSA

Chapter 1—Weed Taxonomy
David W. Hall, Lambert B. McCarty, and Tim R. Murphy
Color Plates 1–1 through 1–105. Photos not available for 1–7, 1–53, 1–78, 1–93, and 1–94

Chapter 7—Application Technology
Thomas Reed and Steve Titko
Color Plates 7–1 through 7–9.

Chapter 8—Control of Turf Weeds
Lambert B. McCarty and Tim R. Murphy
Color Plates 8–1 through 8–14.

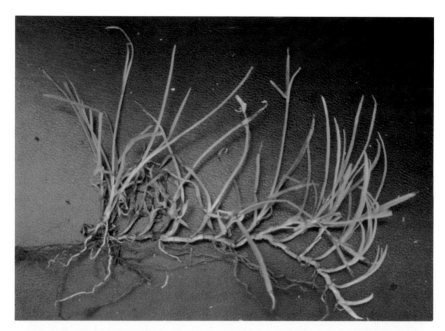

Color Plate 1–1. Green Kyllinga (Perennial Kyllinga); *Cyperus brevifolius* (Rottb.) Hassk.; [*Kyllinga brevifolius* Rottb.].

Color Plate 1-2. Annual Sedge; *Cyperus compressus* L.

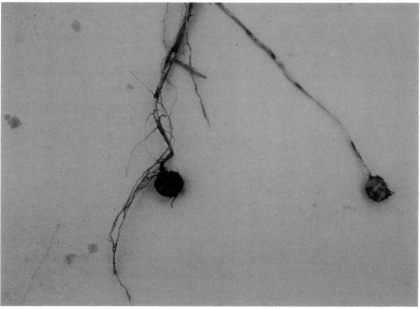

Color Plate 1–3. Yellow Nutsedge (Yellow Nutgrass); *Cyperus esculentus* L.

Color Plate 1-4. Globe Sedge; *Cyperus globulosus* Aubl.

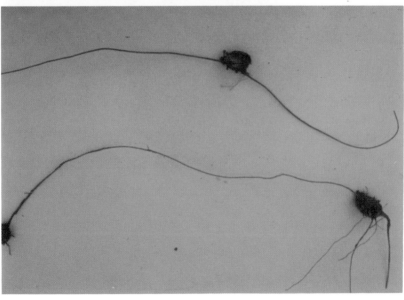

Color Plate 1–6. Quackgrass; *Agropyron repens* (L.) Beauv.; [*Elymus repens* (L.) Gould]. Photo: A.J. Turgeon and T.L. Watschke, Pennsylvania State University.

Color Plate 1–7. Creeping Bentgrass; *Agrostis stolonifera* L. var. *palustris* (Huds.) Farw.; [*A. palustris* Huds.]. Photo not available.

Color Plate 1–8. Bushy Bluestem (Bushy Broomgrass, Bushy Beardgrass); *Andropogon glomeratus* (Walt.) BSP.

Color Plate 1-9. Broomsedge (Broomgrass, Sagegrass); *Andropogon virginicus* L.

Color Plate 1-10. Carpetgrass; *Axonopus affinis* Chase.

Color Plate 1-11. Alexandergrass (Creeping Signalgrass); *Brachiaria plantaginea* (Link) A.S. Hitchc.

Color Plate 1–12. Broadleaf Signalgrass; *Brachiaria platyphylla* (Griseb.) Nash.

Color Plate 1-13. Smallflowered Alexandergrass; *Brachiaria subquadripara* (Trin.) A.S. Hitchc.

Color Plate 1-14. Field Sandbur (Coast Sandspur, Field Sandspur); *Cenchrus incertus* M.A. Curtis; [*C. pauciflorus* Benth.].

Color Plate 1-15. Bermudagrass; *Cynodon dactyon* (L.) Pers.

Color Plate 1-16. Orchardgrass; *Dactylis glomerata* L.

Color Plate 1-17. Crowfootgrass; *Dactyloctenium aegyptium* (L.) Willd.

Color Plate 1-18. Tropical Crabgrass; *Digitaria bicornis* (Lam.) Roem. & Schult. ex Loud.

Color Plate 1-19. Smooth Crabgrass; *Digitaria ischaemum* (Schreb. ex Schweig.) Schreb. ex Muhl.

Color Plate 1-20. Large Crabgrass and Southern Crabgrass; *Digitaria sanguinalis* (L.) Scop. and *Digitaria ciliaris* (Retz.) Koel.

Color Plate 1-21. Goosegrass (Crowfoot, Silver Crabgrass); *Eleusine indica* (L.) Gaertn.

Color Plate 1-22. Tall Fescue; *Festuca arundinacea* Schreb.; [*F. elatior* L., sensu stricto]. Photo: A.J. Turgeon and T.L. Watschke, Pennsylvania State University.

Color Plate 1–23. Nimblewill; *Muhlenbergia schreberi* J.F. Gmel.

Color Plate 1-24. Fall Panicum; *Panicum dichotomiflorum* Michx.

Color Plate 1–25. Torpedograss; *Panicum repens* L.

Color Plate 1–26. Dallisgrass; *Paspalum dilatatum* Poir.

Color Plate 1–27. Bahiagrass; *Paspalum notatum* Fluegge.

Color Plate 1–28. Vaseygrass; *Paspalum urvillei* Steud.

Color Plate 1-29. Annual Bluegrass; *Poa annua* L.

Color Plate 1-30. Yellow Foxtail; *Setaria pumila* (Poir.) Roem. & Schult.; [*S. glauca* auct. non (L.) P. Beauv.; *S. lutescens* (Weig.) F.T. Hubbard].

Color Plate 1–31. Johnsongrass; *Sorghum halepense* (L.) Pers.

Color Plate 1-32. Smutgrass; *Sporobolus indicus* (L.) R.Br.; [*Sporobolus poiretii* (Roem. & Schult.) Hitchc.].

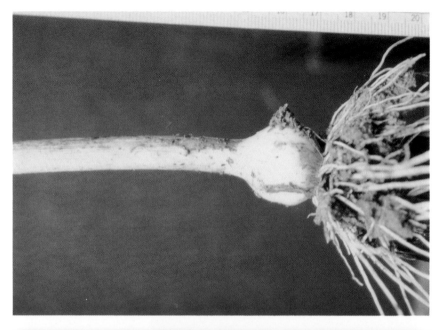

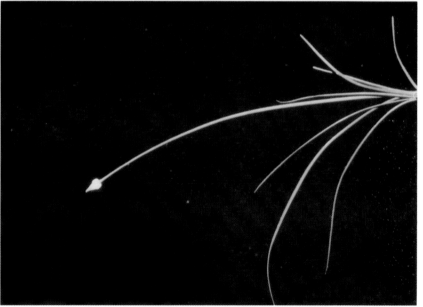

Color Plate 1–33. Wild Onion; *Allium canadense* L. Photo: a and b, Southern Weed Science, A.W. Evans and The DuPont Company; c, N.L. Hartwig and W.S. Curran, Pennsylvania State University.

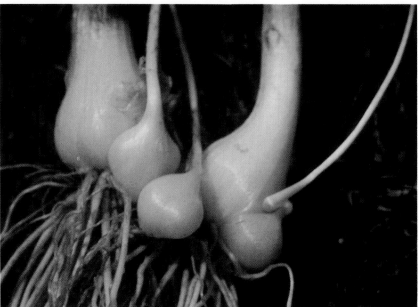

Color Plate 1-34. Wild Garlic; *Allium vineale* L.

Color Plate 1-35. Carpetweed; *Mollugo verticillata* L.

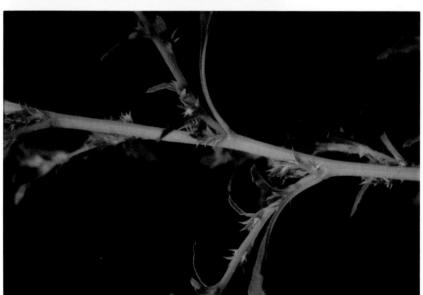

Color Plate 1–36. Tumbleweed (Prostrate Amaranth); *Amaranthus albus* L. [*A. blitoides* S. Wats.; *A. graecizans* of American authors]. Photo: Southern Weed Science, A.W. Evans and The DuPont Company.

Color Plate 1-37. Mouse-ear Chickweed; *Cerastium fontanum* Baumg. ssp. *triviale* (Link) Jalas; C. *holosteoides* Fries; C. *vulgatum* L.].

Color Plate 1–38. Bird's-eye Pearlwort; *Sagina procumbens* L. Photo: a, J.C. Harper, Pennsylvania State University; b, Geigy Weed Tables.

Color Plate 1-39. Knawel; *Scleranthus annuus* L.

Color Plate 1-40. Common Chickweed; *Stellaria media* (L.) Cyrillo.

Color Plate 1-41. Common Lamb's-quarters; *Chenopodium album* L.

Color Plate 1-42. Common Yarrow; *Achillea millefolium* L.

Color Plate 1-43. Common Ragweed; *Ambrosia artemisiifolia* L.

Color Plate 1-44. Mugwort; *Artemisia vulgaris* L.

Color Plate 1-45. English Daisy; *Bellis perennis* L. Photo: A.J. Turgeon and T.L. Watschke, Pennsylvania State University.

Color Plate 1–46. Spotted Knapweed; *Centaurea maculosa* Lam. Photo: a, N.L. Hartwig and W.S. Curran, Pennsylvania State University; b, Southern Weed Science, A.W. Evans and The DuPont Company.

Color Plate 1-47. Oxeye Daisy; *Chrysanthemum leucanthemum* L.; [*Leucanthemum vulgare* L.]. Photo: N.L. Hartwig and W.S. Curran, Pennsylvania State University.

Color Plate 1-48. Chicory; *Cichorium intybus* L.

Color Plate 1–49. Bull Thistle; *Cirsium vulgare* (Savi) Tenore.

Color Plate 1–50. Horseweed; *Conyza canadensis* (L.) Cronq.

Color Plate 1-51. Dogfennel; *Eupatorium capillifolium* (Lam.)

Color Plate 1–52. Purple Cudweed; *Gnaphalium purpureum* L.

Color Plate 1–53. Mouse-ear; *Hieracium pilosella* L. Photo not available.

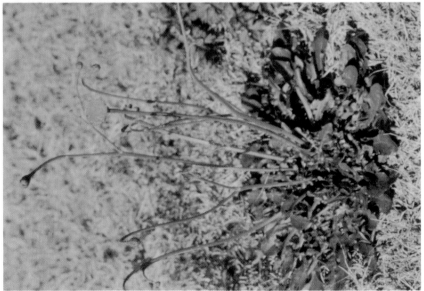

Color Plate 1–54. Catsear Dandelion; *Hypochoeris radicata* L.

Color Plate 1–55. Lawn Burweed (Spurweed); *Soliva prerosperma* (Juss.) Less.

Color Plate 1-56. Spiny Sowthistle; *Sonchus asper* (L.) Hill.

Color Plate 1-57. Dandelion; *Taraxacum officinale* Weber.

Color Plate 1-58. Field Bindweed; *Convolvulus arvensis* L. Photo: A.J. Turgeon and T.L. Watschke, Pennsylvania State University.

Color Plate 1–59. Dichondra (Carolina Dichondra, Ponyfoot); *Dichondra carolinensis* Michx.

Color Plate 1-60. Yellow Rocket; *Barbarea vulgaris* R.Br. Photo: A.J. Turgeon and T.L. Watschke, Pennsylvania State University.

Color Plate 1-61. Wild Mustard; *Brassica kaber* (DC.) Wheeler; [*Sinapis arvensis* L.]. Photo: N.L. Hartwig and W.S. Curran, Pennsylvania State University.

Color Plate 1–62. Shepherdspurse; *Capsella bursa-pastoris* (L.) Medic.

Color Plate 1-63. Hairy Bittercress; *Cardamine hirsuta* L.

Color Plate 1–64. Field Pepperweed; *Lepidium campestre* (L.) R.Br. Photo: N.L. Hartwig and W.S. Curran, Pennsylvania State University.

Color Plate 1–65. Virginia Pepperweed; *Lepidium virginicum* L.

Color Plate 1-66. Field Pennycress; *Thlaspi arvense* L. Photo: a and c, N.L. Hartwig and W.S. Curran, Pennsylvania State University; b, Southern Weed Science, A.W. Evans and The DuPont Company.

Color Plate 1-67. Spotted Spurge (Prostrate Spurge); *Chamaesyce maculata* (L.) Small; [*Euphorba maculata* L.].

Color Plate 1-68. Redstem Filaree; *Erodium cicutarium* (L.) L'Her. ex Ait.

Color Plate 1-69. Carolina Geranium (Wild Geranium; Crane's-bill; Stork's-bill); *Geranium carolinianum* L.

Color Plate 1-70. Ground Ivy; *Glechoma hederacea* L.

Color Plate 1-71. Henbit; *Lamium amplexicaule* L.

Color Plate 1-72. Purple Deadnettle; *Lamium purpureum* L.

Color Plate 1-73. Healall; *Prunella vulgaris* L.

Color Plate 1–74. Florida Betony (Rattlesnake Weed); *Stachys florida Shuttlew.*

Color Plate 1–75. Common Lespedeza (Annual Lespedeza; Japanese Clover); *Lespedeza stria-ta* (Thunb.) H. & A.

Color Plate 1–76. Black Medic; *Medicago lupulina* L.

Color Plate 1-77. Bur-Clover; *Medicago polymorpha* L. Photo: W. Duncan, University of Georgia.

Color Plate 1-78. Large Hop Clover. *Trifolium aureum* Poll.; [*T. agrarium* L., sensu American authors]. Photo not available.

Color Plate 1-79. Crimson Clover; *Trifolium incarnatum* L.

Color Plate 1-80. White Clover; *Trifolium repens* L.

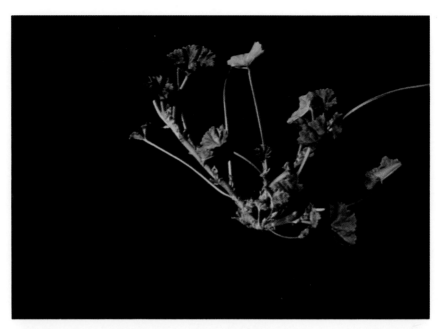

Color Plate 1–81. Roundleaf Mallow; *Malva rotundifolia* L.; [*M. pusilla* Sm.]. Photo: A.J. Turgeon and T.L. Watschke, Pennsylvania State University.

Color Plate 1-82. Cutleaf Evening Primrose; *Oenothera laciniata* Hill.

Color Plate 1-83. Yellow Woodsorrel; *Oxalis stricta* L.; [*O. dillenii* Jacq.].

Color Plate 1–84. Buckhorn Plantain; *Plantago lanceolata* L.

Color Plate 1-85. Broadleaf Plantain; *Plantago major* L.

Color Plate 1-86. Prostrate Knotweed; *Polygonum aviculare* L.

Color Plate 1-87. Red Sorrel (Sheep Sorrel; Sourgrass); *Rumex acetosella* L.

Color Plate 1-88. Curly Dock; *Rumex crispus* L.

Color Plate 1-89. Common Purslane; *Portulaca oleracea* L.

Color Plate 1-90. Creeping Buttercup; *Ranunculus repens* L. Photo: N.L. Hartwig and W.S. Curran, Pennsylvania State University.

Color Plate 1-91. Parsley-piert; *Alchemilla arvensis* (L.) Scop.

Color Plate 1-92. Indian Mockstrawberry; *Duchesnea indica* (Andr.) Focke.

Color Plate 1-93. Woodland Strawberry; *Fragaria vesca* L. Photo not available.

Color Plate 1-94. Common Cinquefoil; *Pontentilla canadensis* L. Photo not available.

Color Plate 1-95. Poorjoe; *Diodia teres* Walt.

Color Plate 1–96. Virginia Buttonweed; *Diodia virginiana* L.

Color Plate 1-97. Florida Pusley; *Richardia scabra* L.

Color Plate 1-98. Oldfield Toadflax; *Linaria canadensis* (L.) Dumont.

Color Plate 1-99. Corn Speedwell; *Veronica arvensis* L.

Color Plate 1–100. Creeping Speedwell; *Veronica filiformis* Sm. Photo: A.J. Turgeon and T.L. Watschke, Pennsylvania State University.

Color Plate 1-101. Purslane Speedwell (Neckweed); *Veronica peregrina* L.

Color Plate 1–102. Wild Carrot (Queen Anne's Lace); *Daucus carota* L.

Color Plate 1–103. Pennywort (Dollarweed), *Hydrocotyle* spp.; Coastal Plain Pennywort, *H. bonariensis* Comm. ex Lam.; Water Pennywort, *H. umbellata* L.; Whorled Pennywort, *H. verticillata* Thunb.

Color Plate 1-104. Mat Lippia (Matchweed); *Phyla nodiflora* (L.) Green; [*Lippia nodiflora* (L.) Michx.].

Color Plate 1–105. Violet; *Viola spp.*

Color Plate 7-1. Typical turf boom sprayer.

Color Plate 7-2. Drift reducing flat spray tip with view of preorifice.

Color Plate 7–3. Turbo Floodjet spray tip with view of preorifice.

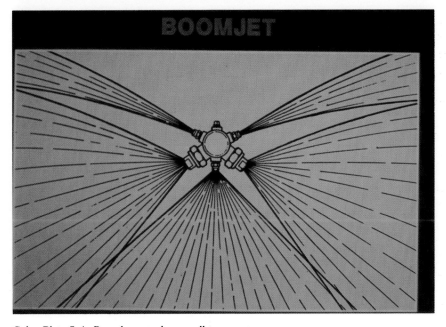

Color Plate 7–4. Boomless nozzle on pull-type sprayer.

Color Plate 7-5. Rotary nozzle on turf sprayer.

Color Plate 7-6. Typical portable compressed air sprayer.

Color Plate 7-7 (to the left). Hand held rotary nozzle.
Color Plate 7-8 (above). Lawn gun with associated showerhead nozzle.

Color Plate 7-9. Typical commercial truck-type sprayer.

Color Plate 8-1. Weed occurrence often results when turf density is thin.

Color Plate 8-2. Annual bluegrass is a profilic producer of seedheads which, in turn, disrupts the appearance and function of a turf area.

Color Plate 8-3. Planting weed free seed and vegetative materials are major methods of preventing the introduction of weeds into a turf area.

Color Plate 8-4. Mechanical equipment should be cleaned before entering a weed free area to prevent the transfer of weed seeds.

Color Plate 8-5. Areas surrounding irrigation sources such as ponds, canals, and open ditches should be as weed free as possible to prevent introduction in a turf area through the irrigation system.

Color Plate 8-6. Weeds uncontrolled along a fence row that provides a seed source to adjacent turf.

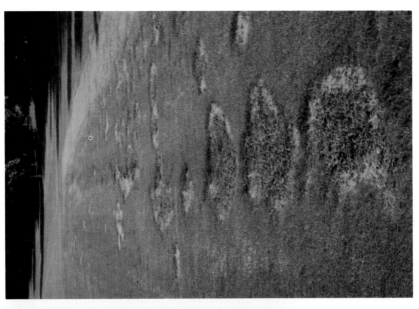

Color Plate 8–7 (above). Goosegrass surviving in thin turf due to compacted soil from excessive cart traffic.

Color Plate 8–8 (to the right). Weed encroachment into turf areas damaged from pest activity.

Color Plate 8-9. Using mulch to prevent weed establishment as well as to conserve water in the landscape.

Color Plate 8-10. Tilling an area before turf establishment reduces weed occurrence and allows soil amendments, such as lime and fertilizer, to be incorporated.

Color Plate 8-11. Hand removal of weeds is still widely practiced on high maintenance or herbicide-sensitive areas such as golf greens.

Color Plate 8–12. A polyethylene tarp used during fumigation to reduce gas volatilization.

Color Plate 8-13. Stage of weed growth and development (two to four leaf stage) that is easiest to control with postemergence herbicides.

Color Plate 8-14. Purple nutsedge leaftip (left) compared with yellow nutsedge (right).

79. Kenaga, E.E., and C.A.I. Goring. 1980. Relationship between water solubility, soil sorption, octanol-water partitioning, and concentration of chemicals in biota. p. 78–115. *In* J.A. Eaton et al. (ed.) Aquatic toxicology. ASTM Spec. Publ. 707, ASTM, Philadelphia.

80. Ketchersid, M.L., R.W. Bovey, and M.G. Merkle. 1969. The detection of trifluralin vapors in air. Weed Sci. 17:484–485.

81. Lappin, H.M., M.P. Greaves, and J.H. Slater. 1985. Degradation of the herbicide mecoprop [2-(2-methyl-4-chlorophenoxy) propionic acid] by a synergistic microbial community. Appl. Environ. Microbiol. 49:429–433.

82. Lee, C.H., P.C. Oloffs, and S.Y. Szetto. 1986. Persistence, degradation, and movement of triclopyr and its ethylene glycol butyl ester in a forest soil. J. Agric. Food Chem. 34:1075–1079.

83. Leistra, M., J.H. Smelt, J.G. Verlaat, and R. Zandvoort. 1974. Measured and computed concentration patterns of propyzamide in field soils. Weed Res. 14:87–95.

84. Loos, M.A., I.F. Schlosser, and W.R. Mapham. 1979. Phenoxy herbicide degradation in soils: Quantitative studies of 2,4-D and MCPA-degrading microbial populations. Soil Biol. Biochem. 11:377–385.

85. MacNamara, G., and S.J. Toth. 1970. Adsorption of linuron and malathion by soils and clay minerals. Soil Sci. 109:234–240.

86. Makary, M.H., M.R. Riskallah, M.E. Hegazy, and M.H. Belal. 1981. Photolysis of phoxim on glass and on tomato leaves. Bull. Environ. Contam. Toxicol. 26:413–419.

87. McAuliffe, D., and A.P. Appleby. 1984. Activity loss of ethofumesate in dry soil by chemical degradation and adsorption. Weed Sci. 32:468–471.

88. McCall, P.J., and P.D. Gavit. 1986. Aqueous photolysis of triclopyr and its butoxyethyl ester and calculated environmental photolysis rates. Environ. Toxicol. Chem. 5:879–885.

89. Menges, R.M., and J.L. Hubbard. 1970. Selectivity, movement, and persistence of soil-incorporated herbicides in carrot plantings. Weed Sci. 18:247–252.

90. Menges, R.M., and S. Tamez. 1974. Movement and persistence of bensulide and trifluralin in irrigated soil. Weed Sci. 22:67–71.

91. Miller, J.H., P.E. Keely, R.J. Thullen, and C.H. Carter. 1978. Persistence and movement of ten herbicides in soil. Weed Sci. 26:20–27.

92. Moreale, A., and R. Van Bladel. 1980. Behavior of 2,4-D in Belgian Soils. J. Environ. Qual. 9.627–633.

93. Nash, R.G. 1988. Dissipation from soil. p. 131–169. *In* R. Grover (ed.) Environmental chemistry of herbicides. Vol. 1. CRC Press, Boca Raton, FL.

94. Nash, A.S., and P.H. Dernoeden. 1982. Effectiveness and persistence of oxadiazon as a preemergence crabgrass herbicide and subsequent effects on overseeded perennial ryegrass. Proc. Northeast. Weed Sci. Soc. 36:301–306.

95. Nash, R.G., and B.D. Hill. 1990. Modeling pesticide volatilization and soil decline under controlled conditions. p. 17–28. *In* D.A. Kurtz (ed.) Long range transport of pesticides. Lewis Publ., Chelsea, MI.

96. Oliver, J.E. 1979. Volatilization of some herbicide related nitrosamines from soils. J. Environ. Qual. 8.596–601.

97. Osman, M.A., and S.A. Faust. 1964. Studies on the fate of 2,4-D and ester derivatives in natural surface waters. J. Agric. Food Chem. 12:541–546.

98. Pal, S., P.N. Moza, and A. Kettrup. 1991. Photochemistry of pendimethalin. J. Agric. Food Chem. 39:797–800.

99. Parker, L.W., and K.G. Doxtader. 1983. Kinetics of the microbial degradation of 2,4-D in soil: effects of temperature and moisture. J. Environ. Qual. 12:553–558.

100. Parochetti, J.V., and G.W. Dec, Jr. 1978. Photolysis of eleven dinitroanaline herbicides. Weed Sci. 26:153–156.

101. Parochetti, J.V., G.W. Dec, Jr., and G.W. Burt. 1976. Volatility of eleven dinitroaniline herbicides. Weed Sci. 24:529–532.

102. Parochetti, J.V., and E.R. Hein. 1973. Volatility and photolysis of trifluralin, benefin, and nitralin. Weed Sci. 21:469–473.

103. Parr, J.F., and S. Smith. 1973. Degradation of trifluralin under laboratory conditions and soil anaerobosis. Soil Sci. 115:55–63.

104. Peter, D.J., and J.B. Weber. 1985. Adsorption and efficacy of trifluralin and butralin as influenced by soil properties. Weed Sci. 33:861–867.

105. Pik, A.J., E. Peake, M.T. Strosher, and G.W. Hodgsen. 1977. Fate of 3,6-dichloropicolinic acid in soils. J. Agric. Food Chem. 25:1054–1061.

106. Probst, G.W., T. Golab, R.J. Herberg, F.J. Holzer, S.J. Parka, C. Van Der Schans, and J.B. Tepe. 1967. Fate of trifluralin in soils and plants. J. Agric. Food Chem. 15:592–609.

107. Que Hee, S.S., and R.G. Sutherland. 1975. Volatilization of formulated butyl esters of 2,4-D from pyrex and leaves. Weed Sci. 23:119–126.

108. Rao, P.S.C., R.E. Green, V. Balasubramanian, and Y. Kanehiro. 1974. Field study of solute movement in a highly aggregated oxisol with intermittent flooding: II. Picloram. J. Environ. Qual. 3:197–202.

109. Rao, P.S.C., R.E. Jessup, and J.M. Davidson. 1988. Mass flow and dispersion. p. 21–43. In R. Grover (ed.) Environmental chemistry of herbicides. Vol. 1. CRC Press, Boca Raton, FL.

110. Savage, K.E. 1978. Persistence of several dinitroaniline herbicides as affected by soil moisture. Weed Sci. 26:465–471.

111. Savage, K.E., and T.N. Jordan. 1980. Persistence of three dinitraniline herbicides on the soil surface. Weed Sci. 28:105–110.

112. Savage, K.E.,and R.D. Wauchope. 1974. Fluormeturon adsorption-desorption equilibria in soil. Weed Sci. 22:106–110.

113. Schweizer, E.E. 1976. Persistence and movement of ethofumesate in soil. Weed Res. 16:37–42.

114. Scott, H.D., and R.E. Phillip. 1972. Diffusion of selected herbicides in soil. Soil. Sci. Soc. Am. Proc. 36:714–719.

115. Skoop, J., W.R. Gardner, and E.J. Tyler. 1981. Solute movement in structured soils: two region model with small interaction. Soil Sci. Soc. Am. J. 45:837–842.

116. Smith, A.E. 1972. The hydrolysis of 2,4-dichlorophenoxyacetate esters to 2,4-dichlorophenoxyacetic acid in Saskatchewan soils. Weed Res. 12:364–372.

117. Smith, A.E. 1973. Degradation of dicamba in prairie soils. Weed Res. 13:373–378.

118. Smith, A.E. 1974. Breakdown of the herbicide dicamba and its degradation product, 3,6-dichlorosalicylic acid, in prairie soils. J. Agric. Food Chem. 22:601–605.

119. Smith, A.E. 1976. The hydrolysis of herbicidal phenoxyalkanoic esters to phenoxyalkanoic acids in Saskatchewan soils. Weed Res. 16:19–22.

120. Smith, A.E. 1978. Relative persistence of di- and tri chlorophenoxyacetic acid herbicides in Saskatchewan soils. Weed Res. 18:275–279.

121. Smith, A.E. 1985. Persistence and transformation of the herbicides [^{14}C] fenoxaprop-ethyl and [^{14}C] fenthiaprop-ethyl in two prairie soils under laboratory and field conditions. J. Agric. Food Chem. 33:483–488.

122. Smith, A.E. 1989. Degradation, fate, and persistence of phenoxyalkanoic acid herbicides in soil. Rev. Weed Sci. 4:1–24.

123. Smith, A.E., and A.J. Aubin. 1989. Persistence studies with the herbicide clopyralid in prairie soils at different temperatures. Bull. Environ. Contam. Toxicol. 42:670–675.

124. Smith, A.E., and A.J. Aubin. 1990. Degradation studies with ^{14}C-fenoxaprop in prairie soils. Can. J. Soil Sci. 70:343–350.

125. Smith, A.E., and B.J. Hayden. 1981. Relative persistence of MCPA, MCPB, and mecoprop in Saskatchewan soils, and the identification of MCPA in MCPB treated soils. Weed Res. 21:179–183.

126. Smith, K.W., and G.R. Stephenson. 1984. Fate of ^{14}C-HOE 00736 in soil. p. 113–126. In P.N.P. Chow and C.A. Grant (ed.) Herbicide action in plants and soils: Proceedings of the 11th workshop on chemistry and biochemistry of herbicides. Agriculture Canada. Brandon, Manitoba, Canada.

127. Smith, A.E., and A. Walker. 1989. Prediction of the persistence of the triazine herbicides atrazine, cynazine, and metribuzin in Regina heavy clay. Can. J. Soil Sci. 69:587–595.

128. Spencer, W.F., and M.M. Cliath. 1990. Movement of pesticides from soil to the atmosphere. p. 1–16. In D.A. Kurtz (ed.) Long range transport of pesticides. Lewis Publ., Chelsea, MI.

129. Spencer, W.F., W.J. Farmer, and M.M. Cliath. 1973. Pesticide volatilization. Res. Rev. 49:1–47.

130. Stahnke, G.K., P.J. Shea, D.R. Tupy, R.N. Stouggard, and R.C. Shearman. 1991. Pendimethalin dissipation in Kentucky bluegrass turf. Weed Sci. 39:97–103.

131. Stephenson, G.R., K.R. Solomon, C.S. Bowhey, and K. Liber. 1990. Persistence, leachability, and lateral movement of triclopyr (Garlon) in selected Canadian forestry soils. J. Agric. Food Chem. 38:584–588.

132. Stewart, D.K.R., and S.D. Gaul. 1977. Persistence of 2,4-D, 2,4,5-T and dicamba in a dykeland soil. Bull. Environ. Contam. Toxicol. 18:210–218.

133. Takade, P.Y., M.S. Seo, T.S. Kao, and T.R. Fukuto. 1976. Alteration of 0,0-dimethyl-s-[α-(carboethoxy)benzo] phosphorodithivate (phenothoate) in citrus, water and upon exposure to air and sunlight. J. Agric. Food Chem. 29:227-230.

134. Tanaka, F.S., R.G. Wein, and E.R. Mansager. 1981. Survey for surfactant effects on the photolysis of herbicides in aqueous solutions. J. Agric. Food Chem. 29:277-230.

135. Torstensson, N.T.L. 1977. Effect of repeated applications on degradation of some herbicides. Proc. EWRS Symp. Methods Weed Control and their Integr. 1977. 113-120.

136. Tweedy, B.G., N. Turner, and M. Achituv. 1968. The interactions of soil-borne microorganisms and DCPA. Weed Sci. 16:470-473.

137. United States Environmental Protection Agency. 1990. Natioanl survey of pesticides in drinking water wells. Phase I report. USEPA Rep. 570/9-90015. U.S. Gov. Print. Office, Washington, DC.

138. Van Hoogstraten, S.D., C. Baker, and S.D. Horne. 1974. Ethofumesate Behavior in the Soil. p. 503-509. In Proc. 17th British Weed Control Conf. Brighton, England. 18-21 Nov. 1974. The Boots Company, Ltd. Nottingham, England.

139. Wagenet, R.J., and J.L. Hutson. 1990. Quantifying pesticide behavior in soil. Annu. Rev. Phytopath. 28:295-319.

140. Wagenet, R.J., and P.S.C. Rao. 1990. Modeling pesticide fate in soils. p. 351-399. In H.H. Cheng (ed.) Pesticides in the soil environment. SSSA Book Ser. 2, SSSA, Madison, WI.

141. Walker, A. 1976. Effect of varying weather conditions on the persistence of three herbicides in soil. p. 635-642. In Proc. 1976 British Crop Protection Conf—Weeds. Brighton, England. 15-18 Nov. 1976. The Boots Company, Ltd. Nottingham, England.

142. Walker, A. 1978. Simulation of the persistence of eight soil-applied herbicides. Weed Res. 18:305-313.

143. Walker, A., and W. Bond. 1977. Persistence of the herbicide. AL 92, 553, N-(1-ethyl-propyl)-2,6-dinitro-3,4-xylidine, in soils. Pestic Sci. 8:359-365.

144. Walker, A., and J.A. Thompson. 1977. The degradation of simazine, linuron, and propyzamide in different soils. Weed Res. 17:399-405.

145. Walker, A., and S.J. Welch. 1991. Enhanced degradation of some soil-applied herbicides. Weed Res. 31:49-57.

146. Wauchope, R.D., T.M. Butler, A.G. Hornsby, P.W.M. Augustyn-Beckers, and J.P. Burt. 1992. The SCS/ARS/CES pesticide properties database for environmental decision-making. Environ. Contam. Toxicol. 123:1-64.

147. Weber, J.B. 1990. Behavior of dinitroaniline herbicides in soils. Weed Technol. 4:394-406.

148. Weber, J.B., and S.B. Weed. 1968. Adsorption and desorption of diquat, paraquat, and prometone by montmorillonitic and kaolinitic clay minerals. Soil Sci. Soc. Am. Proc. 32:485-487.

149. Weed, M.B., J.J. Belasco, and J.L. Ploeg. 1966. Further studies with siduron for the selective control of annual weeds in turf. p. 75. In Weed Sci. Soc. Abstracts. Weed Sci. Soc. of Am, Champaign, IL.

150. Weed Science Society of America. 1989. Herbicide handbook. 6th ed. Weed Sci. Soc. of Am., Champaign, IL.

151. Wehtje, G., L.N. Mielke, J.R.C. Leavitt, and J.S. Schepers. 1984. Leaching of atrazine in the root zone of an alluvial soil in Nebraska. J. Environ. Qual. 13:507-513.

152. Willis, G.H., R.C. Wander, and L.M. Southwick. 1974. Degradation of trifluralin in soil suspensions as related to redox potential. J. Environ. Qual. 3:262-265.

153. Yih, R.H., C. Swithenbank, and D.H. McRae. 1970. Transformation of the herbicie N-(1,1-dimethyl-propynyl)-3,5-dichlorobenzamide in soil. Weed Sci. 18:604-607.

154. Zimdahl, R.L., P. Catizone, and A.C. Butcher. 1984. Degradation of pendimethalin in soil. Weed Sci. 32:408-412.

155. Zimdahl, R.L., and S.M. Gwynn. 1977. Soil degradation of three dinitroanilines. Weed Sci. 25:247-251.

Chapter 6

Herbicide Formulation Technology

G. B. BEESTMAN, *DuPont Agricultural Products, Wilmington, Delaware*

W. J. KOWITE, *Rhone-Poulenc Ag Company, Research Triangle Park, North Carolina*

Of the many herbicides registered in the USA for weed control in turf, none are usable in their technical form; all must be formulated to useful products, and formulating new products is becoming increasingly complex. Modern, rapidly degrading, chemically unstable herbicides must be stabilized. Modifications of the chemical and physical properties of herbicides, such as solubility, physical form, melting point, and chemical reactivity, must be made to achieve desired product characteristics. Living biological control agents must be kept viable during storage and must be activated after application. The formulators must maximize weed control with the least amount of active ingredients, while minimizing damage to turfgrasses. To minimize environmental impact, formulations must conform to emerging delivery systems, and packaging that degrades or recycles, as the public increasingly insists that they do not see, feel, or smell the treatments, nor be negatively impacted in any way.

Formulations technology is emerging to meet these demands with alterations of present product types and creation of new delivery forms. An overview of recent and established formulations is presented below. More exhaustive sources may be consulted for detailed informaiton of generic types of formulations (23, 47, 60).

I. DRY APPLICATION

Virtually all turfgrass herbicides applied dry are formulated as *granulars* (46). These include products for both homeowners and professional turf managers, and are applied through the familiar drop-type and broadcast spreaders. In this formulation, the technical herbicide is usually coated or adsorbed onto the inert carrier. A good deal of ingenuity and imagination have been applied to the choice of materials tried as carriers over the years, with minerals and organically derived by-products being the most popular choices. Commonly used materials in the minerals class include various clays (e.g., attapulgite, montmorillonite, and kaolinite), sand, diatomaceous earth, gypsum, dolomite, vermiculite, oxides, and phosphates. When the herbicide is combined with an appropriate fertilizer blend, the popular Weed and Feed (O.M. Scott & Sons Company, Marysville, OH) product is obtained. The most widely used organic carrier in the USA is ground corn (*Zea mays* L.) cob grit, with others such as walnut (*Juglans nigra* L.) shells and grain or rice (*Oryza sativa* L.) hulls also being utilized.

New carriers are becoming available to meet specific needs. Carriers made from recycled paper are available in small size and low density required for foliar application, or high density for penetration of turf (21). Carriers made from agglomerated powdered peanut (*Arachis hypogaea* L.) hulls (30) or processed organic materials (41) are designed to disintegrate in water, reducing the likelihood of birds ingesting the granules.

Incorporation of herbicides into starch granules has the potential to reduce chemical leaching into groundwater (59, 62) and has been shown to reduce chemical injury to turf (12). Incorporation of herbicides into wheat (*Triticum aestivum* L.) gluten granules (18), lignin (45, 61), and a thermoplastic matrix (9) provide controlled release.

The desired physical properties of the granular formulation must be carefully considered in choosing the inert carrier. For example, for preemergence herbicides that must contact the soil to provide root uptake, a heavy carrier capable of dropping through a dense canopy of shoots is needed. A mineral-type carrier with a large bulk density might be the best choice for this application. In the case of a foliar-active postemergence herbicide, a carrier with a relatively light bulk density might be preferable to help retain the active ingredient on the leaf surface. Particle size is also an important property to consider in light of application techniques and coverage as well as the effect on bioefficacy. Often the size distribution or homogeneity of the particles is as critical as the actual diameter dimensions. Granular products are usually sized in accordance with the U.S. Standard Sieve Classification and are expressed in a mesh-size range. For example, for a carrier to be specified as 20/40 mesh ($<850\ \mu$ openings/>425-μ openings), at least 90% of the material, by weight, should pass through a 20-mesh (850-μ opening) screen and be retained by a 40-mesh (425-μ openings) screen.

Constraints placed upon granule size and granule density to provide weed control might be in conflict with application needs thus presenting a special problem for the formulator. Consistent weed control might require 215 000 particles m^{-2} (20 000 particles ft^{-2}) of turf to prevent weed escapes. Small, light granules can supply the required number of particles for adequate coverage; however, the turf specialist may need large, heavy granules to provide wind resistance and uniform distribution from rotary applicators. Large, heavy granules provide only 21 000 particles m^{-2} (2000 particles ft^{-2}) or one-tenth the number needed for consistent weed control. One solution to this problem is to create large, heavy granules that disintegrate in water to provide postapplication redistribution of the herbicide. Powdered gypsum or other dense mineral, the desired herbicide, and a water-swelling clay can be compressed to form structurally sound granules (32). Such granules provide uniform distribution from rotary applicators and resist being blown by wind. Rainfall or irrigation expands the swelling clay causing immediate disintegration of the granules and redistribution of the herbicide for uniform weed control.

Similarly, properties such as resistance to attrition required to eliminate dustiness, may be in conflict with the requirement for rapid disintegration in water. The breakdown of granules during any stage of processing or handling, resulting in dustiness, is undesirable; however, rapid disintegration and release of herbicides in the presence of water is more rapid with softer granules. Thus, a trade-off in properties may be required. The method of incorporating active ingredients onto the carrier can affect these properties. Special binders can be utilized to adhere chemicals to nonporous surfaces that do not strongly absorb herbicides.

Many biological herbicides require solid substrate to grow or become effective. Granules will probably be a significant form of delivery for these materials.

II. BIOLOGICAL HERBICIDES

Sources of biological herbicides include viruses, bacteria, fungi, insects, and fish (6, 33, 57). The greatest formulations challenge is to satisfy the requirement for free water to maintain and activate biological pesticides, particularly fungal-based pathogens (5, 44, 56). Irrigation is used more intensively for turf management than for agricultural crops; therefore, the turf market may be a better fit for foliar-applied biological herbicides (5). A bacterial-based biological herbicide developed for control of annual bluegrass (*Poa annua* L.) has recently been disclosed (6). A significant formulations challenge is to stabilize living cells in a dry state.

A new system of weed control employs bacterial-based pathogens in combination with low levels of chemical herbicides (15). A broader spectrum of weed control is then achieved. A significant formulations challenge is single-package combinations of chemical and biological herbicides.

Fungal-based pathogens, mycoherbicides, have been most extensively developed (19, 54, 55, 57). Formation of mycoherbicides is the key to more fully exploiting their potential (10, 17, 55). Controlled-release granular formulations using alginate (16) or wheat gluten (20) enhanced herbicide efficacy of soil-applied mycorherbicides. Invert emulsions that retard evaporation of water were developed for delivery of mycoherbicides in foliar applications (19, 44). Dependence on dew or misting, to achieve infection, was significantly reduced.

Starch incorporation technology, developed by USDA scientists, has been utilized to control delivery of biological and chemical herbicides (48). Granules for direct dry application and sprayable formulations have been made.

III. SPRAY APPLICATIONS

Liquid formulations are applied to the target species as a spray. The simplest liquid formulations are solutions. If the solubility of the technical herbicide permits, the active ingredient is dissolved in water or a blend of water and suitable cosolvents, such as alcohols, glycols, and other polar media. If the active ingredient has low water solubility and contains an acidic functional group, water-soluble salts may be formed by neutralizing with amines or alkali hydroxides, typically NaOH or NH$_4$OH. Examples are salts of phenoxy acids, benzoic acid, glyphosate (N-(phosphonemethyl)glycine), and imazaquin [2-[4,5-dihydro-4-methyl-4-(1-methylethyl)-5-oxo-1H-imidazol-2-yl]-3-quinolinecarboxylic acid].

Newer, sulfonylurea herbicides for postemergence weed control are effective at grams per hectare rates. Examples are metsulfuron methyl [2-[[[[(4-methoxy-6-methyl-1,3,5-triazin-2-yl)amino]carbonyl]amino]sulfonyl]benzoic acid methyl ester], and chlorsulfuron [2-chloro-N-[[(4-methoxy-6-methyl-1,3,5-triazin-2-yl)amino]carbonyl]benzenesulfonamide]. Sulfonylureas can be formulated as aqueous solutions; however, they must be stabilized through complexation and pH control (29).

Aqueous-solution products are concentrated and intended for dilution in water by the applicator unless specified as ready-to-use formulations. The latter are generally limited to small volume use by homeowners. Hard water, containing relatively high concentrations of Ca^{2+} and Mg^{2+} cations, may present problems in the dilution of susceptible herbicide salts. The divalent metallic cations displace the amine or monovalent metallic cations from the negatively charged herbicides and precipitate them from the spray solution. This results in uneven treatments, or perhaps total loss of efficacy, and clogged spray nozzles. Sequestering agents or crystal growth inhibitors are added to chemically bind the Ca^{2+} and Mg^{2+} cations in hard water and prevent precipitation of the herbicides. Antifoams or defoamers may be added to control foaming. For most herbicides, emulsifiers are essential to enchance biological efficacy. Emulsifiers are also used to lower surface tension and control coverage of the sprayed solution on plant leaves. Humectants, sticking agents, wetting agents, dyes, and salts might also be utilized to complete a solution formulation.

Emulsifiable concentrates (ECs) are a large and important class of liquid formulations. Technical herbicides that have low water solubility in hydrocarbon solvents are often formulated this way. Low-melting-point herbicides that pass from a solid to a liquid phase after application are difficult to formulate as liquids. Making an EC may be the only direct possibility. Basic components of an EC are the active ingredient, solvent, and emulsifiers. Solvents dissolve the herbicide keeping it liquid during storage and after dilution into water. Emulsifiers disperse both solvent and herbicide in water as tiny droplets, forming an emulsion.

Appropriate solvents for a given herbicide can be identified by mapping herbicide solubility as a function of three solvent parameters: H bonding, dispersivity, and polarity. Other properties that influence the choice of solvent include: flash point, odor, color, and phytotoxicity to plants. Krenek and Rohde (35), in their overview of solvents used for agricultural chemicals, provide details of their use in formulations and describe refinements of solvent properties for meeting current needs. Higher N-alkyl pyrrolidones are a new class of surface-active solvents with good solvency for a wide variety of herbicides as ECs (43). Use of solvents as carriers in place of water can improve herbicide efficacy (35). Emulsifiable concentrates have been developed for waterless, low-volume applications (35). Incorporation of polymers into the active ingredient, prior to adding solvent, achieves sustained release (39).

The emulsifier system is critical to a successful EC. This type of emulsifier is generally a blend of surfactants designed to produce an acceptably stable emulsion of the technical material and solvent across a range of water hardness. Frequently, blends of both nonionic and anionic surfactants are the most useful, with an active-ingredient concentration range of 3 to 8% by weight, being typical. The ability of the product to self-emulsify or *bloom* when added to water with minimal agitation is a desirable, though not necessary, property that is also a function of the emulsifier. In addition to bloom and emulsifier stability, the property of resuspension of the settled emulsion is also important. Emulsions are not thermodynamically stable; hence, they tend to separate over time. A well-balanced herbicide emulsion will separate as a thick creamy layer, while a poorer product will form a layer of oil. In either case, the ease of resuspension is important because of the eventual possibility that a tank full of spray mixture will have to be stored overnight, or perhaps longer, before use. A product that separates as an oil will probably be more difficult to resuspend than a creamy separation. Water hardness often plays a role in emulsion performance, and its effects should be examined carefully by the formulation chemist. Shelf stability, as well as effects of other water parameters such as pH and temperature on the diluted EC, also must be studied during product development. Compatibility with other added tank-mix ingredients is a complex subject and will be addressed later in the chapter.

In order to achieve better solubility or improved physiological responses in plants, chemical modifications of the active ingredient are sometimes made. For example, phenoxy esters are synthesized from their corresponding acids. Low-volatile esters such as butoxyethyl are preferred for turf application over smaller, high-volatile esters to prevent unintentional damage to adjacent, susceptible plants. The concentration of active ingredient in an EC, or any other liquid concentrate, is expressed in weight per volume as well as in weight percent. This practice arose to enable the applicator to prepare dilutions by volume, while still knowing the weight of active per area covered. In the case of ester derivatives of herbicides, the concentrations are given for both the ester and, more importantly, the theoretical amount of active herbicide in the acid form calculated from the ester content. For example, a commercial formulation of the butoxyethyl ester of 2,4,-D [2,4-dichlorophenoxy)acetic acid] containing 60.8% by weight of ester possesses an acid equivalent of 41.9% by weight, or 473g L^{-1} (3.8 lb gal^{-1}) as governed by the specific gravity of the product. This last value actually determines the rate of application to achieve the desire coverage of the herbicide.

A relatively new formulation involving emulsion chemistry is the concentrated emulsion. A recent review describes concentrated emulsion formulations and contrasts their properties with other formulations (14). Unlike the EC, which is formulated in a nonaqueous solvent, the concentrated emulsion is prepared in water. The active ingredient is emulsified at a high concentration to form a stable aqueous system that can be diluted in the field. The inherent concerns of flammability, health risks, expense, odor, and increased phytotoxicity associated with nonaqueous solvents, can be avoided or greatly minimized as little or no solvents are required. Only herbicides that are liquids or readily liquefiable with the addition of a little solvent, and are nonreactive to water over a period of years, are suitable for this formulation. A variation of concentrate emulsions uses urethane resin to improve simazine efficiency in turfgrass, reduce volatilization of turfgrass herbicides, and reduce leaching of atrazine [6-chloro-N-ethyl-N'-(1-methylethyl)-1,3,5-triazine-2,4-diamine] (53).

Another major class of formulation is the liquid flowable, or simply *flowable* in the trade. This product contains a solid form of technical herbicide as a stable suspension or dispersion in a liquid medium, usually water. It offers the convenience of a liquid formulation for technical materials whose solubility in organic solvents is too low for commercial formulation as an EC. Technical herbicides best suited for flowables are high-melting crystalline compounds having very low water solubility. The technical particle size must be reduced to a very small diameter (3–10 μm) in order to obtain a stable dispersion. This may be achieved by dry milling the technical using an efficient method such as air milling prior to formulating in water. More commonly, technical materials are wet milled using media mills. Primary suspension stability is achieved using polymers that provide steric stabilization (52). Polymers are selected to tightly adsorb onto suspended herbicide crystalline particles and that have water-soluble groups to protrude into the water. Resistance to compression of these pendant water-soluble groups prevents suspended crystals from aggregating and dropping out of suspension. Other ingredients, such as thickening agents, antifreeze compounds, antifoamers, and preservatives, help to ensure that the desirable physical properties of the formulation are maintained. A partial listing of these properties include: (i) chemical stability of the technical material, (ii) suspension stability of the concentrated product over a reasonable shelf life, with special emphasis on avoiding hard packing of the technical material, (iii) ease of miscibility in water, (iv) minimization of the rate of settling of diluted flowable, and ease of resuspension of settled solids, (v) stability of the product to as broad a range of temperatures as possible, and (vi) compatibility with liquid fertilizer and other tank mix additives.

Concentrations of active ingredients in liquid flowables are expressed in much the same way as with other liquid formulations, that is, in weight per unit volume. Thus, a flowable product labeled as 4F contains 4 lbs a.i. gallon $^{-1}$ of formulation or 1.8 kg a.i. 3.8 L $^{-1}$. Where metric units are commonplace, concentrations are listed in grams per liter. Rates per given area are then conveniently measured by volume for both the product and water diluent. Two well known examples of turfgrass herbicides formulated as liquid flowables are atrazine and simazine (6-chloro-N,N'-diethyl-1,3,5-triazine-2,4-diamine).

Combination emulsion and suspension formulations have been developed to provide single-package combinations of multiple pesticides. These formulations, called suspoemulsions, consist of an emulsion phase containing one or more active ingredients with a continuous phase also containing active ingredients, but in the form of a solid dispersion. A recent review presents the history of suspoemulsion formulation developments and use of latices in suspoemulsion formulation (42).

Wettable powders (WPs) are a common class of sprayable formulations. To formulate a WP, the technical material is dry milled to a fine powder in the presence of suitable inert ingredients to produce a powdered form of the herbicide that is easily diluted in water for application. High-melting-point crystalline active ingredients, which do not soften during the temperature rise associated with milling, are ideal for WP formulation. To handle low-melting-point or softening technical materials, externally cooled mills are used. For water-sensitive herbicides, mills are blanketed in an atmosphere of dry inert gas. These modifications to process problem herbicides add significantly to the cost of a formulation.

Impact mills are routinely used to reduce particle size to a range of 10 to 20 μm. Milling to a smaller size range is best achieved with an air mill. The optimum size range for a commercial WP is often dictated by the minimum size requirement for biological efficacy. Other considerations to optimize particle size are speed of dispersion into water, bulk density, dustiness, and suspension stability.

In addition to the technical material, a typical WP contains silicate diluent, wetting agents, dispersant, and other inserts with specialized functions. These inerts include antifoams, chemicals stabilizers, humectants, emulsifiers (to facilitate efficacy), and stickers. A controlled-release WP of trifluralin (2,6-dinitro-N,N-dipropyl-4-(trifluoromethyl)benzenamine) incorporated into water-soluble polymers has been developed (40). Molten trifluralin is emulsified into water-soluble polymers and spray dried to form an encapsulated trifluralin powder. Further processing to retain desired crystalline structure produces the finished WP.

Wettable powders gained considerable popularity because of the relative simplicity of formulating them and the attractive economics, with a loading of 80% by weight or more of active ingredient being fairly common. The major disadvantage is the mess and unavoidable dust involved in handling a finely divided powder.

A popular formulation that overcomes the dustiness of powders is the sprayable granule, pioneered by Albert (2). Typical formulations and methods of preparing sprayable granules are described (22). Sprayable granules are also known as dry flowables (DFs) or water-dispersible granules (WDGs). These are formulations of essentially water-insoluble technical materials and may be regarded as an agglormerated form of WP, at least in a functional sense. In addition to the ingredients common to WPs, a binder is usually needed to hold the fine particles of herbicide and inerts together.

The ingredients are agglomerated into larger particles by methods such as disk or pan granulation, fluidized bed, spray drying, or extrusion. The DF formulations can now be manufactured in a new heat activated binder process that eliminates the need for drying of the granules (25). Eliminating the drying step saves the major costs of air purification systems to handle waste water from drying. By selection of small binder particles, dustless WPs can be formulated. A good process and formulation should yield granules that are uniform, dust free and of sufficient hardness to resist size reduction by normal abrasion and crushing during storage, transport, and handling. At the same time, the granules must soften and disperse quickly in water to form a spray mixture comparable to that of WPs or liquid flowables.

A DF formulation was made to modify the performance of turfgrass herbicides (34). Clay-based minigranules containing turf herbicides were dispersed in a matrix of soluble fertilizer. Granules were wetted into suspension as the fertilizer salts dissolved. As a consequence, benefin [N-butyl-N-ethyl-2,6-dinitro-4-(trifluoromethyl)benzenamine] was protected from ultraviolet light-induced decomposition, and foliar burn of oxadiazon was eliminated. The DFs will probably continue to be a preferred formulation for turf herbicides as they are inherently more stable than suspensions, solutions, or other solvent-containing formulations.

An emerging herbicide formulation for turf is the tablet (49). Tablets are prepared by compressing powders to dry, solid form. Effervescent tablets contain a bicarbonate base and an organic acid; when added to water, reaction to the organic acid with the bicarbonate base produces CO_2 gas that facilitates dispersion or solution into water. Noneffervescing tablets are formulated with water-swelling clays, or polymers, and wicking agents to promote dispersion into water. Tablets may also contain wetting agents, disintegrates, binders, die-release agents, antifoams, and emulsifiers. Roundup Quick Stik, an effervescent tablet formulation of glyphosate, is an example.

Formulations described so far constitue the majority of commercial products. One new liquid formulation deserves mention, however; this is the microemulsion. This system combines features of both true solutions and emulsions by dissolving the herbicide technical material in water by use of large quantities of surfactant or appropriate cosurfactants or solvents. While economically unattractive for many applications, microemulsions are used extensively in aerosol ready-to-use products.

IV. SPRAY TANK COMPATIBILITY

New product forms and large numbers of increasingly complex formulations can result in undesirable interactions when mixed together. These interactions, either chemical or physical, are unpredictable and require concerted efforts to be resolved. Instructions from product labels should be read and followed. Manufacturers should be notified of compatibility problems and their advise should be sought.

Chemical incompatibility often results in decomposition of an active ingredient. Temperature, solution, pH, and length of time that a spray mixture is held before spraying will affect the degree of herbicide decomposition. Chemical decomposition is difficult to detect and can occur without a recognizable physical change. Extremes in spraying conditions are required to realize decomposition through significant losses in efficacy. Only then can a problem be recognized and corrected.

Conversely, most physical incompatibilities are very apparent to the user. They may be symptoms of chemical degradation or incompatibility of the active ingredient, but often the problem lies with the inert ingredients of a formulation. Even though the active ingredient is chemically unaffected, the mixture may become unusable due to the formation of crystals, flakes, gel, oil, grease, or sludge that can act to clog spray equipment. Usually, ionic interactions or complexations, coupled with solubility characteristics of the chemicals, are fundamental to the occurrence of these problems. Liquid fertilizers are particularly notorious for causing compatibility problems, mainly because of their high use concentration and strong ionic nature.

The simplest and most practical approach to predicting and avoiding problems is to utilize the time-honored jar test. This basically involves adding the components of a questionable spray mixture to a 473 mL (one-pint) wide-mouth jar fitted with a tightly sealing screw cap (e.g., a common canning or preserving jar). The ingredients are tested in appropriately scaled-down quantities so as to retain their relative concentrations. The order of mixing of the ingredients is carefully noted and followed on a larger scale if no problems are observed in the jar. After mixing or shaking the components, the jar is usually allowed to remain undisturbed for at least 15 min. The absence of any flocculated solids, grease, or crystals is a favorable indicator that larger scale mixing will be satisfactory. The formation of finely divided flocculated material that readily disperses on mild agitation and passes cleanly through a fine mesh screen or strainer is usually not a serious indicator of trouble. One note of caution is that the water and other materials used in the jar test should be of the same source and temperature as those to be used later on a larger scale; otherwise, an inaccurate assessment of the tank mix may result. The order of addition is often quite important in evaluating incompatibilities. The water or liquid fertilizer is added first, followed by dry formulations such as WPs or DFs. Some mixing may be required at this point to aid dispersion. Next, liquid flowables are added, followed by solutions and ECs. Variations may be tried in the jar test if the above generally accepted order of additions does not work. If at all possible, any problem formulations should be prediluted with water before mixing in order to lessen the shock effect.

A number of compatibility agents are marketed that claim to aid in stabilizing tank mixes (27). These are usually surfactants or blends of surfactants in solvents, in which the surfactants are selected from classes known to impart additional stability to formulations in liquid fertilizers. They may or may not be of benefit to a particular mixing problem, and the above jar test is once again an excellent means of testing their effectiveness. These products bring an additional degree of uncertainty about possibly increased phototoxicity due to the additional surfactants. Still, they have a place in the area of spray applications stability. The issues of compatibility and spray adjuvants will continue to be of great interest in the foreseeable future.

V. TRENDS

Trends that will assist, as well as challenge, formulators of turfgrass herbicides in the future include: (i) adaptation of formulations for packaging and application systems, (ii) increased use of encapsulation, and (iii) cell immobilization of biological herbicides. Each of these trends is discussed below.

Closed-mixing and handling-transfer systems are emerging as preferred means to deliver pesticides (1). Closed systems and applications equipment will put additional demands on the formulator. One example, available to turf professionals, is the Expidite system (63); this system is gravity fed and requires that formulation rheology be controlled to provide both consistent flow and a good spray pattern across the range of temperatures in which the herbicides will be used.

An emerging closed system for single dosages of pesticides is water-soluble bags; these eliminate user contact during pesticide mixing. Packaging for water-soluble bags is easier to dispose of than plastic and metal containers. It has not been in direct contact with the products and can be disposed of as nonhazardous waste. Examples of turfgrass herbicides in water-soluble bags are: Solution-dry dimethylamine 2, 4-D; Dissolve-amines of 2, 4-D, mecoprop [(± -2-(4-chloro-2-methylphenoxy)propanoic acid] and dichlorprop [(±)-2-)2,4-dichlorophenoxy)propanoic acid]; Lesco TFC-chlorsulfuron [2-chloro-N-[[(4-methoxy-6-methyl-1,3,5-triazin-2-yl)amino]carbonyl]benzenesulfonamide]; and PRE-M-pendamethalin[N-(1-ethylpropyl)-3,4-dimethyl-2,6-dinitrobenzenamine]. Larger container water-soluble jugs are also available.

Gels are an emerging type of formulation well suited to returnable closed systems. Herbicide gels have been packaged in water-soluble bags. The gels can be formulated to be nonflowing so that minimal leakage would occur even if a bag developed a pinhole (28). Solventless and waterless gels based upon solution or suspension of herbicides into emulsifiers are being developed.

Microencapsulation is a tool with which formulators can create microcontainers of biological and chemical herbicides. Within these microcontainers, herbicides have reduced phytotoxicity, reduced acute toxicity and reduced leaching, are protected from dissipation, yet, are highly efficacious. Microencapsulation is gaining increased use in the formulation of pesticides.

Common microencapsulation techniques are explained in detail in a study by Marrs and Scher (38), but the most commercially successful method for chemical herbicides is interfacial polymerization (8). The breakthrough in interfacial-polymerization microencapsulation to create directly usable suspensions of microcapsules, with a larger volume of pesticides inside of microcapsules than the volume of water suspending them, has made this technology commercially viable for herbicides (7).

Microencapsulating one or more pesticides to isolate them from chemical or biological herbicides can be used to combine incompatible pesticides in a single formulation. Liquid and low melting point herbicides in microencapsulated form can be processed to dispersible dry solids (51). This eliminates the need for large amounts of inert absorbants to convert the liquids to a dry form; thus, dry flowable formulations of microencapsulated liquid herbicides can be formulated to contain much higher levels of active ingredients.

Modification of microcapsule shellwall composition to obtain desired formulation properties is possible. Microcapsule shellwalls can be modified to improve suspension properties of the microcapsules (50). Microcapsules can be made to release active ingredients at prescribed temperatures (11). Other modifications of shellwall composition to enhance the efficiency of herbicides or achieve desired formulation properties are attractive features of this technology, which is now emerging in crop and turf formulations.

Interfacial polymerization has been used to microencapsulate biological materials (13, 37), although matrixing techniques using water soluble natural or synthetic polymers are more common (24). Use of aminated glucosaccharide gelled with anionic polymers encapsulates viable cells with minimal damage (31). Live cells can be encapsulated in polysaccharide, a permanent shellwall fixed with polyamino acids, and further processed to liquify interiors of the microcapsules to perform biological functions when inserted into the body (26). The pore size of such microcapsules can be tailored to produce desired rates of release (36). A laboratory scale MicroDropper is available to simplify laboratory encapsulation of living cells (3). A larger-scale process utilizes water-soluble polymers to encapsulate microbes or other biological materials (4). This process achieves high recovery rates of viable (but dormant) active microbes encapsulated in polymer beads that can then be applied dry as granules or wet through spray nozzles.

Use of these techniques will continue to expand. Some of the benefits might be storage-stable biological herbicides, microenvironments that promote infection of biological herbicides, tailored delivery of chemical or biological herbicides, and multicomponent chemical and biological turf products.

In conclusion, the future of herbicide formulations for the turfgrass market is assurd as evidenced by the range and diversity of recent products, new chemical and biological herbicides, and novel delivery technologies. Increased emphasis will probably be seen on solventless formulations, closed-mixing, and handling-transfer systems, degradable or reusable packaging, and maximizing herbicide efficacy. Both professional turf managers and homeowners will benefit from improved generations of herbicide products to come.

REFERENCES

1. Akesson, N.B., R.W. Brazelton, R. Rutz, D.L. Anderson, Jr., R. Reynolds, and W.W. Jacobs. 1987. Closed mixing, handling and application systems. p. 13–55. In G.B. Beestman and D.I.B. VanderHooven (ed.) Pesticide formulations and application systems. Vol. 7. ASTM Spec. Tech. Publ. 968. Am. Soc. for Testing Materials, Philadelphia, PA.

2. Albert, R.E., and G.B. Weed. 1975. Water-dispersible pesticide aggregates. U.S. Patent 3 920 442. Date issued: 18 November.

3. Arneodo, V., D. Koka, F. Spenlehauer-Bonthonneau, P. Hundelt, and C. Thies. 1990. Curing of droplets to form microparticles. p. 447–448. In Vincent H.L. Lee (ed.) Proc. Int. Symp. Control. Rel. Bioact. Mater., Reno, NV. 22–25 July. Controlled Release Society, Washington DC.

4. Baker, C.A., A.A. Brooks, R.Z. Greenley, and J.M. Henis. 1992. Encapsulation of biological materials in non-ionic polymer beads. U.S. Patent 5 089 407. Date issued: 18 February.

5. Bannon, J.S., J.C. White, D. Long, J.A. Riley, J. Baragona, M. Atkins, and R.H. Crowley. 1990. Bioherbicide technology: An industrial perspective. p. 305–319. In R.E. Hoagland (ed.) Microbes and microbial products as herbicides. ACS Symp. Series 439. Am. Chem. Soc., Washington, DC.

6. Baragona, J.S., and J.C. White. 1992. Colonization of the bacterial biocontrol agent Xanthomonas Camperstris in annual bluegrass (Poa annua L.). p. 148. In WSSA Abstracts. Weed Sci. Soc. of Am., Champaign, IL.

7. Beestman, G.B. and J.M. Deming. 1988. Developments in microencapsulation, high concentration. p. 25–35. In D.A. Hovde and G.B. Beestman (ed.) Pesticide formulations and application systems. Vol. 8. ASTM Spec. Tech. Publ. 980. Am. Soc. for Testing Materials, Philadelphia, PA.

8. Beestman, G.B., and J.M. Deming. 1990. Commercial development of microencapsulated pesticides. p. 91–98. In R.M. Wilkins (ed.) Controlled delivery of crop-protection agents. Taylor & Francis, London.

9. Boehm, N., and T.P. Anderson. 1990. Soil-applied controlled-release products and suscon technology. p. 125–148. In R.M. Wilkins (ed.) Controlled delivery of crop-protection agents. Taylor & Francis, London.

10. Boyette, C.D., P.C. Quimby, Jr., W.J. Connick, Jr., D.J. Daigle, and F.E. Fulgham. 1991. Progress in the production formulation, and application of mycoherbicides. p. 209–222. In D.O. TeBeest (ed.) Microbial Control of Weeds. Chapman & Hall, New York.

11. Carter, D.H., P.A. Meyers, and C.L. Greene. 1992. Temperature-Activated release of trifluralin and diazinon. p. 57–72. In L.E. Bode and D.G. Chasin (ed.) Pesticide Formulations and application systems. Vol. 11. ASTM Spec. Tech. Publ. 1112. Am. Soc. for Testing Materials, Philadelphia, PA.

12. Chalmers, D.R., H.J. Hopen, and A.J. Turgeon. 1987. Controlled-release preemergence herbicide formulations for annual grass control in Kentucky bluegrass (Poa pratensis) Turf. Weed Sci. 35:533–540.

13. Chang, T.M.S. 1964. Semipermeable microcapsules. Science (Washington, DC) 146:524–525.

14. Chasin, D.G. 1987. Pesticide concentrated emulsion formulations. p. 32–38. In D.I.B. VanderHooven and L.D. Spicer (ed.) Pesticide formulations and application systems. Vol. 6. STM Spec. Tech. Publ. 943. Am. Soc. Testing and Materials, Philadelphia, PA.

15. Christy, A.L., K.A. Herbst, J.P. Kostka, J.P. Mullen, and P.S. Carlson. 1992. Synergizing chemical herbicides with microbes. p. 87–99. In S.O. Duke et al. (ed.) Pest control with enhanced environmental safety. ACS Symp. Series 524. Am. Chem. Soc. Washington, DC.

16. Connick, W.J., Jr. 1990. Microbial pesticide controlled-release formulations. p. 233–243. In R.M. Wilkins (ed.) Controlled delivery of crop-protection agents. Taylor & Francis, London.

17. Connick, W.J., Jr., C.D. Boyette, and J.R. Mc Alpine. 1992. Formulation of mycoherbicides using a pasta-like process. Biol. Control 1(4):281–287.

18. Connick, W.J., Jr., D.J. Daigle, and P.C. Quimby, Jr. 1991. An improved invert emulsion with high water retention for mycoherbicides delivery. Weed Technol. 5:442–444.

19. Connick, W.J., Jr., J.A. Lewis, and P.C. Quimby. Jr. 1990. Formulation of biocontrol agents for use in plant pathology. p. 345–372. *In* R.P. Baker and P.E. Dunn (ed.) New directions in biological control: Alternatives for suppressing agricultural pests and diseases. Liss Inc., New York.

20. Connick, W.J., Jr., A.B. Pepperman, Jr., J.W. Kuan, W.R. Nickle, and C.D. Boyette. 1991. A new process to make granular products containing chemical and biological pesticides. p. 8. *In* ASTM Abstracts. 11th Symp. on Pesticide Formulations and Applications Systems, San Antonio, TX. 14–15 Nov. Am. Soc. for Testing Materials, Philadelphia, PA.

21. Dill, R.A. 1992. Biodac offers flexibility to formulators. Agric. Chem. 14:22.

22. Fleming, J.P., and J.L. Hazen. 1983. Development of water-dispersible granule system. p. 141–146. *In* T.M. Kaneko and N.B. Akesson (ed.) Pesticide formulations and application systems. Vol. 3. ASTM Spec. Tech. Publ. 828. Am. Soc. for Testing Materials, Philadelphia, PA.

23. Foy, C.L. (ed.). Adjuvants for agrichemicals. CRC Press, Boca Raton, FL.

24. Fravel, D.R., and J.A. Lewis. 1992. Production, formulation and delivery of beneficial microbes for biocontrol of plant pathogens. p. 173–182. *In* L.E. Bode and D.G. Chasin (ed.) Pesticide formulations and application systems. Vol. 11. ASTM Spec. Tech. Publ. 1112. Am. Soc. for Testing Materials, Philadelphia PA.

25. Geigle, W.L., L.S. Sandell, and R.D. Wysong. 1991. Water-dispersible or water-soluble pesticide granules from heat-activated binders. World Patent 91/13545. Date issued: 19 September.

26. Goosen, F.A., G.M. O'Shea, and A.M.F. Sun. 1989. Microencapsulation of living tissue and cells. U.S. Patent 4 806 355. Date issued: 21 February.

27. Harvey, L.T. 1991. A guide to agricultural spray adjuvants used in the united states. Thomson Publ., Fresno, CA.

28. Hodakowski, L.E., C.R. Chen, S.T. Gouge, and P.J. Weber. 1992. Containerization system for agrochemicals and the like. U.S. Patent 5 080 226. Date issued: 14 January.

29. Hyson, A.M. 1990. Stabilized aqueous formulations of sulfonylurea salts. U.S. Patent 4 936 900. Date issued: 26 June.

30. Ivie, S.I. 1991. Method of processing peanut hulls. U.S. Patent 5 041 410. Date issued: 21 August.

31. Jarvis, A.P., Jr. 1989. Microencapsulation with polymers. U.S. Patent 4 803 168. Date issued: 7 February.

32. Johnson, C.E. 1987. Production of granular products by roll compaction. p. 199–202. *In* G.B. Beestman and D.I.B. VanderHooven (ed.) Pesticide formulations and application systems. Vol. 7. ASTM Spec. Tech. Publ. 968. Am. Soc. for Testing Materials, Philadelphia PA.

33. Julien, M.H. (ed.) 1992. Biological control of weeds. 3rd ed. University of Arizona Press, Tucson.

34. Kotz, M.E. 1986. Functional formulation for prescription performance. p. 3–12. *In* L.D. Spicer and T.M. Kaneko (ed.) Pesticide formulations and application system. Vol. 5. ASTM Spec. Tech. Publ. 915. Am. Soc. for Testing Materials, Philadelphia PA.

35. Krenek, M.R., and W.H. Rohde. 1988. An overview-solvents for agricultural chemicals. p. 13–27. *In* D.A. Hovde and G.B. Beestman (ed.) Pesticide formulations and application systems. Vol. 8. ASTM Spec. Tech. Publ. 980. Am. Soc. for Testing Materials, Philadelphia PA.

36. Lim, F.R. 1988. Production of sustained released system. U.S. Patent 4 789 516. Date issued: 6 December.

37. Lim, F.R., and R.D. Moss. 1982. Process for producing controlled porosity microcapsules. U.S. Patent 4 322 311. Date issued: 6 December.

38. Marrs, G.J., and H.B. Scher. 1990. Development and uses of microencapsulation. p. 65–90. *In* R.M. Wilkins (ed.) Controlled delivery of crop-protection agents. Taylor & Francis, London.

39. Meyers, P.A., and L.C. Forman. 1989. Emulsifiable concentrate. U.S. Patent 4 828 835. Date issued: 9 May.

40. Misselbrook, J., E.F. Hoff, Jr., E. Bergman, L.J. Mc Kinney, and J.H. Lefiles. 1991. Microencapsulated agriculturally active material. U.S. Patent 5 073 191. Date issued: 17 December.

41. Moechnig, B.W., and B.L. Wilhelm. 1990. Development and properties of transport—A new inert carrier. p. 38–41. *In* L.E. Bode et al. (ed.) Pesticide formulation and application systems. Vol. 10. ASTM Spec. Tech. Publ. 1087. Am. Soc. for Testing Materials, Philadelphia PA.

42. Mulqueen, P.J., E.S. Paterson, and G.W. Smith. 1990. Recent development in suspoe-mulsions. Pestic. Sci. 29:451–465.

43. Narayanan, K.S., and R.K. Chadhurl. 1992. Emulsifiable concentrate formulations for mul-tiple active ingredients using N-alkylpyrrolidones. p. 73–96. *In* D.G. Chasin and L.E. Bode (ed.) Pesticide formulations and application systems. Vol. 11. ASTM Spec. Tech. Publ. 1112. Am. Soc. for Testing Materials, Philadelphia PA.

44. Quimby, P.C., Jr., F.E. Fulgham, C.D. Boyette, and W.J. Connick, Jr. 1989. An Invert Emulsion Replaces Dew in Biocontrol of Sickepod—A Preliminary Study. p. 264–270. *In* D.A. Hovde and G.B. Beestman (ed.) Pesticide formulations and application systems. Vol. 8. ASTM Spec. Tech. Publ. 980. Am. Soc. for Testing Materials, Philadelphia PA.

45. Riggle, B.E., and D. Penner. 1988. Controlled release of three herbicides with the kraft lignin PC940C. Weed Sci. 36:131–136.

46. Sawyer, E.W. 1983. Introduction to granular carriers, granular pesticide formulations and processing. p. 26–44. *In* K.G. Seymour (ed.) Pesticide formulations and application sys-tems: Second conference. ASTM Spec. Tech. Publ. 795. Am. Soc. for Testing Materials, Philadelphia PA.

47. Scher, H.B. (ed.). 1984. Advances in pesticide formulations technology. ACS Symposium Series 254. Am. Chem. Soc., Washington, DC.

48. Shasha, B.S., and M.R. Mc Guire. 1992. Starch matrices for slow release of pesticides. p. 33–40. *In* D.G. Chasin and L.E. Bode (ed.) Pesticide formulations and application sys-tems. Vol. 11. ASTM Spec. Tech. Publ. 1112. Am. Soc. for Testing Materials, Philadel-phia PA.

49. Somlo, J. 1990. Herbicidal Compound Concentrate. U.S. Patent 4 933 000. Date issued: 14 January.

50. Stern, A.J. 1993. A photometric study of dilute microcapsule suspensions. p. 145–154. *In* B.N. Devisetty and D.G. Chasin (ed.) Pesticide formulations and application systems. Vol. 12. ASTM Spec. Tech. Publ. 1146. Am Philadelphia PA.

51. Surgant, J.M., and J.M. Deming. 1990. Formulations of water-dispersible granules and process for preparation thereof. U.S. Patent 4 936 901. Date issued: 26 June.

52. Tadros, T.F. 1991. Steric stabilization and flocculation by polymers. Polym. J. (Tokyo) 23(5):L683–696.

53. Takematsu, T., M. Konnai, and Y. Takeuchi. 1987. Research on efficient use of simazine by adding resin emulsion in turfgrass. Agrochem. p. 129–132.

54. Templeton, G.E. 1982. Biological herbicides: Discovery, development, deployment. Weed Sci. 30:430–433.

55. Templeton, G.E. 1986. Specific weed control with mycoherbiciees. p. 601–608. *In* 1985 British Crop Protection Conference Weeds, Brighton, Metrople. 18–21 Nov. BCPC Publ., England.

56. Templeton, G.E. 1990. Weed control with pathogens: Fugure needs and directions. p. 320–329. *In* R.E. Hoagland (ed.) Microbes and microbial products as herbicides. ACS Sym-posium Series 439. Am. Chem. Soc., Washington, DC.

57. Templeton, G.E., and K.K. Heiny. 1990. Mycoherbicides. p. 279–286. *In* R.P. Baker and PE. Dunn (ed.) New directions in biological control: Alternatives for suppressing agricul-tural pests and diseases. A.R. Liss, New York.

58. Templeton, G.E., R.J. Smith, D. Long, J.A. Riley, J. Baragona, M. Atkins, and R.H. Crowley. 1990. Bioherbicide technology: An industrial perspective. p. 305–319. *In* R.E. Hoagland (ed.) Microbes and Microbial Products as Herbicides ACS Symp. Series 439. Am. Chem. Soc., Washington, DC.

59. Trimnell, D., and B.S. Shasha. 1990. Controlled release formulations of atrazine in starch for potential reduction of groundwater pollution. J. Controlled Release 12:251–256.

60. Valkenburg, W.V. (ed.). 1973. Pesticide formulations. Marcel Dekker, New York.

61. Wilkins, RM. 1990. Biodegradable polymer methods. p. 149–160. *In* R.M. Wilkins (ed.) Controlled delivery of crop-protection agents. Taylor & Francis, London.

62. Wing, R.E., W.M. Doane, and M.M. Schreiber. 1990. Starch-encapsulated herbicides: Ap-proach to reduce groundwater contamination. p. 17–25. *In* L.E. Bode et al. (ed.) Pesticide formulations and applicatino systems. Vol. 10. ASTM Spec. Tech. Publ. 1078. Am. Soc. for Testing Materials, Philadelphia PA.

63. Wright, D.R. 1992. The expedite pesticide application system. A more efficient, safer way to apply pesticides. p. 183–192. *In* D.G. Chasin and L.E. Bode (ed.) Pesticide formula-tions and application systems. Vol. 11. ASTM Spec. Tech. Publ. 1112. Am. Soc. for Test-ing Materials, Philadelphia PA.

Chapter 7

Application Technology

THOMAS REED, *Spraying Systems Company, Wheaton, Illinois*

STEVE TITKO, *O.M. Scott & Sons Company, Marysville, Ohio*

The goal of herbicide application is three fold: to deliver the proper rate of chemical to the target weed, to adequately and uniformly cover the target, and to ensure that chemical drift is kept to a minimum. Successful application may involve either liquid (sprayable) or dry (spreadable) materials. The choice of which to use is dependent upon several factors. Certain herbicides may only be available in either a dry or liquid form. The availability of equipment at some locations may determine the type of application. In many cases the specific weed species may require a particular type of application to obtain satisfactory control. Also, the turf manager may base his decision of dry or liquid application upon budget considerations or the ease with which the material can be handled.

Once a method of application is chosen, the proper equipment to accomplish the task must be selected. Equipment selection is based upon the intended function and its intensity of use. Golf course, professional lawn care, or roadside application equipment is intensely used and must be ruggedly built. Homeowner equipment is designed to be simple and economical. This chapter discusses the different types of liquid and granular systems, the components in those systems, and their proper operation.

I. LIQUID APPLICATION SYSTEMS

A. Boom Sprayers

Liquid application systems can vary from simple hand-held pressurized sprayers to large self-propelled boom sprayers (Color Plate 7–1). Regardless of their complexities, the function of all hydraulic boom sprayers is to provide a uniform application of the spray material to the target area. Every hydraulic sprayer consists of several components. Each component may affect the performance of the spray system. Therefore, it is important to match the appropriate components of a boom sprayer to the particular application or applications desired.

1. Tanks

Tanks are used to transport the liquid being sprayed. Size and material from which a tank is constructed are important factors to consider. The construction material should be corrosion resistant with respect to the material being applied. Common materials used in tank construction include fiberglass, molded plastics, and stainless steel (Table 7–1).

The tank should be designed to minimize leftover spray mix so as to reduce waste and disposal problems; some tanks have a built-in sump for this purpose. The tank must also have a drain at the lowest point. The capacity at various levels should be clearly marked on the tank or be determined by a sight gauge visible from the operator's position. When using a centrifugal pump the tank should be mounted above the pump to facilitate easy priming.

Tank size selection is a compromise between weight to be transported and supported by the soil and the time required for refilling. The extra weight of larger tanks may cause more soil compaction but the effects can be reduced by using flotation tires. Hectares (acres) per tankful are determined by tank size and application rate.

2. Sprayer Pumps

The pump must deliver adequate flow and pressure and handle the desired chemicals without rapid corrosion and wear. Pumps are of two types: positive displacement and nonpositive displacement. Positive displacement pumps provide a constant output regardless of spraying pressure; included in this type are the piston pump, diaphragm pump, and the roller pump operating at low pressures. The output of nonpositive displacement pumps is dependent upon the spraying pressure required; included in this type are centrifugal pumps and roller pumps operating at higher pressures. The type

Table 7-1. Tank materials and their characteristics.

Consideration	Plastic	Fiberglass	Stainless steel
Corrosion proof	Yes	Yes	Yes
Repairable	Some with kits	Kit with resin	Welding
Weight	Light	Medium	Heavy
Sizes gallons	10–1350	25–2000	50–2000
liters	38–5103	95–1560	189–7560
Liquid level visible	Yes	Some	No, sight gauge required
Cost	Low	Medium	High
Comments	Not easy to repair Sunlight can breakdown some tank materials Mounting is critical	Can break or crack under impact Mounting is critical	Strong and durable but most ex- pensive

of pump needed depends upon the intended use; no pump is ideal for all purposes. Four of the most common pumps used on turf and landscape sprayers are discussed below.

Roller Pump. Roller pumps produce medium flows and pressures and are adequate for many applications. The rollers are held in a slotted rotor revolving in an eccentric case. As the rollers pass the pump inlet, the cavities between and under the rollers enlarge and draw in liquid. When nearing the outlet, the cavities contract due to the eccentric housing, and force the liquid out of the pump (Fig. 7–1).

Roller pumps have a low initial cost, a low maintenance cost, and they are suitable for a variety of pesticides. These pumps are very efficient; however, as pressure is increased, the volume (output) decreases slightly, especially after the pump becomes worn. Pump capacity is a function of pump design and rotational speed.

Roller pumps are not well suited for abrasive material such as wettable powders. Abrasives rapidly wear the pump housing, the slots in the rotor, and the rollers. Replacing the rollers is easy, but may not restore the pump to a satisfactory working condition. Nylon rollers work well with most chemicals, but rubber rollers are slightly better if abrasive materials must be used.

Centrifugal Pump. A centrifugal pump creates flow and pressure by centrifugal force from an impeller to the fluid. They are considered high-volume, low-pressure pumps. Liquid enters through the center of the impeller and, as the impeller spins, the liquid is thrown by centrifugal force into a spiral passage leading to the outlet. The only moving parts in a centrifugal pump are the shaft and impeller (Fig. 7–2).

The impeller must operate between 2000 and 4200 rpm to give rated performance. If pump speed decreases by 10%, volume drops by 10% and pressure decreases by 19%. Power-take-off-powered centrifugal pumps require speed-up drives and high engine revolutions per minute, which can waste fuel when spraying. An alternative is to power the pump by a hydraulic motor connected to the sprayer's hydraulic system or by an auxiliary gasoline engine.

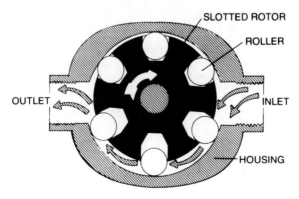

Fig. 7–1. Cutaway view of roller pump.

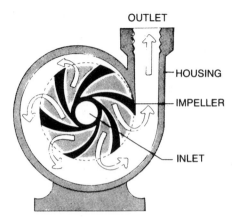

Fig. 7-2. Cutaway view of centrifugal pump.

Centrifugal pumps are long lasting (even with wettable powders) and produce a high volume of flow that is ideal for hydraulic (jet) agitation in the sprayers tank. They can develop pressures up to 690 kPa or (100 lb in. $^{-2}$), but pump output falls very rapidly above 207 to 276 kPa (30–40 lb in. $^{-2}$). Typical maximum working pressure is 345 to 414 kPa (50–60 lb in. $^{-2}$).

Piston Pumps. Piston pumps are low-volume, high-pressure pumps. With a piston pump, liquid is propelled by a piston moving in a cylinder. The intake stroke draws the liquid in through one valve, and the output stroke forces the liquid out through another valve (Fig. 7-3). Piston pumps develop high pressures that can increase the versatility of a sprayer; however, the relative capacity of piston pumps is usually low. Because the higher-volume piston pumps are expensive, mechanical agitation is normally used instead of hydraulic agitation. Larger-capacity pumps driven by gas engines are better suited for professional applicators. The large pumps achieve higher flow rates with two to eight cylinders, and the multicylinder design produces a more even flow. Piston pumps should have either an internal or external air cham-

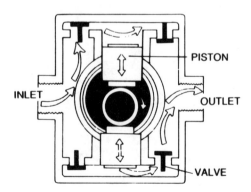

Fig. 7-3. Cutaway view of piston pump.

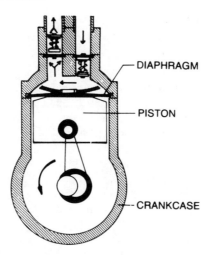

Fig. 7-4. Cutaway view of diaphragm pump.

ber, sometimes referred to as a surge tank or accumulator, to dampen pulsations in the liquid flow associated with each pump stroke.

Diaphragm Pumps. Diaphram pumps have medium output and medium to high pressures. The diaphragm pump has at least one chamber sealed at one end by a membrane or diaphragm. The other end has inlet and outlet valves. The diaphragm is connected to a piston. As the piston moves, the liquid is drawn by suction through the inlet valve by movement of the diaphragm, which enlarges the chamber. Return of the piston forces the diaphragm inward shrinking the chamber and propelling the liquid out (Fig. 7-4). An external compression chamber is required to smooth out line pulses if one is not incorporated in the pump. Connection and operation of the diaphragm pump is similar to the piston pump system.

Diaphragm pumps require minimal maintenance because there is no contact between the spray material and moving parts other than the diaphragm. The diaphragm should be resistsnt to the chemical used. Abrasive materials are less likely to damage this type of pump.

Pump Capacity. An important factor in pump selection is required pump capacity. The pump should have sufficient capacity to supply all of the nozzles, provide jet agitation (if used), and offset pump wear. If hydraulic (jet) agitation is used, allow at least 1.13 m^3 h^{-1} (5 gal min^{-1}) equivalent mixing action for each 378 L (100 gal) of tank capacity. This can be obtained by pumping 1.13 m^3 h^{-1} (5 gal min^{-1}) per 378-L (100-gal) tank capacity through a submerged standard agitator, or by running 0.45 m^3 h^{-1} (2 gal min^{-1}) from the pump through a siphon (venturi) agitator that increases the flow through the agitator 2.5 times.

Finally, when selecting a pump allow for normal pump wear. Pump capacity should be 20 to 25% higher than the combined application and agitation volumes required to compensate for wear loss. A summary of the pumps and their characteristics is presented in Table 7-2.

3. Hoses

Hoses carry liquid throughout the spraying system. They should be as short as possible to reduce pressure losses that can occur as fluids flow through the hose. They should also be sized to allow for a liquid velocity of 1.52 to 1.83 m (5 to 6 ft) per second to prevent wettable powders from settling out of the tank suspension.

The hose between the tank and pump should be very short and larger in diameter than the downstream hoses. This will eliminate negative pressure which can develop causing the supply hose to collapse and starve the pump disrupting fluid flow in the system. Many supply hoses are wire reinforced to prevent collapse.

Hoses-to-boom sections should be of equal length to minimize differences in pressure loss. Hose size between nozzles should be large enough to maintain uniform pressure through all nozzles across the boom.

4. Controls and Plumbing

When spraying turfgrass the operator must constantly monitor and control the spraying operation. Numerous devices are available to aid in operating the sprayer. Figures 7-5 and 7-6 illustrate typical plumbing arrangements for positive and nonpositive pumping systems.

Sprayer Monitors and Controls. System monitors sense the operating conditions of the total sprayer such as travel speed, pressure, or flow; these inputs are fed into a microcomputer along with other inputs such as swath width, or liters (gallons) of spray mixed in the tank. The console displays the pressure and travel speed. The most important function of the monitor is to continuously compute and display the application rate in liters per hectare (gallon per acre). In addition, the monitor will compute and display important information such as field capacity in hectares per hour (acres per hour), amount applied, amount remaining in tank, area covered, and distance traveled. Of course, sensors must be installed and the unit accurately calibrated before they will function. Once that job is completed, however, proper operation requires actuating switches or pushing buttons. In many cases, more accurate rate monitoring will result in better pest control, lower likelihood of pollution, and less pesticides applied.

Many units have the additional capability of automatic rate control. This may be a built-in or an add-on function. The controller receives the actual application rate from the monitor and compares it with the preset desired rate. If there is a difference (error) of at least 1%, the controller will adjust the application rate automatically (usually by adjusting pressure) to reduce the error. If the error becomes large (e.g., 10%) the unit will signal the operator to indicate that the controller is unable to correct the problem. This may happen if speed varies too much for pressure compensation, a hose or connection breaks, a line strainer plugs, or some other serious problem occurs.

Table 7-2. Pumps for boom sprayers.

	Roller	Centrifugal	Piston	Diaphragm
Materials handled	Nonabrasive materials	Most	Most	Most: some chemicals may damage diaphragm
Relative purchase price	Low	Medium	High	High
Durability	Pressure decreases with wear	Long life	Long life	Long life
Pressure ranges				
psi	0-300	0-100	0-1000	0-850
kPa	0-2068	0-690	0-6900	0-5862
Operating speeds RPM†	300-1000	2000-4200	600-1800	200-1200
Flow rates GPM†	1-35	20-120	1-60	1-60
LPM†	4-133	76-455	4-227	4-227
Advantages	Low cost. Easy to service. Operates at power take off speeds. Medium volume. Easy to prime	Handles all materials. High volume. Long life	High pressure. Wear resistant. Handles all materials. Self-priming	Wear resistant. Resistant to most chemicals. Self-priming
Disadvantages	Short life if material is abrasive	Low pressure. Not self-priming. Requires speed-up drive or high speed hydraulic motor	High cost. Needs surge tank	Needs surge tank. High cost

† RPM, revolutions per minute; GPM, gallons per minute; LPM, liters per minute.

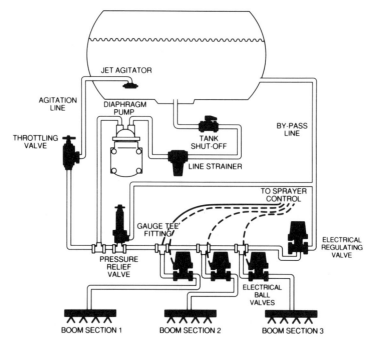

Fig. 7–5. Typical plumbing system for positive displacement pump.

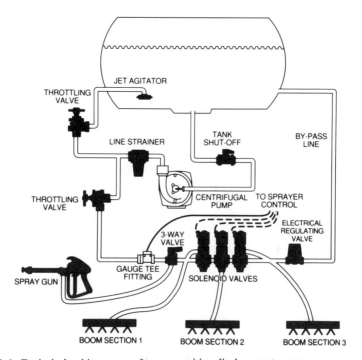

Fig. 7–6. Typical plumbing system for non-positive displacement pump.

Pressure Gauge. The pressure gauge should be one designed to measure liquid pressure. The range should be ≈ 1.5 to 2.0 times the maximum anticipated pressure. A damper installed between the gauge and sprayer will smooth pressure pulsations and make the gauge easier to read as well as prolong the life of the moving parts. Liquid filled gauges are preferred over dry gauges because they dampen vibrations caused by pressure spikes in the system. The pressure gauge should be installed so that it can be read from the operator's position.

Boom Control Valves. Sometimes it is desirable to use less than the full boom for narrow turf areas or when finishing a putting green. Booms are often divided into sections with individual valves. The valves, either manual or electrical, control the flow to either the left, center, or right boom section, or any combination of these.

Pressure Regulating Valves. Pressure relief (by-pass) valves are needed in systems with positive displacement pumps to control the spray pressure and prevent excessive pressure buildup. The valves open as pressure increases to some adjustable level; this controlled flow relieves the pressure and permits some of the flow to bypass back into the sprayer tank. Since the valve controls the pressure in the system, its adjustment also determines the operating pressure; thus, the valve is often referred to as the pressure regulator. Sometimes this same line is used for agitating the tank solution; however, this practice should be avoided as the flow through the bypass can fluctuate due to changes in the system's pressure requirements. Electric (remote control) pressure regulating valves are also available for easy pressure adjustment by the operator while spraying.

Throttling Valves. Pressure in spraying systems supplied by nonpositive displacement pumps (centrifugal pumps) should be controlled by using a throttling valve. The valve restricts flow to the boom and nozzles without creating excessive pressure buildup due to the nature of the pumping system. A throttling valve is also a good choice for regulating hydraulic agitation flow.

Agitators. The amount of agitation depends largely upon the formulation of the chemical being applied. Separation of chemical from carrier in the tank causes the concentration of the pesticide spray to change as the tank empties. Therefore, uniform application requires a uniform tank mix. All sprayers should have a tank agitator to maintain a uniform mix. Agitation may be produced by a hydraulic jet or mechanical apparatus.

Agitation by a hydraulic jet (commonly called jet agitation) uses a portion of the liquid flow to create a mixing action in the tank. The pump must be large enough to provide the extra volume required by the jet agitator. The flow can be through a standard agitator nozzle or a specally designed siphon nozzle. The siphon nozzle creates a *venturi effect* or vacuum that increases the discharge from the nozzle. This increases the mixing action by 2.5 times and is very effectie when liquid flow is otherwise marginal.

Jet agitation may also utilize a pipe or tube with several discharge holes, called a sparger, near the bottom of the tank. A sparger is desirable for large, long tanks.

When using jet agitation, the agitator orifices should receive liquid from a separate line on the discharge side of the pump and not merely from the bypass line.

Mechanical agitation is produced by paddles or propellers located in the bottom of the sprayer tank. These mixers are driven mechanically from the power source for the pump or by a 12 V electrical motor. Mechanical agitators are often used on sprayers with piston pumps, since jet agitation requires a larger, more expensive piston pump.

Any agitator, when properly designed and operated, will adequately mix most pesticides. Adjustable agitators are desirable to minimize foaming that may occur with vigorous agitation of certain chemicals. The amount of flow needed for agitation can be determined in the section on pump capacity.

Strainers. Strainers and filters should be used at three places within a spraying system. Basket strainers are found at the tank's filler hatch. This is followed by a strainer between the tank and pump or between the pump and valves on the downstream side, depending on the type of pump. A growing practice is to place small in-line strainers on the supply line to each boom section. This practice greatly reduces the chance of nozzles clogging. Strainers should also be placed at the nozzle as a final measure to prevent clogging of the tip orifice.

Strainers are made using wire screens of various mesh size supported by stainless steel or plastic frames and placed inside a holding container or bowl. Screens for line strainers and nozzles are also available in corrosion-resistant thermoplastics. The mesh size of the strainer screens refers to the number of openings per linear distance. Generally, the screen area of the strainer between the tank and pump should be 57 cm^2 for each m^3 h^{-1} (2 in.^{2} for each gal min $^{-1}$) of flow.

A new type of strainer with a self-cleaning feature is available. The strainer uses excess capacity to continually wash down the screen element, bypassing the contaminants and undissolved chemical back to the tank (Fig. 7–7). A throttling valve should be used to regulate the bypass flow from the strainer.

Nozzle Screens and Check Valves. Screens at the nozzle should be no larger than the tip orifice and can be wire mesh or slotted. Some screens have a ball check valve to prevent nozzle dripping. These are needed when the boom is shut off during turns or if the operator stops in the field as excessive residues may damage the turf. Another available anti-drip device is a diaphragm check valve. This check valve allows the nozzle tip to be changed without letting spray material leak from the boom. Also, the diaphragm helps protect the device from chemical corrosion which could cause a ball check valve to fail (Fig. 7–8).

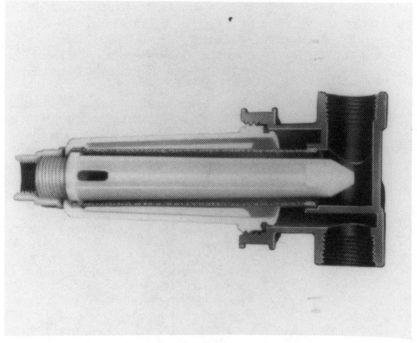

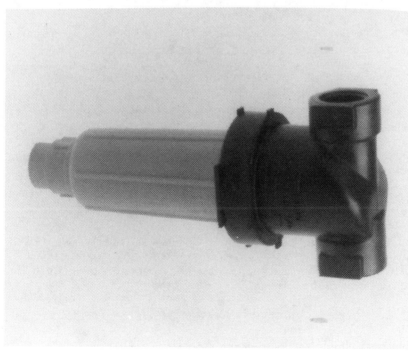

Fig. 7-7 Self-cleaning strainer with cutaway view.

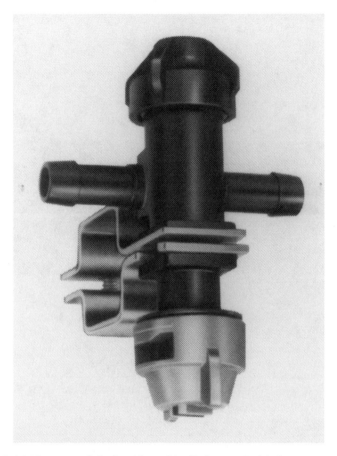

Fig. 7–8. Quick change nozzle body with no-drip diaphragm check valve.

4. Nozzles

Proper selection and operation of spray nozzles are important steps in precision application. Incorrect application rates or poor spray distribution can be very evident in fine turf areas.

Spray tips have three important functions: to regulate flow, to form droplets, and to disperse the droplets in a specific pattern. Flow regulation is extremely important as it contributes to the application rate. Nozzle flow rate conforms to the formula:

$$m^3\ h_1^{-1}/m^3\ h_2^{-1} = \sqrt{kPa_1}\,/\sqrt{kPA_2} \qquad \text{or}$$

gallons per minute$_1$/gallons per minute$_2$

$$= \sqrt{\text{pounds per square inch}}\,/\sqrt{\text{pounds per square inch}_2}$$

This formula indicates that in order to double the flow rate through an orifice the pressure must be increased four-fold. Therefore, orifice size and liquid pressure are the key properties affecting the flow rate through nozzles. These factors are easily changed by selecting a different nozzle size or by adjusting the pressure. Additional factors affecting flow rate relate to the properties of the fluid passing through the nozzle such as viscosity, liquid density, and surface tension. These properties are not readily changed by the operator unless adjuvants are added to the tank mixture or the carrier is something other than water (e.g., liquid fertilizer).

Droplet formation at the nozzle orifice results from the collapse of unstable fluid sheets, jets, and strings or from the tearing action of air. These actions usually produce droplets that vary widely in size. Droplet size in a spray pattern is measured in micrometers. From the droplet spectrum, one is able to determine the characteristics of the nozzle's spray through various statistical parameters. The parameter most frequently reported is the volume median diameter ($Dv_{0.5}$). The $Dv_{0.5}$ is the diameter that divides the droplet spectrum into two equal portions by volume. For example, if a droplet spectrum is found to have a $Dv_{0.5}$ of 250 μm, this indicates that half the volume of the spectrum is in droplet sizes smaller than 250 μm and the other half is in droplet sizes larger than 250 μm.

Droplet size is affected by nozzle pressure and spray angle as well as the spray pattern shape (nozzle design). Increasing pressure at the nozzle will decrease droplet size. Increasing the spray angle of the tip will also decrease droplet size. As nozzle capacity (orifice size) is increased, there is a corresponding increase in the droplet size.

Nozzle spray patterns are of three basic types: flat sprays, hollow cone, and full cone patterns. Each type of spray pattern has certain characteristics which favor its use for specific applications.

Flat Spray Nozzle. The spray droplets from a flat spray tip form a fan-shaped pattern as they leave the elliptical orifice (Fig.7-9). As the edges of the pattern have a lower spray volume, the patterns of adjacent nozzles must be overlapped to obtain uniform coverage along the spray boom. Minimum proper overlap is 30% on each edge of the spray pattern. Tables in nozzle manufacturers' catalogs provide data on spray tip height to achieve proper overlap.

Flat spray tips are commonly manufactured in 80 and 110° spray angles. Wider angle nozzles produce smaller droplets, but they can be spaced further apart on the spray boom or operated closer to the target. Narrow-angle spray tips produce a more penetrating spray and are less susceptible to clogging. The characteristics of the flat spray tip make it ideal for broadcast applications of herbicides where uniformity is critical. Typical operating pressure should be 207 to 414 kPa (30–60 lb in. $^{-2}$) for the most uniform coverage. Lower pressures will reduce drift but may also result in less uniformity along the boom.

Several new types of flat spray tips are also available to turf managers. The extended range flat spray tip has been designed to provide better spray

Fig. 7-9. Flat spray tip and pattern.

distribution over an extended range of spraying pressures from 104 to 414 kPa (15–60 lb in. $^{-2}$). At low pressure, systemic herbicides can be uniformly applied with reduced risk of drift.

Higher pressures can be used for applications of contact herbicides where more complete coverage is essential (Fig. 7-10).

Another variation of the flat spray tip utilizes a preorifice to reduce liquid velocity and lower spraying pressure, resulting in larger spray droplets. This spray tip is being used in applications where drift control is a dominant factor. Typical operating pressure for maximum drift control is 207 to 276 kPa (30–40 lb in. $^{-2}$) (Color Plate 7-2).

Fig. 7-10. Extended range flat spray tip and pattern.

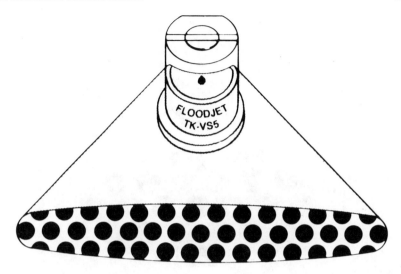

Fig. 7-11. Flooding spray tip and pattern.

The twin orifice flat spray is designed for applications requiring thorough spray coverage and good spray penetration. The spray tip has two orifices that direct one flat spray pattern 30° to the front and a second pattern 30° to the rear. By atomizing with two orifices, the droplet size is smaller than an equivalent capacity standard flat spray tip. The smaller droplets increase coverage potential and make the nozzle suitable for applying contact herbicides. Typical operating pressure is 207 to 414 kPa (30–60 lb in.$^{-2}$).

Flooding Nozzle. The standard flooding nozzle produces a wide, flat spray pattern as the liquid is atomized at the leaving edge of the deflector surface (Fig. 7-11). The wide spray angle (110 to 130°) allows wider nozzle spacings and lower boom heights in broadcast applications. Both the wider spacings, which allow a larger orifice and the round shape of the orifice, make it less suceptible to clogging.

While popular because of its low maintenance, the standard flooding nozzle does not provide the most uniform spray distribution. The edges of the spray pattern typically exhibit higher volumes known as *spray horns*. These heavy edges require that adjacent spray patterns be double overlapped to optimize broadcast coverage. Angling the nozzles at 15 to 45° also improves the uniformity of coverage. Typical operating pressure is 69 to 173 kPa (10–25 lb in.$^{-2}$).

A new type of flooding nozzle has been designed to overcome the deficiencies of the standard flooding nozzle. The Turbo FloodJet (Spraying Systems Co., Wheaton, IL) spray tip utilizes a preorifice and patented atomization chamber to produce a uniform tapered edge pattern (Color Plate 7-3). The droplets from this spray tip are very large making it an appropriate choice for drift control. Unlike the standard flooding nozzle, the Turbo FloodJet spray tip produces very uniform coverage in broadcast applications.

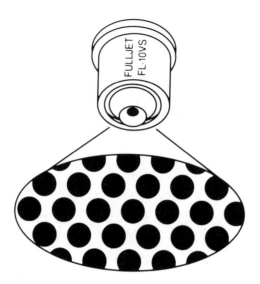

Fig. 7-12. Wide angle full cone spray tip and pattern.

For maximum drift control typical operating pressures are 104 to 207 kPa (15–30 lb in. $^{-2}$).

Wide Angle Full Cone Nozzle. The wide angle full cone nozzle produces large droplets distributed uniformly in a full cone pattern (Fig. 7-12). Its primary purpose is to control drift. The uniform spray pattern is maintained over a pressure range of 69 to 276 kPa (10–40 lb in. $^{-2}$). This nozzle is well suited for soil-applied and systemic herbicides. Maximum drift control is obtained at pressures of 104 to 138 kPa (15–20 lb in. $^{-2}$). The nozzle can be operated spraying straight down with a 10 to 30% overlap of the spray pattern. To optimize broadcast uniformity, however, spray patterns should be overlapped 30 to 50% on each edge with the nozzles spraying at a 30 to 45° angle from the vertical.

Hollow Cone Nozzle. A hollow cone nozzle produces a spray pattern with the liquid concentrated on the outside of a conical pattern. The typical spray distribution is saddle-shaped with less liquid in the center of the distribution and the amount of liquid tapering off rapidly at the edges. For this reason proper overlap is more difficult to achieve in broadcast applications with hollow cone nozzles.

With the exception of the Raindrop nozzle (Delevan Corp., West Des Moines, IA), hollow cone nozzles generally produce the smallest droplets of any nozzle type. They are used mainly to apply insecticides, fungicides, or growth regulators where penetration and coverage are critical. Spray drift can be high due to the number of small droplets produced. Typical operating pressure of these nozzles is 276 kPa (40 lb in. $^{-2}$) and above. The Raindrop nozzle is a drift reducing hollow cone nozzle (Fig. 7-13). Its design reduces many of the small droplets typically produced by a hollow cone noz-

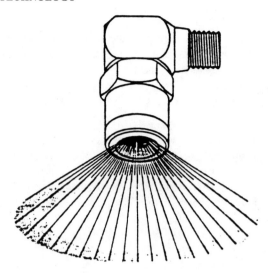

Fig. 7-13. Raindrop nozzle and pattern.

zle. Typical operating pressure is 138 to 414 kPa (20–60 lb in. $^{-2}$). For optimum uniformity the nozzles are tilted 15 to 45° and spray patterns are overlapped 100%.

Boomless Nozzle. In some areas the terrain or obstructions may make operation of a boom sprayer difficult or impossible. The boomless or cluster nozzle is typically used in these situations (Color Plate 7-4). This compact nozzle assembly mounted at the rear of the sprayer can deliver a spray swath 9.1 to 18.2 m (30–60 ft) depending upon pressure and capacity. The nozzle assembly consisting of up to five separate nozzles produces a wide, flat spray pattern. Atomization is as fine as possible in relation to the distance the spray must travel to outside edges of the swath. Angle mounting can be used to allow a lower nozzle height thus decreasing the effect of wind on spray drift, while maintaining the swath width. Spray distribution is not as uniform as with a boom sprayer; however, double overlapping swaths can compensate for this to some degree.

Oscillating Solid Stream. The oscillating solid stream nozzle utilizes a cluster of many small openings arranged on a cylinder. The cylinder oscillates in a back and forth motion from a variable speed electric motor. This motion distributes the spray and facilitates droplet formation. The pattern width can vary from 4.6 to 10.6 m (15–35 ft) depending upon the number and location of openings in the cluster. Since the spray is projected from the unit at these distances, it is essentially boomless and, therefore, desirable where a boom sprayer cannot operate. Droplet size is controlled by the speed of the motor and is inversely proportional to the speed. The orientation of the nozzle can change from horizontal to vertical. A horizontal arrangement produces a fan or arc pattern emitted parallel to the ground. A vertical position projects the arc perpendicular to the ground for covering trees and brush. This versatility, its boomless nature, and the ability to manipulate droplet size, has found particular favor with the roadside and railway spraying industry. Although suitable for spraying certain herbicides on turf, its use is somewhat limited to open areas and where precision and uniformity are not required. Its principle advantage is its boomless design and the ability to spray large droplets where drift is a concern.

Rotary Nozzle. Rotary nozzles utilize centrifugal force to atomize the spray. Although there are many designs of rotary nozzles, the most common is the spinning disk (Color Plate 7–5). The disk is driven electrically by a variable speed motor; it may have grooves, teeth, or both. The liquid enters the base of the disk through a metered orifice; it is then channeled through the grooves where individual droplets are formed by the centrifugal force of the disk. The droplets are propelled away from the disk horizontally and drop to the surface to form a circular pattern.

Spinning disk nozzles are among the most accurate nozzles for producing droplets of consistent size; as a result, they have also been called controlled droplet applicators, or CDAs. Droplet size is a function of the speed of the disk, the liquid flow rate and surface tension, and the design of the disk. Increasing motor speed decreases droplet size. Increasing flow rate generally increases droplet size, while other factors, such as liquid viscosity and surface tension, affect the precise mechanism of droplet formation.

Spinning disk nozzles are popularly used for applying postemergence herbicides to turf. Research has shown that the optimum droplet size for these applications is ≈ 250 μm. This size droplet is small enough to provide adequate coverage of the target plant while resisting evaporation and drift. Since these nozzles are highly efficient in optimizing droplet size, little of the spray material is wasted as runoff from droplets that are too large or as drift from droplets that are too small. Therefore, compared with other nozzles, adequate spray coverage is obtainable at a lower spray volume with spinning disk nozzles, and comparable efficacy has been demonstrated at application volumes of 46.8 L ha^{-1} (5 gal acre^{-1}) or less with some translocated chemicals.

Although spinning disk nozzles are gaining popularity with turf managers, their disadvantages have kept many from this technology. These include their mechanical complexity and reliability, cost per unit, and limited versatility for the higher-volume applications required for fertilizers or preemergence herbicides. Also, since the droplets produced by these nozzles are not propelled downward by pressure they can move laterally with wind gusts. Such a phenomenon is known as *swath displacement* where the entire swath or pattern may predictably move a few centimeters (inches) to few meters (feet) according to the wind direction and velocity. Finally, as low-volume applications of herbicides from spinning disks using a concentrated spray solution, each droplet contains significantly more herbicide than a droplet of the same size from a conventional higher-volume application. Although quantitatively spinning disks produce less driftable fines than most nozzles, the lethality to nontarget plants and ornamentals from a few stray droplets is much higher. For these reasons, spinning disks and CDA have seen comparatively little use in turf applications.

Spray Tip Materials. There is sufficient evidence that spray tips may be the most neglected component in the spraying system; yet, they are among the most critical in ensuring proper application of agrichemicals. In some cases, overapplication by as much as 50% has been traced to worn spray tips.

Nozzle tips are available in a variety of materials, including: ceramic, hardened stainless steel, stainless steel, thermoplastic, and brass. Ceramic is the most wear-resistant material, and though more expensive, it may be the best investment. Stainless steel nozzles have excellent corrosion and abrasion resistance. Thermoplastic tips have good abrasion resistance; however, they are easily damaged when clogged orifices are cleaned. Brass tips are low cost but wear rapidly with abrasive mixtures and are corroded by some liquid fertilizers.

During the last 25 yr, researchers have tried to quantify the differences in wear life of different spray tip materials. This has been done in an attempt to determine the useful life of the various materials and to show applicators the economic advantages of longer wearing materials.

The results of these tests are expressed using a term known as the *wear number*. The wear number is the relative wear life of a spray tip material using brass as a reference. Brass is given a wear number of 1. Thus, if stainless steel has a wear number of 3, it is assumed that a spray tip of this material will wear three times longer than brass. Wear numbers hold true only for the conditions under which the spray tips are tested. Unfortunately, when comparing data from various researchers there is considerable variability in the reported results. This variability between different wear life tests probably reflects the factors that influence spray tip wear: orifice shape and size, spraying pressure (velocity), spray liquid (abrasive media), and nozzle material.

5. Markers

A helpful accessory to aid uniform spray application is a foam or dye marker system for marking the edge of the spray swath. This mark shows the operator where to drive to the next pass to reduce skips and overlaps. The mark may be continuous or intermittent. Turf colorants are also available. When added to the tank and sprayed these indicate uniformity across the entire swath. They are also used to indicate coverage from hand gun sprayers.

6. Spray Distribution and Calibration

A carefully calibrated sprayer that uniformly distributes the spray mixture will help maximize the effectiveness of an herbicide. The following information will help to fine tune the spray application.

Distribution. Distribution tests for boom sprayers check the uniformity and accuracy of pesticide application. Time spent on evaluating a sprayer pays off in good pest control at minimum cost. The following three tests each require only a few minutes, but they assure the sprayer's performance.

1. *Nozzle uniformity.* Nozzles should be equally spaced on the boom. All nozzles should be the same, with respect to manufacturer, type, size, and part number.
2. *Nozzle flow.* Each nozzle should have the same output. Spray should be collected from each nozzle simultaneously and the amounts compared. Identical glass jars make comparisons easy. Output from each nozzle should be within 5% of the average.
3. *Boom height.* After adjusting boom height according to recommendations in the nozzle section, a trial run should be made with water on a dry concrete or asphalt surface. The area should be sprayed and the drying pattern observed to evaluate uniformity. Streaking at the same spacing as the nozzles indicates incorrect boom height or worn nozzles. Heavy streaks under the nozzles mean the boom is too low or the tips have been damaged by improper cleaning.

Calibration with New Spray Tips. The size of the nozzle tip will depend upon application rate in liters per hectare (gallons per acre), ground speed in meters per seconds (miles per hour), and the effective sprayed width (W) that you plan to use. Some manufacturers advertise gallons per acre nozzles, but this rating applies only to certain conditions (207 kPa [30 lb in. $^{-2}$], 1.78 m s $^{-1}$ [4 mi h $^{-1}$], and 50.8-cm [20-in.] spacings). The gallons-per-acre rating is useless if any one of the conditions deviates from the standard.

A more exact method of choosing the correct nozzle tip is to determine the cubic meter per hour (gallons per minute) required for a specific set of conditions; then, select nozzles that provide this flow rate when operated within the recommended pressure range. By following the steps described in Table 7-3 (Steps 1-5), the nozzles required for each application can be selected well ahead of the spraying season.

After selecting the proper spray tips, sprayer calibration can be completed. Check the calibration every few days during the season. New nozzles do not lessen the need to calibrate because some nozzles wear in, and will increase their flow rate rapidly during the first few days of use. See Table 7-3 (Steps 6-8), for the proper steps to calibrate with new spray tips, and Table 7-4 for the proper steps to calibrate with existing spray tips.

Boom Sprayer Application Techniques. The application of herbicides to turfgrasses can be stressful, especially during hot and dry weather conditions. It is essential, therefore, that procedures are followed for minimizing excessive application, while maintaining the proper application rate for improved efficacy. Excessive swath overlap, inadequate overlap, and speed are the most important variables to consider during an application.

Proper swath overlap with a boom sprayer is facilitated if the sprayer is equipped with a foam marking system. Passes of the sprayer are made by aligning the foam marks of the previous pass to within a specified distance of the foam marks of subsequent passes. Although weather conditions can affect the duration that the foam remains visible in the turf, the opera-

Table 7–3. Calibration procedure with new spray tips.

Step 1. Select the spray application rate in L ha^{-1} (or gal acre^{-1} [GPA]) for use.

Step 2. Select or measure an appropriate ground speed in m s^{-1} (or mi h^{-1} [MPH]) according to existing field conditions. Do not rely upon speedometers as an accurate measure of speed. Slippage and variation in tire sizes can result in speedometer errors of 20% or more. To determine ground speed, see the section on speed measurement in Table 7–5.

Step 3. Determine the effective sprayed width per nozzle (W) in cm or in. For broadcast spraying, W = the nozzle spacing. For boomless spraying, W = the swath width.

Step 4. Determine the flow rate required from each nozzle in L min^{-1} (LPM) (or gal min^{-1} [GPM]) by using a nozzle catalog, tables, or the following equation:

Metric: $LPM = L\ ha^{-1} \times m\ s^{-1} \times W(cm)/16\ 660$

English: $GPM = GPA \times MPH \times W(in.)/5940$

Step 5. Select a nozzle that will provide the flow rate determined in Step 4 when the nozzle is operated within the recommended pressure range.

Step 6. Change the required flow rate for each nozzle from LPM (GPM) to mL min^{-1} (ounces min^{-1} [OPM]), as shown:

Metric: $mL\ min^{-1} = LPM \times 1000$

English: $OPM = GPM \times 128$

Step 7. Collect the output from one of the nozzles. Adjust the pressure until the LPM (OPM) collected is the same as the amount calculated for their outputs. If it becomes impossible to obtain the desired output within the recommendation range of operating pressures, select larger or smaller nozzle tips and recalibrate. It is important for spray nozzles to be operated within the recommended pressure range. The range of operating pressures is for pressure at the nozzle tip; line losses, nozzle check valves, etc., may require the main pressure gauge at the boom or at the controls to reach a much higher level.

Step 8. Operate the sprayer at the speed measured and at the pressure determined. After spraying a known area, check the liquid level in the tank to verify that the application rate is correct. For example, the desired application rate is 187 L ha^{-1} (20 GPA) at a measured speed of 2.68 m s^{-1} (6 mi h^{-1} [MPH]). To use flat spray tips on 50.8-cm (20-in.) spacings:

Metric: $LPM = 187 \times 2.68 \times 50.18/16\ 660 = 1.53$

English: $GPM = 20 \times 6 \times 20/5940 = 0.40$

From the charts selected, an 8004 flat spray tip which provides 1.53 LPM (0.40 GPM) at 5.6 kPa (40 psi) is selected. The flow rate is then converted to mL min^{-1} (OPM):

Metric: $mL\ min^{-1} = 1.53 \times 1000 = 1530$

English: $OPM = 0.40 \times 128 = 51$

Finally, the flow rate is collected and spray pressure adjusted to provide the desired rate.

tor should not depend on the foam's persistence to adequately guide the spraying of areas in which a considerable amount of time has passed since the last strip was sprayed. In such cases, the use of flags and other markers provide a more permanent demarcation of sprayed areas. Also, spray dyes and colorants can be used to delineate the areas sprayed. Exercise particular care when using colorants near fences and sidewalks as they can leave a stain on these surfaces.

Table 7-4. Calibration procedure with existing spray tips.

Step 1. Operate the sprayer at the desired operating pressure. Use a container marked in millimeters (ounces) to collect the output of a nozzle for a measured length of time such as 1 min. Check several other nozzles to determine the average number of mL min^{-1} (ounces min^{-1} [OPM]) to output from each nozzle.

Step 2. Convert mL min^{-1} (or OPM) of flow to L min^{-1} (LPM) (or gal min^{-1} [GPM]) by dividing the mL min^{-1} by 1000 (or ounces per minute [OPM] by 128).

Step 3. Determine the spraying speed. For mounted boom sprayers the speed in m s^{-1} (or miles h^{-1} [MPH]) can easily be measured. For hand operated booms, lay out 100 m^2 (1000 ft^{-2}) and record the time it requires to cover the area uniformly. See Table 5 for speed measurement procedures.

Step 4. Determine the sprayed width per nozzle (W) in centimeters or inches. For broadcast spraying, W = the nozzle spacing.

Step 5. Calculate the sprayer application rate:

Metric: L ha^{-1} = LPM × 16 660/(m s^{-1} × W)

English: GPA = GPM × 5940/MPH × W

For example, if the measured nozzle output is 1600 mL min^{-1} (54 OPM), ground speed is 2.69 m s^{-1} (6 MPH), and nozzle spacing (W) is 50.8 cm (20 in.):

Metric: LPM = 1600/1000 = 1.6

English: GPM = 54/128 = 0.42

Metric: L ha^{-1} = 1.6 × 16 660/(2.68 × 50.8) = 26 656/136 = 196

English: GPA = 0.42 × 5940/6 × 20 = 2495/20 = 20.8

The application rate can be adjusted by changing the ground speed or nozzle pressure and calibrating. Changes in nozzle pressure should be used only to make small changes in output and must be maintained within the recommended pressure range.

Whatever method is used, proper swath overlap is achieved by maintaining the correct distance between nozzles on the boom. For instance, if the proper nozzle spacing is 50.8 cm (20 in.), then a 50.8-cm (20-in.) gap should be maintained between the end nozzles on successive passes of the sprayer.

The speed of the sprayer (see Table 7-5 for the procedure for determining ground speed) directly affects application rate and should be held constant while spraying. Doubling the speed halves the application rate and vice versa. An accurate speedometer or speed monitor is essential for measuring this variable. Additionally, many monitors have the capability of providing other valuable information, such as area and amount sprayed.

Boom sprayers should ideally spray in straight lines and never while turning. Spraying while turning will cause an excessive application of product toward the inner areas and deficient application toward the outer areas. This is because the speed of turning of the inner nozzle is much slower than that of the outer nozzle.

The first step in spraying an area is to survey the property. Remove any movable objects and make a mental note of permanent obstacles and sloping or rough terrain. Sloped terrain requires measures for allowing the boom

Table 7-5. Procedure for determining ground speed.

To determine ground speed, measure a distance with similar surface conditions. Suggested distances are 30.4 m (100 ft) for speeds up to 2.23 m s^{-1} (5 MPH), 60.8 m (200 ft) for speeds from 2.23 to 4.46 m s^{-1} (5 to 10 MPH), and at least 91.2 m (300 ft) for speeds above 4.46 m s^{-1} (10 MPH). At a normal walking speed for manual sprayers, or at the engine throttle setting and gear planed for use during spraying with a loaded power sprayer, determine the travel time between the measuring stakes in each direction. Average these speeds and use the following equation to determine ground speeds:

Metric: Speed (m s^{-1}) = distance (m)/time (s)

English: Speed (MPH) = distance (ft) × 60/time (s) × 8.8

For example, in measuring a 60.8-m (200-ft) course, it is determined that 22 s are required for the first pass and 24 s are required for the return pass.

Average time = (22 + 24)/2 = 23 s

Metric: m s^{-1} = 60.8/23 = 2.6

English: MPH = 200 × 60/23 × 88 = 12 000/2024 = 5.9 MPH

to remain parallel to the ground at the correct nozzle height. This can be accomplished by carefully selecting the manner in which the slope is traversed, or through mechanical adjustments of the height of the boom sections.

It is best to spray parallel to the length of the field, starting against some square end if possible. This will minimize turning time, as well as the need for turning the sprayer on and off. Additionally, a straight starting strip will facilitate maintaining straight subsequent passes which are easier to follow and provide proper overlap.

Allow enough room at the short ends of the field for turning the sprayer. As mentioned earlier, do not spray while turning. These ends are referred to as *headers* and should be sprayed after the main body of the field has been completed. Spraying the headers before completing the main body of the field is a common mistake and necessitates driving through wet foliage. Turfgrass phytotoxicity can result from an accumulation of herbicide on the tires of the sprayer when driving through previously sprayed, wet foliage. For the same reason, spraying should be done in a back and forth motion across a field, not in a continuous perimeter working inward.

Finally, the operator should monitor the sprayer pressure to ensure that the unit is operating correctly as determined during calibration. The operator should also periodically inspect the sprayer during the application to look for obvious leaks, nozzle blockage from foreign material, and proper tank agitation. Any discrepancies from normal conditions should be immediately corrected.

B. Hand-Held Liquid Application Equipment

1. Hose-End Sprayer

The hose-end sprayer, or proportioner, is attached to the end of a garden hose and meters out concentrated pesticide into the passing stream of water.

Hose-end sprayers are most commonly identified with homeowner use and are readily seen in garden stores with ready-to-use formulas or with pesticide concentrates. They are not particularly accurate but are sufficiently effective for controlling some broadleaf weeds for most homeowners.

Proportioners for professionals are not commonly used, however, the commercial lawn care industry has experimented with such devices in an attempt to develop a system that will allow their operators to spot treat weeds, while applying liquid fertilizers. Such a development would increase application efficiency, productivity, and reduce pesticide use. Refinements in these professional model proportioners will no doubt lead to increase use in the industry.

2. Wick Applicator

Wick applicators can vary from homemade to commercial units. In general, an absorbent material such as a sponge, rope, or wick, is saturated with a herbicide mixture. The wick is then brushed over the target weed to transfer the herbicide to the foliage. More sophisticated applicators have a reservoir and flow control device for automatic wetting of the wick. A similar device is a wax applicator that rubs a wax bar impregnated with the herbicide across the target weed.

An obvious advantage associated with these applicators is that there is no drift. Also, nonselective systemic herbicides such as glyphosate can be cleverly used as a selective herbicide when invasive weeds are taller than the surrounding turfgrass. Brushing the tips of the weeds without contacting the turfgrass leaves can effectively control weeds for which no selective herbicides are available. Care should be exercised to ensure that rainfall is not likely within 48 h after application to prevent washing the herbicide into the turf.

3. Portable Compressed Air Sprayer

Compressed air sprayers come in a variety of shapes and sizes that range from 3.78 to 18.9 L (1–5 gal). The smaller units are generally carried with one hand while a spray wand is operated with the other. Larger units are generally carried as a knapsack or backpack (Color Plate 7–6).

Most compressed air sprayers pressurize the spray tank by pumping air into it with a mechanical hand pump. The compressed air in turn exerts pressure on the spray solution. Some backpack-type sprayers pressurize only a small amount of liquid in a chamber beneath the tank. A diaphragm pump is operated by a lever, while spraying to achieve the proper pressure.

Compressed air sprayers are extremely versatile and useful for a variety of spraying. A wide variety of lances and nozzles can be fitted to nearly any sprayer to accommodate different applications. Perhaps the most popular nozzle equipped on these sprayers is a multipurpose nozzle. It can be adjusted to produce a fine spray in a cone pattern or coarse stream. These nozzles are useful for spot treatments of individual weeds; however, they are inefficient for groups of weeds or larger areas. It is very difficult to evenly spray an area with this type of nozzle.

A flat fan-type nozzle can be used with greater success and accuracy for larger areas and is preferred by most professionals. Distribution of the spray is even across the pattern. Furthermore, the application volume can be varied by selecting a different size with a known output. This leads to a more accurate calibration and ultimately better results.

Finally, there are no provisions for agitation within a portable compressed air sprayer. Frequent shaking of the unit is recommended as the best solution, although this is not possible with backpack units when attached to the operator. Liquid herbicide formulations are preferred in these sprayers because they require minimal agitation. Substantial application rate variability can occur when wettable powder or dispersible granule formulations are used in these sprayers from product settling in the tank.

4. Low-Volume Spinning Disk Applicator

A number of manufacturers now market hand-held spinning disk applicators. Their development was a result of the need for crop protection in undeveloped countries without the benefit of tractors and plentiful water. Today the spinning disk applicator lance is a popular form of weed control in many areas of Africa, Southeast Asia, and South America. Although their use in turfgrass weed control has been limited in the USA, use among landscapers, lawn care companies, and golf course managers is increasing (Color Plate 7–7).

The primary benefits of these units are their portability and high efficiency. Many units can spray up to one acre with as little as 3.78 L (1 gal) of spray. Although this results in less filling time and more acres per day sprayed, such ultra-low volumes present difficulties in visualizing the spray pattern. Operators have complained that they lose total sight of the spray and, therefore, are uncomfortable using these units. Certain herbicide formulations, principally the emulsifiable concentrates (ECs), are more easily seen when spraying because of their tendency to form milky-white emulsions that reflect light. When clear or light-colored formulations are used that are not ECs, certain adjuvants such as those containing emulsifiers can be added in sufficient volume to color the mixture. Some manufacturers sell ready-to-use formulations for their lances that contain white pigments to provide excellent spray visibility.

As discussed in the section addressing boom-mounted spinning disk applicators, these units produce a narrower range of droplet sizes which increases their spray efficiency. The relatively small droplets produced are best suited for foliar-active herbicides, including selective herbicides for broadleaf weed control and nonselective systemic herbicides for general weed control.

5. Hand-Held Sprayer Application Techniques

One of the most common mistakes an operator can make while operating a portable compressed air sprayer is failure to maintain the proper pressure in the tank. Operating the unit under extremely low pressure results in coarse size droplets that can be wasteful. Conversely, extremely high pressure can produce driftable fine droplets. Some portable sprayers have pressure indicators on them to provide some indication of pressure.

The nozzle type installed in the sprayer's wand will determine the application technique. Adjustable cone nozzles may be suitable for spot spraying individual weeds. Usually, the target is sprayed to the point at which there is complete wetting of the foliage but not run-off of droplets. Spraying large clusters of weeds or areas with this type of nozzle results in uneven coverage and is discouraged.

Flat-fan nozzles provide superior coverage and droplet control for spraying larger areas. If the operator is able to maintain a fairly constant pressure, then the sprayer will have a known output similar to boom sprayers. This results in better application accuracy, as long as the speed and technique of the operator are appropriate.

Flat-fan nozzles should not be waved in a back-and-forth, side-to-side motion. Instead, the nozzle should be held stationary at the proper height with the orifice and fan pattern perpendicular to the forward direction of the operator. The operator's walking speed and direction should be the only variables that affect coverage and rate. This technique is sufficient for larger areas or clusters of weeds.

The uniqueness of spinning-disk (controlled droplet applicators, CDA) requires specialized application techniques. Unlike conventional hydraulic nozzles that project the spray downward, spinning disks emit the spray horizontally while gravity pulls the droplets down. The width of the pattern is not dependent on nozzle height and, therefore, these units are operated close to the surface of the target (5–20 cm or 2–8 in.) to provide better protection from drift.

Another unique difference of spinning-disk applicators is their circular pattern. The width of the pattern, or ring, is determined by the design and speed of the disk, and flow rate of the spray mixture. While some spinning-disk applicators allow for adjustment of these variables, others designed for specific purposes do not and any attempt to change the variables would adversely affect the units performance.

Although all nozzles, regardless of design, should be moving while spraying, failure to provide adequate movement of spinning disk applicators, which results in excessive application, can be especially phytotoxic to the turfgrass. Because of the low spray volume and the resultant concentration of the spray droplets, there is increased potential for herbicide burn from these sprayers.

As with compressed air sprayers, motions involving side to side arm movements results in uneven coverage. Instead, the lance should be held stationary by the arms while the operator walks forward. The operator should completely pass the target to insure that the entire ring traverses the area.

The best method for providing complete coverage of an area is to provide visual markers at the ends of the area and walk straight toward them. This may involve the use of removable flags, or siting on distant objects such as trees, posts, a leaf, or some other landscape feature. Lawns measuring 929 m^2 (10 000 ft^2) or less that have trees and other features are much easier to adequately spray than larger, more open areas that may be better covered by boom sprayers.

C. Commercial Lawn Care Equipment

Since its beginnings in the late 1960s, the commercial lawn care industry has adapted a number of application technologies. Perhaps none is more significant than the development of the lawn gun. This device is simply an on-off trigger mechanism molded in the form of a gun for operator comfort. The nozzle is the shape of a typical bathroom shower head that forms many streams of spray (Color Plate 7-8). The gun is typically connected by long lengths of hose to the spray truck. The truck houses the tank and pumping system which are similar in design and operation to those used on boom sprayers (Color Plate 7-9). The spray is distributed by the applicator waving the gun in a back and forth motion while walking across the lawn.

The characteristics of the lawn gun include the ability to deliver high volumes of spray mixture, precise placement of spray on the lawn, and the production of relatively large droplets with few driftable fines. A careful analysis of these characteristics is necessary to understand the mechanisms of this application technology and how they are related to each other.

First, it is important to clarify what is meant by high volume since this is a relative term. Before the mid-1980s large trucks carrying up to 4536 L (1200 gal) of product were the industry standard. It was also common practice to apply 16.3 L 100 m^{-2} (4 gal 1000 ft^{-2} or 175 gal acre^{-1}) of lawn area. These high volumes of product were necessary because applications of soluble-fertilizer and pesticide mixtures could be stressful to turfgrasses in lower volumes. Also, it was an absolute necessity to spray close to ornamental plants without potential drift and subsequent nontarget injury. Therefore, large droplets were necessary as they are far less subject to drift. As the size of the droplet increases, the volume necessary to provide adequate application coverage also increases.

Recent trends in the industry have shown a movement away from large tanker trucks to smaller units utilizing low volume applications. The development of slowly available, sprayable fertilizers in combination with careful planning and better applicator training and techniques allowed volumes as low as 4.1 L 100 m^{-2} (1 gal 1000 ft^{-2} or 43 gal acre^{-1}). One obvious benefit of this application method is reduced equipment cost and increased road safety from smaller, pickup-size trucks.

Finally, low and high volumes in this context apply only to lawn gun applications for commercial lawn care. Compared with typical agricultural applications averaging ≈ 1.9 L 100 m^{-2} (20 gal acre^{-1}), or spinning-disk technology at <0.5 L 100 m^{-2} (5 gal acre^{-1}), low volume lawn care application with the lawn gun is still relatively high volume.

D. Commercial Lawn Care Application Techniques

Lawn gun applications require considerable skill by the operator to evenly distribute the spray mixture. Most of the techniques involving a lawn gun are the same for both high- and low-volume applications; however, a few important differences exist and will be discussed.

Proper spray delivery and uniformity of lawn-gun applications are dependent upon walking speed and gun motion. Gun motion consists of waving the gun in a back and forth, side to side manner using the wrist, arm, or both, depending upon operator preference and fatigue. The gun can be held at any angle, from perpendicular to nearly parallel, relative to the ground. The speed at which the gun is oscillated side to side is determined by the operator's walking speed; the faster the walking speed, the faster the gun motion required to obtain adequate spray distribution.

Gun motion can be tested by using what many industry professionals call the *hit two three* method. In this technique, a weed or test target should be hit at least two to three times with a spray pattern as the operator moves forward and over it. For example, if a target is hit only once for a given walking speed, then the gun motion speed should increase in order to move the pattern back across the target one or two more times. These are minimum guidelines; a faster gun motion is almost always desirable for achieving proper spray distribution, however, operator fatigue is likely when faster gun motions are used and, thus, a compromise resulting in greater consistency throughout the spraying day should be sought. Similarly, a comfortable walking speed should be employed to reduce operator error due to fatigue. Sprayer output should be adjusted to this speed to provide proper application rate. Most operators will walk at speeds ranging from 0.9 to 1.1 m s^{-1} (2.0 to 2.5 mi h^{-1}) during an application.

One of the most versatile features of a lawn gun application is the ability to vary swath width. This allows precise placement of the spray around typical lawn obstacles such as flower beds, trees and sidewalks. The width is varied by changing the arc of gun motion. Increasing the arc, or widening the side to side motion, increases the overall spray swath. Similarly, decreasing the arc decreases the swath.

Typically, open spraying is done with an 2.4- to 3.0-m (8- to 10-ft) swath; therefore, this is the swath width that other calibration factors, such as walking speed and sprayer output, are based for delivering the proper application rate. As the swath width is narrowed, however, application rate will increase if operator speed remains constant. This is a common error that often results in over application, and associated turfgrass phytotoxicity, in confined areas. Two methods are used to offset this problem: increasing walking speed, and reducing sprayer output by partially depressing the trigger of the gun.

As stated previously, an increase in walking speed requires a more rapid gun motion to improve distribution. In very confined areas, this requires a very fast motion, typically with the wrist. *Half-triggering* reduces sprayer output so that a slower walking pace and wrist motion can be utilized; this is accomplished by sliding the index finger behind the trigger to prvent it from being fully depressed while the trigger is operated by the middle finger. Although these methods may not be perfectly accurate, they have prevailed as the best available technology for dealing with the myriad of situations encountered in professional lawn care.

Another very significant factor in lawn gun applications is proper swath overlap. This is perhaps the most common error encountered in these applications. At least one ft of the swath should overlap the previous pass to provide adequate coverage. Failure to provide overlap will result in poor weed control and, where a combination fertilizer and herbicide products are used, streaking will usually result. Excessive overlap can result in phytotoxicity, especially where combination products are used.

A good training technique for demonstrating how swath width, overlap, walking speed, and gun motion affect proper application rate is to practice on paved areas spraying water. A 93 m^{-2} (1000-ft^{-2}) area should be covered in the appropriate time as determined by the calibration procedure. Dry pavement allows the operator to visualize coverage and uniformity. A uniform application will evaporate evenly, while uneven applications will become obvious, especially during drying. Adjustments in timing, swath and overlap can then be made until a satisfactory distribution and proper application rate are achieved (See Table 7-6 for calibration procedure for a commercial lawn gun).

In actual spraying, the farthest point of the lawn from the truck is sprayed first. This allows the operator to remove the proper amount of hose from the reel at one time and to end with the gun at the truck so that the hose can be reeled up without dragging the gun through the turf. Front lawns should be sprayed parallel with the road frontage to provide a more even appearance, especially when the spray mixture contains a fertilizer.

The operator should always look ahead when spraying, concentrating on an object to walk towards. At the end of each pass, a couple of steps are taken toward the area not sprayed, and a new strip started to provide the proper amount of overlap with the previous pass. A perimeter pass around the ends of the lawn is routinely done by many applicators, while some ap-

Table 7-6. Calibration procedure for a commercial lawn gun.

Step 1. Select a desired application volume in L 93 m^{-2} (gal 1000 ft^{-2}).

Step 2. Determine a comfortable walking speed to cover 93 m^2 (1000 ft^2). Most applicators will cover this area in between 40 and 50 s (0.66 to 0.83 min).

Step 3. Divide the application volume (Step 1) by the time (Step 2) to determine proper sprayer output min^{-1}:

Metric: 3.78 L 93 m^{-2}/0.8 min 93 m^{-2} = 4.73 L min^{-1}

English: 4 gal 1000 ft^2/0.8 min 1000 ft$^{-2\times}$ = 5 gal min^{-1}

Step 4. Collect the output of the lawn gun for 1 min in a measuring pail.

Step 5. Use a combination of nozzle size and pressure variation to adjust the output to the desired level.

plicators spray the borders as they end each strip of the lawn. Finally, spraying next to flower beds, sidewalks, and other features requires the operator to walk next to the object and direct the spray away from the feature. This provides better control of the pattern for preventing nontarget spraying and improving spray distribution of lawn edges.

As stated previously, lawn gun applications can either be high volume or low volume. High-volume applications are characterized by higher pressures that direct the spray away from the gun. This force, coupled with larger spray droplets, allows for greater resistance to pattern distortion than with low-volume applications. Also, high-volume applications are more forgiving with respect to coverage as more droplets are produced. High-volume applications may also involve walking at slower speeds, resulting in better coverage.

A few techniques are helpful to compensate for the relative disadvantages of low-volume applications. By holding the gun nearly parallel to ground, the spray disperses better and avoids blow-back onto the operator. Great care must be utilized, however, in the vicinity of ornamental plants. Also, a more rapid gun motion improves spray distribution. Usually, the lighter hoses associated with low-volume equipment offsets the fatigue resulting from rapid-motion spraying.

E. Operating Procedures

1. Drift Control

The main objective in spraying agrichemicals is to direct the spray droplets to the intended target. In every spraying application the possibilty exists that spray materials will move away from the target area. Controlling the drift of spray droplets has become more essential with the increased biological activity of today's herbicides and increasing concern about the environment.

The only way to eliminate spray drift is to stop spraying; however, spray drift can be minimized by utilizing proper spray equipment and operational procedures as well as by carefully selecting chemical formulations.

Spray can drift in two ways: small droplets can be carried short distances by wind, and vapor from highly volatile chemicals can move great distances following application and can continue long after the spraying operation. The former is referred to as physical drift and the latter is called vapor drift.

In particular, ester formulations require extra precautions for avoiding vapor drift. Amine salt formulations are essentially nonvolatile and are preferred over esters when spraying near shrubs, gardens, flowers and other sensitive, nontarget species. Also, using chemical additives and avoiding applications on hot days can minimize vapor drift.

Physical drift is related to droplet size. The smaller the droplets, the further they can be carried from the target by wind. Anything that affects droplet size and distance to the target influences physical drift.

To minimize spray drift, the following precautions should be taken:

- Use lower spraying pressures to reduce the number of fine spray droplets produced.
- Keep boom height as low as possible while maintaining uniform coverage
- Use nozzles that are more resistant to drift, such as extended-range flat sprays, low-pressure flat sprays, or wide-angle full-cone spray tips.
- Replace and clean faulty or plugged nozzles that may cause fogging.
- Use spray additives to increase the liquid viscosity at the nozzle orifice so that fewer fine droplets are produced.
- Spray when wind speeds are < 5 mi h^{-1}; early morning or early evening are often good choices.

2. Mixing

Carelessness during mixing operations is all too common. Many mixing errors occur because turf managers do not know their exact tank volumes, or tanks have been incorrectly marked. Volume markings should appear on all tanks in locations where they can easily be read. The accuracy of all volume markings should be checked.

When labeling the tank or taking readings, be sure the sprayer is parked with the tank level.

The active ingredients of a pesticide are diluted with water, oil, or inert solids so they can be handled by application equipment and applied properly. The resulting product is a formulation. A pesticide often is sold in several different formulations. Choose the formulation that best meets the needs of a particular application. Next, determine how much of the formulation to use, based on tank size, spray application volume, acreage, and the recommended dosage on the label. Mix only what is needed for that day.

When mixing, always check the label for any precautions. Some chemicals can form an invert emulsion if mixed incorrectly. Known as *buttering out*, this thick paste will not spray and is very difficult to clean out of the sprayer. Correct mixing also ensures against chemical damage to sprayer parts.

Never add concentrated chemicals to an empty tank. Fill the tank half full with clean water. In addition to providing a medium for the formulation, the water primes the pump and tank filter. Be sure there is no direct connection between the water source and the sprayer tank to avoid back-siphoning of chemicals. Start the agitation before adding any chemicals to ensure it is functioning properly. Incomplete mixing can result in nonuniform application.

Measure the chemicals and add them to the tank. Rinse the chemical containers and pour the rinsate into the tank. Wear protective clothing, especially when handling concentrated chemicals. Some mixing problems can be eliminated by premixing a chemical to form a slurry. Fill the premix container half full with water, then add the pesticide. Mix the slurry until it is uniform and then add it to the sprayer tank.

Systems that directly inject undiluted herbicide into the spray lines are now available. The chemicals are metered according to travel speed using adjustable metering pumps. These systems have the potential to improve application accuracy as well as operator safety. Operators do not have to handle the concentrated herbicides during mixing, there is no excess mixture requiring disposal, and the tank does not have to be cleaned. While a few systems are being marketed, they are not currently suitable for handling all chemical formulations, especially wettable powders.

3. Records

A record of each spraying operation is very helpful and may be required. Keep track of calibration data such as date, speed, pressure, nozzle type, and application rate. When a turf area is sprayed, record temperature, the calibration data, approximate wind speed and direction, ground speed, pressure, application rate, material or materials applied, acreage covered, and exact location. Such information can prove invaluable in evaluating pest control, or in case of accidents or legal action.

F. Maintenance

1. Cleaning

Sprayers must be cleaned to prevent cross-contamination of pesticides and plant injury. Trace amounts of one pesticide can react with another or carry over to the next spraying and cause damage; this is particularly true for herbicides. Long exposures with even small amounts of some pesticides can damage sprayer components, including stainless steel tips and fiberglass tanks. If spraying crops that are very susceptible to herbicide injury, such as ornamentals, use two sprayers: one for herbicides only, and one for all other pesticides. No cleaning method is entirely foolproof, but careful cleaning will usually remove all but insignificant amounts of insecticides and fungicides.

Always try to end the day with an empty tank to avoid excess spray material that might contaminate water supplies or cause injury to plants or animals. Flush with clean water, preferably after each day's operation, however, if planning to use the same material over several days, most pesticides may be kept in the tank overnight. The label usually indicates which ones may not. Also, rinse the outside of the sprayer. Surfactants combined with pesticides, when they are compatible, will provide some cleaning action in the sprayer.

Some pesticide combinations may produce an invert emulsion in the sprayer tank. Flushing with water after each load may prevent an accumulation. If water alone does not dissolve and remove the buildup, add Stoddard solvent, kerosene, or other low-flammable solvent; allow paste to dissolve, then agitate and flush. Next, flush with detergent and, finally, with clean water.

Before the sprayer is stored and whenever pesticides are changed, clean the tank thoroughly with a cleaning solution. The solution used depends upon the pesticides to be removed from the sprayer. Check the pesticide label for cleaning instructions. Add the cleaning solution to the tank and thoroughly agitate before flushing. Always flush with clean water to remove the cleaning solution. Remove nozzle tips and screens; clean them in a strong detergent solution or kerosene, using a soft brush such as an old toothbrush. Follow the same safety precautions during cleaning as for applications. Use respirator, rubber gloves, or other protective gear as may be directed by label instructions.

2. Storage

If the sprayer has no rubber parts, such as gaskets, diaphragms, hoses, or pump rollers, add new motor oil in the tank prior to the final flushing to help prevent corrosion. As the water is pumped from the sprayer, the oil will leave a protective coating on the inside of the tank, pump, and plumbing. Remove nozzle tips, screens, and check valves and store them to prevent corrosion. Close nozzle openings with tape to prevent dirt, insects, or mice from entering.

In all cases, protect the pump. If the pump has rubber parts, disconnect the lines, and pour one tablespoon of radiator rust inhibitor into the inlet and outlet ports. If the pump has no rubber parts, engine oil is satisfactory. Rotate the pump four or five revolutions by hand to completely coat the interior surfaces. An alternative is to put automotive antifreeze with rust inhibitor in the pump and other sprayer parts. This protects against corrosion and prevents freezing in case all of the water has not been drained.

During the final cleaning, completely check the sprayer. Look at the hoses, clamps, connections, nozzle tips, and screens for needed replacements. Store the sprayer in a reasonably clean and dry building. With trailer sprayers, consider putting blocks under the frame or axle and reduce tire pressure and relieve tire stress.

3. Safety

The label on the pesticide container best tells how to apply the pesticide safely. It contains an array of information such as who may apply the chemical, special safety gear, specific mixing procedures, and approved container rinsing and disposal methods.

Avoid exposure to pesticides when mixing and spraying by using protective clothing and equipment. Applicators should wear long-sleeve shirts, trousers, gloves, waterproof boots, brimmed hats, goggles, and, if necessary, respirators. Consult the pesticide label for specific recommendations. Do not smoke or eat when handling pesticides. Always carry a supply of fresh water for rinsing safety gear after handling chemicals, cleaning clogged tips, or for emergency washing in the event of direct exposure to chemicals.

A competent applicator must know the signs and symptoms of pesticide poisoning and know what to do about them. Always post the name of the chemical you are using and the number of the nearest poison control center before spraying.

Mix only the amount of spray material needed for each day's use. If emptying a container, be sure it is triple rinsed and drained into the tank. Return any unused chemicals to an approved locked storage area in the original labeled containers.

Empty pesticide containers can pose a threat to the environment if proper disposal procedures are not followed. Check the pesticide label for container disposal instructions. Many large tanks can be recycled back to the chemical manufacturer. Dispose of small triple-rinsed containers in an approved landfill.

Safe transport of chemicals to the field should not be overlooked. Display a slow-moving-vehicle sign on the sprayer, but don't use this as a substitute for lights and reflectors. Limit sprayer driving to daylight hours only. Also, be sure the tank lid and sprayer connections are secured to avoid any chemical spills.

Consider constructing a concrete wash down area that slopes to a collection point for disposal of rinsate. The area could also drain to a plastic lined gravel and soil evaporation pit. In many states, plans are available to aid in the construction of approved wash down sites. Check with the State Department of Agriculture and Cooperative Extension Service for the latest information before constructing any collection facility.

II. GRANULAR APPLICATION EQUIPMENT

There are two basic types of granular applicators available for turf use: drop-type (gravity) spreaders and broadcast spreaders. Drop-type spreaders have a hopper width equal to the spreading width and a full length agitator. Broadcast spreaders throw granular materials out beyond the spreader. Virtually all drop-type spreaders for turf use are mounted on wheels and may be pushed or pulled, depending upon the design. Broadcast spreaders are of two general types: rotary (or centrifugal), in which a spinning impeller distributes the product, or pendulum, in which an oscillating spout or pendulum distributes the product. Figures 7–14 and 7–15 show typical drop-type and broadcast spreaders. Variations of broadcast spreaders include air-blast spreaders and hand-carried rotaries; these are not recommended for turf use since their precision is highly variable and depends completely on the skill of the operator.

Selecting the proper spreader or spreaders can improve application quality, minimize total costs, and minimize labor.

The basic decision is between drop-type and broadcast spreaders. Drop-type spreaders are generally more precise and deliver a better pattern. Since the product drops straight down, there is less herbicide drift and better control, with less chance of applying product to nontarget areas. Some drop-type spreaders will not handle larger granules, and ground clearance in wet turf may be a problem. Since the edge of a drop-type spreader pattern is sharp, any steering error will cause missed strips or doubled strips. Drop-type spreaders usually require more effort to push.

Fig. 7–14. Push-type rotary spreader.

Broadcast spreaders cover a wider swath and thus covering a given area faster; however, they provide less uniformity of distribution than drop-type spreaders. Because of pattern feathering, they are more forgiving of steering errors. Since they do not have a full width agitator to turn like a drop-type spreader, they require less push force. Broadcast spreaders normally handle large particles well but drift is a problem with fine particles, especially when wind is present. Ground clearance in turf is usually no problem for a broadcast spreader. Since patterns vary, more calibration time is needed. A major advantage of broadcast spreaders is that they are better suited to the use of plastic and fiberglass in their construction; thus, they are usually more corrosion resistant. Broadcast spreaders are also more durable in com-

Fig. 7-15. Push-type drop spreader.

mercial use and less likely to be knocked out of calibration than some drop-type spreaders.

The size of the spreader needed for a particular purpose is determined largely by the size of the areas to be covered, the transportation requirements, and the number of obstacles in the areas to be covered. While generally faster, a large spreader is not necessarily best in small, irregular lawns with trees, flower beds and other landscape features. One factor to consider is that, even for large open areas, doubling their swath width will not double the area covered per day. As a general rule of thumb, swath width must be at least tripled to double the area covered per unit time. The ability to deliver an acceptable pattern with a wide range of products is important. Some means of pattern adjustment is certainly an asset.

Manufacturing uniformity is a serious consideration. All spreaders of a given model should be manufactured to provide as close to the same rate and pattern with each product as possible. If several spreaders are to be used, it is certainly desirable to have them all delivering the same rate and pattern at the same setting. Even if only one spreader is in use, the setting on the product label is more likely to be correct for the particular spreader if that spreader was manufactured under close quality control specifications.

Durability of a spreader is important. Lawn care service use has been found to be the most abusive use to which push-type commercial spreaders are put. The spreader should be structurally sound and as corrosion resistant as possible. Epoxy powder coating, used by some manufacturers, will at least double the useful life of sheet metal parts, while stainless steel offers the most durability.

Any spreader used for lawn care service applications will eventually need replacement parts, so reliable parts service should be a consideration. Easy serviceability is another factor.

A final factor to consider in selecting a spreader is availability of settings for a large number of products in that spreader model. Even though these settings should always be checked and may occasionally need revision to suit particular conditions, they are generally correct and are a real time saver.

A. Granular Application Principles

There are two important aspects to the precision application of granular products. The first is the product *application rate*. This refers to the average amount of product applied, usually expressed in kilograms per 100 square meters (pounds per 1000 square feet). Every herbicide is recommended for application at some specific rate. Overapplication is costly, increases the risk of phytotoxicity, and may be illegal. Underapplication can reduce the efficacy of the product and, thus, cause customer dissatisfaction. Equally important is *uniform distribution*. This is different from the application rate. For example, a herbicide might be labeled for application at 2 kg 100 m $^{-2}$ (4 lb 1000 ft $^{-2}$). If a spreader applies 9 kg 465 m $^{-2}$ (20 lb 5000 ft $^{-2}$) lawn, the apparent rate of application is correct, but it is possible that some areas of the lawn received twice as much herbicide as other areas. It is impossible to achieve absolutely uniform distribution with any granular applicator, but the most uniform distribution possible is particularly important with turf. Under the right conditions, small differences in rate on different areas can result in very obvious stripes, spots and other nonuniform responses of the turf.

It would be desirable for all spreaders to deliver the same rate of product per unit area regardless of ground speed. This characteristic is referred to as *volumetric metering*. The opposite is *gravimetric metering*, in which the flow rate of product out of the spreader remains constant with time, regardless of speed. With gravimetric metering, the application rate is inversely proportional to speed. Most drop-type spreaders are a cross between volumetric and gravimetric metering, i.e., the application rate increases somewhat as the speed decreases. Most broadcast spreaders are essentially gravimetric; therefore, a uniform ground speed is necessary to achieve a steady delivery rate, and the proper speed is needed if spreader settings are to be accurately used.

With drop-type spreaders the pattern is normally the same, regardless of speed, product physical characteristics, or environmental factors. Rotary spreader patterns, on the other hand, are very sensitive to these variables and severe pattern skewing can result if proper precautions are not taken. The pattern applied by a rotary spreader is dependent on impeller characteristics (height, angle, speed, shape, and roughness), ground speed, drop point of the product on the impeller, product physical parameters (density, shape, and roughness of particles), and environmental factors (temperature and humidity). Most of these factors are beyond the control of the spreader operator. Design engineers normally try to develop rotary spreaders that provide an acceptable pattern with a fairly broad range of products and operating conditions. Small rotaries, particularly homeowner models, usually do not have any pattern adjustment and are designed to perform well with average products, and acceptably with a fairly wide range of products. This is possible because of the very limited swath width. The wider pattern of the larger commercial rotaries makes them more susceptible to skewing; thus, a means of pattern adjustment is usually provided. This adjustment typically consists of blocking off part of the metering port or ports on smaller units and moving the metering point or changing the impeller geometry on larger units. It is essential that the operator be aware of the need for pattern adjustment and the means of accomplishing this on a particular spreader. The operator should first follow the manufacturer's recommendations on pattern adjustment. If skewing cannot be fully corrected this way, there are other means that can be used such as varying the speed or tilting the impeller. In extreme cases where a product is so heavy or so light that skewing cannot be eliminated, it may be necessary to use a wider swath width on one side than on the other.

1. Operating Procedures

Some drop-type spreaders provide a means of mechanically verifying and correcting the calibration. If the spreaders being used offer this feature, the operators should take advantage of it. It is suggested that calibration be checked and corrected according to the manufacturer's directions at least weekly when the spreader is in regular use, and more often if the spreader has suffered any abuse or mechanical damage (See Table 7–7 for spreader rate calibration procedure). Obviously, the manufacturer's specifications should be followed in calibrating after any disassembly.

Most commercial broadcast spreaders do not provide a means for recalibration because the ports are larger and less sensitive to minor variations than are drop-type spreader ports. Nevertheless, it should not be assumed that a broadcast spreader will always deliver exactly the desired rate and pattern. Because of variables in the product, operator variables such as walking speed, and environmental and spreader variables, it is highly recommended that each spreader be checked for proper delivery rate with the specific operator and product to be used. Many product suppliers furnish recommended settings and swath widths. These are as precise as the manufac-

Table 7-7. Spreader rate calibration process.

Step 1. Spread a weighted amount of product on a measured area, preferably at least 93 m^2 (1000 ft^2) for a drop spreader and 465 m^2 (5000 ft^2) for a small broadcast spreader.

Step 2. Weigh the product again to determine the rate actually delivered. A laboratory test stand that allows the spreader to remain stationary, while the drive wheel is spun at the correct speed is faster, more precise, and avoids the risk of improper application to a test area, but is usually not available. Another method of rate verification that can be used with drop spreaders is to fasten a catch pan under the spreader and push the spreader a measured distance at the proper speed. This method can be precise, but it is essential that the pan be fastened to the spreader in such a way that there is not interference with the shut-off bar or rate control linkage.

turer can make them, but the factors just mentioned can result in significant rate variations. Label settings should be use only as the initial setting for verification runs by the operator prior to large-scale use (See Table 7-8 for spreader pattern calibration procedure).

Header strips at each end of the turf area provide a place to turn around and realign the spreader and also serve to make the border of the turf area more uniform. The operator should always get the spreader moving at rated speed (normally 1.3 m s^{-1} [3.0 mi h^{-1}] for walk-behind spreaders and 2.0 m s^{-1} [4.5 mi h^{-1}] for tractor powered units) on the header strip or on a driveway or sidewalk, then open the spreader when crossing into the turf area to be treated. At the other end, the spreader should be closed while moving, then stopped and turned while in the header strip. A spreader should never be open while stopped as excessive product will be applied to a small

Table 7-8. Spreader pattern calibration procedure.

With broadcast spreaders, it is also necessary to check and correct, if necessary, the distribution pattern. Again, the product label may give a recommended setting and width, but a custom applicator is foolish not to verify the setting and width before treating a large turf area. A quick pattern check can be made by operating the spreader over a paved area and observing the pattern. This method is not highly accurate since even major distribution errors may not be visible and because of particle bounce and scatter. A preferred method is to lay out a row of shallow cardboard boxes on a line perpendicular to the direction of travel. Boxes 2.5 to 5.0 cm (1-2 in.) high, with an area of 0.093 m^2 (≈ 1 ft^{-2}) spaced on 0.3 m (1 ft) centers, and good for commercial push-type rotaries. The row of boxes should cover 1.5 to 2 times the anticipated effective swath width. To conduct the test, pour some product into the spreader, set it at the label setting for rate and pattern, and make three passes over the boxes, operating in the same direction each time. The material caught in each box can be weighed and a distribution pattern plotted, but a simpler procedure is to pour the material from each box into a test tube, vial, or small bottle. When the bottles are stood side by side in order, a plot of the pattern is visible. This pattern can be used to detect and correct skewing and to determine swath width. The effective swath width is twice the distance out to the point where the rate is one half the average rate at the center. For example, if the center three to four bottles have material 5 cm (2 in.) deep, and the bottles from the 1.8 m (6 ft) positions (i.e., 1.8 m [6 ft] left of the spreader centerline and 1.8 m [6 ft] right of the spreader centerline) have material 2.5 cm (1 in.) deep, the effective swath width is (3.7 m (12 ft). A more detailed test procedure is spelled out by the American Society of Agricultural Engineers in their standard S341.1, *Test Procedure for Dry Fertilizer Spreaders*.† Note that with any of the preceding pattern tests, the product should be swept up after the test.

† TSAE. 1980-81 Agricultural Engineers Yearbook, published by ASAE, St. Joseph, MI.

area. The end turns should never be made with the spreader open as the resulting pattern will be very irregular. Normally a back and forth pattern is preferred, particularly for small areas. A circuitous pattern may be used on large areas, but uniform distribution is difficult to achieve at the corners. The main advantage of a circuitous pattern is compensation for skewing.

Occasionally, it may be impossible to obtain a completely acceptable pattern with a broadcast spreader; striping of the turf may result, particularly if fertilizer and herbicide combination products are used. A common reaction to this problem is to reduce the spreader setting to a half rate and make two applications at right angles; however, this may not be a valid solution to the problem as this will merely change the stripes into a diagonal checkerboard. If pattern problems cannot be corrected, the proper procedure is to reduce the setting to a half rate, reduce the swath width by half, and apply the materials in parallel swaths.

A spreader should not be operated backwards. It is obvious with most broadcast spreaders that pulling the spreader backwards delivers an unacceptable pattern. With drop-type spreaders, a considerably different rate will be delivered at the same setting when operated backwards. In some cases, such as for applying materials to new seedings in loose soil, the spreader may be easier to pull than to push. If it is desired to operate a spreader backwards, a different setting should be determined.

Some broadcast spreaders are provided with a means of partially cutting off one side of the pattern. This feature is desirable when edging along driveways or sidewalks.

Finally, it is usually best to set and fill the spreader on a paved surface rather than on the lawn. If a spill occurs, a driveway is much easier to sweep clean than is turf.

A spreader should never be operated in a strong wind; 2.2 m s^{-1} (5 mi h^{-1}) is generally the maximum for broadcast spreaders. In general, if the leaves of trees are fluttering in the wind, there is too much wind for safe application. Drop-type spreaders provide more protection from the wind and can therefore be operated under winter conditions.

When a foliar application to wet turf is necessary, adhesion of the granules to the foliage can be improved by allowing the turf to grow fairly long. This will improve the efficacy of foliar-active products applied with broadcast spreaders. With drop-type spreaders, it may be necessary to mow just prior to application to prevent moisture buildup on the spreader bottom.

2. Care and Maintenance

Proper care and maintenance will not only prolong the life of a spreader, it will also keep the spreader operating properly and make the operator's job easier. Once again, the spreader manufacturer's instructions should be followed, but the recommendations given here are generally applicable. Even though many spreaders now have an epoxy powder coating for corrosion resistance or are partially plastic or fiberglass, corrosion is still a problem with fertilizers and herbicides. A spreader should normally be washed thoroughly after each day's use and then be allowed to dry. If material is caked on the spreader, hot water may be needed to break it loose. After the spreader has been washed and dried, it should be oiled according to the manufacturer's instructions. Tests have shown that proper washing, drying, and oiling can extend the corrosion life of metal parts on a spreader by a factor of three to four, even under adverse storage conditions.

It is generally not desirable to oil or grease the gears on rotary spreaders since the lubricant attracts dirt and causes premature wear unless a protective gear cover is used. Dry graphite lubricant can be used if desired, but many spreader gears have a lubricant impregnated in them and do not require further lubrication.

When not in use, spreaders should be stored in a clean, dry place, out of direct sunlight. Nothing should be piled on the spreaders while stored, since even moderate weight can, over a few months, distort the tires or cause permanent damage to the plastic parts.

Most commercial spreaders are designed to take the normal stresses of continuous lawn care service use, but occasional maintenance and parts replacement will always be needed. Abusive use will shorten the life of the spreader and raise maintenance costs.

3. Safety

The primary safety factors to consider in the application of granular herbicides have been discussed. Application should not be attempted under windy conditions. Care should be taken to keep broadcast spreaders well away from nontarget plants or soil areas. Remember that, with broadcast spreaders, material is actually thrown much farther than the effective swath width. In some cases, the total throw width is two or three times the effective swath width.

Proper rate and pattern control is essential for safe application of herbicides.

REFERENCES

1. Bode, L.E., and S.L. Pearson. 1983. The calibration of commercial pesticide application equipment for ornamentals and turfgrass. Manual M444-4, Cooperative Extension Service, Univ. of Illinois, Urbana, IL.

Chapter 8

Control of Turfgrass Weeds[1]

LAMBERT B. McCARTY, *University of Florida, Gainesville, Florida*

TIM R. MURPHY, *University of Georgia, Griffin, Georgia*

Weeds most often become established in a weakened turf; thus, knowing turf weaknesses often helps to understand the reason for weed encroachment and how it may be reduced (Color Plate 8–1). Weak turf and bare areas exist because of: (i) improper turf species for a given area; (ii) damage from pests such as diseases, insects, nematodes, and animals; (iii) environmental stresses such as excessive shade, drought, heat, cold, and poor drainage; (iv) improper turf management practices such as misuse of fertilizer and chemicals, improper mowing height or frequency and lack of proper soil aeration; and (v) physical damage and compaction from concentrated traffic. Unless factors contributing to turf decline are corrected, continued weed encroachment should be expected.

Weed control techniques include prevention, as well as cultural, mechanical, biological, and chemical control.

I. PREVENTION

Weeds are prolific seed producers (Color Plate 8–2). A single plant can produce from 1000 to 500 000 seeds (Table 8–1). Seed can easily be transported to nearby turf areas by way of wind, water, and animals. Prevention is avoiding introduction of weeds within an area. There are national, state, and local prevention efforts against the introduction and spread of weeds. A local preventive program is one of the best methods of avoiding future weed problems. Many of these methods are common sense approaches that ensure sanitary conditions and minimize weed introduction. Some of these methods include use of weed-free turf seeds, stolons, sprigs, plugs, or sod.

---

[1] Contribution from the Florida Agric. Exp. Stn. J. Ser. No. R-02830.

Table 8-1. Approximately number of seeds produced per plant.†

Weed	Seeds produced per plant
Annual bluegrass	2 000
Black medic	2 400
Broadleaf plantain	36 000
Common lambsquarters	72 000
Common purslane	52 000
Curly dock	40 000
Dandelion	12 000
Giant foxtail	10 000
Knotweed	6 000
Redroot pigweed	117 000
Sandbur	1 000
Veronica or speedwell	2 900
Witchweed	500 000
Yellow nutsedge	2 400

† Compiled from Ross and Lembi (97); and Emmons (34).

The use of clean mulch, topdressing materials, and the avoidance of manure also are examples of preventative methods.

A. Clean Seed

Only cleaned seed should be planted since most weed seeds have been removed. The Federal Seed Act of 1939 regulates the seed trade to protect consumers from mislabeled or contaminated crop seed. The following information is required by this act to be listed on seed labels in interstate commerce.

1. Percentage of pure seed of the named crop.
2. Percentage of other crop weed.
3. Percentage of weed seed.
4. The name and occurrence of noxious weed seed.

The following is an example of a typical turf seed label:

> Brand name: XYZ Centipedegrass Seed
> 98.75% Pure Seed
> Other Ingredients:
>   0.00% Other Crop Seed
>   1.00% Inert Matter
>   0.25% Weed Seed
>   85.00% Germination
> Tested: 1/94
> Lot 0001-A
> Net Wt. 50 Lbs.

Noxious weed seed are prohibited from entering the USA by the Federal Seed Act. Also prohibited from entering the country are crop seeds containing in excess of 2% weed seeds of all kinds.

Table 8-2. Longevity of weed seeds buried in the soil.[†]

Weeds	Years viable
Quackgrass	1 to 6
Cocklebur	16
Foxtail	20
Johnsongrass	20
Canada thistle	21
Common lambsquarters	40
Redroot pigweed	40

[†] Compiled by Ross and Lembi (97).

B. Vegetative Materials

It is important to purchase weed-free vegetative materials (Color Plate 8-3). Weeds are not always evident in a commercial production field but become more obvious when cultural practices change after planting.

The American Sod Producers Association (1) has proposed maximum weed infestation numbers in nursery and field grown grass. Nursery grown sod is considered weed-free if less than five weeds are found per 9.3 m^2 (100 ft^2). No more than 10 weeds are allowed per 100 ft^2 for field sod to be considered a weed-free product. In addition, sod is considered unacceptable if common bermudagrass, quackgrass, or bromegrass are present (1).

Once established, certain weeds cannot selectively be controlled with herbicides. For example, common bermudagrass is the primary weed problem in St. Augustinegrass sod production (106). This is the result of unavailable selective herbicides and unsatisfactory control from nonselective herbicides. Inspection of planting material for weed should occur before purchase.

C. Sanitation Practices

Sanitation practices include the prevention of weed seed movement by mechanical or human means. Mechanical devices, such as mowers or cultivators, pick-up weed seeds, and transport them to adjacent areas. Annual bluegrass, crabgrass, chickweed, and goosegrass are weed seeds easily transported and deposited by these devices, especially when shoes and mowers are wet (Color Plate 8-4). Equipment should be rinsed before being transported from infested to weed-free areas during weed seed production season.

Frequently, weeds are introduced into turf through the addition of contaminated topsoil. Most weed seed are located near the soil surface (96) and can remain viable for an extended time period (Table 8-2). When contaminated topsoil soil is used for topdressing, prolific weed seed germination and subsequent emergence often results. Therefore materials used for soil modification or topdressing should be free of viable weed seeds or vegetative propagules through fumigation or heat treatment prior to use.

Irrigation systems fed by open ditches, canals, and ponds also contribute to the spread of weeds. One study found that >130 weed species in irrigation sources. The researchers concluded irrigation from the source would deposit > 35 000 seeds per acre (69). Therefore, turf managers should strive to keep irrigation sources and embankment areas weed free (Color Plate 8-5). Areas periodically flooded by streams, canals, or rivers also are subject to weed infestation. Another source of weed seed is from unmowed adjacent areas such as fence rows, roadsides, and open fields (Color Plate 8-6). Cultural practices minimizing seed production, or the use of herbicides, should be a regular part of a maintenance program.

II. CULTURAL CONTROL

Cultural practices promoting vigorous, dense turf are the most important and least recognized means of preventing weed establishment and encroachment. Since high light intensity is required for germination of some weeds such as crabgrass and goosegrass (38), cultural practices increasing turf density will prevent light from reaching the soil surface. Exclusion of light from the soil surface also delays germination of weed seeds in spring since the soil surface is better insulated and remains cooler. Soil fertility, soil aeration, and soil moisture levels should therefore be maintained at optimal levels for turfgrasses.

An example of the cultural practices mowing height and fertilization influencing weed occurrence involves smooth crabgrass in a red fescue lawn. Red fescue mowed at 5.6 cm (2.2 in.) had better turf coverage and less crabgrass occurrence (4 to 14%) during 4 yr than turf mowed at 3.2 cm (1.25 in.) (18 to 39%) (49). The yearly addition of N fertilization at 49 or 98 kg N ha^{-1} (44 to 88 lb N acre^{-1}) further strengthened the turf stand; thus, crabgrass occurrence was reduced. Heavy weed infestation and poor turf quality resulted at a low fertility rate and excessively low (1.9 cm or 0.75 in.) mowing height.

Soil nutrient levels also may favor one plant species over another (Table 8-3). For example, P fertilization repeatedly used at high rates increased annual bluegrass populations in bentgrass (42). Bentgrass apparently is better able to absorb P in low P-containing acidic soils and can out compete annual bluegrass under these conditions (71). The application of S to acidify soil,

Table 8-3. Examples of weeds that often indicate poor growing conditions.

Weeds	Conditions
Algae	Excessive surface moisture, too low mowing height
Goosegrass, knotweed, *Poa annua*	Soil compaction, low soil oxygen levels
Legumes (e.g., clover, chickweed)	Low soil nitrogen levels
Plantains	High soil pH
Sedges, rushes	Poor drainage, overwatering
Sorrel	Low soil pH
Spurges, pusley, knotweed	Excessive nematodes
Quackgrass, poorjoe, sandspur	Poor and/or sandy soil

or limiting P application, is suggested to decrease annual bluegrass density (42). Bentgrass also has a competitive advantage over annual bluegrass when N fertilization is withheld (29). A range of soil pH between 5.8 and 7.2 is recommended to favor a dense and competitive turf (104) although weed growth varies with different soil pH (15, 48, 63).

Maintaining proper soil moisture through irrigation and soil drainage encourages vigorous turf growth. Excessive irrigation and poor surface and subsurface soil drainage results in low soil O_2 levels. Soil compaction also reduces O_2 diffusion and restricts rooting. Turf density decreases with compaction and weeds such as annual bluegrass, goosegrass, prostrate knotweed, and various sedges often invade because they can tolerate these conditions (Color Plate 8-7).

Pest damage also decreases turf density and allows weed encroachment. Insects, diseases, and nematodes are common pests that effect turf density and should be controlled when possible (44). If pests are not controlled, weeds easily infest damaged areas (Color Plate 8-8).

Specific weed occurrence also may provide insight to specific pest presence. For example, weeds commonly associated with nematode-thinned turf include prostrate spurge, prostrate knotweed and Florida pusley (Table 8-3).

Other cultural means of control involve covering a weed infested area with mulches to exclude light (Color Plate 8-9). Commonly used mulching materials are straw, wood chips, sawdust, grass clippings, and various synthetic covers. These materials generally are useful only on small, specific areas. If organic mulches are used, a minimum of 5 to 7.6 cm (2 to 3 in.) is required to prevent weed germination. Care must be taken to prevent these materials from moving into mowed areas as they may become a hazard to equipment operation and personnel.

Fire also is used to remove undesirable brush and weeds. For example, bermudagrass sod production fields can be burned in late winter or early spring just prior to green-up. This burns the weed tops and reduces thatch and mat accumulation. It also controls some insects and disease. Heat generated from burning, however, may break seed dormancy of certain weeds. This may be true because: (i) less competition from dominate vegetation results in greater fluctuations in day and night soil temperatures, while more light reaches the soil surface; and (ii) removal of plants having probable alleopathic effects (70). In most areas, open burning now is regulated or is restricted by local governmental agencies.

III. MECHANICAL CONTROL

Mechanical control of weeds involves hand pulling or various types of tractor-powered tillage operations. The most commonly used mechanical weed control methods in turf are tillage (preplant), hand pulling, hoeing, and mowing.

A. Tillage

Tillage, or cultivation, usually is practiced before turfgrass establishment. Weeds are destroyed by breaking them apart, removing them from the soil, disturbing their root systems, causing desiccation and smothering or burying tender tissue. Depleting stored food reserves and reducing soil reserves of vegetative propagules also destroy weeds (97).

Other potential benefits from proper tillage are increased soil aeration and water penetration, breakage of surface crusts and soil clods, surface smoothing for planting, and incorporation of surface applied fertilizer, liming material and soil amendments (Color Plate 8–10). Best results from tillage are obtained when the soil surface is dry so the disturbed weeds are subjected to desiccation. When soils are too wet or water is applied shortly after tillage, the disturbed plants are more likely to survive. Tillage of wet soils also increases the incidence of clods, crusts, and compaction layers that may interfere with subsequent planting and turf seed germination.

Repeat tillage usually is necessary for control of perennial weeds and the continued emergence of annuals. Multiple growing seasons of intensive tillage normally are required to deplete the vegetative reproductive structures of most perennial weeds. Tillage should be repeated on a 2- to 3- wk interval and continued through the end of the growing season in order to deplete the underground carbohydrate food reserves of tubers, rhizomes, and bulbs. Tillage should be performed when the effects of water and wind on soil erosion can be avoided.

Implements used to work the soil commonly are referred to as primary and secondary tillage equipment (2). Primary equipment is used to break and loosen the soil at depths of 15.3 to 91.5 cm (6 to 36 in.). Moldboard, disk, rotary, chisel, and subsoil plows are examples of primary tillage equipment. These pieces are designed to break up hardpan layers or compacted zones. Secondary equipment is used to work the top 15.3 cm (6 in.) of soil. Power driven tillers, harrows, cultivators, tandem disks, and rotary hoes are examples of secondary tillage equipment. This equipment provides control of weeds, prepares the seedbed, and incorporates soil amendments.

Tillers normally are powered by a tractor's power-takeoff or an auxiliary mounted engine. Nonpowered equipment usually are pulled or dragged through the soil. A disk harrow or a nonpowered preplant unit, are probably the most commonly used tillage implement in turf operations. The disk harrow provides both cutting and burying of weeds as a method of control.

Disadvantages of tillage include exposed soil being subjected to wind and water erosion. Also, if weeds are mature when tilled, their seeds are buried and become a future source of weeds. Other possible disadvantages of tillage are scheduling to coincide with proper soil moisture, and the cost of tractors, tillage implements, labor, and fuel.

B. Hand Pulling, Hoeing, and Rouging

Manual weed control often is performed by hand pulling, hoeing, and rouging. Manual weed control is not widely practiced and is generally impractical on large turfgrass areas. Because of herbicide sensitive constraints on certain small turf areas and landscapes with sensitive ornamental species, however, manual weed control practices still are used on a limited basis.

Hand pulling and hoeing effectively controls annual and biennial seedling weeds. These practices are less effective on established perennial weeds, because underground reproductive parts often remain in the soil and can regenerate.

Roughing often is used in combination with hand pulling and involves the use of a special implement that has a hooked and sharpened metal blade-end. The implement is pushed into the soil to sever the roots and the plant then is pulled from the soil. Roughing still is widely used to remove weeds such as goosegrass from creeping bentgrass golf greens because the turfgrass species has low tolerance to postemergence herbicides (Color Plate 8-11).

C. Mowing

Proper mowing practices are a valuable weed control method. When frequently repeated at the appropriate height (Table 8-4), mowing depletes underground weed food reserves, prevents weed seed maturation, and favors the growth of turfgrass species. Usually, tall annual broadleaf weeds are the ones most weakened or eliminated by mowing. Stem tips of these weeds produce growth-inhibiting substances. These substances, when present, inhibit bud growth on the lower and underground stems as well as roots. This is known as *apical dominance*. Once mowed, apical dominance is reduced with the removal of the stem tips. Buds may then grow, resulting in a bushier appearance. Once these stems are removed by mowing, new stem growth occurs at the expense of below-ground food reserves. Over time, repeated clipping essentially causes the plant to become weakened through starvation of these underground root reserves.

Table 8-4. Recommended mowing heights for turfgrass species.†

Turfgrass species	Inches	Centimeters
Bahiagrass	2.0–4.0	5.0–10.2
Bentgrass		
colonial	0.5–1.0	1.3–2.5
creeping	0.2–0.5	0.5–1.3
Bermudagrass		
common	0.5–1.5	1.3–3.8
hybrid	0.25–1.0	0.6–2.5
Blue grama	2.0–2.5	5.0–6.4
Buffalograss	0.7–2.0	1.8–5.0
Carpetgrass	1.0–2.0	2.5–5.0
Centipedegrass	1.0–2.0	2.5–5.0
Fine fescue	1.5–2.5	3.8–6.4
Kentucky bluegrass	1.5–2.5	3.8–6.4
Perennial ryegrass	1.5–2.5	3.8–6.4
St. Augustinegrass	2.0–3.0	5.0–7.6
Tall fescue	1.5–3.0	3.8–7.6
Zoysiagrass	0.5–2.0	1.3–5.0

† Emmons (34).

Lambsquarters, pigweed, and ragweed are common weeds in newly established turfs intolerant of frequent mowing. They will be eliminated as mowing commences. Weeds should be mowed in the bud stage or earlier to prevent seed development. Prostrate or rosette type broadleaf weed species, as well as grasses, have their primary growing point, or crown, located at or just below the soil surface. Therefore, mowing does not injure the growing point but does remove the oldest portion of the leaf. New growth resumes because the growing point is unaffected. If the crown is injured by other means, the plant may not recover. Examples of weeds tolerant to mowing include goosegrass, annual bluegrasss, common purslane, spotted and prostrate spurge, Virginia buttonweed, and prostrate knotweed.

IV. BIOLOGICAL CONTROL

Biological methods use weeds' natural antagonists as control agents. The objective of biological control is not weed eradication, but rather the reduction of the population below a level of economic or aesthetic injury. Unfortunately for turf managers, a high percentage of control of a weed species is necessary to satisfy their clientele. Goals of a successful biological weed control agent include (70): (i) weaken or kill the weed; (ii) injure only the intended species and no other; (iii) be mobile anough to reach the weed; (iv) reproduce faster than the weed; (v) be adapted to the weeds environment; and (vi) be free of predators or pathogens.

Biological control agents rarely have been used in turf because they often are pathogenic to the turf. An example involves the use of leaf spot pathogens [*Bipolaris setariae* (Saw.) and *Piricularia grisea* (Cke.) Sacc.] as potential biological control agents of goosegrass (37). With either pathogen, however, intricate and exact conditions must exist for disease infection or control is lost. In addition, various species of these pathogens are disease-causal agents of turfgrass including grey-leaf spot of St. Augustinegrass and various leaf spots of bermudagrass; however, progress in using pathogenic fungi for weed control in turfgrasses has been achieved. Riddle et al. (95) reported that selected strains of *Sclerotinia sclerotiorum* (Lib.) de Bary, effectively controlled dandelion without injuring Kentucky bluegrass, creeping bentgrass, or annual bluegrass.

Interest has increased on the potential use of bacterium as a biological means of weed control. Various strains of *Xanthomonas campestris* recently have been isolated and screened for control of annual bluegrass (88). Much work on using various rust (*Puccinea* spp.) organisms for nutsedge control also has been done. Future work on these and other biological control agents will continue, resulting in alternatives to current methods.

A recent successful and commercially available biological control agent for aquatic weeds involves the white amur, or grass carp (*Ctenopharyngodon idella*). This fish feeds mostly on filamentous algae, chara, submersed weeds, and duckweed. It does not, however, feed extensively on emergent vegetation or large free-floating weeds such as water hyacinth. Stocking rates range from 2 to 8 fish ha^{-1} (5 to 20 fish acre^{-1}). It has a life span of ≈ 16 yr (97).

Although some outstanding successes have been achieved with biological agents in other commodities, additional research is needed to identify biological weed control agents for turfgrasses. Through wide publicity the general public has incorrectly viewed this as a viable and immediately available alternative for the control of all types of turfgrass pests.

V. CHEMICAL CONTROL

One of the major contributing factors to the advancement of man's way of life during the 20th century has been the development of pest control compounds. The first major selective pest controlling compound used was a lime–Cu–S mixture known as the Bordeaux mixture. It was discovered to have properties on powdery mildew of grapes in 1896. Selective broadleaf weed control also was investigated with this mixture.

Attempts in developing selective weed controlling chemicals during the period from 1900 to 1915 emphasized solutions of $CuNO_3$, ammonium salts, H_2SO_4, $FeSO_4$, and K salts (94). These were investigated for selective weed control in cereal crops. Compounds developed between 1900 and 1940 included the arsenicals, chlorates, borates, ammonium sulfamate and the dinitrophenols (45, 98). The organic arsenicals (MSMA, monosodium salt of methylarsonic acid; DSMA, disodium salt of methylarsonic acid; AMA, ammonium salt of methylarsonic acid; and CMA, calcium salt of methylarsonic acid) were developed during this time and still are used for selective grass control in turf. The trigger for development of modern herbicide technology, however, did not occur until World War II.

The discovery of the herbicidal properties of 2,4-D [(2,4-dichlorophenoxy)acetic acid] during World War II began the area of modern herbicide technology. Perennial broadleaf weed control was provided by 2,4-D. These weeds previously were controlled by hand labor or land fallow. The first use of 2,4-D was for dandelion control in Kentucky bluegrass. The compound proved to be economical, reasonably predictable and consistent, and highly efficacious. Most importantly, it was safe and relatively easy to use. It still is one of the most widely used herbicides.

VI. HERBICIDE CLASSIFICATION AND NOMENCLATURE

Herbicides may be classified by several criteria. These include selectivity and movement in plants, chemistry, application method, application timing, persistence, and mode of action. Selectivity and movement in plants, as well as method and timing, tend to be the most important classification criteria for turf managers to follow.

A. Selectivity and Movement

1. Selective

A selective herbicide controls or suppresses certain plant species without seriously affecting the growth of another plant species. Selectivity may be due to differential absorption, translocation, metabolism, morphological, or physiological differences between turfgrasses and weeds. The majority of turfgrass herbicides are selective. For example, 2,4-D is used for selective control of many broadleaf weeds, such as dandelion, without significant injury to most turfgrasses.

2. Nonselective

Nonselective herbicides control all plants. These generally are used in the renovation or establishment of a new turf area, as spot treatments of isolated weed patches, or for sidewalk trimming. Glyphosate [N-(phosphomethyl)glycine] and diquat (6,7-dihydrodipyrido[1,2-α:2′,1′-c]pyrazinediium ion) are examples of nonselective herbicides. Herbicides such as atrazine (6-chloro-N-ethyl-N′-(1-methylethyl)-1,3,5-triazine-2,4-diamine) or MSMA can be nonselective at rates higher than those used for selective control.

3. Systemic

Systemic herbicides are translocated in the plant's vascular system. A plant's vascular system translocates the nutrients, water and organic materials necessary for normal growth and development. In contrast to the quick-kill accomplished with contact herbicides, systemic herbicides require several days or even a few weeks to be fully translocated through the plant's vascular system before death. Systemic herbicides also are classified as selective or nonselective. Glyphosate is a nonselective, systemic herbicide while 2,4-D, dicamba (3,6-dichloro-2-methoxybenzoic acid), imazaquin [2-[4,5-dihydro-4-methyl-4-(1-methylethyl)-5-oxo-1H-imidazol-2-yl]-3-quinolinecarboxylic acid], and sethoxydim [2-[1-(ethoxyimino)butyl]-5-[2-(ethylthio)propyl]-3-hydroxy-2-cyclohexen-1-one] are examples of selective, systemic herbicides.

4. Contact

Contact herbicides affect only the portion of green plant tissue contacted by the herbicide spray. These herbicides are not translocated or are limited in the vascular system of plants. Therefore, underground plant parts such as rhizomes or tubers are not killed. Repeat applications usually are needed with contact herbicides to kill regrowth from underground plant parts. Adequate spray volumes and thorough coverage of the weed foliage are necessary for effective control. Contact herbicides kill plants quickly, often within a few hours of application. Contact herbicides may be classified as selective or nonselective. The contact herbicides bromoxynil (3,5-dibromo-4-hydroxybenzonitrile) and bentazon [3-(1-methylethyl)-(1H)-2,1,3-benzothiadiazin-4(3H)-one 2,2-dioxide] are classified as selective herbicides. Diquat is a nonselective contact herbicide.

B. Timing of Herbicide Application

Herbicides also are classified by application timing with respect to turfgrass and weed seed germination.

1. Preplant

These are applied to provide nonselective control of all weeds before turfgrass is planted. Soil fumigants, such as metam-sodium and methyl bromide, and nonselective herbicides such as glyphosate, often are used as preplant herbicides.

2. Preemergence

Preemergence herbicides generally are applied to an established turfgrass site prior to weed seed germination. This group of herbicides controls weeds during the germination process. Emerged weeds visible at the time of application are not controlled by preemergence herbicides. Although the majority of herbicides may be classified as preemergence or postemergence, atrazine, simazine, (6-chloro-N, N'-diethyl-1,3,5-triazine-2,4-diamine), dithiopyr [S,S-dimethyl 2-(difluoromethyl)-4-(2-methylpropyl)-6-(trifluoromethyl)-3,5-pyridinedicartothioate], ethofumesate [($\pm$)-2-ethoxy-2,3-dihydro-3,3-dimethyl-5-benzofuranyl methanesulfonate], pronamide (3,5-dichloro(N-1,1-dimethyl-2-propynyl)benzamide), and others are exceptions. These herbicides have preemergence and postemergence activity on selected annual weeds.

Preemergence herbicides form the base of a chemical weed control program in turfgrasses and are used primarily to control annual grasses and certain annual broadleaf weeds. They are persistent in the soil and control susceptible weeds for an extended period of time. Turfgrass preemergence herbicides generally are effective for 60 to 120 d. The length of efficacy depends on the specific chemical being used, soil, physical and chemical properties, soil moisture levels, temperature, and application placement. The soil persistence of these herbicides is advantageous in terms of length of weed control; however, it may be a disadvantage if seeding, sprigging, or sodding operations are planned for a treated site. Newly-seeded and sprigged turgrasses have a low tolerance to most preemergence herbicides. Siduron [N-(2-methylcyclohexyl)-N'-phenylurea] and oxadiazon (3-[2,4-dichloro-5-(1-methylethoxy)phenyl]-5-(1,1-dimethylethyl)-1,3,4-oxadiazol-2-($3H$)-one) are noted exceptions. Appropriate waiting periods after herbicide application are required before reestablishing the site with turf. The herbicide label should be consulted to determine the length of time required before establishment operations can be conducted safely.

3. Postemergence

Postemergence herbicides are applied directly to emerged weeds. In contrast to preemergence herbicides, this group provides little, if any, residual control of weeds. A complete chemical weed control program can be accomplished with postemergence herbicides provided multiple applications are used. Because of the necessity for repeat applications, possible temporary turfgrass injury may occur. As a result, most turfgrass managers use postemergence herbicides in conjunction with a preemergence weed control program. Postemergence herbicides are useful to control perennial grass and broadleaf weeds not controlled by preemergence herbicides. Certain postemergence herbicides may be used on newly established turfgrasses or within 3 to 4 wk after its establishment.

C. Nomenclature

Three types of names normally are associated with an herbicide. The chemical name describes the chemistry of the compound. These usually are a lengthy technical description of the chemical. The common name is a generic name assigned to the chemical and often is a simpler version of the chemical name. Chemical and common names must be approved by an appropriate authority before being accepted by the scientific community. The trade name, used by the chemical company for marketing purposes to promote the sale of a specific product, often is the most recognizable name of an herbicide.

An example of chemical nomenclature would involve the herbicide oryzalin. Oryzalin is the common name, while the chemical name is 4-(dipropylamino)-3,5-dinitrobenzenesulfonamide. Surflan is the trade name for oryzalin. Due to the number and constant change of trade names, most scientific journals and university publications use the common name of a herbicide.

D. Herbicide Registration

Registering a new pesticide has become expensive and time consuming. Only one out of 20 000 compounds tested reaches the market (47). Developing a new herbicide may cost $35 million. An additional $40 million to $100 million is required to build a production plant. Seven to ten years of testing normally are required before a compound reaches the market. Chemical companies obtain a product patent prior to the release of the herbicide. After the product is patented, a company retains exclusive or proprietary rights for 17 yr. After the patent has expired, other chemical companies are free to market the herbicide under a different trade name. Since a patent protects a compound for 17 yr, and it takes an average of 7 yr for testing, patenting, and facility building, only 10 yr of exclusive marketing can be expected. Much of the money for herbicide development is used to generate data from extensive and rigorous testing. These examine crop and weed efficacy, environmental hazards, and a wide array of toxicological tests. Environmental and toxicological data are submitted to the U.S. Environmental Protection Agency (EPA) for review and registration. The EPA has the responsibility of insuring the pesticide poses no undue environmental and health hazards when used as instructed. A label providing sufficient information and warnings on the safe and proper handling, environmental precautions, as well as use of the product must accompany each product.

E. Experimental Use Permits

Late in a pesticide's development process, the EPA can be requested to allow the use or sale of a limited amount of the product under an experimental use permit (EUP). This usually is sought 1 to 2 yr prior to the anticipated full registration and usually is done in order to gather performance information based on real use conditions.

F. General and Restricted Use Pesticides

Pesticides are classified into general and restricted use categories. General use pesticides are those not causing adverse environmental effects and are safe for application by the general public. Restricted use pesticides represent minor risk to human health or to the environment. They only are sold to certified applicators trained in pesticide handling. Two categories of certification exist. A Private Applicator Certificate is required for those who use restricted-use pesticides on their own or rented land. A Commercial Applicator Certificate is required for those who apply either restricted or general use pesticides for compensation.

VII. NONSELECTIVE WEED CONTROL

If perennial weeds such as nutsedge and bermudagrass are present, it is advisable that weed control be implemented before planting or establishing a turf area. Once the turf is established, control becomes more difficult and expensive.

A. Soil Fumigation

Soil fumigants are volatile liquids or gases that control a wide range of soil-borne pests. Soil fumigants such as methyl bromide, are highly toxic and expensive. Their use is limited to small, high cash crops such as tobacco, certain vegetables, fruits, bedding plants, and turf. The expense results from a plastic cover necessary to trap the fumigant vapors in the soil. Fumigants control both weeds and many nematodes, fungi and insects; however, weed species that have a hard, water-impermeable seed coat such as sicklepod, white clover, redstem filaree, and morninglory are not effectively controlled with soil fumigants. Important considerations before choosing a particular soil fumigant include its expense, soil moisture level, soil temperature, and the time delay before planting.

Several compounds are used as fumigants (97). The two most commonly used materials in turf are methyl bromide and metham (methylcarbamodithioic acid) or metam-sodium (sodium methyl-dithiocarbamate).

1. Methyl Bromide

Methyl bromide is a colorless, nearly odorless liquid or gas. At 3.4 °C (38 °F), the liquid turns into a gas and is 3.2 times heavier than air at 20 °C

(68 °F). These properties require a gas impermeable cover be used with it (Color Plate 8–12) or the material will escape. Methyl bromide is extremely toxic and commonly is combined with a odor detectable warning agent such as chloropicrin (teargas).

When using a fumigant, the soil should be in a condition suitable for planting. Weed control normally is achieved only as deep as the soil is properly prepared. The soil should be moist for adequate fumigant penetration and dispersion. Moisture-saturated or extremely dry soils limit penetration and dispersion that subsequently affects weed seed absorption. Soil temperature at 10 cm (4 in.) should be a minimum of 15.6 °C (60 °F). Fumigation is not effective if soil temperatures are below 10 °C (50 °F).

A plastic or polyethylene cover should be placed with ends properly secured prior to application to prevent gas leakage. Once the area is treated, it should remain covered for 24 to 48 h. The cover then may be removed and the soil aerated for 24 to 72 h before planting.

2. Metham

Metham or metam-sodium is a member of the thiocarbamate herbicide family. Metham is water-soluble and upon contact with moist soils, breaks down to form the highly toxic and volatile chemical methyl isothiocyanate. Like methyl bromide, metham should be applied to moist soils with temperatures of at least 15.6 °C (60 °F). It is most effective when its vapors are confined by a tarp. A water-based soil seal method may also be used. With this method, the soil is cultivated and kept moist for a week before treatment. The material is applied, rototilled, and watered-in immediately to the depth of desired control 10 to 15 cm ($\approx$ 4 to 6 in.). Approximately 7 d after treatment, the area should be cultivated to help release any residual gases. One to two weeks later (2 or 3 wk after initial application), the treated area may be planted. The longer preplanting waiting period and lowered effectiveness in the absence of using a tarp are the primary disadvantages of metham.

3. Dazomet

Dazomet (tetrahydro-3,5-dimethyl-2H-1,3,5-thiadiazine-2-thiane) recently has been reintroduced as a soil fumigant. Unlike methyl bromide and metham, dazomet is a granular product and is not a restricted use product. Being a granular, dazomet must be evenly applied and incorporated for maximum effectiveness. Its breakdown characteristics, application preparation, and effectiveness are closely associated to metham, as are its advantages and disadvantages.

B. Nonselective Herbicides

Nonselective herbicides (e.g., glyphosate) also are used for preplant weed control. Normally, multiple applications, spaced 2 to 4 wk apart, are needed for control of existing weeds. For example, a minimum of three applications of glyphosate were necessary to completely control bermudagrass (62).

Control of subsequent germinating weeds as well as other soil-borne pests is not achieved with this method.

VIII. SELECTIVE WEED CONTROL

A. Proper Herbicide Selection, Application, and Record Keeping

Knowledge of the safety, effectiveness at certain weed growth stages, stage of turf establishment, tolerance or susceptibility of treated turf species, time required for control, and economics are important considerations when trying to choose between herbicides. Enormous amounts of information on these is available from local cooperative county extension offices, state turfgrass specialists, colleagues, and representatives of the chemical company; however, even the best herbicide is only as good as its application. Many variables influence successful herbicide application. These include: pesticide formulation, proper equipment, environmental factors at the time of application, proper and constant calibration, and adequate agitation. Most herbicide failures involve applying the wrong products or applying the chemical at an improper time, rate, or manner.

Once a particular herbicide is chosen and applied, accurate, detailed information should be kept. In addition to listing what and where a material was applied, information on how and at what rate it was applied, who made the application, and the environmental conditions at the time of application are needed. Environmental information should include: soil and air temperatures; soil moisture and pH; relative humidity; wind speed and direction; water pH; cloudiness; weed growth stage and turfgrass condition at the time of application; time and amount of irrigation or rainfall following application; and dew presence. By having this information, turf managers can determine the effectiveness of a material when applied under specific environmental conditions and can more accurately pinpoint contributing factors if unsatisfactory results occur.

B. Preemergence Herbicides

Preemergence herbicides are applied to the turfgrass site prior to weed seed germination. The mode of action for most preemergence herbicides [e.g., DCPA, bensulide [O,O-bis)1-methylethyl) S-[2-[(phenylsulfonyl)amino]ethyl]phosphorodithioate], benefin [[N-butyl-N-ethyl-2,6-dinitro-4-(trifluoromethyl)benzenamine], oryzalin, and pendimethalin [N-)1-ethylpropyl)-3,4-dimethyl-2,6-dinitro-benzenamine]] is the inhibition of certain phases of cell division (mitosis) or inhibition of cell elongation. As the weed seedling germinates, its root and shoot absorbs the herbicide, stops growth and eventually dies.

Preemergence weed control was first suggested by Leach and Lipp (72) and Sprague and Evaul (102). Some of the first chemicals evaluated for preemergence weed control included calcium cyanide (103), arsenate (105), and naphthylacetic acid (100). The first true and consistent preemergence herbicide was available for turf producers by 1959. Dimethyl tetrachloroterephthalate (DCPA) provided more consistent weed control with less turf damage than was previously available (35). With subsequent release of dinitroaniline chemistry in 1962, the widespread acceptance of preemergence weed control in turfgrass was established.

When considering any herbicide, the first consideration is the tolerance of the desirable turfgrass species to the chemical in question. As a general rule, preemergence herbicides are not as phytotoxic to established turfgrass species as postemergence herbicides. Notable exceptions are atrazine, simazine, and pronamide on cool-season grasses. Table 8–5 lists the most widely used turfgrass species and their tolerance to preemergence herbicides.

The effectiveness of preemergence herbicides vary. Reasons for this include timing in relation to weed seed germination, soil types, and the environmental conditions (e.g., rainfall and temperature) during and immediately following herbicide application. Other factors are the target weed species and biotypes, and the cultural factors (e.g., aerification) following application. Preemergence herbicides generally, are most effective for annual grass control, although some annual broadleaf weeds also are suppressed.

1. Timing

An important consideration in preemergence herbicide use is its application timing. Most preemergence herbicides are ineffective on visible weeds. Applications, therefore, should occur prior to seed germination. However, if applied too soon, the degradation of the herbicide in the soil may reduce its concentration to an ineffective level. Crabgrass and goosegrass are two of the most troublesome annual grass weeds in turf. If preemergence herbicides are used for control, application timing is critical. Crabgrass initiates spring germination from February through May when soil temperatures at a 10-cm (4-in.) depth reach 11.7 to 14.4 °C (53–58 °F) (75). Alternating dry and wet conditions at the soil surface as well as light intensity also encourage crabgrass germination. Goosegrass, meanwhile, germinates at soil temperatures of 15.6 to 18.3 °C (60 to 65 °F). Goosegrass also requires high light intensity for seed germination (38). Because of higher temperature requirements for germination, goosegrass normally germinates 2 to 8 wk later in spring than crabgrass (9, 75). Therefore, when developing an exclusive goosegrass weed control program, preemergence herbicide application should be delayed ≈ 3 to 4 wk in spring later than a crabgrass program.

Annual bluegrass is a winter grass weed that starts germination in late summer and continues germination through the fall and winter when soil temperatures at the 10 cm (4-in.) level drop to the low- to mid-20s °C (70s °F). Preemergence herbicide application should be timed just prior to expected period of peak germination. Annual bluegrass often has a second germination flush in mid- to late-winter. This is important for turf managers to recognize because fall herbicide applications normally do not provide season-long control and repeat application may be necessary.

Table 8-5. Established turfgrass tolerance to preemergence herbicides.†

Herbicides	Bahiagrass	Bentgrass	Bentgrass golf green	Bermudagrass	Bermudagrass golf green	Centipedegrass	Kentucky bluegrass	Perennial ryegrass	St. Augustinegrass	Tall fescue	Zoysiagrass
Atrazine	D‡	D	D	I	D	T	D	D	T	D	I-T
Benefin	T	I	D	T	D	T	T	T	T	T	T
Benefin + oryzalin	T	D	D	T	D	T	D	D	T	T	T
Benezin + trifluralin	T	D	D	T	D	T	T	T	T	T	T
Bensulide	D	T	T	T	D	T	T	T	T	T	T
Bensulide + oxadiazon	D	I-T	I-T	T	T	D	T	D	D	T	T
DCPA	T	I	D	T	D	T	T	D	T	T	T
Dithiopyr	T	T	T	T	T	T	T	T	D	D	D
Ethofumesate	D	D	D	I	D	D	D	T	D	D	T
Fenarimol	D	T	T	T	T	T	T	T	T	D	T
Isoxaben	T	T	T	T	D	T	T	T	T	T	T
Metolachlor	T	D	D	T	D	T	D	D	T	D	D
Napropamide	T	D	D	T	D	T	D	D	T	T	D
Oryzalin	T	D	D	T	D	T	D	D	T	T	T
Oxadiazon	D	D	D	T	T	D	D	D	T	D	D
Pendimethalin	T	I-T	D	T	T	T	T	T	T	T	T
Prodiamine	D	D	D	T	D	D	T	T	D	D	D
Pronamide	D	D	D	T	D	D	D	D	D	D	D
Siduron	D	I	I	D	D	T	T	T	T	D	T
Simazine	D	D	D	I	D	T	D	D	T	D	I-T

† Adapted from Lewis (77), McCarty (80), and Murphy (93).
‡ T = Tolerant at labeled rates; I = Intermediate tolerance; D = damaging or not registered for use on this turfgrass.

2. Efficacy

Various literature citings discuss several herbicidal control levels for annual grasses commonly found in turf (5, 11, 28, 51). Most states have turfgrass specialists who periodically report and update such a list. Table 8-6 lists the expected control of common turf weeds for various preemergence herbicides.

Continued use of a particular preemergence herbicide may control the intended species but also may increase the cover of other weed species. For example, bensulide provides good crabgrass control, but may increase the cover of clover and speedwell (55). In this same study, benefin and DCPA increased lawn burweed, wild parsnip and clover, while oxadiazon increased wild parsnip and sandwort populations.

3. Sequential Applications

For season-long control, repeat applications are necessary, especially in the southern areas of the USA. Most herbicides begin to degrade when exposed to the environment. Degradation generally is enhanced by increasing soil moisture and warm weather, and with soils having low cation exchange and water holding capacities. Most herbicides are effective in preventing subsequent weed seed germination during 60 to 120 d after application. Afterwards, through losses from degradation and other means, repeat applications become necessary for continued preemergence weed control. Turf managers must recognize and understand that most preemergence herbicides will prevent the germination and establishment of desirable turfgrasses as well as weeds during 60 to 120 d after application. Timing, therefore, is important on those areas to be turf-established. It must be noted that on those areas to be turf-established, most preemergence herbicides should not be used 2 to 4 mo prior to planting. Severe turf root damage and turf germination reduction may result.

Some evidence suggests that after initial normal herbicide application rates during 1 or 2 yr, subsequent yearly rates may be reduced. When proper mowing height (5.7 cm or 2.25 in.) and N fertilizer (98 kg N ha^{-1} or 88 lb N acre^{-1}) were maintained, the application of a preemergence herbicide in a red fescue lawn, in the first year, maintained low crabgrass populations (1 to 3%) during the next 4 yr (49). Similarly, herbicide rates required to control crabgrass or goosegrass could be halved or eliminated in subsequent years when an normal rate was applied the first year (55).

4. Aerification

Core aeration generally has not been recommended or practiced following a preemergence herbicide application. Core aeration was believed to disrupt the herbicide barrier in the soil and stimulate weed emergence. Johnson (59) reported that core aeration immediately prior to or 1, 2, 3, or 4 mo after applications of benefin, bensulide, DCPA, and bensulide plus oxadiazon to common bermudagrass did not stimulate large crabgrass emergence.

Table 8-6. Expected control of selective weeds with preemergence herbicides.†

Herbicide	Crabgrass	Goosegrass	Annual bluegrass	Common chickweed	Henbit	Lawn burweed	Corn speedwell
Atrazine	P-F‡	P	E	G	G	E	G
Benefin	G-E	F	G-E	G	G	F	G
Benefin + oryzalin	E	G	E	G	G	—	—
Benefin + trifluralin	E	G	E	G	G	F	F
Bensulide	G-E	P-F	F	F	F	F	F
Bensulide + oxadiazon	E	G-E	—	—	—	—	—
DCPA	G-E	F	G	E	F	P	E
Dithopyr	E	G-E	G-E	—	—	—	E
Fenarimol	P	P	G	P	P	P	P
Isoxaben	F	P	F	G	G	G	—
Metolachlor	F-G	F	F-G	—	—	—	—
Napropamide	G-E	G	G	E	P	E	E
Oryzalin	E	F-G	G-E	G	G	—	—
Oxadiazon	G	E	G	P	P	P	G
Pendimethalin	E	G-E	G-E	E	G	—	E
Prodiamine	G-E	G-E	G	—	—	—	—
Pronamide	F	P	G-E	E	P	P	G
Siduron	F	P	P	P	P	P	P
Simazine	F	P	E	G	G	E	G

† Adapted from Iewis (77), McCarty (80), and Murphy (93).
‡ E = Excellent, >89% control; G = Good, 80 to 89% control; F = Fair, 70 to 79% control; P = Poor, <70% control.

Aeration at 4 or 8 wk after application increased large crabgrass cover 5% for oxadiazon at 2.2 kg ha^{-1} (2 lb acre^{-1}), but not at 4.4 kg ha^{-1} (4 lb acre^{-1}). In a related study, it was shown that core aeration at 1, 2, or 3 mo after an application of oxadiazon did not decrease goosegrass control on a 'Tifgreen' bermudagrass putting green (56). Branham and Rieke (13) reported core aeration, or vertical mowing, immediately or 1 mo after an application of benefin, bensulide, or DCPA did not affect large crabgrass control in annual bluegrass. Monroe et al. (91) noted that aeration did not affect the activity of several preemergence herbicides in controlling crabgrass species in either Tifgreen or common bermudagrass. In creeping bentgrass, however, significantly greater amounts of crabgrass occurred in aerified plots with the cores returned than in plots not aerified, or aerified plots with the cores removed.

5. Annual Bluegrass Control in Golf Greens

Annual bluegrass is the most troublesome winter annual weed in golf greens. Its low growth habit and ability to thrive in moist conditions and compacted areas make it difficult to control. Annual bluegrass has a lighter green color than most grass species used to overseed golf greens. It also produces numerous seedheads that reduce the quality of the putting surface (Color Plate 8–2). Because of its low tolerance to heat, annual bluegrass dies quickly in warm weather, leaving many playing areas bare until the bermudagrass has time to fill-in (35). Chemical control of annual bluegrass is difficult due to: (i) the majority of preemergence herbicides cannot selectively prevent annual bluegrass germination while allowing the overseeded grass to establish itself, and (ii) most effective postemergence herbicides for annual bluegrass also injure the overseeded grass species.

Preemergence control of annual bluegrass in turf was first noted in the 1930s when the insecticide lead arsenate was discovered (101). Since then, preemergence annual bluegrass control has been reported with numerous herbicides.

Bermudagrass Golf Greens. Preemergence control in bermudagrass golf greens currently is available with several herbicides. Each has its own use precautions. If these are not followed, unsatisfactory results may occur. Bingham et al. (10) reported bensulide would provide preemergence annual bluegrass control and that acceptable stands of ryegrasses could be obtained when seeding was delayed 1 mo after its application. This could, however, be influenced by environmental and management practices resulting in a narrow tolerance range. Label directions dictate that bensulide application should be no sooner than 120 d prior to overseeding. This waiting period allows enough bensulide to be in the soil to control the germination annual bluegrass, but be low enough to not interfere with germination of the grasses used for overseeding.

Benefin, like bensulide, can be applied before annual bluegrass and overseeding if proper timing is followed. At the low application rate, a minimum of 6 wk are necessary after treatment before overseeding should be attempted. Twelve to fourteen weeks are necessary between application of the high rate and overseeding.

Pronamide also provides preemergence control of annual bluegrass in bermudagrass. Like bensulide, pronamide must be applied in advance of annual bluegrass germination and seeding cool-season grasses. The minimum recommended period between application and overseeding is 60 to 90 d. It also is recommended that application not be made where drainage flows onto areas planted with cool-season grasses.

Activated charcoal has been used successfully to prevent injury to the desirable overseeded grass when pronamide was applied closer than 60 d to overseeding (89). High rates (e.g., 122–195 kg ha^{-1} or 2.5–4 lb 1000 ft^{-2}) of charcoal are necessary. A disadvantage of this method is the inability to reestablish the ryegrass in the event the charcoal treatment fails. Current formulations of activated charcoal also are messy to handle and apply.

Ethofumesate [(±)-2-ethoxy-2,3-dihydro-3,3-dimethyl-5-benzofuranyl methanesulfonate] also provides preemergence and early postemergence annual bluegrass control in bermudagrass overseeded to ryegrass (30, 59, 73). To prevent turfgrass injury, application rate, time and frequency are important. In general, an initial 1.1 kg ha^{-1} (1 lb acre^{-1}) is applied 30 to 45 d after overseeding. A sequential application at similar rates may be required 30 d after the initial application for season-long control. If ethofumesate is applied before bermudagrass dormancy in the fall, the bermudagrass stops growing (30). A delay in spring transition from ryegrass to bermudagrass also occurs when ethofumesate is applied in early fall (57) or in February.

Fenarimol [α-(2-chlorophenyl)-α-(4-chlorophenyl)-5-pyrimidine-methanol], a systemic fungicide used to control several turfgrass diseases, gradually reduces annual bluegrass populations without adverse effects to overseeded grasses or bermudagrass (21). Its application should occur prior to overseeding and prior to the germination of annual bluegrass. A treatment scheme has been suggested consisting of one, two, or three applications with the single or final application being 2 to 4 wk prior to overseeding (21). Fenarimol does not appear to deleteriously effect either overseeded perennial ryegrass or bermudagrass, but the necessity of properly timed repeat applications can be a drawback for managers who have limited budgets and labor. Inconsistent annual bluegrass control following fenarimol treatments has been noted (39, 61).

Bentgrass Golf Greens. Bentgrass is sensitive to most postemergence grass herbicides and many are ineffective against annual bluegrass. As a result, preemergence herbicides are the most common means of controlling this weed. Dithiopyr and bensulide are currently available materials for preemergence annual bluegrass control in bentgrass golf greens. Erratic control of annual bluegrass, however, has been reported (10, 11, 16, 99). It has been suggested that the presence of perennial biotypes of the species may contribute to this erratic control (41). Low growing, creeping perennial types become dominant compared with the annual biotype under frequent close mowing. Moist soil conditions and high soil nutrient levels, which are conditions normally maintained with creeping bentgrass golf greens, also contribute to creeping perennial biotype dominance (16). As a result, preemergence herbicides may control the annual biotype, allowing the perennial biotype to further dominate the green.

Limited research on preemergence control of the perennial biotype suggests poor short-term control (16). Repeat application over multiple years (minimum of 4 yr) are necessary for significant reduction of perennial weeds in bentgrass golf greens. Multiple-year treatments during February and March are considered superior for control compared with August or September treatments.

Ethofumesate has been used safely to control annual bluegrass in bentgrass golf greens (78). Best control with minimum turf injury has been achieved with application rates at 0.56 kg ha^{-1} (0.5 lb acre^{-1}) per application for a total of five applications or at 0.84 kg ha^{-1} (0.75 lb acre^{-1}) per application for three applications. Applications should be 30 d apart. Control seems consistent when treatments begin in October. Applications in late December or in January increases bentgrass injury. Bentgrass, with a shallow root system, grown under stress conditions or in compacted soils, is more prone to injury from the ethofumesate treatments.

With the realization that elimination of annual bluegrass in golf greens is not always achievable with current herbicide technology, research recently has focused on suppressing its growth and seedhead production (32). The turf growth regulators (TGRs) paclobutrazol and flurprimidol are currently available for annual bluegrass suppression in bentgrass golf greens. Other materials (e.g., mefluidide, maleic hydrazide) also are available, but only for higher mowed turf (31). Generally, paclobutrazol or flurprimidol are applied to actively growing bentgrass in mid-fall or early spring. Differential species susceptibility to the herbicide is attributed to a greater uptake of the TGR by the shallower-rooted annual bluegrass when compared with the deeper rooted bentgrass (67). Paclobutrazol and flurprimidol are considered Type II growth regulators since they inhibit gibberellin biosynthesis and suppress internode elongation (68). These materials are root-absorbed (xylem-mobile) and work by reducing the competitive ability of the annual bluegrass for 3 to 8 wk after application. This allows the creeping bentgrass to out compete the weed. These materials should only be applied during periods of active bentgrass root growth. Flurprimidol at rates >0.56 kg ha^{-1} (0.5 lb acre^{-1}) can reduce germination of annual bluegrass seed as well as bentgrass (40), thus, should be applied only to established greens. Prevention of annual bluegrass seedhead formation may be inconsistent with these materials but they do prevent seedhead stalk elongation (68), which may result in improved turf uniformity and appearance.

6. Newly Established Turf.

Preemergence herbicides such as bensulide, dithiopyr, and members of the dinitroanaline family (e.g., benefin, oryzalin, pendimethalin, prodiamine [N^3,N^3-di-N-propyl-2,4-dinitro-6-(trifluoromethyl)-m-phenylenediamine], and trifluralin [2,6-dinitro-*N*,*N*-dipropyl-4-(trifluoromethyl)benzenamine]) should only be used in well established turfgrasses, since these may inhibit rooting of immature or newly-established turfgrasses (8, 79). A waiting period of 12 to 20 wk normally is required between the last herbicide application and establishment of the turfgrass.

Oxadiazon generally is the safest preemergence herbicide when vegetatively establishing grass (9), while siduron is the safest on seeded grasses. Oxadiazon functions by inhibiting shoot emergence of susceptible weeds and does not prevent cell division of roots as do most other preemergence herbicides. Minimal effects therefore occur on the rooting of vegetatively established turf species, but selective weed control of goosegrass occurs.

Siduron is a member of the substituted urea herbicide family. It appears to interfere with photosynthesis of the developing weed. Since siduron does not appreciably inhibit rooting, it safely can be applied to newly seeded turf. Siduron effectively controls annual grass weeds such as crabgrass and foxtail but does not effectively control annual bluegrass, goosegrass, or most broadleaf weeds (4). Siduron should not be used on bermudagrass.

C. Postemergence Herbicides

Postemergence herbicides are effective only on visible weeds. The timing of the application should be when weeds are young, preferably during the two-to-four leaf stage (Color Plate 8–13). Herbicide uptake and translocation is favored at this time. Turfgrasses also are then better able to fill in voids left by the dying weeds.

Generally, postemergence herbicides have a much greater likelihood of injuring a turf species than preemergence herbicides. Turf managers must be careful about the herbicide they select and how they use it. Turf injury usually is more likely when the turf is under stress from temperature, moisture, and pests such as nematodes. Turfgrass species tolerance to postemergence herbicides are listed in Table 8–7.

1. Broadleaf Weed Control.

Broadleaf weed control in turf has been traditionally with members of the phenoxy herbicide family [e.g., 2,4-D, dichlorprop [(±)-2-(2,4-dichlorophenoxy)propanoic acid] (2,4-DP)], MCPA [4-chloro-2-methylphenoxyl-acetic acid], and mecoprop [(±)-2-(4-chloro-2-methylethenoxy)propanoic acid] and the benzoic acid herbicide family (e.g., dicamba). All are selective, systemic and foliar-applied herbicides. Broadleaf weeds, especially perennials, often are not adequately controlled with just one of these materials. Usually, two- or three-way combinations of these herbicides, and possible repeat applications 7 to 14 d apart, are necessary for satisfactory control. Combinations of 2,4-D, MCPP, and dicamba appear to be synergistic, therefore, require less of each than if applied alone. Turf safety with this combination depends on the herbicide mixture, its rate, and its formulation as well as environmental conditions at the time of treatment.

Table 8–7. Turfgrass tolerance to postemergence herbicides.†

Herbicides	Bahia-grass	Bentgrass	Bermuda-grass	Carpet-grass	Centipede-grass	Kentucky bluegrass	St. Augustine-grass	Perennial ryegrass	Tall fescue	Zoysia-grass
Asulam	D‡	D	I-T	D	D	D	I	D	D	D
Atrazine	I	D	I	T	T	D	T	D	D	I
Bentazon	T	T	T	T	T	T	T	T	T	T
Bromoxynil	T	T	T	–	T	T	T	T	T	T
Chlorflurenol	T	D	T	–	D	T	D	D	D	T
Chlorsulfuron	T	I	T	–	D	T	D	D	D	D
Clopyralid	D	D	I-T	–	D	T	D	T	I-T	I-T
2,4-D	T	D-I§	T	I-T	D-I	T	D-I	I§	T	T
2,4-D + dicamba	T	D-I§	T	I-T	D-I	T	D-I	I§	T	T
2,4-D + dichlorprop (2,4-DP)	T	D-I§	T	I-T	I-T	T	D-I	I§	T	T
2,4-D + mecoprop (MCPP)	T	I§	T	I-T	D-I	T	D-I	I§	T	T
2,4-D + MCPP + dicamba	D	D-I§	D-I	I-T	D	T	D-I	I§	T	D
2,4-D + triclopyr	T	I	T	T	I-T	T	D-I	T	I-T	T
Dicamba	D	I§	T	D	D	I-T	D	I	I-T	I
DSMA, MSMA¶	I§	D	D	–	D	T	D	I	T	I
Fenoxaprop	I§	I§	D	–	D	I-T	D	I	I-T	I
Halosulfuron	–	–	S	–	S	I	I	I	I	S
Imazaquin	D	D	T	I-T	T	D	T	D	D	T
MCPP	T	T	T	I-T	D-I	T	D-I	T	T	T
Metsulfuron	D-I	D	T	I	I-T	I-T	I-T	D	I-T	I
Metribuzin	D	D	T	–	D	D	D	D	D	D
Pronamide	D	D	T	–	D	T	D	T	T	D
Quinclorac	D	D	D	D-I	T	D	D	T	D	T
Sethoxydim	D	D	I	T	T	D	T	D	D	I
Simazine	I	D	I	T	T	D	T	D	D	I

† Adapted from Lewis (77), McCarty (80), McCarty and Colvin (83), and Murphy (93).
‡ T = tolerant at labeled rates; I = intermediate tolerance, use at reduced label rates; D = damaging, do not use this herbicide or is not registered for use on this turfgrass.
§ Tolerance depends on specific product formulation, timing of its application and its applied rates.
¶ DSMA = disodium salt of methylarsonic acid, MSMA = monosodium salt of methylarsonic acid.

Table 8-8. General characteristics of different forms of 2,4-D.[†]

Form	Solubility in water	Solubility in oil	Color when mixed with water	Precipitates formed in hard water	Volatility potential
Acid	Low	Low	Milky	Yes	Low
Amine salts					
Water soluble	High	Low	Clear	Yes	None
Oil soluble	Low	High	Milky	Yes	None
Esters					
Low volatile	Low	High	Milky	None	Medium
High volatile	Low	High	Milky	None	High
Inorganic salts	Medium	Low	Clear	Yes	None

[†] After Ashton and Monaco (4).

Many formulations and mixtures of the phenoxy herbicides are available (Table 8-8). These include the parent acid, amine salts, esters, and inorganic salts. The water-soluble amine formulations are the most common because of their lack of volatility, high water solubility, ease of handling and overall low cost. Although more effective, high-volatile esters normally are not used in turf. The likelihood these will volatilize and drift to nearby desirable plant species is high.

In areas where bermudagrass exhibits dormancy due to cold temperatures, various members of the triazine herbicide family are used. Usually these are applied in the mid to late fall months at 1.12 kg ha^{-1} (1 lb acre^{-1}) and possibly repeated in 60 d. Simazine is a widely used material for this and provides good to excellent control of many winter broadleaf weeds such as parsely piert and lawn burweed. In addition, simazine also controls annual bluegrass. Timing is somewhat important as too early of an application may result in turf phytotoxicity and less weed control, while applications too late (e.g., during spring transition) may result in unacceptable thin or weakened bermudagrass.

Until recently, these various herbicide or herbicides were the main chemicals for broadleaf control. Metsulfuron [2-[[[[(4-methoxy-6-methyl-1,3,5-triazin-2-yl]carbonyl]amino]sulfonyl]benzoic acid], triclopyr [[(3,5,6-trichloro-2-pyridinyl)oxy]acetic acid], and clopyralid (3,6-dichloro-2-pyridinecarboxylic acid) have been introduced as alternatives to phenoxy herbicides for broadleaf control. Metsulfuron belongs to the sulfonylurea herbicide family and is noted for its broadleaf weed control at extremely low rates [e.g., 0.0175–0.105 kg ha^{-1} (0.25–1.5 oz product acre^{-1})]. Metsulfuron also has activity on certain bahiagrass cultivars but its total spectrum of weed control has not yet been determined.

Triclopyr and clopyralid belong to the pyridine herbicide family. Compounds in this family have been noted for their high degree of activity. For example, members of this herbicide family are up to ten times more potent than 2,4-D on some broadleaf weed species (70). These herbicides rapidly are absorbed by the roots and foliage of broadleaf plants. They are readily translocated throughout the plants via both xylem and phloem tissues. Problems with this herbicide family include soil mobility and the extreme sensitivity to them by many desirable ornamental. Triclopyr is used alone and in combination with 2,4-D, or clopyralid, for broadleaf weed control. These are used on primarily in cool-season grasses. Table 8.9 lists the effectiveness of commonly used postemergence herbicides for broadleaf weed control.

2. Grass Weed Control.

Postemergence grass weed control traditionally has been through single and repeat applications of the organic arsenicals (e.g., MSMA, DSMA, and CMA). Two to four applications, spaced 7 to 14 d apart are required for complete weed control (50, 52, 53). Repeat applications are needed for control of annual weeds and for most perennial weeds. The rate and number of applications necessary for control also increases as weeds mature. Organic arsenicals can be phytotoxic on cool season turfgrasses, especially when used during high temperatures ($>32\,°C$; $90\,°F$). Control also is reduced if rainfall occurs within 24 h of treatment (9). Recently, new herbicide releases have provided alternatives to the arsenicals for postemergence grass weed control. Decreased phytotoxicity, as well as reduced number of applications, often are associated with these herbicides. The following discusses herbicides available for various turfgrass species.

Bermudagrass and Zoysiagrass. Postemergence control of crabgrass species and goosegrass species usually have been with organic arsenicals (12, 50, 74). As previously mentioned, repeat applications with a short interval between applications are required, especially for mature weed control, but may result in short-term phytotoxicity. Increasing phytotoxicity usually results in bermudagrass and zoysiagrass with repeat applications. *Zoysia* spp. tend to be more sensitive to organic arsenical applications.

In order to increase herbicidal activity on goosegrass, various combinations of arsenicals with other herbicides have been tested. Higher rates (e.g., 0.28–0.56 kg ha^{-1} or 0.25–0.5 lb acre^{-1}) of metribuzin (an asymmetrical triazine [4-amino-6-(1,1-dimethylethyl)-3-(methylthio)-1,2,4-triazin-5(4H)-one]) have provided excellent control of goosegrass when used alone but resulted in marginal bermudagrass tolerance. Lower rates (e.g., 0.14 kg ha^{-1} or 0.125 lb acre^{-1}) of metribuzin with arsenical herbicides have shown good to excellent goosegrass control (9, 12, 52, 54, 74). This combination is only used safely on well established bermudagrass maintained at mowing heights >1.25 cm (0.5 in.). The use of metribuzin increases herbicide activity on goosegrass, but a certain degree of phytotoxicity and a number of escaped weeds may exist. Metribuzin also may inhibit photosynthesis of bermudagrass for a certain period of time (108).

Diclofop-methyl [($\pm$)-2-[4-(2,4-dichlorophenoxy)phenoxy]propanoic acid], a member of the aryl-oxy-phenoxy herbicide family, is superior in goosegrass control when compared with individual and combinations of the organic arsenicals and metribuzin. Little damage to bermudagrass has resulted

Table 8-9. Susceptibility of broadleaf weeds to turf herbicides.†

Weed	Lifecycle	Atrazine/ Simazine	2,4-D	Mecoprop (or MCPP)	Dicamba	2,4-D + MCPP	2,4-D + dichlorprop	2,4-D + MCPP + dicamba	2,4-D + triclopyr	Metsulfuron	Quinclorac
Betony, Florida	P‡	S-I§	I	I	I-S	I	I	I-S	-	-	-
Bittercress, hairy	WA	-	S	I	S	S	S	S	-	-	-
Bindweed, field	P	-	S-I	i	s	S-I	s	S	-	-	-
Black medic	A	-	R	i	I-R	i	s	s	I-R	-	R
Burclover	A	I	I-R	S	I	S-I	S	S	-	-	-
Buttercups	WA,B&P	-	S-I	I	I-R	S	S	S	I-R	-	-
Buttonweed, Va.	P	S	S-I	I	I	I	S-I	S-I	S	S	-
Carpetweed	SA	S	S	I	S	S	S	S	-	-	S
Carrot, wild	A, B	-	I	I	S	I	S-I	S	-	-	S
Catsear	P	S	S-I	I	S-I	S	S	S	S	S	R
Chickweed, common	WA	I	R	S-I	S	S	S	S	S	S	R
Chickweed, mouse-ear	WA,P	I	I-R	S-I	S	S	S	S	S-I	S-I	R
Chicory	P	-	S	S	S	S	S	S	S	S	-
Cinquefoil, common	P	S	S-I	S-I	S-I	S-I	S-I	S-I	-	-	S
Clover, crimson	SA	S	S	S	S	S	S	S	-	-	S
Clover, hop	WA	S	I	S	S	S	S	S	S	S	S
Clover, white	P	S	I	S	I	I	I	S	S-I	-	S
Daisy, English	P	I-R	R	I	I	I	I	S-I	-	-	-
Daisy, oxeye	P,B	S-I	I	I	S	S	S	S	I-S	S	I
Dandelion	P	I	S	S	S-I	S	S	S	I-S	-	-
Dichondra	P	S-I	S	I	S	I	I	S-I	I	I	-
Dock, broadleaf & curly	P	I	I	I-R	S-I	S-I	S-I	S-I	I	I	R
Garlic, wild	P	-	S-I	R	S-I	S	S-I	S-I	-	S-I	R
Geranium, Carolina	WA	-	S	S-I	S-I	S-I	S-I	S	-	S-I	-
Hawkweed	P	-	S	R	S-I	S-I	S	S-I	-	-	-
Healall	WA	S	I-R	I	S	I	S-I	S	S	S-I	R
Henbit	P	-	I-R	I	S-I	I	I-S	S-I	S	-	R
Ivy, ground	WA	-	R	I	S	I	S-I	S-I	-	S-I	-
Knawel	WA	S	R	I	S	S-I	S-I	I	S	-	S-I
Knotweed, prostrate	SA	-	S	I	S	S-I	S	S	S	S-I	I
Lambsquarter, common	SA	S	I-R	S-I	S	S-I	I	S	-	-	-
Lespedeza	SA	S	I-R	S	S	S-I	I	S	-	-	-

(continued on next page)

Table 8-9. Continued.

Weed	Lifecycle	Atrazine/ Simazine	2,4-D	Mecoprop (or MCPP)	Dicamba	2,4-D + MCPP	2,4-D + dichlorprop	2,4-D + MCPP + dicamba	2,4-D + triclopyr	Metsulfuron	Quinclorac
Mallow	P	--	I-R	I	S-I	S-I	S-I	S-I	--	--	--
Mugwort	P	--	I	I-R	S-I	I	I	I	--	--	--
Mustard, wild	WA	S	S	I	S	S	S-I	S	--	I	I
Onion, wild	P	--	I	R	S-I	I	I	S	S	S-I	R
Parsley-piert	WA	S	R	S-I	S-I	S-I	R	S-I	S	--	--
Pearlwort	WA	--	S-I	S-I	--	S-I	S-I	S-I	--	--	--
Pennywort, lawn	P	S	S-I	S-I	S	S-I	S-I	S-I	--	--	--
Pepperweed	A	--	S	S	S	S	S	S	--	--	--
Pigweed	A,P	--	S	S	R	S	S	S	--	S-I	I
Plantains	P	I-R	S	I-R	S	I	I	S	I-R	I	I
Purslane, common	SA	--	I	R	S	I	I	S-I	--	I	R
Red sorrel	P	--	R	S	S	S-I	I	S	--	--	R
Shepherd's-purse	WA	--	S	S-I	S-I	S-I	I	S	--	--	R
Speedwell, corn	WA	S	I-R	I-R	I-R	I-R	I-R	I-R	S-I	--	I
Spurge, prostrate	SA	S-I	I	I	S	I	S-I	S-I	S-I	--	I
Spurge, spotted	SA	S	I-R	S-I	S-I	S-I	S-I	S	S	--	I
Spurweed (lawn burweed)	WA	S-I	I	S-I	S	I	I	S	S	--	I
Strawberry, India mock	P	--	R	I	S-I	R	R	S-I	--	--	--
Thistles	B,P	--	S-I	I	S	S-I	S-I	S	--	I	--
Violet, johnny-jumpup	WA	--	I-R	I-R	S-I	I-R	I	I-R	--	--	--
Violet, wild	P	--	I-R	I-R	S-I	I-R	I	I-R	I-R	--	R
Woodsorrel, yellow	P	I	R	R	I	I-R	I-R	I-R	--	S-I	--
Yarrow	P	--	I	I-R	S	I-R	I	S-I	--	S-I	--
Yellow rocket	WA	--	S-I	I	S-I	S-I	S-I	S	--	--	--

† Adapted from Lewis (77), McCarty (80), Murphy (93), and Turgeon (104).

‡ A = annual; B = biennial; P = perennial; SA = summer annual; WA = winter annual.

§ S = susceptible; I = intermediately susceptible, good control sometimes with high rates, however, a repeat treatment 3 to 4 wk later each at the standard or reduced rate is usually more effective; R = resistant in most cases. Not all weeds have been tested for susceptibility by each herbicide listed.

and repeat applications usually are not necessary (86, 92). This herbicide seems to be more active on goosegrass maintained at lower mowing heights (82). The addition of MSMA is possibly antagonistic for goosegrass control, while the addition of metribuzin to diclofop injures the turf. Goosegrass control is relatively slow and often requires 2 to 3 wk to become effective. Weed control spectrums also appear to be limited, with goosegrass being the most susceptible annual grass weed. Treated areas should not be overseeded with perennial ryegrass for at least 6 wk after application (87). Diclofop-methyl's registration currently is limited to certain states under Section 24c of the EPA's herbicide registration category (97). Zoysiagrass tolerance to diclofop-methyl has not been reported.

An experimental material, quinclorac (3,7-dichloro-8-quinolinecarboxylic acid), has shown potential for postemergence crabgrass control in bermudagrass. Quinclorac also has provided selective torpedograss suppression in bermudagrass, an option previously not available (81). A series of two or three applications are normally required for these suppression. Selective broadleaf weed control also is available with quinclorac but goosegrass control appears to be lacking.

Fenoxaprop-ethyl [(±)-2-[4-[(6-chloro-2-benzoxazolyl)oxy]phenoxy]propanoic acid], another member of the aryl-oxy-phenoxy herbicide family, has been shown to control annual grass weeds, crabgrass species in particular (6, 76). Zoysiagrass has shown good tolerance to fenoxaprop (23), while bermudagrass has not (46).

Centipedegrass. The triazine herbicides were used traditionally for postemergence grass weed control in centipedegrass. However, repeat applications necessary for control often resulted in turfgrass injury (90). Triazine herbicides provided variable postemergence grass weed control but lost their effectiveness as weeds matured. The organic arsenicals, commonly used in other turfgrass species, are highly injurious to centipedegrass.

Sethoxydim, a member of the aryl-oxy-phenoxy herbicide family, provides good to excellent control of many annual grass weeds and also provides suppression of several perennial grass weeds, including bahiagrass (18). Centipedegrass tolerance to sethoxydim is excellent (84, 107). The discovery of sethoxydim's tolerance has been a major break through in postemergence annual grass control in centipedegrass.

St. Augustinegrass. One major problem in producing St. Augustinegrass is its relatively poor tolerance to most postemergence herbicides (104). Triazine herbicides (e.g., atrazine and simazine) provide fair control of some annual grass weed species, but only in its juvenile growth stage. Repeat applications often are necessary for satisfactory control, usually resulting in some turf phytotoxicity.

Asulam [methyl[(4-aminophenyl)sulfonyl]carbamate], a member of the carbamate herbicide family, provides control of some annual grass weeds without serious damage to St. Augustinegrass (21). Repeat applications 7 to 14 d apart may be required for control of older weeds. This increases the likelihood of damage to St. Augustinegrass. As with most other postemergence herbicides, asulam should be applied when temperatures are below 29.4 °C (85 °F) and when the turf is actively growing.

Bahiagrass. Bahiagrass, like St. Augustinegrass, is somewhat sensitive to most postemergence herbicides. This sensitivity limits the number of herbicides available for use on it. Although labeled on bahiagrass, most postemergence broadleaf (e.g., 2,4-D, dicamba, or mecoprop) herbicides will cause turf yellowing, especially if it is applied when temperatures are hot, or the growing turf is under stressful conditions. Normally, the phytotoxicity is not lethal and turf recovery can be expected within 1 to 2 wk.

Postemergence grass weed control, in bahiagrass is possible with hexazinone [3-cyclohexyl-6-(dimethylamino)-1-methyl-1,3,5-triazine-2,4(1H, 3H)-dione] (14). Only low maintenance, well established bahiagrass areas on roadsides, railroads, and utility rights-of-way should be treated. Various broadleaf and grass weeds are controlled if there is adequate soil moisture to activate the herbicide. Early spring applications are recommended. Temporary turf phytotoxicity can be expected following application. On high maintenance bahiagrass, no selective postemergence herbicide is available to control grass weeds. Spot spraying or selective placement such as rope-wicking, with a nonselective herbicide such as glyphosate, are the only means of chemical control of grass weeds.

Cool-Season Turfgrasses. Postemergence grass weed control in cool-season turfgrasses traditionally has been limited to various members of the organic arsenicals (e.g., calcium salt of monosodium methylarsonic acid) (3). Specific formulations and specific rates are necessary for its use on most cool-season turfgrasses or injury may result. Proper timing at a young weed-growth stage, during mild environmental conditions, and while turfgrass actively is growing should be considered before using any of these herbicides.

More recently, fenoxaprop has been shown to control tillered crabgrass (7, 19) when adequate soil moisture is present and also is tolerated by some cool-season turfgrasses. Seedling and mature perennial ryegrass and tall fescue have shown little injury from fenoxaprop (24, 43, 85). Kentucky bluegrass also is tolerant (19), but sometimes can be injured when applied in the spring (7, 20). Mono seedling stands of Kentucky bluegrass have been shown to be injured by fenoxaprop; however, when it is in competition with a severe infestation of crabgrass, the loss through injury may be outweighed by the improved turf cover the following fall (26). Creeping bentgrass also is injured by fenoxaprop (7), but recovers within several weeks of application (46). Safeners may reduce fenoxaprop damage on bentgrass (7) as may the addition of iron with and without methylene urea (26). A low rate of fenoxaprop (0.027 kg ha^{-1} or 0.025 lb acre^{-1}) reduces the degree of bentgrass discoloration (17) but may result in inconsistent crabgrass control.

3. Nutsedge Control.

The predominant nutsedge species in turfgrasses are yellow and purple nutsedge. Other, more local members of the *Cyperus* genus include annual or water sedge, perennial and annual kyllinga, globe sedge, Texas sedge, flathead sedge, and cylindrical sedge. Path or slender rush, a member of the rush (*Juncus*) family, also can occur in some turf situations.

Yellow and purple nutsedge are low-growing perennials that resemble grasses. Nutsedges, in general, are yellow-green to dark-green, with triangular stems bearing three-ranked leaves, unlike the two-ranked leaves of the grass family. The root systems are fibrous with deep-rooted tubers or nutlets. Seedhead color is often used to distinguish between the two major nutsedges. Leaf tip shape is another distinguishing characteristic. Leaf tips of purple nutsedge are generally wider and more rounded. Conversely, yellow nutsedge leaf tips are narrow, forming a needle-like tip (Color Plate 8–14). Yellow and purple nutsedge are not believed to produce viable seed but due to their underground tubers and rhizomes, these species have the capacity to reproduce and spread.

Nutsedge generally thrive in soils that remain wet for extended periods of time. The first control step is to correct the cause of continuously wet soils. Do not overirrigate an area, and if necessary, provide surface and subsurface drainage. Preemergence control of sedges is available from several materials. Triazine herbicides (e.g., atrazine and simazine) provide fair preemergence control of select annual sedges, but generally are ineffective on perennial species. Metolachlor provides preemergence control of most annual sedges and selective control of perennial species. One notable exception is purple nutsedge. Preemergence control of purple nutsedge is currently unavailable. Metolachlor often is combined with triazine herbicides for nutsedge, broadleaf and certain annual grass control.

Historically, postemergence chemical control of most sedges was attempted with repeat applications of 2,4-D, the organic arsenicals, or a combination of the two. Although effective, treatments were slow to kill and repeat applications generally were necessary. Extensive damage resulted with certain turf species, such as centipedegrass and St. Augustinegrass.

Control of yellow nutsedge and annual sedges is possible with bentazon with minimal turf damage (21). Purple nutsedge can be suppressed with imazaquin (22). Control may increase when it is tank-mixed with MSMA (66). Certain broadleaf and monocot weeds, such as wild garlic, also are controlled with imazaquin (36), however, spring green-up of bermudagrass may be delayed following fall or winter treatments.

Repeat applications with either herbicide normally are required to completely control an established nutsedge stand. Treatments during multiple years also may be required to eradicate nutsedges. For example, when applied annually, 3 yr of imazaquin plus MSMA treatments were required for complete purple nutsedge control (66).

Immature annual sedges can be suppressed with triazine herbicides. Atrazine commonly is used in centipedegrass and St. Augustinegrass sod production shortly after harvesting. As the weeds mature, control with atrazine decreases dramatically. Repeat applications of atrazine may be necessary for season-long control.

A recently introduced material, halosulfuron, belongs to the sulfonyl-urea herbicide family and appears to provide good postemergence control of most major sedges. Halosulfuron is used at low rates (e.g., 0.035–0.07 kg ha^{-1} or 0.03–0.06 lb acre^{-1}) and should be repeated in 4 to 6 wk for increased control. It is not known if tank-mixing with other compounds will increase nutsedge activity of halosulfuron.

Postemergence herbicides often slightly to moderately discolor (injure) turf species, even though these herbicides are labeled for turf use. Injury generally is temporary (2–4 wk), but increases with moisture, heat or pest stress. It is desirable to minimize injury to turf, especially where high quality turf is expected. Iron and N have been used in conjunction with postemergence herbicides to minimize turf injury (58, 65). Although these additives have shown some short-term prevention of postemergence herbicide injury, complete elimination of turf injury for all grasses or for all herbicides may not occur.

4. Mixed grass stands.

Because of incompatible leaf texture and color, it normally is undesirable to have a mixture of grass species in the same area. Selectively controlling one species of grass appearing within a stand of another species generally is more desirable than using a non-selective herbicide and then re-planting the turf. Table 8–10 summarizes current knowledge on selectively controlling a particular turf species in a mixed stand. As with most postemergence herbicides, multiple applications normally are required for complete eradication of a certain species, which may result in some injury to the desired turf. Selective control of bermudagrass in St. Augustinegrass, bentgrass and bahiagrass still is difficult to achieve with today's herbicides.

An increasing problem for many golf course superintendents is the encroachment of collar region bermudagrass into bentgrass greens. Siduron and ethofumesate have suppressed bermudagrass (30), however, varying levels of bentgrass injury were noted (33).

Temporary (up to 90 d) bermudagrass suppression has been achieved with combinations of siduron with flurprimidol, as well as ethofumesate plus flurprimidol (64). This suppression was superior to that achieved by the standard practice of using siduron alone. April treatments were less injurious to bentgrass and provided a level of bermudagrass retardation similar to a September followed by an April application.

All chemicals mentioned are for reference only and are reported for 1994. Not all are available for turf use. Some may be restricted by some states, provinces, or federal agencies. Always read and follow the manufacturer's label as registered under the Federal Insecticide, Fungicide, and Rodenticide Act (97). Mention of a proprietary product does not constitute a guarantee or warranty of the product by the authors or the publishers of this book and does not imply approval to the exclusion of other products that also may be suitable.

Table 8-10. Postemergence herbicides which selectively remove undesirable turf species from a mixed stand.

Herbicide	Tolerant turf	Susceptible turf	Reference
Arsenicals (MSMA/DSMA)‡	Bermudagrass Zoysiagrass	Centipedegrass St. Augustinegrass	McCarty (80)
Asulam	St. Augustinegrass Bermudagrass (Tifway 419)	Centipedegrass	McCarty (80)
Atrazine, simazine, pronamide	Bermudagrass Centipedegrass St. Augustinegrass	Bentgrass Bluegrass Fine fescue Ryegrass	McCarty (80)
Chlorsulfuron	Bermudagrass Kentucky bluegrass	Tall fescue	Dernoeden (27)
Ethofumesate plus atrazine, simazine	St. Augustinegrass	Bermudagrass	McCarty (80)
Fluazifop	Tall fescue	Bermudagrass Centipedegrass Zoysiagrass	Johnson (60)
Fenoxaprop	Bentgrass† Kentucky bluegrass Ryegrass Zoysiagrass (Meyer) Tall fescue	Bermudagrass Centipedegrass St. Augustinegrass	Dernoeden (24, 25, 26) Higgins et al (46) Johnson (60) McCarty (80)
Metsulfuron	Bermudagrass Centipedegrass Kentucky bluegrass St. Augustinegrass Zoysiagrass (Meyer, Emerald)	Bahiagrass Tall fescue	Dernoeden, (27) McCarty (80)
Sethoxydim	Centipedegrass Fine fescue	Bermudagrass	McCarty et al. (84)

† Herbicide rate or mowing height dependent.
‡ DSMA = disodium salt of methylarsonic acid, MSMA = monosodium salt of methylarsonic acid.

APPENDIX A.

COMMON AND SCIENTIFIC NAMES OF PLANTS DISCUSSED

Common Name	Scientific Name
bahiagrass	*Paspalum notatum* Fluegge
barnyardgrass	*Echinochloa crus-galli* (L.) Beauvois
bentgrass	*Agrostis* spp.
bentgrass, colonial	*Agrostis tenuis* Sibth
bentgrass, creeping	*Agrostis stolonifera* L.
bermudagrass	*Cynodon dactylon* (L.) Pers.
betony, Florida	*Stachys floridana* Shuttlew
bindweed, field	*Convolvulus arvensis* L.
bittercress, hairy	*Cardamine hirsuta* L.
blue grama	*Bouteloua gracilis* (Willd. ex Kunth) Lagasca ex Griffiths
bluegrass, annual	*Poa annua* L.
bluegrass, Kentucky	*Poa pratensis* L.
bromegrass	*Bromus* spp.
buffalograss	*Buchloe dactyloides* (Nutt.) Engelm.
burclover	*Medicago* spp.
buttercup, creeping	*Ranunculus repens* L.
buttonweed, Virginia	*Diodia virginiana* L.
carpetgrass	*Axonopus affinis* Chase
carpetweed	*Mollugo verticillata* L.
carrot, wild	*Daucus carota* L.
cat's-ear	*Hypochoersis radicata* L.
centipedegrass	*Eremochloa ophiuroides* (Munro) Hackel
chickweed, common	*Stellaria media* (L.) Villars
chickweed, mouse-ear	*Cerastium vulgatum* L.
chicory	*Cichorium intybus* L.
cinquefoil, common	*Potentilla canadensis* L.
clover, white	*Trifolium repens* L.
clover, crimson	*Trifolium incarnatum* L.
clover, hop	*Trifolium aureum* Pollich
cocklebur	*Xanthium strumarium* L.
crabgrass	*Digitaria* spp.
daisy, English	*Bellis perennis* L.
daisy, oxeye	*Chrysanthemum leucanthemum* L.
dallisgrass	*Paspalum dilatatum* Poiret
dandelion	*Taraxacum officinale* Weber
dichondra	*Dichondra micrantha* Urban
dock, broadleaf	*Rumex obtusifolius* L.
dock, curly	*Rumex crispus* L.
duckweed	*Lemna* spp.
fescue, red	*Festuca rubra* L. *commutata*
fescue, tall	*Festuca arundinacea* Schreber
foxtail	*Setaria* spp.
garlic, wild	*Allium vineale* L.
geranium, Carolina	*Geranium carolinianum* L.
goosegrass	*Eleusine indica* (L.) Gaertner
grape	*Vitis* spp.

(continued on next page)

Common Name	Scientific Name
hawkweed, mouse-ear	*Hiedracium pilosella* L.
heal-all	*Prunella vulgaris* L.
henbit	*Lamium amplexicaule* L.
hyacinth, water	*Eichhornia crassipes* (C. Martius) Solms-Laub.
ivy, ground	*Glechoma hederacea* L.
jimsonweed	*Datura stramonium* L.
johnsongrass	*Sorghum halapense* (L.) Pers.
knawel	*Scleranthus annuus* L.
knotweed, prostrate	*Polygonum aviculare* L.
kyllinga, annual	*Cyperus sesquiflorus* (Torr.)
kyllinga, perennial (green)	*Cyperus brevifolius* (Torr.) (Rottb.) Hassk.
lambsquarters, common	*Chenopodium album* L.
lespedeza, common	*Lespedeza striata* (Thunb. ex Murray) Hook. & Arn.
mallow	*Malva rotundifolia* L.
medic, black	*Medicago lupulina* L.
morningglory	*Ipomoea* spp.
mugwort	*Artemisia vulgaris* L.
mustard, wild	*Brassica kaber* (DC.) L. Wheeler
nimblewill	*Muhlenbergia schreberi* Gmelin
nutsedge, purple	*Cyperus rotundus* L.
nutsedge, yellow	*Cyperus esculentus* L.
onion, wild	*Allium canadense* L.
parsley-piert	*Alchemilla arvensis* (L.) Scop.
parsnip, wild	*Pastinaca sativa* L.
pearlwort	*Sagina decumbens* (Ell.) T. & G.
pear, prickly	*Opuntia* spp.
pennywort	*Hydrocotyle* spp.
pepperweed, Virginia	*Lepidium virginicum* L.
pigweed, redroot	*Amaranthus retroflexus* L.
pigweed	*Amaranthus* spp.
plantain	*Plantago* spp.
plantain, broadleaf	*Plantago major* L.
poison ivy	*Toxicodendron radicans* (L.) Kuntze
purslane, common	*Portulaca oleracea* L.
pusley, Florida	*Richardia scabra* L.
quackgrass	*Agropyron repens* (L.) Beauvois
ragweed, common	*Ambrosia artemisiifolia* L.
rocket, yellow	*Barbarea vulgaris* R. Br.
rush, path (slender)	*Juncus tenuis* Willd.
ryegrass, perennial	*Lolium perenne* L.
sandbur	*Cenchrus* spp.
sandwort	*Arenaria serpyllifolia* L.
sedge, cylindric	*Cyperus retrorsus* Chapm.
sedge, flathead, annual or water	*Cyperus compressus* L.
sedge, globe	*Cyperus globulosis* Aubl.
sedge, Texas	*Cyperus polystachyos* Rottb.
shepherd's-purse	*Capsella bursa-pastoris* (L.) Medikus
sicklepod	*Cassia obtusifolia* (L.) H. Inwin & Barneby

(continued on next page)

Common Name	Scientific Name
smartweed, Pennsylvania	*Polygonum pensylvanicum* L.
smutgrass	*Sporobolus indicus* (L.) R. Br.
sorrel, perennial	*Rumex* spp.
sorrel, red	*Rumex acetosella* L.
speedweed, corn	*Veronica arvensis* L.
spurge, prostrate	*Euphorbia [Chamaesyce] supina* Raf.
spurge, spotted	*Euphorbia [Chamaesyce] maculata* L.
spurweed (lawn burweed)	*Soliva sessilis* R. & P. and *S. pterosperma* (Jussieu) Lessing
St. Augustinegrass	*Stenotaphrum secundatum* (Walter) Kuntze
strawberry, India Mock	*Duchesnea indica* (Andreus) Focke
thistles	*Cirsium* and *Carduus* spp.
vaseygrass	*Paspalum urvillei* Steudel
velvetleaf	*Abutilon theophrasti* Medic.
veronica (speedwell)	*Veronica peregrina* L.
violet	*Viola* spp.
witchweed	*Striga asiatica* (L.) Kuntze
woodsorrel, yellow	*Oxalis stricta* L.
yarrow	*Achillea millefolium* L.
zoysiagrass	*Zoysia* spp.

Appendix B. Weed Identification Guides for Turf Managers

Title	Authors
Weeds of Southern Turfgrass SP-79	Murphy, T.R., L.B. McCarty, D.L. Colvin, R. Dickens, J.W. Everest, and D.W. Hall. 1992. Univ. of Florida Cooperative Extension Service, Gainesville, FL 32611-0011
Weeds of Arkansas. MP 169.	Baldwin, FL, and E.B. Smith, 1981. Univ. of Arkansas Cooperative Extension Service Printing, Little Rock, AK 72203
Weed Identification Guide	Southern Weed Science Society, 309 W. Clark St., Champaign, IL 61820
Weeds of the Southern United States	Georgia Cooperative Extension Service, Univ. of Georgia, Athens, GA 30602
Growers Weed Identification Handbook (Pub. 4030)	Fisher, B.B., A.H. Lange, J. McCaskill, B. Crampton, and B. Tabraham. Div. of Agricultural Information. University of California, Berkeley, CA 94720
Identify Seedling and Mature Weeds Common in the Southeastern United States	Stucky, J.J., T.J. Monaco, and A.D. Worsham. 1980. North Carolina State Univ. 318 Ricks Hall, Raleigh, NC 27650
Weeds of the West	Whitson, T.D., L.C. Burrill, S.A. Dewey, D.W. Cudney, B.E. Nelson, R.D. Lee, and R. Parker. 1991. Western Weed Science Society, Univ. of Wyoming. Pioneer of Jackson Hole, 132 West Gill St., Jackson, WY 83001

REFERENCES

1. American Sod Producers Association. Guidelines specifications to sodding. Am. Sod Producers Assoc., New Brunswick, NJ.

2. Anderson, W.P. 1983. Weed science: Principles. 2nd ed. West Pub. Company, St. Paul, MN.

3. Ashburn, E.L. 1988. Lawn weeds and their control. Univ. Tenn. Agric. Ext. Ser. PB 956. Knoxville, TN.

4. Ashton, F.M., and T.J. Monaco. 1991. Weed science principles and practices. John Wiley & Sons, New York.

5. Barrett, L.H., and J.A. Jagschitz. 1975. Control of crabgrass and goosegrass with pre-emergence chemicals in turfgrass. Proc. Northeast Weed Sci. Soc. 29:359–364.

6. Bhowmik, P.C. 1986. Fenoxaprop-ethyl for postemergence crabgrass control in Kentucky bluegrass turf. HortScience 21:457–458.

7. Bhowmik, P.C., and M. Eichenlaub. 1986. Influence of safeners on bentgrass tolerance to fenoxaprop-ethyl. Proc. Northeast. Weed Sci. Soc. 40:283.

8. Bingham, S.W. 1974. Influence of selected herbicides on rooting of turfgrass sod. p. 372–377. In E.C. Roberts (ed.) Proc. 2nd Int. Turf. Res. Conf. Blacksburg, VA. ASA and CSSA, Madison, WI.

9. Bingham, S.W. 1985. Effectiveness of herbicides for *Eleusine indica* control during *Cynodon dactylon* improvement in golf course fairways. p. 705–715. In F. Lemaire (ed.) Proc. 5th Int. Turf. Res. Conf., Avignon, France, 1–5 July 1985.

10. Bingham, S.W., R.E. Schmidt, and C.K. Curry. 1969. Annual bluegrass control in over-seeded bermudagrass putting green turf. Agron. J. 61:908–911.

11. Bingham, S.W., and R.L. Shaver. 1979. Effectiveness of herbicide programs for annual bluegrass (*Poa annua*) control in bermudagrass (*Cynodon dactylon*). Weed Sci. 27:367–370.

12. Bingham, S.W., and R.L. Shaver. 1980. Goosegrass control in bermudagrasses. 1980. p. 237–245. In J.B. Beard (ed.) Proc. 3rd Int. Turf Res. Conf., Munich, West Germany. 11–13 July 1977. ASA, CSSA, SSSA, and ITS, Madison, WI.

13. Branham, B.E., and P.E. Rieke. 1986. Effects of turf cultivation practices on the efficacy of preemergence grass herbicides. Agron. J. 78:1089–1091.

14. Brecke, B.J. 1981. Smutgrass (*Sporobolus poiretii*) control in bahiagrass (*Paspalum notatum*) pastures. Weed Sci. 291:553–555.

15. Buchanan, G.A., C.S. Hoveland, and M.C. Harris. 1975. Response of weeds to soil pH. Weed Sci. 23:473–477.

16. Callahan, L.M., and E.R. McDonald. 1992. Effectiveness of bensulide in controlling two annual bluegrass (*Poa annua*) subspecies. Weed Technol. 6:97–103.

17. Carroll, M.J., M.J. Mahoney, and P.N. Dernoeden. 1992. Creeping bentgrass (*Agrostis palustris*) quality as influenced by multiple low-rate applications of fenoxaprop. Weed Technol. 6:356–360.

18. Chernicky, J.P., B.J. Gossett, and T.R. Murphy. 1984. Factors influencing control of annual grasses with sethoxydim and RO-13-8895. Weed Sci. 32:174–177.

19. Chism, W.J., and S.W. Bingham. 1991. Postemergence control of large crabgrass (*Digitaria sanguinalis*) with herbicides. Weed Sci. 39:62–66.

20. Cisar, J.L., and J.A. Jagschitz. 1984. Turfgrass tolerance to post and preemergence herbicides. Proc. Northeast Weed Sci. Soc. 38:298–302.

21. Coats, G.E. 1986. Turfgrass weed control. Mississippi Agric. and Forestry Exp. Stn. Bull. 95. Mississippi State.

22. Coats, G.E., D.C. Heering, and J.W. Scruggs. 1987. Wild garlic and purple nutsedge control in turf. Proc. South. Weed Sci. 40:98.

23. Dernoeden, P.H. 1985. Controlling crabgrass with reduced rates of herbicides. Grounds Mainten. 20:12–22, 94.

24. Dernoeden, P.H. 1987. Tolerance of perennial ryegrass and tall fescue seedlings to fenoxaprop. Agron. J. 79:1035–1037.

25. Dernoeden, P.H. 1989. Bermudagrass suppression and zoysiagrass tolerance to fenoxaprop. p. 285–290. In H. Takatoh (ed.) Proc. 6th Int. Turf. Res. Conf., Tokyo. 31 July–5 Aug. 1989. Int. Turf. Soc, Tokyo.

26. Dernoeden, P.H. 1989. Mature creeping bentgrass and seedling Kentucky bluegrass tolerance to fenoxaprop. p. 279–283. In H. Takotoh (ed.) Proc. 6th Int. Turf. Res. Conf., Tokyo. 31 July–5 Aug. 1989. Int. Turf. Soc., Tokyo, Japan.

27. Dernoedon, P.H. 1990. Comparison of three herbicides for selective tall fescue control in Kentucky bluegrass. Agron. J. 82:278–282.

28. Dernoeden, P.H., T.L. Watschke, and J.K. Mathias. 1984. Goosegrass (*Eleusine indica*) control in turf in the transition zone. Weed Sci. 32:4–7.

29. Dest, W.M., and K. Guillard. 1987. Nitrogen and phosphorus nutritional influence on bentgrass-annual bluegrass community composition. J. Am. Soc. Hortic. Sci. 112:769–773.

30. Dickens, R. 1979. Control of annual bluegrass (*Poa annua*) in overseeded bermudagrass (*Cynodon* spp.) golf greens. Weed Sci. 27:642–644.

31. DiPaola, J.M. 1992. Turf growth regulators. Pest control recommendations for turfgrass managers. North Carolina Agric. Ext. Serv. AG-408. Raleigh, NC.

32. DiPaola, J.M., and W.M. Lewis. 1989. Growth regulators and *Poa annua* suppression. p. 22–23. *In* Proc. 27th Annual North Carolina Turf Conf. Turfgrass Council of North Carolina, Raleigh.

33. Duble, R.L. 1974. Bentgrass greens in the hot, humid south. Golf Superintendent 42(3):36–38.

34. Emmons, R.D. 1984. Turfgrass science and management. Delmar Publ., Albany, NY.

35. Engel, R.E., and R.D. Ilnicki. 1969. Turf weeds and their control. p. 240–287. *In* A.A. Hanson and F.V. Juska (ed.) Turfgrass science. Agron. Monogr. 14. ASA, CSSA, and SSSA, Madison, WI.

36. Ferguson, G.P., G.E. Coats, G.B. Wilson, and D.R. Shaw. 1992. Postemergence control of wild garlic (*Allium vineale*) in turfgrass. Weed Technol. 6:144–148.

37. Figliola, S.S., N.D. Camper, and W.H. Ridings. 1988. Potential biological control agents for goosegrass (*Eleusine indica*). Weed Sci. 36:830–835.

38. Fulwider, J.R., and R.E. Engel. 1959. The effect of temperature and light on germination of seed of goosegrass, *Eleusine indica*. Weeds 7:359–361.

39. Gaul, M.C., and N.E. Christians. 1988. Selective control of annual bluegrass in cool-season turfs with fenarimol and chlorsulfuron. Agron. J. 80:120–125.

40. Gaussoin, R.E., and B.E. Branham. 1987. Annual bluegrass and creeping bentgrass germination response to flurprimidol. HortScience 22:441–442.

41. Gibeault, V.A., and N.R. Goetze. 1972. Annual meadow-grass. J. Sports Turf Res. Inst. 48:1–11.

42. Goss, R.L., S.E. Brauen, and S.P. Orton. 1975. The effects of N, P, K and S on *Poa annua* L. in bentgrass putting green turf. J. Sports Turf. Res. Inst. 51:74–82.

43. Grande, J.A., A.S. Harrison, and P.W. Robinson. 1984. HOE-A25.01. A new postemergence crabgrass herbicide for turfgrass. Proc. Northeast Weed Sci. Soc. 38:281.

44. Halisky, P.M., C.R. Funk, and R.E. Engel. 1966. Melting-out of Kentucky bluegrass varieties by *Helminthosporium vagans* as influenced by turf management practices. Plant Dis. Rep. 50:703–706.

45. Hansen, A.A. 1921. The use of chemical weed killers on golf courses. U.S. Golf Assoc. Bull. 1:128–131.

46. Higgins, J.M., L.B. McCarty, T. Whitwell, and L.C. Miller. 1987. Bentgrass and bermudagrass putting green tolerance to postemergence herbicides. Hort Science 22:248–250.

47. Hill, G.D. 1982. Impact of weed science and agricultural chemicals on farm productivity in the 1980s. Weed Sci. 30:426–429.

48. Hiltbold, A.E., and G.A. Buchanan. 1977. Influence of soil pH on persistence of atrazine in the field. Weed Sci. 25:515–520.

49. Jagschitz, J.A., and J.S. Ebdon. 1985. Influence of mowing, fertilizer and herbicide on crabgrass infestation in red fescue turf. p. 699–704. *In* F. Lemaire (ed.) Proc. 5th Int. Turf. Res. Conf., Avignon, France. 1–5 July 1985.

50. Johnson, B.J. 1975. Postemergence control of large crabgrass and goosegrass in turf. Weed Sci. 23:404–409.

51. Johnson, B.J. 1976. Dates of herbicide application for summer weed control in turf. Weed Sci. 24:422–424.

52. Johnson, B.J. 1976. Turfgrass tolerance and weed control with methazole and metribuzin. Weed Sci. 24:512–517.

53. Johnson, B.J. 1977. Sequential herbicide treatments for large crabgrass and goosegrass control in bermudagrass. Agron. J. 69:1012–1014.

54. Johnson, B.J. 1980. Goosegrass (*Eleusine indica*) control in bermudagrass (*Cynodon dactylon*) turf. Weed Sci. 28.378–381.

55. Johnson, B.J. 1982. Frequency of herbicide treatments for summer and winter weed control in turf grasses. Weed Sci. 30:116–124.

56. Johnson, B.J. 1982. Oxadiazon treatments on overseeded putting-green turf. Weed Sci. 30:355–338.

57. Johnson, B.J. 1983. Response to ethofumesate of annual bluegrass (*Poa annua*) and overseeded bermudagrass (*Cynodon dactylon*). Weed Sci. 31:385–390.

58. Johnson, B.J. 1984. Influence of nitrogen on recovery of bermudagrass (*Cynodon dactylon*) treated with herbicides. Weed Sci. 32:819–823.

59. Johnson, B.J. 1987. Effects of core cultivation on preemergence herbicide activity in bermudagrass. HortScience 22:440–441.

60. Johnson, B.J. 1987. Turfgrass species response to herbicides applied postemergence. Weed Tech. 1:305–311.

61. Johnson, B.J. 1988a. Fenarimol for control of annual bluegrass in dormant bermudagrass turf. Georgia Agric. Exp. Stn. Res. Rep. 552. Athens.

62. Johnson, B.J. 1988b. Glyphosate and SC-0224 for bermudagrass (*Cynodon* spp.) cultivar control. Weed Tech. 2:20–23.

63. Johnson, B.J., and R.E. Burns. 1985. Effect of soil pH, fertility, and herbicides on weed control and quality of bermudagrass (*Cynodon dactylon*) turf. Weed Sci. 33:366–370.

64. Johnson, B.J., and R.N. Carrow. 1989. Bermudagrass encroachment into creeping bentgrass as affected by herbicides and plant growth regulators. Crop Sci. 29:1220–1227.

65. Johnson, B.J., R.N. Carrow, and T.R. Murphy. 1990. Foliar-applied iron enhances bermudagrass tolerance to herbicides. J. Am. Soc. Hortic. Sci. 115:422–426.

66. Johnson, B.J., and T.R. Murphy. 1992. Purple nutsedge control with imazaquin in bermudagrass turf. Georgia Agric. Exp. Stn. Res. Rep. 408. Athens.

67. Kegeyama, M.E., L.R. Widell, D.G. Cotton, and G.R. McVey. 1989. Annual bluegrass to bentgrass conversion with a turf growth retardant (TGR). p. 387–390. *In* H. Takatoh (ed.) Proc. 6th Int. Turf. Res. Conf., Tokyo. 31 July–5 Aug. 1989. Int. Turf. Soc., Tokyo.

68. Kaufman, J.E. 1989. How turfgrass biology affects responses to growth regulators. p. 83–88. *In* H. Takatoh (ed.) Proc. 6th Int. Turf. Res. Conf., Tokyo. 31 July–5 Aug. 1989. Int. Turf. Soc., Tokyo.

69. Kelley, A.D., and V.F. Burns. 1975. Dissemination of weed seeds by irrigation water. Weed Sci. 23:486–493.

70. Klingman, G.C., and F.M. Ashton. 1982. Weed science principles and practices. John Wiley & Sons, New York.

71. Kuo, S., S.E. Brauen, and E.J. Jellum. 1992. Phosphorus availability in some acid soils influences bentgrass and annual bluegrass growth. HortScience 27:370.

72. Leach, B.R., and J.W. Lipp. 1927. Additional experiments in grub-proofing turf. U.S. Golf Assoc. Bull. 7:28.

73. Lee, W.D. 1977. Winter annual grass control in Italian ryegrass with ethofumesate. Weed Sci. 25:252–255.

74. Lewis, W.M. 1981. Metribuzin for preemergence and postemergence control of crabgrass and goosegrass in bermudagrass turf. p. 383–390. *In* R.W. Sheard (ed.) Proc. 4th Int. Turf. Res. Conf., Ontario, Canada. 19–23 July 1981. Int. Turf. Soc. and Univ. of Guelph, Guelph, Ontario.

75. Lewis, W.M. 1985a. Weeds in turf. p. 18–34. *In* A.H. Bruneau (ed.) Turfgrass pest management manual. North Carolina Agric. Ext. Serv., Raleigh.

76. Lewis, W.M. 1985b. Fenoxaprop-ethyl for smooth crabgrass and goosegrass control in turf. Proc. South. Weed Sci. Soc. 38:104.

77. Lewis, W.M. 1992. Weed control. Pest control recommendations for turfgrass managers. North Carolina Agric. Ext. Serv., Raleigh.

78. Lewis, W.M., and J.M. DiPaola. 1989. Ethofumesate for *Poa annua* control in bentgrass. p. 303–305. *In* H. Takatoh (ed.). Proc. 6th Int. Turf. Res. Conf., Tokyo, 31 July–5 Aug. 1989. Int. Turf. Soc., Tokyo.

79. Lewis, W.M., J.M. DiPaola, and A.H. Bruneau. 1988. Effects of preemergence herbicides on turfgarss rooting. Grounds Maint. 23(2):48–49.

80. McCarty, L.B. 1993. Weed identification and control. Univ. of Florida's pest control recommendations for turfgrass managers. Univ. of Florida Coop. Ext. Serv. SS-ORH-004. Gainesville.

81. McCarty, L.B. 1992. Qunclorac evaluations in warm-season turfgrasses. Proc. South. Weed Sci. Soc. 45:136.

82. McCarty, L.B. 1991. Goosegrass (*Eleusine indica*) control in bermudagrass (*Cynodon* spp.) turf with diclofop. Weed Sci. 39:255–261.

83. McCarty, L.B., and D.L. Colvin. 1991. Carpetgrass response to postemergence herbicides. Weed Technol. 5:563–565.

84. McCarty, L.B., J.M. Higgins, L.C. Miller, and T. Whitwell. 1986. Centipedegrass tolerance to postemergence grass herbicides. HortScience 21:1405–1407.

85. McCarty, L.B., J.M. Higgins, T. Whitwell, and L.C. Miller. 1989. Tolerance of tall fescue to postemergence grass herbicide. HortScience 24:309–311.

86. McCarty, L.B., L.C. Miller, and D.L. Colvin. 1991. Bermudagrass (*Cynodon* spp.) cultivar response to diclofop. MSMA, and metribuzin. Weed Technol. 5:27–32.

87. McCarty, L.B., and T.R. Murphy. 1993. Perennial ryegrass (*Lolium perenne*) establishment following diclofop application timings and rates. p. 246–249. *In* R.N. Carrow et al. (ed.) Int. Turfgrass Soc. Res. Intertec Publ. Corp., Overland Park, KS.

88. McCarty, L.B., and J.S. Weinbrecht. 1992. Annual bluegrass control with *Xanthomonas campestris*. p. 327–328. *In* T.E. Freeman (ed.) Turfgrass research in Florida: A technical report. Inst. of Food and Agric. Sci., Univ. of Florida, Gainesville.

89. Meyers, H.G., W.L. Currey, and D.E. Barnes. 1973. Deactivation of Kerb with sewage sludge, topdressing and activated charcoal. p. 442–444. *In* W. Grierson (ed.) Proc. Florida State Hortic Soc. Miami Beach, FL. 6–8 Nov. 1973. Univ. of Florida, Gainesville.

90. Miller, L.C., J.P. Krausz, C.L. Parks, and C.S. Gorsuch. 1985. Centipedegrass and its problems. South Carolina Coop. Ext. Serv. Cir. 583. Clemson.

91. Monroe, J.H., W.M. Lewis, and J.M. DiPaola. 1990. Aerification effects on preemergence herbicide activity. p. 27. *In* Weed Sci. Soc. Am. Abstr. Champaign, IL.

92. Murdoch, C.L., and R.K. Nishimoto. 1982. Diclofop for goosegrass control in bermudagrass putting greens. HortScience 17:914–915.

93. Murphy, T.R. 1988. Turfgrass weed control for professional managers. Univ. Georgia Coop. Ext. Service. Bull. 991. Athens.

94. National Research Council, Committee on Plant and Animal Pests. 1968. Principles of Plant and Animal Pest Control. Vol. 2. Weed control. Natl. Acad. Sci., Washington, DC.

95. Riddle, G.E., L.L. Burpee, and G.J. Boland. 1991. Virulence of *Sclerotinia sclerotiorum* and *S. minor* on dandelion (*Taraxacum officinale*). Weed Sci. 39:109–118.

96. Robinson, R.J. 1949. Annual weeds and their viable seed population in the soil. Agron. J. 41:513–518.

97. Ross, M.A., and C.A. Lembi. 1985. Applied weed science. Macmillan Publ. Company, New York.

98. Scott, R. 1929. Preventing crabgrass seed. U.S. Golf Assoc. Bull. 4:118–119.

99. Shearman, R.C. 1986. Kentucky bluegrass and annual bluegrass response to ethofumesate. HortScience 21:1157–1159.

100. Slade, R.E., W.G. Templeman, and W.A. Sexton. 1945. Plant growth substances as selective weed killers. Nature (London) 155:497–498.

101. Sprague, H.B., and G.W. Burton. 1937. Annual bluegrass (*Poa annua* L.) and its requirements for growth. New Jersey Agric. Exp. Stn. Bull. 630. Rutgers Univ., New Brunswick.

102. Sprague, H.B., and E.E. Evaul. 1930. Experiments with turfgrasses. New Jersey Agric. Exp. Stn. Bull. 803. Rutgers Univ., New Brunswick.

103. Starkie, G. 1933. Control of weeds in lawns with calcium cyanamid. J. Am. Soc. Agron. 25:82–84.

104. Turgeon, A.J. 1991. Turgrass management. 3rd ed. Reston Publications Company, Reston, VA.

105. Welton, F.A., and J.C. Carroll. 1938. Crabgrass in relation to arsenicals. J. Am. Soc. Agron. 30:816.

106. White, R.W., and P. Busey. 1988. History of turfgrass production in Florida. p. 100–113. *In* Proc. 36th Annual Florida Turf. Conf. Florida Turf. Assoc., Orlando.

107. Willard, T.R., and W.L. Currey. 1985. Selectivity of postemergence grass herbicides in warm-season turfgrass. Proc. South. Weed Sci. Soc. 38:96.

108. Yang, Y.S., and S.W. Bingham. 1984. Effects of metribuzin on net photosynthesis of goosegrass (*Eleusine indica*) and bermudagrass (*Cynodon* spp.). Weed Sci. 32:247–250.

SUBJECT INDEX

Aatrex 4L. *See* Atrazine
Aatrex 80W. *See* Atrazine
Aatrex Nine-O. *See* Atrazine
Acclaim 1EC. *See* Fenoxaprop
Acetohydroxy acid synthase. *See* Acetolactate
synthase
Acetolactate synthase, 40, 58
Acetyl CoA carboxylase, 51
Achillea millefolium L. *See* Yarrow, common
Activated charcoal, 229
Additive action, of herbicides, 38
Aerification, 226–228
After-ripening, 34
Agitators, boom sprayer, 175–176
Agropyron repens (L.) Beauv. *See* Quackgrass
Agrostis palustris Huds. *See* Bentgrass,
creeping
Agrostis stolonifera L. *See* Bentgrass, creeping
Air-blast spreader, 200
Alchemilla arvensis (L.) Scop. *See* Parsley-piert
Alexandergrass, 6
smallflowered, 7
Algae, 212
Allelopathic effects, 35
Allium canadense L. *See* Onion, wild
Allium vineale L. *See* Garlic, wild
Alopecurus myosuroides Huds. *See* Foxtail,
slender
Alternanthera pungens HBK. *See* Khakiweed
AMA, 41, 50
Amaranth, prostrate. *See* Tumbleweed
Amaranthaceae, 11
Amaranthus spp. *See* Pigweed
Amaranthus albus L. *See* Tumbleweed
Amaranthus blitoides S. Wats. *See* Tum-
bleweed
Amaranthus graecizans. *See* Tumbleweed
Amaranthus retroflexus L. *See* Pigweed,
redroot
Ambrosia artemisiifolia L. *See* Ragweed,
common
Andropogon glomeratus (Walt.) BSP. *See*
Bluestem, bushy
Andropogon virginicus L. *See* Broomsedge
Angiosperm, 3
Anion exchange, 110
Annual bluegrass. *See* Bluegrass, annual
Annual kyllinga. *See* Kyllinga, annual
Annual lespedeza. *See* Lespedeza, common
Annual sedge. *See* Sedge, annual
Annual sowthistle. *See* Sowthistle, annual
Ansar 6.6. *See* MSMA
Antagonism, between herbicides, 38
Apical dominance, 215
Aquatic weeds, 216–217
Aqueous-solution products, 156
Arenaria serpyllifolia L. *See* Sandwort

Arsenicals, 40, 50, 52, 89–90, 217, 234, 239
Artemisia vulgaris L. *See* Mugwort
Arylphenoxypropionates, 50–52
Asulam, 41, 50, 55–57, 232, 237–238, 241
Asulox. *See* Asulam
Atrazine, 41, 50, 63, 82, 112, 114, 116, 119,
144–146, 158–159, 218–219, 224–225,
227, 232, 235–239, 241
Axonopus affinis Chase. *See* Carpetgrass

Backpack-type sprayer, 190–191
Bahiagrass, 10, 102
grass weed control in, 238
Balan 2.5G. *See* Benefin
Banvel. *See* Dicamba
Barbarea vulgaris R. Br. *See* Rocket, yellow
Barricade. *See* Prodiamine
Basagran. *See* Bentazon
Basamid granular. *See* Dazomet
Beardgrass, bushy. *See* Bluestem, bushy
Bellis perennis L. *See* Daisy, English
Benefin, 41, 49–50, 57, 85–86, 114, 123–125,
160, 223, 225–231
Bensulide, 41, 50, 58–60, 95, 114, 123,
130–131, 223, 225–231
Bensumec. *See* Bensulide
Bentazon, 38–39, 42, 50, 54, 218, 232, 239
Bentgrass, creeping, 5, 31–33
Bentgrass golf greens, 229–230
Benzamides, 50, 52–53
Benzofurans, 78–81
Benzoic acids, 50, 53, 156
Benzonitriles, 50, 53
Benzothiadiazoles, 50, 54
Bermudagrass, 7, 102
collar region, 240
grass weed control in, 234–237
Bermudagrass golf greens, 228–229
Betasan. *See* Bensulide
Betony, Florida, 20, 235
Bindweed, field, 16–17, 235
Biological weed control, 155, 163, 216–217
Bipolaris setariae (Saw.), 216
Bipyridyliums, 50, 54–55
Bird's-eye pearlwort. *See* Pearlwort, bird's-eye
Bittercress, hairy, 17, 235
Black medic. *See* Medic, black
Blackseed plantain. *See* Plantain, blackseed
Bloom (emulsifiable concentrate), 157
Bluegrass, annual, 10, 31–34, 79, 134–135,
210–213, 216, 224, 227, 231, 233
control in golf greens, 228–230
Bluestem, bushy, 5–6
Boom height, 186
Boom sprayer, 167–189
agitators, 175–176
application techniques, 186–189

249